SO
CLOSE
TO
GREATNESS

SO
CLOSE
TO
GREATNESS

A BIOGRAPHY OF William C. Bullitt

BY WILL BROWNELL
AND RICHARD N. BILLINGS

Macmillan Publishing Company

NEW YORK

Collier Macmillan Publishers

LONDON

Macmillan Publishing Company
866 Third Avenue, New York, N.Y. 10022
Collier Macmillan Canada, Inc.

Library of Congress Cataloging-in-Publication Data
Billings, Richard N.
So close to greatness.
Bibliography: p. 333
Includes notes, index.
1. Bullitt, William C. (William Christian), 1891–
1967.   2. Ambassadors—United States—Biography.
3. United States—Foreign relations—20th century.
I. Brownell, Will.   II. Title.
E748.B8837B55   1987   327.2′092′4 [B]   86-28439
ISBN 0-02-517410-X

Macmillan books are available at special discounts for bulk purchases
for sales promotions, premiums, fund-raising, or educational use.
For details, contact:

Special Sales Director
Macmillan Publishing Company
866 Third Avenue
New York, N.Y. 10022

10 9 8 7 6 5 4 3 2 1

Designed by Jack Meserole

Printed in the United States of America

CONTENTS

ACKNOWLEDGMENTS

Thanks especially to Ambassador Elbridge Durbrow, Ambassador Angier Biddle Duke, Ambassador Clare Boothe Luce, Ambassador Jacob Beam, Allen Grover, Hubert P. Earle, Beatrice Farnsworth, Robert K. Straus, George Elsey, Grace Tully, Eleanor Lansing Dulles, Virginia Gardner, Nathan Miller, Benjamin Welles, Eleanor Davies Ditzen, Dr. Richard Friedman, Rosemary Sheehan.

Finally, to the editor of this book, Edward T. Chase of Macmillan.

FOREWORD

William C. Bullitt was a man of mystery and paradox. He is still remembered as one of the outstanding American diplomats of this century, yet his government career spanned less than a dozen years. He was a prodigy: Wilson's emissary to Lenin at twenty-eight; Roosevelt's ambassador to the Soviet Union at forty-two; but at fifty he had dropped from sight. In 1941 he was still castigated as a leftist—for his early support of the Russian Revolution, but more for his marriage to Louise Bryant, the widow of John Reed—when in fact he was a conservative and moving further right. He was a prophet who predicted in 1943 a postwar confrontation with the U.S.S.R., a "cold war," but his credibility had diminished, and his warning went unheeded. He was envied as an acquaintance of most of the important figures of his time—Roosevelt, Churchill, Eisenhower, de Gaulle, Chiang Kai-shek—yet he died virtually friendless. And he was regarded as a person of great wealth—worth $9 million, it was reported in his obituary in *The New York Times*—though his estate actually came to $223,000.

As a young man, Bill Bullitt could look to high horizons: he was voted "most brilliant" in his class at Yale, 1912; he was, in the opinion of Walter Lippmann, "the sharpest of the American correspondents" covering the war in Europe; his journalistic prowess earned him a responsible position in the State Department in 1917; and in 1919 he led an official mission to Moscow, seeking to negotiate an end to the civil war in Russia. Even as a dissident, Bullitt commanded attention. When he resigned from the U.S. delegation to the Paris peace talks and aired his objections to the Treaty of Versailles before a Senate committee, he was widely denounced as a radical. It was a treaty "which makes certain future wars . . ." he insisted, and it turned out he was right.

In the 1920s, Bullitt was an expatriate in Paris along with Ernest Hemingway, F. Scott Fitzgerald, and the others. In a letter to Fitzgerald, Hemingway called him a "fellow novel writer," somewhat sarcastically because the book Bullitt had written, a withering sketch of a decadent society in a city that closely resembled his native Philadelphia, was popular pulp (150,000 copies sold). It was while in Paris that Bullitt and Bryant were married, though they were divorced less than seven years later.

Bullitt decided to try his hand at writing history, directing his effort to the period of the world war. He revealed his plan to Sigmund Freud, whom he had sought out in Vienna—some say he became a patient, though Bullitt denied it—

and Freud expressed an interest in collaborating on the chapter about Woodrow Wilson. Bullitt called the idea "an impossible monstrosity," telling Freud "the part would be greater than the whole." As it turned out, the part became the whole, a psychological study of Wilson by Bullitt and Freud.

As he had with Freud, Bullitt made a point of getting to know men of influence. He once said that if you deal with bright people, you will know all the important people in the world. He nearly did, as the *Times* noted in his obituary: "He knew every European statesman from Georges Clemenceau of France and Lenin of Russia to Winston Churchill of Britain . . ."

Anticipating the election of Franklin D. Roosevelt in 1932, Bullitt contacted Louis B. Wehle, a New York lawyer and old friend of Roosevelt. Wehle introduced Bullitt to FDR, and after the election he proposed him as the ambassador to France, not realizing the job had been promised to Jesse I. Straus, the president of Macy's. Wehle then suggested that if the United States recognized the Soviet Union, Bullitt would be the best man for Moscow, and Roosevelt agreed. They made "an ideal team," Wehle wrote.

The Soviet Union was recognized in November 1933, and Ambassador Bullitt showed he had an eye for talent by recruiting top-flight assistants such as George F. Kennan and Charles E. Bohlen, both future ambassadors to Moscow and among the ablest articulators of U.S. foreign policy. Bullitt was welcomed at a Kremlin reception by Stalin himself, but relations soon turned sour—between the two governments and between Bullitt and the Soviet foreign minister, Maxim Litvinov. Bullitt blamed Litvinov personally for the failure to reach a settlement of Russia's war debt, though in fact Stalin was responsible for the stalemate. Also, it was while Bullitt was in Moscow that Stalin started the purges of officials he considered disloyal. Several of Bullitt's contacts were among the victims, and he felt isolated and alone.

Bullitt left Moscow with relief in the spring of 1936, though he was headed for no particular post. He returned to Washington as a writer for Roosevelt's reelection campaign and he inspired FDR's famous speech: "I have seen war. . . . I hate war." By chance, Jesse Straus fell ill that summer, and Bullitt was named ambassador to France. He was delighted, and so were the French, as he let Roosevelt know by letter from Paris: members of the French government "seem to be greatly pleased by my appointment." It was not an empty boast, as officials in Washington took note: "Bullitt practically sleeps with the French cabinet," wrote Harold L. Ickes, the secretary of the interior.

Bullitt became particularly close to Edouard Daladier, the premier of France when war with Germany was declared. ". . . he asks my judgment about nearly everything of great importance," Bullitt wrote Roosevelt. His influence with Daladier was such that he was able in April 1939 to assure the Polish foreign minister, Jozef Beck, that Poland could depend on French military support in the event of an attack by Germany. Joseph P. Kennedy, the ambassador to Great Britain, later charged that France and Britain would not have gone to war with Germany, had they not been goaded by Bullitt.

Bullitt was often criticized for rash, impulsive action. He was not fazed, though, if he believed he was right, as he did when he insisted on remaining in Paris when the French government, as the Germans advanced in June 1940, fled south to Vichy. "No American ambassador in Paris has ever run away from anything," he wrote Roosevelt. Even Harold Ickes, an admirer of Bullitt, called it a foolish move, and Secretary of State Cordell Hull argued that Bullitt, had he been present when the Council of Ministers met, might have influenced a decision to continue the war from Algeria, rather than bow to Hitler. As for Roosevelt, he did not admonish Bullitt, who had advised him that if he got an order to leave Paris, he would disobey it.

When he was not offered a cabinet post—secretary of war or secretary of the navy—Bullitt felt let down by Roosevelt, probably with justification. The president had made a commitment, or so Bullitt thought, at a meeting at the White House in February 1940; however, in July, in an election year maneuver, he named two Republicans, Henry L. Stimson and Frank Knox. Bullitt's ambition was to be secretary of state—Hull was nearing seventy and hinting he was ready to retire—so he decided to be a good soldier. Roosevelt asked him to make a foreign policy speech in Philadelphia, and Bullitt spoke in blunt terms that for the president, while he agreed, would have meant a political risk. War was inevitable, Bullitt declared, and he asked: "When are we going to say . . . that we don't want to hear any longer about what we can get from our country, but we do want to hear what we can give to our country?" One imagines that a young John F. Kennedy, who had been a guest at Bullitt's embassy in the summer of 1938, paid close attention to those words.

Roosevelt was unwilling to make Bullitt secretary of state—he talks too much and is too quick on the trigger, FDR said to Ickes. So Bullitt was relegated to odd jobs: ambassador-at-large in North Africa and the Middle East, assistant to Secretary of the Navy Knox. Understandably, Bullitt was restless: "For eighteen months I have been doing double time," he wrote a friend in 1941, "and the administration has been going half time."

In frustration, Bullitt made a great mistake: he attacked the undersecretary of state, Sumner Welles. Welles was vulnerable. In September 1940, on a train to Alabama for the funeral of Speaker of the House William B. Bankhead, Welles got drunk and propositioned a porter. Word of the incident, while withheld from the public, circulated in Washington, and in April 1941 Bullitt met with Roosevelt and urged him to dismiss Welles. He suggested there might be a call for a criminal prosecution, and he confided that Hull "considered Welles worse than a murderer." The president refused to act, and the issue simmered for two years, as

Bullitt stoked the coals. Finally, Welles resigned. This unfortunate incident caused a distinct cooling in the relationship between Bullitt and the president.

When Bullitt went to Russia in 1919, he shared an expression with his companion Lincoln Steffens, who used it in slightly altered form in his autobiography: "We have seen the future, and it works." Bullitt would later, in his second thoughts about communism, happily give Steffens credit for the aphorism, but he was a seer still and all. He did see the future, in 1919, and again in 1943. "When Germany collapses," he wrote in a memorandum to Roosevelt, "we must be in a position to prevent . . . the flow of the Red amoeba into Europe. . . . We shall never again have as much influence on Great Britain and the Soviet Union as we have today. . . . On the day Germany surrenders, our influence . . . will reach zero." George Kennan wrote that the Bullitt memo "deserves a place among the major historical documents of our time."

Bullitt saw his prediction come true, and he wrote in a book, *The Great Globe Itself*: "The events of 1945 proved beyond . . . doubt that the Atlantic Charter and Yalta Declaration had been to Stalin merely . . . ready-made suits of sheep's clothing which he could wear until he no longer needed a camouflage." Bullitt made another prediction in that book, which proves the relevance of his thinking even today. "After the next war," he wrote, "there may be no after."

THE AUTHORS

Washington, D.C.
March 1987

I

American Aristocrat

Home to Philadelphia

FOLLOWING his death in Paris on February 15, 1967, the body of Ambassador Bullitt was brought to Philadelphia for a funeral service and burial in Woodlands Cemetery, and he was at rest after a long and stormy journey. He had come from Old Philadelphia, which was less a piece of geography than it was a social phenomenon, for it had been the habitat of the first American aristocracy. Bullitt had never quite fit in, not that he failed to measure up, for he was of early colonial stock with forebears of fame and fortune; but he was restless and ambitious and had really returned to Philadelphia only occasionally during his adult life: to speak on foreign policy, as he had in August 1940; to shepherd his debutante daughter in 1941; and to run for mayor in 1943. Nathaniel Burt, a local historian, wrote that professions such as politics, the military, and the divinity were not for the Philadelphia well-born: "For one thing, . . . one stands a good chance of being moved *away* from Philadelphia. A career *away* from Philadelphia is out of bounds, doesn't count." Who were the exceptions? Benjamin Franklin, the first emissary to France, was not, for he was originally from Boston and came to Philadelphia as a printer, a trade that disqualified him as a member of the gentry. George Mifflin Dallas was, however: a Princeton graduate and a lawyer, Dallas was named minister to Russia in 1837; he was elected vice president in 1844 (the city in Texas that bears his name had been settled in 1841); and he was minister to Great Britain from 1852 to 1860. And so was Richard Rush, who served four presidents as attorney general, secretary of state, secretary of the treasury, and minister to France. Still, a University of Pennsylvania sociologist, E. Digby Baltzell, concluded in 1958 that "the American upper class . . . has produced few great statesmen," and "this has been especially true of Philadelphia."

The first fathers of Old Philadelphia families emerged as distinct groups over successive stages: the merchants and statesmen of the eighteenth century, Philadelphia's "golden age"; the heads of family manufacturing companies and investment banking houses of the years before the Civil War; and the entrepreneurs—merchandisers, transportation magnates, and so on—who amassed enormous wealth in the late nineteenth and early twentieth centuries. A new bourgeois ethic, Baltzell wrote, "entered the genteel drawing rooms around Washington and Independence Squares" shortly after the War of 1812; "Proper Philadelphia was busy assimilating the pioneers of America's soon-to-be predominant class. These were the days of the founding of family firms; . . . the

3

consolidation of coal-mining interests; and the founding of such Proper Philadelphia institutions as the Pennsylvania Railroad and the Philadelphia Club." Philadelphia had become by 1870 a conservative city, in which a business aristocracy was able to pass control of institutions from generation to generation, and social connections were more important than anywhere in America. As Mark Twain wrote in 1899: "In Boston they ask, How much does he know? In New York, How much is he worth? In Philadelphia, Who were his parents?"

Old Philadelphians, while accumulating fortunes, established upper-class institutions, which, as Baltzell put it, "structured the process of assimilation by providing ways and means for the . . . rich to play and learn and worship together. . . ." The institutions also provided "an important means of consolidating a continuity of . . . power in the serious world of affairs." New England boarding schools were established in the latter half of the nineteenth century, but they presented a risk: "In Philadelphia," Burt wrote, "it used to be a bit swank to go off to boarding school, and being swank in Philadelphia is one of those things that one has to be cautious about. . . . To be traditionally swank, . . . is wonderful, but parvenu swank makes people snicker." So many Philadelphians sent their young to local day schools, such as De Lancey, which was merged with the city's oldest private school, Episcopal Academy. Ivy League universities had long been upper-class institutions, with most Philadelphia collegians choosing Princeton or the University of Pennsylvania, although Harvard and Yale were favored by a special sort of student. ". . . it is almost a tradition," Burt wrote, "that . . . those Philadelphians active in politics and civic causes should be graduates of Harvard or Yale."

The neighborhood was the most obvious emblem of wealth and position, notably the cluster of mansions around Rittenhouse Square, the first of which were built shortly after the Civil War, protected by the Broad Street station of the Pennsylvania Railroad, opened in 1881. "At the very center of town, . . ." Burt explained, "this great brick castle . . . stood as the Bastille. . . . To get the trains from the main tracks, . . . a massive elevated stone causeway was built, cutting the city in two. . . . This was the Chinese Wall. . . ." South of the wall, below Market Street, lay Rittenhouse Square; north of the wall lay "the Mongolia of 'North of Market,' where Nobody lived."

Most of them Quakers originally, Old Philadelphians became Episcopalians and worshiped at Holy Trinity; Presbyterianism was "respectable, solid and worthy," as Burt phrased it, "though a little bourgeois"; Lutherans held sway in the Germantown section, but other Protestant sects were scorned, as was Catholicism. Anti-Semitism was quite prevalent, but it applied to "emigrant, unassimilated, synagogue-going, Polish-Russian Jews," who were flatly excluded; however, descendants of old families with names like Rosengarten, Etting, and Horwitz were, Burt wrote, "members in good standing" and were "mostly pillars of the right Episcopalian churches." Burt might have had the Bullitts in mind—Ambassador Bullitt's mother was a Horwitz—when he wrote, ". . . a little touch of Jewishness is almost requisite."

At the turn of the century most Old Philadelphians were Republicans in the image of President McKinley. Philadelphia had been the site of the first Republican national convention, in 1856, and from the founding in 1862 of the Union League, a social club but a political force, the city was a bastion of the Grand Old Party for ninety years. (The patrician elite also numbered a few Democrats, according to Baltzell: Richard Rush and Charles Jared Ingersoll, a congressman in the 1840s, for example, and "a few contemporary members of the Ingersoll, Bullitt, and Biddle families.") The Republican who personified power in Philadelphia was Boies Penrose, who started out as a reformer in the 1870s—it was in that decade that a city charter was drafted by a commission headed by John C. Bullitt, the grandfather of the ambassador—but who abandoned his principles for practical purposes. In 1884 Penrose was elected to the state legislature from a district that included Rittenhouse Square and adjacent neighborhoods, defeating William C. Bullitt, Sr., Baltzell wrote, "because of his ability to cultivate the hardly fashionable voters . . . east of Broad Street."

Penrose was elected to the U.S. Senate in 1897, serving there until his death in 1921, and he was succeeded by George Wharton Pepper, who was an epitome of Old Philadelphia: a lawyer but an unsuccessful politician, who was shunted aside by state party leaders when he was up for reelection in 1927. Pepper opposed power politics, as it had been exemplified by Boss Penrose; he never wavered in his support of President Harding (he regarded the Teapot Dome scandal as only an "unhappy event"); and when Roosevelt took office in 1933, he held him in contempt as a traitor to his class. On the contrary, Baltzell argued, Roosevelt perpetuated upper-class influence, and in the 1930s several political leaders with upper-class backgrounds emerged—from Philadelphia they were William C. Bullitt and Francis B. Biddle—who by no accident were Democrats. They were "deviants in a predominantly Republican . . . subculture."

"Since colonial times," Baltzell wrote, "when John Dickinson and Joseph Gallaway were leading members of the bar, the Philadelphia lawyer has always been a leader in both civic and business affairs. . . ." Many of the best bankers were trained originally as lawyers, such as Thomas S. Gates, who became the president of the Philadelphia Trust Company and then a partner of J. P. Morgan &

Company. Medicine was as respected as the law, though its influence, as measured by corporate board memberships and civic positions, was never as great. George Pepper's father and grandfather had been doctors, and Samuel Gross, the famous surgeon, practiced in Philadelphia, although he came from Easton, which "is right far from Philadelphia socially," Burt wrote. "Dr. Gross's son became a doctor, . . . and . . . two Gross girls married Horwitzes, still another medical family. . . . Then a Horwitz married a Bullitt, a Bullitt descendant [the ambassador's brother, Orville] married an Ingersoll, and so it goes." After law and medicine the favored professions were insurance and banking, which included the brokerage business, and it was considered most proper to run the family enterprise, "especially if it falls in the area of the Iron Triangle—iron and steel making, railroads and coal."

For over fifty years following the Revolution Philadelphia banks were the equivalent of the federal treasury: Thomas Willing, known as the father of American banking—he was the president of the First Bank of the United States—and his partner, Robert Morris, literally subsidized the war for independence. Nicholas Biddle was appointed president of the Second Bank of the United States by President Monroe in 1823, but President Jackson was determined to end Philadelphia's banking monopoly; and he did, when the Second Bank's charter expired in 1836. "Philadelphia's gradual decline from its Golden Age," wrote Baltzell, "was now complete: it had lost the political leadership of the nation when the capital moved to Washington, in 1800; its commercial dominance passed to New York after the opening of the Erie Canal, in 1825; and Jackson's defeat of the Second Bank ended its financial monopoly." Two successful private banking houses were established in the aftermath of the Panic of 1837, which had been precipitated by the closing of the Second Bank: the House of Drexel, eventually the Philadelphia branch of J. P. Morgan & Company; and Jay Cooke & Company, whose collapse—Cooke squandered his fortune on railroad speculations—caused the Panic of 1873.

Coal: "It has been a dirty business in every sense of the word," Burt wrote, "yet it also involved . . . some fine pioneering courage and inventiveness." Anthracite would become the most profitable product in Pennsylvania—Old Philadelphia families, among them the Bullitts, made fortunes as a result—but not until a railroad was built across the Alleghenies. "A few far-sighted Philadelphians," Baltzell wrote, "had been concerned . . . for some time, but the majority were still preoccupied with running factories, building canals, and opening up coal mines. . . . Finally, in 1846, a group of prominent Philadelphia capitalists . . . organized what is now the Pennsylvania Railroad."

Coal and railroading were appropriate commercial endeavors by Old Philadelphia standards, but other businesses were not, such as merchandising and street transportation. The most successful Philadelphia merchant was John Wanamaker, the son of a bricklayer, who opened his first store in 1861 and was a multimillionaire when he died in 1922. The leading transit operator was Peter A. B. Widener, who started buying streetcar lines with money he made selling mutton to the Union Army; by 1883 he and a partner, William L. Elkins, owned all the lines in the city. Widener, whose great-grandfather arrived in Philadelphia from Rotterdam in 1752, admired the Dutch masters; he became the owner of the finest private collection of Rembrandts and Van Dycks, which he displayed at Lynnewood Hall, his estate in a Philadelphia suburb.

Widener's descendants did not become lawyers and doctors in the Old Philadelphia tradition, although his elder son did run the family business. George D. Widener cared no more than his father had about being accepted by society: he too had known hardship as a youth, and he identified with everyday people; nor did he marry into the Philadelphia upper class, choosing instead Eleanor Elkins, the daughter of William Elkins. They had two sons: Harry Elkins Widener, who became a collector of valuable books; and George D. Widener, Jr., who did marry "well," became a member of the Philadelphia Club, and was a well-known breeder of thoroughbred racehorses. George Widener, Sr., his wife, and their son Harry went abroad in 1912, and they returned in April on the *Titanic*; George was lost, as was Harry, who assured his mother, as she was about to board a lifeboat, that a rare edition of Francis Bacon's *Essays*, purchased in London, was secure in his pocket. Harry Widener left his literary collection to Harvard, from which he had graduated in 1907, and his mother donated the Widener Library to the university, with a room set aside for his books.

Peter Widener's other son, Joseph E. Widener, was deeply offended at being shunned, especially after he married Ella Pancoast, who came from one of Philadelphia's oldest families. "Mother lived on the right side of the Market Street tracks," wrote her son, Peter A. B. Widener II. "The Pancoast family address was 1911 Walnut Street, . . . in what is known as the Rittenhouse Square section. But Father? It made no difference that Grandfather had built one of the finest mansions in the city at Broad Street and Girard Avenue. It was twelve squares north of Walnut Street, and that would never do." His mother had been ostracized: "As Mrs. Joseph E. Widener, she was never again invited to the Assembly Ball." The Assembly, wrote Nathaniel Burt, was the most venerated Philadelphia institution: "Admission to the Assembly is . . . strictly hereditary in the male line. . . . If a daughter marries out, . . . she stays out. A son however can marry anybody and stay in." (When one such son asked if he could bring Grace Kelly, the actress and a Philadelphian and later Princess Grace of Monaco, he was told he would have to marry her first.)

Joseph Widener was all the more furious in 1919 when his debutante daughter, Fifi, was not invited to the Assembly, and he threatened to withhold support of a civic project sponsored by prominent citizens, members of the Assembly. An invitation was issued to Fifi, sent to the Widener home across the line in Montgomery County, so she could be listed as an out-of-town guest. Ella Widener, however, was still rejected.

Bullitt Family Origins

"HIS FAMILY TREE is ornamented by the father of George Washington, the sister of Patrick Henry, Pocahontas herself," it was noted in *Time* in 1943, when William C. Bullitt was running for mayor of Philadelphia, adding that a statue of his grandfather, John C. Bullitt, "stands outside the drab, over-columned City Hall." Bullitt could indeed be proud of his heritage, which began in the New World with Joseph Boulet, a French Huguenot from the province of Languedoc, who fled the tyranny of Cardinal Richelieu and settled at St. Mary's City on the Maryland shore of the Potomac River, "the birthplace of religious freedom," as it had been named in 1634 by its British Catholic colonists. Boulet arrived in 1637, and exactly three hundred years later his descendant, United States Ambassador to France William Bullitt, was made an honorary citizen of Nîmes, his ancestral home. It was the occasion of a nostalgic journey to the city in southern France, but Bullitt's delight was qualified—he was highly chagrined, his brother recalled years later—by the realization that all the relatives he encountered were of peasant stock. Bullitt had been raised in the tradition of Old Philadelphia: every civilization is dominated by a few aristocrats, and Bullitt counted himself one of them. He could cite the lineage created by the marriages of the heirs of Joseph Boulet, which enabled him to claim prominent ancestors in American colonial history: Pocahontas and her husband, John Rolfe, who introduced tobacco farming in Virginia; Annie Henry, the sister of Patrick Henry; Augustine Washington, the father of the first president; Thomas Walker, a friend and neighbor of Thomas Jefferson; and Thomas Bullitt, the founder of Louisville, Kentucky. Bullitt remembered years later walking with Mrs. Charles E. Ingersoll, his brother's mother-in-law: "Come, Mrs. Ingersoll," said Bullitt, "just take my arm as we cross the street. No one will dare to run us down." Mrs. Ingersoll was not so sure: "But they might not know who we are," she said.

———————

The first Bullitt of the American dynasty was Benjamin, who moved up the Potomac to Port Tobacco, Maryland, in 1685. From there the family fanned over the colonial territory—to Virginia, then Kentucky, and eventually Pennsylvania—leaving its imprint on each region it reached. The second Bullitt, also Benjamin, settled in Fauquier County, Virginia, where he married Elizabeth Harrison of the noted Virginia family (Carter Bassett Harrison, brother of William Henry Harrison, the ninth president, was a congressman from Virginia, 1793–99), and their son John, a distinguished officer in the French and Indian Wars, led a surveying party in 1773 from Virginia westward along the Ohio River and laid out a settlement, which became Louisville. The youngest son of Benjamin and Elizabeth Bullitt, Cuthbert, remained in Virginia, where he was the commonwealth attorney, a judge of the General Court, and a member of the Virginia Convention of 1776. His son, Alexander Scott Bullitt, followed his uncle, John Bullitt, to Kentucky in 1785 and started a farm near Louisville, called Oxmoor, a name he took from *Tristram Shandy*, the novel by Laurence Sterne. Oxmoor, consisting of some 1,500 acres on Beargrass Creek, was to remain in the Bullitt family for at least two centuries, although it was vacated during the Civil War and not reclaimed until 1909. Alexander Scott Bullitt became the first speaker of the Kentucky Senate and the state's first lieutenant governor, from 1800 to 1808; and Bullitt County, south of Louisville, was named for him.

The same year he built his house at Oxmoor, Alexander Scott Bullitt married Priscilla Christian, the fifteen-year-old daughter of William Christian and Annie Henry, sister of Patrick Henry, the patriot and orator. William Christian was killed in an ambush in 1786 while he and John Bullitt were leading the pursuit of an Indian band suspected of stealing horses, and Priscilla Christian lived to be only thirty; but a feeling of pride in this brief association with the renowned English family resulted in the retaining of its name, often as the middle name of the first-born male, by Bullitts for generations to come. Originally the name was Kristin, and it identified a clan of pirates who swept down from Iceland in the thirteenth century. The William Christian killed in the Indian skirmish in 1786 was a descendant of another William Christian, who in 1651 organized an armed challenge to the leadership of Oliver Cromwell, the lord protector, on the Isle of Man, for which he was hanged; and he was a relative of Fletcher Christian, who in 1789 led the mutiny aboard *H.M.S. Bounty*.

William Bullitt of the twentieth century never hesitated to express pride in his ancestral ties to the American Revolution: in August 1940 he signed a jesting letter to Franklin Roosevelt, "T. Jefferson," adding a serious postscript in which he declared, mistakenly, that "one of my great-grandfathers was the boy's guardian." The facts of the Jefferson connection are these. Thomas Walker, a physician and explorer—he wrote an account of an expedition in 1750, claiming to have been the first white man to cross the Appalachian Mountains—was a close associate of Peter Jefferson, father of the third president, and his son, John Walker, was a boyhood friend of Thomas Jefferson himself. Thomas Walker married Mildred Thornton in 1741, and their daughter, Peachy Walker, married Joshua Fry (an heir to the Joshua Fry who led the Virginia regiment in the Indian wars in which George Washington served and who was succeeded by Washington as commander when he died in 1751). In 1819 Mildred Ann Fry, the daughter of Peachy and Joshua Fry, married William Christian Bullitt, the son of Priscilla Christian and Alexander Scott Bullitt and the great-grandfather of William C. Bullitt, the ambassador. (It was via the Walker line of ancestry that Bullitt could claim kinship with "Grandma Pocahontas," whose descendant, Susanna Eldridge, was the grandmother of Thomas Walker.)

Bullitt's grandfather, John C. Bullitt, was born at Oxmoor on February 10, 1824, and he recorded his memories of the farm in his diary:

> The entrance to the place was . . . through the "Big Gate," and thence an avenue, . . . with rows of locust trees on either side for a quarter of a mile, where it opened into a lawn of some twenty-five or thirty acres. . . . In this lawn and well removed from the house . . . were the negro cabins, and to the northeast of the house the stables, corn crib, etc. were located. It was a genuine southern or Kentucky farm. . . . Altogether it was almost an ideal agricultural neighborhood. The profits were not very great. But the habits of the people were simple and their expenses very moderate. . . . The negroes . . . raised broom corn—two outer rows in the cornfields being always reserved for this purpose. At night we would find them busy in their cabins making . . . brooms of broom corn and on Saturday night they went off to Louisville . . . with their . . . brooms for sale.

While it provided a livelihood, farming was a Bullitt family avocation; their profession was the law—the firm established by William C. Bullitt in Louisville in 1815 still exists in 1987. John C. Bullitt studied law at Transylvania University in Lexington, Kentucky, then worked as an apprentice in his father's firm, and was admitted to the bar in Louisville in 1845. Getting from Louisville to Philadelphia in 1849 was itself a challenge—a long riverboat ride along the winding Ohio and then across the state of Pennsylvania by carriage on the turnpike, as it would be another three years before the railroad was operating—but for John Bullitt there was the lure of a case that would set his career in motion. Three years earlier the Bank of Kentucky had won a $1.3 million judgment against the

Schuylkill Bank of Philadelphia in a suit over a fraudulent stock issue, and John Bullitt was going east "to effect collection of said judgment." He was successful, and owing to the prominence of his client he gained immediate attention and was soon retained by other important business establishments. Although torn by the Civil War—twenty members of his family fought for the Confederacy, and a brother was killed—he decided to remain in Philadelphia, or according to his descendants he was stranded there; and it was during the war that he engaged in a debate with the redoubtable Horace Binney over the issue of habeas corpus. "A Review of Mr. Binney's Pamphlet on the Privilege of the Writ of Habeas Corpus," written by John C. Bullitt in 1862, was regarded by lawyers as a masterpiece of legal logic.

John Bullitt was retained by Anthony J. Drexel and Jay Cooke, as the financial partners had noticed "that young lawyer across the street—burning the midnight oil"; and when Jay Cooke & Company failed, having overinvested in the Northern Pacific Railroad, Bullitt maneuvered an escape from the worst consequences of forced liquidation, and he even managed the reorganization of the Northern Pacific. Jay Cooke survived—he did not go broke and did not go to prison—thanks to John Bullitt, who neglected to learn a lesson from the experience: he himself became a heavy investor—in railroads, coal, and real estate—and he became very wealthy, for a while.

Best remembered for his public service, John Bullitt was appointed in 1876 by the governor of Pennsylvania, John F. Hartranft, to a commission on city planning; as a result he proposed a new charter for Philadelphia—it soon became known as the Bullitt charter—which, as Lincoln Steffens, the famed journalist, wrote, "had been drawn by an expert of experience, intelligence, and integrity, to meet and to defeat the typical ills of the corrupt politics of old." (Steffens was ultimately disillusioned, however: "And yet, back of this charter and working with and through it, there were the same old boss, ring, and machine, governing Philadelphia as St. Louis, Minneapolis, New York, and Pittsburgh were governed.") The charter bill was passed by the State Legislature in 1885, and John Bullitt was memorialized by a bronze statue, placed on the south front of City Hall Plaza.

John C. Bullitt, who married a Kentucky woman, Therese Langhorne, in 1850, had seven children, the second of whom was William C. Bullitt, who was born in Philadelphia on June 18, 1856. A graduate of the University of Pennsylvania in 1876, he studied law at the University of Virginia, was admitted to the Philadelphia bar in 1878, and began his practice in his father's office. In 1882 he was elected to the state legislature, and he promptly introduced the Bullitt charter bill, which was passed, but not until after he had retired from politics, having lost his seat in the legislature, in 1884, to Boies Penrose. (Originally a Democrat in the family tradition, William C. Bullitt, Sr., broke with the party over the issue of the gold standard, supported McKinley in 1896, and became a Republican after that year's election.) In 1885 he joined the Norfolk & Western Railroad and served as a vice president, from 1887 to 1893, and as general manager until he resigned in 1898; he then became a partner in Castner, Curran and Bullitt, sales agent for producers of steam coal that was sold to the navies of various nations and to steamship companies; and he was also the president of the Pocahontas Coal Company and a director of affiliated producers of coal and iron. John C. Bullitt, when he died in 1902, was virtually insolvent, having lost most of what he had invested, the bulk of it in real estate—he had speculated heavily and disastrously in the resort town of Cape May, New Jersey. His son, however, who lived another dozen years, was able to restore the family fortune, at least to the extent that there was still the appearance of wealth.

The maternal ancestry of William C. Bullitt, Jr., the Horwitz-Gross line, is as rich in lore as the Bullitt line, granted there are not so many links to figures in American history. As with John C. Bullitt, the great forebears—family founders in the Old Philadelphia sense—became by the time they died entrenched Philadelphians, although they had come from somewhere else. In the case of Samuel D. Gross the parallel to John Bullitt extends further: both were accomplished professionals, Gross a physician and Bullitt an attorney; both came to Philadelphia in the mid-nineteenth century; and both were accepted socially with little delay. For Haym Salomon it had been an altogether different matter: born a poor Polish Jew, Salomon came to Philadelphia in the 1770s, and while he too was skilled at his profession—a financier, he actually kept America afloat at the end of the Revolution—social acceptance of his family would not come for several generations.

Haym Salomon was born in Lezno in the province of Poznan, Poland, in 1740; shortly thereafter the town was annexed by Prussia and given the name Lissa. Little is known of Salomon's early life because a fire destroyed much of the Jewish section of Lissa, dispersing its inhabitants and destroying records, though there is evidence that he traveled widely and learned to speak French, German, and Russian. He returned to Poland in about 1770 and joined the movement for independence, but in 1772—it was the year that much of Poland was partitioned by Russia, Austria, and Prussia—he was forced to flee and went first to England, then to New York, where he went into business as a broker and merchant. As he had been in Poland, Salomon was drawn to the cause of liberty, and he was arrested as a spy during the British occupation of New York, in 1776; however, his linguistic ability got him assigned to the Hessian mercenary contingent as an interpreter and commissary manager, and he was soon paroled. On January 2,

1777, Salomon married Rachel Franks, the daughter of an influential Jewish merchant, and two weeks after the birth of their first child—a son, Ezekiel, on July 28, 1778—he was arrested again, imprisoned, and sentenced to death. But he escaped by bribing a jailer and made his way, through the American lines, across New Jersey.

"If Haym Salomon had not escaped the British, his life would have been as worthless as the fiat continental currency," wrote Edwin Wolf and Maxwell Whiteman in *The History of the Jews of Philadelphia*. "He arrived in Philadelphia in 1778 penniless, and shortly thereafter . . . helped chart the course of the country's finances." Salomon applied to Congress for employment, claiming he was destitute, but to no avail, and he had no choice but to go into business for himself. "With foreign money in the form of bills and drafts coming into Philadelphia as a result of loans negotiated by Franklin and others in Europe," wrote Wolf and Whiteman, "there was opportunity for a broker who knew foreign exchange. It seems logical that Salomon with his European financial background should have chosen this field, . . . and by 1781 he had established himself firmly."

In May 1781—the war was about to end, but the financial woes of the government would only worsen—Robert Morris was appointed superintendent of the Office of Finance; and in June he named Haym Salomon the broker of the office, and as such Salomon became the sole person responsible for turning foreign bills of exchange, "which the United States was receiving in the form of loans, into usable cash without losing so much in discount that the loans failed in their purpose." With peace—the British surrendered at Yorktown, Virginia, on October 19, 1781—arose another problem, inflation, as Wolf and Whiteman wrote: "Continental currency, English counterfeits, Pennsylvania paper bills and the like from each of the new states circulated at unequal values with no gold or silver to back them." To maintain the government's credit, Salomon made large contributions of his own resources, which were documented in the diary of Robert Morris in the form of seventy-five transactions between August 1781 and April 1784; Salomon had advanced Morris $211,678 in cash, and he held government obligations amounting to $353,729.33, as well as six promissory notes coming to $92,600—a total of $658,007.33. Having suffered heavy financial losses in the year of his death, 1785, Salomon died broke—as did Morris. Salomon's estate was valued at $44,732, against an indebtedness of $45,292; and attempts by his heirs to obtain a settlement of their claim for the money he loaned the government—one in 1864 was termed by a Senate committee to be of "undeniable merit"—were unsuccessful. All Salomon received for saving the nation from bankruptcy was tribute, as he did from James Madison, who wrote on September 30, 1781, to his fellow Virginia delegate to the Continental Congress, Edmund Randolph: "The kindness of our little friend in Front Street . . . is a fund which will preserve me from extremities, but I never resort to it without great mortification, as he obstinately rejects all recompense. The price of money is so usurious that he thinks it ought to be extorted from none but those who aim at profitable speculations. To a necessitous delegate he gratuitously spares a supply out of his private stock."

The first Horwitz to come to America was Jonas, who arrived in Philadelphia soon after 1800 and changed his name to Jonathan. His origins were quite similar to those of Haym Salomon, as he was a Polish Jew who had traveled extensively in Europe, becoming adept at several languages, but the parallel ends there: Horwitz was not a financier but a scholar, who, when his plan to publish the first American Bible in Hebrew went awry, decided to become a physician. He received a degree from the University of Pennsylvania medical college in 1815—while in medical school, he met Joseph Andrews, a trader and part-time teacher of Hebrew, who had married Sarah Salomon, a daughter of Haym and Rachel Salomon—and he opened an office on Vine Street, in the Jewish section of the city. In 1817 Jonathan Horwitz, age thirty-four by this time, and Deborah Andrews, the seventeen-year-old daughter of Joseph and Sarah, were married.

Jonathan Horwitz did not remain satisfied with his medical practice, perhaps because he was located in a less-than-prosperous neighborhood, and through an intermediary, a lawyer named Thomas Cooper, he attempted to contact Thomas Jefferson, who was recruiting a faculty for the University of Virginia. "Thomas Cooper informed me," Horwitz wrote Jefferson in 1818, "that when in Virginia he mentioned my name to you as professor . . . in the College of Charlotte-Ville, . . . and that you replied to him . . . such a professorship might be instituted. This induces me to take the liberty of addressing you. . . ." The application was never answered, calling into question later accounts of the life of Jonathan Horwitz—one appeared in a magazine profile of Ambassador Bullitt in 1939—in which Horwitz was described as "a Baltimore physician and friend of Thomas Jefferson's," who during Jefferson's presidency "was twice sent abroad on diplomatic missions." Jonathan Horwitz did move to Baltimore, in 1830—four years after Jefferson's death—but he had forsaken medicine and had returned to Hebrew scholarship: in 1839 he published *A Defence of the Cosmogony of Moses.* As for the diplomatic missions abroad, they could not have occurred, since the letter from Horwitz to Jefferson—from which it can be deduced the two men had never met—was written in 1818, nine years after the end of Jefferson's two terms as president.

Jonathan Horwitz died in 1852. "Whether or not he himself abandoned Judaism for Christianity is not known," Wolf and Whiteman wrote, but he was buried in an Episcopal cemetery, "and his children, from whom are descended the

Horwitz and Bullitt families of Philadelphia, were all brought up in that faith." (According to Bullitt family genealogical records, this account of the marriage of Jonathan Horwitz to the daughter of Joseph Andrews is incorrect, and Jonathan Horwitz instead was born in Berlin and married the daughter of Major John Andrews [1746–1813] of New York. Both he and his descendants were Episcopalians.)

Jonathan and Deborah Horwitz had three sons, all of whom studied medicine at the University of Pennsylvania, but only one, Phineas, went into practice; he became the surgeon general of the United States Navy during the Civil War. His two brothers, Orville and Benjamin, settled in Baltimore, where they practiced law and entered business—Orville Horwitz, the grandfather of William C. Bullitt, Jr., made a fortune from the ownership of a streetcar company—and they were wed to sisters, the daughters of Samuel D. Gross: Orville married Maria Gross, and Benjamin married Louisa Gross.

The undisputed leader in academic surgery of his era, Gross was born in 1805 on a farm near Easton, Pennsylvania, and he studied at the Jefferson Medical College in Philadelphia, graduating in 1828. By age twenty-five he had translated several medical works from French and German, and in 1830 he published an original work, a treatise on injuries of bones and joints. He left Philadelphia for financial reasons, and after practicing in Easton for a few years he went to Ohio, where, in 1835, he was appointed professor of pathological anatomy at Cincinnati Medical College. In 1839, the year Maria Gross was born, he published his best-known work, *Elements of Pathological Anatomy*, the first attempt in English at a systematic presentation of the subject, and it established him as an authority without equal. In 1840 Dr. Gross was named professor of surgery at the University of Louisville, a post he held, except for a brief stint in New York City, until 1856. In that year he returned to Philadelphia as professor of surgery at Jefferson Medical College, and he remained there for the balance of his career, which ended with his death in 1884. In 1910, four years before she died, Maria Gross Horwitz endowed a chair at Jefferson in honor of her father, and it is at Jefferson that "The Gross Clinic"—the painting that established Thomas C. Eakins, a Philadelphia artist, as a leading exponent of a new naturalistic form—is displayed. Gross was succeeded as professor of surgery at Jefferson by his son, Samuel W. Gross, who shortly before his father died had persuaded William Osler, the noted Canadian physician and professor of medicine—he was Sir William Osler, as he had been knighted for his accomplishments—to come to the University of Pennsylvania. The younger Dr. Gross died in 1889, and his widow, Grace Revere Gross, married Dr. Osler.

William C. Bullitt, Sr., and Louisa Gross Horwitz, the daughter of Orville and Maria Horwitz, were married on June 4, 1889, in Baltimore; it was his second marriage—a first wife had died at the time of the birth of a son, John C. Bullitt, in October 1886—and her first. Louisa Horwitz was twenty-five, the sheltered daughter of wealthy parents, who was alone: her father had died two years before, and her mother was going to Europe to live. Baltimore had been just a way station for the Horwitz family (interestingly, though, the Orville Horwitz of Ambassador Bullitt's generation, his cousin who was born in 1909, studied medicine at Johns Hopkins, not the University of Pennsylvania), which was really a Philadelphia family. The Horwitz homes in Baltimore had been designated for public use, one as an art gallery, the other, a country estate, as a memorial to Maryland's war dead; and Louisa Horwitz was happy to be going home to Rittenhouse Square. (Actually their first home was at 1322 Locust Street, a seven-block walk from the square, but they later moved to 222 Rittenhouse Square West, where both William Bullitt, Sr., and Louisa Bullitt lived out their years.) Louisa had just two interests in life, her family and the church—she was so devoted to her husband and fundamentally devout that when he died, she wanted to follow him to heaven forthwith, for fear that he would be reunited with his first wife—and she worshiped regularly at Holy Trinity, at Nineteenth and Walnut. On January 25, 1891, her first child, a son named William Christian Bullitt, Jr., was born at home, and he nearly met with immediate disaster: he was placed on a chair shortly after birth, and Lady Grace Osler, his great aunt by her previous marriage to Samuel W. Gross, sat on him and all but suffocated him.

Growing Up Rich

THE PHILADELPHIA of January 1891, the Old Philadelphia into which William Bullitt was born, was a land of privilege: "hansom cabs with snow-frosted windows and with coats of arms on each door," Bullitt wrote in a novel published in 1926; ". . . earnest young men in silk hats with silver-handled canes and elegant young women in thick fur capes." It was a far cry from the Philadelphia of some of young Bullitt's less fortunate contemporaries, such as W. C. Fields, the comic actor ("On the whole, I'd rather be in Philadelphia," Fields supposedly said on his deathbed); Marian Anderson, the great contralto; and John

B. Kelly, the father of Princess Grace of Monaco, who made millions as a building contractor but who was an Irish Catholic (a world champion oarsman, Kelly was not permitted to compete in the Diamond Sculls at Henley, England, in 1920 because he had worked with his hands). Rittenhouse Square, originally Southwest Square—it was laid out in the Philadelphia plan of 1682 in response to William Penn's desire for a "Greene Towne, which will never be burnt, and always be wholesome"—was renamed around 1825 in memory of David Rittenhouse, an astronomer-philosopher and first director of the United States Mint. Covering an area of approximately six and three-quarters acres, the square was first inhabited in 1840 when a house was built by James Harper, a brickmaker and a politician, who served in Congress from 1833 to 1837; it was used during the Civil War as a drill field for Union recruits; and by the end of the 1860s several red brick and white marble structures had appeared, the homes of railroad magnates, textile tycoons, well-to-do merchants (including John Wanamaker), plus a few eminent lawyers and doctors. (Despite the population growth cows, pigs, and chickens were still kept on small farms on the south side of the square.) So, at first, living on the square signified new wealth—it was plainly not on a social par with Society Hill, an older neighborhood fifteen blocks to the east—but as new-rich upstarts developed into Old Philadelphians and became accepted, Rittenhouse Square became more than a pleasant place to live: it was their symbol. "Is there any other city, . . ." Bullitt wrote in retrospect, "in which every one who counts lives in an area three streets by eight surrounding a Sacred Square?" There was also the country place in Devon, on the Main Line—Bill Bullitt's grandfather had named it Oxmoor, after the Kentucky plantation on which he was raised—where the family spent summers and celebrated Christmas. "Silver plates on heavy linen," Bullitt remembered, "mountains of fruit and trees of roses, forests of candles, deep cut glass. Twenty-dollar gold pieces under the children's napkins. . . . Grapefruit, black bean soup, terrapin, turkey with cranberries, roast beef, asparagus, canvasback duck, salad, . . . coffee ice cream, plum pudding blazing. . . . Champagne, . . . glacés, chocolates, peppermints, raisins, walnuts, figs and dates."

Louisa Bullitt was a diminutive woman, dark-haired and finely featured; she had an agile mind and a tart tongue, though her gentle nature softened the sting of her criticism. With her sons she was strict and quick to reprove: "Tu m'as compris," she would say sharply, "Hear what I say" (French was spoken at her luncheon table, always), and the boys would obey. It was a ritual for them to say morning prayers in her bedroom, and hymns were sung regularly on Sunday evening, the mother singing and playing the piano and little Willie, as he was known then, joining her, for he was the musically talented one. Willie was her favorite—Jack was not regarded as a half brother by the younger boys, but *she* made the distinction—and Orville, born three years after Bill, learned to live with her preference: he was the ugly duckling who cried a lot, while cheerful Willie got to go places with Mother. Bill Bullitt revered his father, but from a distance, for Jack was his favorite: "Bill always insisted that he wanted to be buried at Father's feet," Orville said after his brother died, and he was.

William Bullitt, Sr., was the opposite of his wife: an imposing man, though not large in stature, he was reserved, even taciturn. He would come to the dinner table and announce that stocks were up or stocks were down, whatever—that was that; and his advice to his sons did not extend beyond basic honesty and morality: "Go straight, boy," was how he would put it, simply. He did not share his wife's religious fervor, but he would take her to Holy Trinity on Sundays, at least in the winter, and stay through the first twenty minutes of the sermon; in the summer, though, he preferred to play golf. The elder Bullitt was an Old Philadelphian through and through (in appearance, with his heavy black mustache and bristling gray beard, he was the image of a tycoon); he resigned from the Norfolk & Western, in fact, because the railroad ordered him to move to Roanoke, Virginia, where the company was headquartered (he then formed Castner, Curran and Bullitt, where for ten years he never addressed his partners by any familiar name, only Mr. Castner or Mr. Curran); and he firmly believed that to be good one had to be rich. He nevertheless impressed upon his sons the importance of humility, reminding them repeatedly how fortunate they were to be able to live comfortably and to attend the schools of their choice; he preached *noblesse oblige*, but the story he told that Bill Bullitt remembered the best was about a Spartan boy whose sense of duty was such that he stood at attention while a fox ate out his insides.

The Willie of his tender years—at seven or so, even with long curly hair and dressed in a sissy suit, there was a swagger in his pose for a formal photograph (thumb hitched to his pants pocket, an impish smirk on his face)—became Billy as a teenager, and by the time he was off to college he preferred to be Bill. (Nevertheless, longtime associates, including Franklin D. Roosevelt and Felix Frankfurter, called him Billy, not to his face but in referring to Bullitt, more likely when they were irritated by something he had said or done.) Willie was spoiled and at the same time sternly disciplined by his mother—he was taken to Europe each summer, but adventures on his own were tightly controlled—and the results were predictable: he was a talented child, already ambitious, but he was restless and often rebellious. The tours of the Continent were a rare treat for someone his age—through his grandmother, who lived in Paris, and an aunt in Rome, who was the Duchess d'Assergio, he met people of nobility and official stature, "people who count," his father said—and there was an educational advantage: as a boy Bullitt was fluent in French and German, and his knowledge of European history was such that he could recite the career of Napoleon, battle by battle. In Philadelphia, though, he was scolded for going to the waterfront with "bad boys," that is, boys of lower-class families, and his ability to negotiate the city streetcar system was considered just too precocious by parents, both his and his playmates'. "My earliest recollection of Bill," R. Sturgis Ingersoll wrote seventy years later, "was . . . in 1898 or 1899. We took the 18th Street trolley to Girard Avenue, changed cars at the intersection, and went to the Zoo. We were alone and certainly not more than eight years old. . . ." What really roused Willie's mother's wrath, however, was an incident involving a little girl he had met on the street, "not like the nice girls you meet at dancing school," she chided. (Willie certainly understood, for dancing school was a weekly event: boys in blue suits and girls in white and pink and blue chiffons, and an orchestra playing "The Blue Danube.") He had brought the girl into the house, where his mother had caught them doing what children innocently do to satisfy their sexual curiosity; and he had been made to promise he would never again have anything to do with such a person. Willie did promise, having been reduced to tears by the rebuke, though it was a promise he would not keep.

"I'm going to be a lawyer and Governor and Secretary of State and President," Bullitt proclaimed early in life, and while he realized none of them, they were real ambitions and not farfetched. "I'm going to show people how they ought to live and have a great civilization." He meant it, for he was first of all a patriot, which may seem a contradiction in that he would live abroad for much of his life; but he would be an expatriate in the tradition of his "star-spangled grandmother," who unfurled the American flag each Fourth of July from the window of her apartment in Paris. Bill Bullitt was seven when the war with Spain was fought in Cuba, and he remembered it when he was the ambassador to France: "I was so excited . . . that I had pictures of the poor Cubans tacked up in my room, as well as one of Teddy Roosevelt. I thought nothing would be smarter than to go out and shoot down two or three Spaniards, because they were so wicked. . . . My emotions had been stirred and my idealism aroused." However, Bullitt's tendency to heated emotions also fostered his rebellious streak: the restlessness had been dismissed as a symptom of his being high-strung, and he would mellow in time; this was different, for Willie Bullitt was the kind of boy who would pull a rose apart to see what was inside. Perhaps it was hereditary, as he was descended from those Kristin pirates, and there happened to be some fairly famous rebels in his ancestry: William Christian, who died in the cause of liberty for the Isle of Man; Fletcher Christian, the mutinous officer of the *Bounty*; and Patrick Henry, whose oratory incited revolt in the American colonies. Billy Bullitt's first real rebellion occurred the day he was to leave for Groton, a school in Massachusetts for sons of the rich (Franklin D. Roosevelt was a Groton graduate, class of 1900): "Every Groton fellow I know is a snob," he declared, and he refused to go.

Bullitt went to De Lancey, a private school in Philadelphia, which offered "to the city boy almost all the advantages of boarding-school life, while he still has the home associations, which should play so important a part in his proper growth and development." Is there a clue in that statement, which appeared in the 1905 school catalog, to the real reason for Bullitt's defiance? He was never known to abhor snobbery, and, in fact, he was quite capable of being an intellectual and social elitist himself; so a better explanation might be that he was fearful of losing the affection of his parents, his mother especially, and simply wished to remain at home, though he was unwilling to admit it and found a pretext. It is also quite likely that he preferred not to leave his Philadelphia stamping ground, both the sanctioned social activities—the parties, plays, and other diversions—and the forbidden territory: "Ask Bullitt who's the girl at the book counter at Wanamaker's and why he goes there so much," quipped a gossip writer in an issue of the school magazine in 1907. If nothing else, it is evident that he was happy and active at De Lancey: "We wish to call attention to the fact," another magazine item went, "that Bill Bullitt has the time to study, play, go out for baseball, and write romantic verses. How does he do it?"

Bullitt was an all-around youngster—versatile and able, clever and well liked. As a student he consistently won an honorable mention in an annual test of general proficiency; as an athlete he made the baseball team, and he excelled at all sports he tried, football pointedly being not one of them: "legalized assault and battery," he called the game in a commentary written for *The De Lancey Monthly* in 1903. Billy Bullitt's writings for the magazine provide the best insight into his character—they show his turn of mind, his fears and misgivings, his prejudices—and they call attention to his never fully realized potential as a brilliant writer. His romantic verses were parodies of the popular romanticists of the day, such as one he wrote in 1905, "with apologies to Henry Wadsworth Longfellow":

> Tell me not in mournful numbers
> That baseball is a worthless game,
> For although there's *foul* about it,
> It's got a *diamond* just the same.

He took the same license with the poem, "Maud Muller," by John Greenleaf Whittier:

> For all sad words of tongue and pen,
> The saddest are these:

It will cost you ten!
(Demerits, that is. . . .)

Bullitt's concern over getting in trouble, his attitude toward authority, was a repeated theme, one he tried to treat with a sense of humor, but not really successfully:

"You!" demanded the teacher, "to whom are you talking?"
"Sir, I was talking to myself."
"Five demerits."
"But, sir, why?"
"For not talking to someone more sensible."

In the fall of 1904 he wrote a poem to that year's graduating seniors, the class of 1905 (Bullitt was in the class of 1908), and he betrayed his premonitions of death, as he would many times in his life:

There are many, all told boys,
The class of 1905,
But twenty years from now, boys,
Will they all be alive?

And thirty years from now, boys,
The ranks will thinner grow,
And the winds will spread our ashes, boys,
Wherever the winds can blow.

The product of a region (Kentucky-north-to-Philadelphia) and a generation (old attitudes, not easily forsworn), Bullitt was brought up to be intolerant of minorities, and his inability to come to terms with equality would at times annul his effectiveness as a writer and as a person. "De Lord he lub de nigger well," he wrote for the *Monthly* in 1905; and in 1907 he wrote a "put-down" of Amelia Jenks Bloomer, an early proponent of women's liberation, for whom a pantlike garment had been named: "The only bloomers a woman should wear are those that grow in her garden."

There were at least two incidents during Bullitt's years at De Lancey that reminded his parents that he was combative and not to be taken lightly. "You're a damned liar," Billy Bullitt said to a German teacher who had accused him of cheating, and the teacher was dismissed by the school, upon complaint of William Bullitt, Sr. On the other occasion Bullitt was beaten in a playground fistfight by George Earle—Earle would later be a good friend of Bullitt's, and a political ally—and Billy demanded boxing lessons as a way to settle the score. Father agreed, and thanks to the tutelage of Freddie Walsh, a professional fighter from Philadelphia, Bullitt was able to whip George Earle and all other comers.

Most Faithful Boy

WHILE willing to yield on the issue of boarding school, Bullitt's parents sensed that their restless son could do with institutional training away from home, and starting in 1904, his thirteenth year, Billy spent summers at Camp Pasquaney in New Hampshire, which while a recreational camp was run in the tradition of a strict English academy: a morning "soak" in the frigid lake was required, and boys whose conduct was substandard were subjected to ridicule (a slob at the dinner table, for example, was ordered to wear a cowbell). Young Bullitt's letters home were not preserved, so his reaction to being shipped off to the woods must be left to conjecture, but there is sound evidence it was positive: first of all, his record as a camper over five summers was excellent; and second, in an evaluation years later he wrote that Camp Pasquaney was "the best educational institution in the United States." He also offered an opinion, interesting if oversimplified, of the Philadelphia of his childhood, which betrayed a frightening supposition of what might have become of him: "The city was totally corrupt. The streets were gang ridden, . . . and many children of prominent families were tough little gangsters, who later achieved prison sentences."

Camp Pasquaney—the name was adopted from the Indians who had inhabited the region around Newfound Lake and means "land of the white birch"—was the idea of Edward Simpson Wilson, who founded the camp in 1895. Wilson's father, John Wall Wilson, a Marine officer in the Civil War and an inventor—he had made a small fortune by devising a way to dump garbage at sea and selling the idea to New York City—had bought a large tract of land that extended up a mountain from the east shore of the lake. Captain Wilson, by this time retired, built a home on the property and called it Eastbourne, for his ancestral estate in Sussex, England; and he and his wife, Lavinia, spent summers there, returning to their apartment in New York for the winter. Their son, Ned—he would be "Mr. Ned" to Pasquaney boys for over thirty-five years—was thirty-two years old in 1895, but he had never discovered a life, either personal or professional, that suited him: he was a bachelor, still very attached to his mother, and unemployed. Ned had gone to Yale, graduating in 1885, but had not been happy there; he had studied medicine for a year at Columbia; he had escorted young boys on trips to Europe; and he had tried his hand at creative writing. However, as a younger colleague at the camp, Charles F. Stanwood, put it, Ned Wilson "was, in the terminology of the day, a 'gentleman.' . . ." Stanwood, who would become the director of the camp eight years after Wilson's death, further wrote: "He drifted, somewhat aimlessly, in and out of medicine, tutoring, and

creative writing. . . . He was, to be sure, successful in making lasting friendships, and he acquired much more than a . . . passing interest in the theater and
in music. But there is nothing in his life to this point to foreshadow the great
qualities which made him only a year or two later a strong and beloved leader of
youth and teacher of moral values."

When Ned Wilson, in 1893, first walked over his father's property, he became, in the words of an official history of the camp, "fired with an ambition. . . ." His father was delighted and ceded to him ample acreage for the site;
Wilson spent the summer of 1894 learning the ropes by working at an established
camp nearby; and in June 1895, he sailed from New York on the boat for Fall
River, Massachusetts—from there to Boston and to Bristol, New Hampshire, by
train—with his first group of boys. One of those boys, C. Mifflin Frothingham,
wrote the history of the camp, in which he explained Wilson's original premise:

> . . . Ned saw the boy of his day wasting his time doing less than nothing during the sum-
> mer. He saw him idling at hotels. Could these boys follow in the footsteps of their fathers?
> Their fathers had not built their success by mere inheritance. They had been brought up in a
> more serious atmosphere, their boyhood had been spent in an office. . . . Now, this
> generation was living on large estates, and frittering its time away at fashionable resorts.

Writing in *The Pasquaney Annual* in 1907, Ned Wilson elaborated on his ideal:

> The closer my association with boys the more intense was my sympathy in their trials
> and temptations, and I soon became impressed with the fact that the gentleman's son, at
> least, was a misunderstood and often much neglected young individual. Here I felt was a
> field, almost untrodden, for the noblest work in the world—the making of the man! My
> very soul cried out with enthusiasm and earnestness to do my part here. . . . With an
> innate love for boys and sincere desire to help them over the many pitfalls, . . . I felt this
> must be a call, and therefore I abandoned every other project and ambition in my life and
> dedicated myself, soul and body, to this work.

Charles Stanwood acknowledged that in its early years, at least, Camp
Pasquaney was a place for "more or less wealthy boys of what was considered
good social pedigree," and he noted that Mr. Ned, as late as the 1920s, was
seeing to it that Pasquaney was being described in promotion brochures to parents
as "the most socially acceptable of the summer camps." Stanwood attributed this
in large measure to the influence of Lavinia Wilson, citing a letter she wrote in
1899, "in which she urges her son to be careful to take 'only nice boys,' "
warning that he would otherwise "run the serious risk of offending those nice
parents who had entrusted their sons to him." Stanwood admitted, rather
ruefully: "The idea that there could be any value in mixing boys from dissimilar
economic and social backgrounds had not yet been widely introduced and accepted." He was, however, quick to defend Wilson and other founders of private

institutions, who were "committed almost exclusively to the education of boys from families of wealth and social standing." It was first of all an economic necessity, but "beyond this mundane reason . . . there was a high idealism in their motivation: privileged boys needed a special kind of education, which would teach them that in terms of character and service they owed more to their country and to society . . . than did those who had not been so blessed." Looking back many years later, Bullitt revealed no concern for the problem of social selection: "When I reached Camp for the first time in 1904," he wrote, "I met a large number of boys of the highest quality."

Bullitt remembered Mr. Ned from the first day he arrived at camp, for he was assigned a bed next to Wilson's. He later recounted, "I was immediately told by the other boys that I should not be able to get any sleep because he *snored*! The first night, therefore, I committed a sacrilege. I placed a sneaker on the floor between our beds, and each time he began to trumpet and awakened me, I rapped him on the nose with the sole of my sneaker. He never realized what was going on—but found he was sleeping fitfully. About a week later he retired for the rest of the summer to his shack just built that year next to his office."

The "most faithful boy" award was considered by Ned Wilson—therefore *it was*—the honor of most significance, especially since it had been his mother's idea. Lavinia Wilson had given the silver cup on which the name of each year's winner was inscribed, and she had decreed, as Wilson wrote in 1907, that the names were to be those of campers who were loyal to the activities and aims of the camp.

Nor was it her wish that anyone should be considered most faithful who was merely passively so; that is, who was good simply because he was not energetic enough to be anything else. Instead, she meant it as a recognition of an inclination on the part of the boy to understand the great benefit resulting from a life led in strict conformity to the principles of the camp, and of devotion on his part to the one object of improving its opportunities as far as it was possible for him to do so. Such a boy must have the highest type of loyalty, that of obedience for love of the principle that he obeys.

Billy Bullitt was named "most faithful boy" that year, and he was the best all-around camper: an outstanding athlete, who won prizes in water sports and was the camp tennis champion; one of the select few to be made a member of Sigma Alpha, an honor society patterned after Skull and Bones at Yale; and the most popular among his peers. He was liked because he was well-behaved without being faultless; in fact, he was a prankster, who was often called Awful Bullitt, and he was notorious for his fascination with intrigue. "Arrival of Billy Bullitt," went a report in *The White Birch*, the camp newspaper, in 1905. "Craze of deciphering secret codes strikes several of the intellects of camp."

There was more to Pasquaney than sports, as interest was encouraged—and ability rewarded—in nonathletic pursuits, such as acting, singing, and nature studies. "I was skeptical at first," wrote Charles Stanwood, who was a first-year camper in 1921, "but in the course of the nine weeks I had to do a lot of rearranging of my earlier notions about conformity. Evidently 'queerness' was not only tolerated at Pasquaney, it was actually encouraged." Bullitt's preferred form of "queerness" was dramatics: in 1907 he played the male lead in the camp play, and according to a review in *The Pasquaney Annual* he "won much applause for his efforts." Female roles were played by younger boys, as Bullitt had in previous years, handling them with remarkable finesse, both in appearance and in mannerisms.

It was customary for the winner of the "most faithful boy" award to call an end to his days as a camper, but Bullitt, at age seventeen, returned for the summer of 1908 and lived in a cabin he had marked as his own by carving his name on the ceiling (he would also be back as a counselor in 1910, following his sophomore year at Yale); and he was elected president of the Camp Society, having been secretary the year before. Anticlimactically, he was defeated for the tennis championship by a first-year fifteen-year-old named Paul B. Watson, Jr. The match was described in *The Annual*:

As a mere question of skill the differences in style of the two make it impossible to say where the advantage lay. Bullitt certainly had all the speed, and his excellent overhead game made him very formidable at the net. Watson, on the other hand, though less brilliant, was far steadier and was so hopelessly certain in the back court that he frequently exasperated his opponent into attempting greater speed than he could control. . . . Watson's real superiority lay in his judgment. Early in the match the evenness of the players made it apparent that the contest would become a test of endurance, and Watson had the good sense to spare himself and keep his opponent busy on the sidelines, while Bullitt wore himself down by unnecessary activity and the violence of his game. The final score was 9–7, 7–5, 5–7, 12–10.

Ned Wilson evidently exerted enormous influence on Bullitt. "The extraordinary quality of the boys at Camp," Bullitt wrote later, "was, of course, due to Mr. Ned, whose passion for the Camp was such that it lifted his qualities above his defects." The defects were manifest: Ned Wilson was a prig and a snob; he was a simplistic moralist, ever condescending to the boys; he was a bigot and a misogynist, who had revered his mother but barely tolerated other women, save servants. (The boys at camp one year nicknamed him "The Merry Widow.") Yet he was an impressive presence, an effective speaker, and the sermons he preached each Sunday in a chapel in the woods were what most Pasquaney boys remembered best. Charles Stanwood attempted to explain Mr. Ned's mastery:

He was magnificently—terrifyingly—intolerant of anything second-rate. Cheapness in speech or in action was anathema to him, and he blasted it without the slightest consideration for any other person concerned. He was sparing with his praise; yet when occasionally he patted one of us on the back and said a few, half-embarrassed words of approval, we knew that every syllable had been honestly earned. Mr. Ned was absolutely sincere in his dealings with boys. He treated us as people. . . . It was simple and direct; above all, it was spoken as one man to another.

"True manliness is not the possession of any one quality, however fine and perfect," Mr. Ned declared one morning in July 1902, as he would on summer Sundays for some thirty years to come,

without the other good qualities embraced in the one greatest of all titles, "Christian Gentleman." It is my purpose . . . to talk . . . of these qualities that make the man. . . . Success . . . depends largely on thorough preparation. . . . If you have been careless in your preparation, your college life will be hard, leading probably to discouragement and failure. . . . In the same way those who go on the Long Walk [a week-long, hundred-mile hike initiated by Wilson in 1895] . . . are those who have shown themselves thoroughly prepared by short walks . . . and by weeks of hardship. . . . In just the same way, though of vastly greater importance, your life of ten weeks here is in preparation for your whole life beyond. . . . I said that boys often have a one-sided idea of manliness. I well remember a simple phrase, . . . which gives a very good idea of what I mean by all-round manliness, . . . "good, strong, and beautiful." These simple words . . . can only apply to one who is of an all-round development. . . .

. . . I want to speak of bravery. We all know and admire physical bravery. . . . However, I wish now to speak of a kind of bravery which is far more important and rare; that is, moral bravery. To be firm and fearless in the doing of duty and to stand bravely by your convictions are the greatest kinds of bravery. I never tire of talking of one of my dearest boy friends, who by strength of character refused to countenance immoral stories. Though he did so at first at the cost of popularity, he soon so won the respect of his classmates as to be regarded as one of the most popular men in his class at college. . . . I wish to mention . . . gentleness, the most beautiful of the Christian graces. Many of the most truly great and manly men have had the gentleness of women. Heartlessness is unmanly. It is the true spirit of a man to defend, not to destroy life. . . .

On successive Sundays Wilson returned to his theme, and there was a cogency and a continuity to it, which he developed and perfected over the years:

Manhood is impossible without honor. . . . It is the fundamental and crowning element of the true man. . . . You cannot be too careful of this particular, for it is the basis of all your other qualities. . . . Tell the truth boldly, frankly. . . . As the old saying has it, "Tell the truth, and shame the Devil." . . .

Speaking from the perspective of middle age, Bullitt said: "I am sure that whatever has proved to be sound in my character derives from my parents and Pasquaney—and not from . . . any other institution."

II

Collegian,
Journalist,
Public Servant

Most Brilliant at Yale

BILL BULLITT, class of 1912, arrived in New Haven in the fall of 1908, a time when there was little to suggest that Yale would one day be a great academic institution. ". . . the professional spirit prevails in Yale athletics," wrote Edward E. Slosson, the respected educator, in *Great American Universities*, "and the amateur spirit prevails in Yale scholarship." Football, an adaptation of English rugby, was introduced at Yale by the legendary Walter Camp, who coached the team from 1888 to 1892, winning sixty-seven games and losing only two; and while the competition had improved by Bullitt's day, the 1909 team was an undefeated national champion. The undergraduate campus, Yale College it was called, was a caricature of itself—especially on a warm spring day, with young men sucking lollypops, shooting marbles, and tossing the lids of Mother Frisbee's cookie cans to each other (not realizing that they were inventing a popular American game). Studious pursuits were even frowned upon, which accounts for the dilemma of Sinclair Lewis, a graduate of Yale in 1907, who went on to become the first American to win the Nobel Prize for literature. Lewis was at a distinct disadvantage: he was midwestern, having come from Sioux City, Iowa; he was ugly, his face scarred by acne; and worst of all he was serious about a superior education, which earned him the nickname "God Forbid Lewis." Yale was establishing a pattern for its rival Princeton, as it was described a decade later by another noted novelist, F. Scott Fitzgerald, with undue emphasis on birthright and social hierarchy. "I'm frankly aristocratic . . . ," an upperclassman advised in *Stover at Yale*, by Owen Johnson, who graduated in 1900, "and what I say, others think. You may think the world begins outside of college. It doesn't. It begins right here."

Superb athlete though he was, Bullitt did not go out for Yale teams, as he had realized after an ordering of priorities that sports would interfere with his more important interests in literary and dramatic activities. As for the college social structure he was well-qualified, with his handsome appearance and facile mind, not to mention his ample bank account. Bullitt had already learned that a quick wit was more appreciated than academic prowess, yet good grades were expected by his parents as well as his peers, so he found a way to beat the system—how to achieve those grades with a minimum of study time. He was an accomplished linguist, owing to his frequent trips to Europe, and he spoke French and German better than his teachers; but instead of advanced languages, which would have been a challenge, he signed up for beginning and intermediate courses, and as a classmate who sat next to him in freshman German testified years later, he "literally never cracked a book." Of the twenty-six courses Bullitt took over four years at Yale, fifteen were in languages, including English in which he excelled, and not surprisingly he was elected to Phi Beta Kappa; but the experience did not markedly mature his mind or develop his character. Attitudes at Yale were similarly smug and therefore reinforcing of those of Old Philadelphia, so instead of seeing one set of values smashed by another, enabling him to construct a set of his own out of the ruins, Bullitt found his old illusions being supported by new ones. The danger was that he would emerge a genteel sophisticate, not the fine thinker for which he had the potential: "Bill Bullitt was very witty and good company," said a classmate, Norman H. Reed, who added that "the repartee was scintillating." Reed remembered an English teacher "who himself was quite a wit, and he and Bill would try to outdo each other in class." It was for his wit and for his extracurricular success that Bullitt was voted the most brilliant member of the class of 1912.

Bullitt was also noted for his tremendous energy—as his classmates recalled, he was able to work up to twenty hours a day—and this was indicated by his range of activities, as they were summarized in the history of his class.

> . . . Bill Bullitt so monopolized debating that he alone from the class finally made the team and was subsequently elected captain. . . . He debated . . . against Princeton, 1911, and was a member of Delta Sigma Rho, an honorary debating society. He was an editor of the *News*, secretary of the Debating Union, president of the Debating Association, . . . and president of the Dramatic Association. He was a member of the City Government Club and the Elizabethan Club.

He also founded the Mince Pie Club, along with his friend Cole Porter of the class of 1913; it was a forum for satire and other forms of humor. "I like anything as long as it is different," said Porter in an apparent explanation of the club's inane purpose.

What prompted such an effort? To a degree it was Bullitt's intellectual appetite, but it was also his desire to demonstrate his mental superiority and thereby gain social recognition. "There was no fiercer competition in the business world than the undergraduate competition for social awards," wrote Henry Seidel Canby, a professor of English when Bullitt was at Yale. "Besides its strenuosities the pursuit of marks or even scholarship glowed dimly." There were, according to a poll of Bullitt's class, four most valued "social" awards—a Phi Beta Kappa key, a varsity "Y," a *Daily News* badge, and a *Yale Lit* emblem—and as a "Phi

Bete" and a member of the editorial board of the *News* Bullitt won two of them; just one would have assured his acceptance in an honor society. "The seniors have fifteen in each," said the upperclassman in *Stover at Yale*; "they give out their elections end of junior year. . . . That's what we're all working for." In May 1911 Bill Bullitt was "tapped" for membership in Scroll and Key, one of the more prestigious societies.

The stage was Bullitt's most consuming interest, and he directed the Dramatic Association, the "Dramat," with the help of two friends who would become theater professionals: Cole Porter, the composer of hit musicals, and Monty Woolley, the actor. In his junior year, as president of the Dramat, Bullitt was pushing himself to exhaustion: up at 5 A.M. after a few hours of sleep, calisthenics and breakfast, a few hours of classes, a stint at the *News* and maybe a meeting of the Elizabethan Club, and then on to the vital work of the Dramat. He appeared in many student-produced plays, taking female roles for the most part: Mistress Page in *The Merry Wives of Windsor*, Lady Gay Spanker in *London Assurance*, Katharine in *The Taming of the Shrew*. "He made a hell of a good-looking girl," said a classmate, Henry B. Richards. "I remember a picture of Bullitt in a program for a play. I cut it out, and it made a hell of a good-looking girl. For a year or two I would bring it out of my wallet and say, as a joke, 'Want to see my best girl?' They were always fooled, and all of the guys wanted to meet her." Bullitt's most memorable role, though, was not as a woman but as Ralph, the grocer's apprentice who pretends knighthood, in *The Knight of the Burning Pestle*, a seventeenth-century comedy by Francis Beaumont and John Fletcher. (Orville Bullitt remarked much later that his brother was "at his most typical" when playing the tragicomical knight, a character based on Cervantes's Don Quixote de la Mancha.) It is a difficult role logistically, especially late in the play, when the knight, in gray satin and silver armor, appears on a stunning white horse and announces in a resonant voice:

> London, to thee I do present the merry month of May;
> Let each true subject be content to hear me what I say:
> For from the top of conduit-head, as plainly may appear,
> I will both tell my name to you, and wheretofore I came here.

Bullitt, wishing to make the most of an impressive moment, had decided on an outdoor setting. A stage had been constructed between two student living quarters, Connecticut and Vanderbilt halls, and a white horse had been borrowed from the New Haven Fire Department. Meticulous to a tee, Bullitt had asked a member of the supporting cast to walk the horse just before the curtain, but what he had feared would happen did: the horse misbehaved. There were whispers in the audience, first of astonishment, then of amusement, as Bullitt gave the knight's oration. "Look the horse is shitting," someone said. "He's shitting on the stage."

In the summer of 1911, between his junior and senior year at Yale, Bullitt saw his college career come to a jolting, if temporary, halt: he suffered a physical collapse. Bullitt was exhausted and very ill from overwork. The disorder was difficult to diagnose—the symptoms were acute intestinal pain and failing hearing and sight—so Bullitt went home to Philadelphia and checked into the University of Pennsylvania Hospital. The doctors were baffled but agreed that he had little time to live, perhaps six months; they put him on a diet of spinach and milk and suggested he move to a warm, remote region. Bullitt chose Redlands, California, east of Los Angeles, which was in keeping with a habit of Philadelphians to retreat to areas of the Far West. (Owen Wister, for example, at his doctor's urging had gone to Wyoming in the 1880s and found there the setting for his best-selling novel, *The Virginian*.) Bullitt outlived the six-month prediction but felt little better and was bored with California, so he returned to Philadelphia, where surgery revealed adhesions. When as a boy Bullitt had suffered a severe stomach upset, an appendectomy was performed, and it could have resulted in the later development of adhesions. The doctors did what they could, told Bullitt to stay on his bland diet, and sent him home to his family, where he might live out his days in comfort. (For some reason an extensive course of X-ray therapy was carried out when such therapy was in its infancy, and it could have been a factor in the later development of leukemia, in the view of Orville Horwitz, Bullitt's cousin and physician. Bullitt died of leukemia at age seventy-six.) It was not a good time for Bullitt to live at home, though, for his father was disabled by heart disease, and his mother was distraught; so he was off to Europe for the summer, feeling much better, since he was eating lobster and drinking champagne instead of spinach and milk. He had found a cure, or so he believed, and he arranged for readmission to Yale in September 1912: "At present he is traveling in Europe . . . to recuperate," it read in the 1912 yearbook, in which Bullitt was listed as an ex-member of the class, though in addition to being voted most brilliant he got votes for most likely to succeed, hardest worker, most versatile, and most entertaining.

"Bill Bullitt is still holding forth at the Elizabethan Club," wrote the historian of the class of 1913, "electing to membership whom he pleases and setting the pace of undergraduate thought in general." He had acquired an eminence that was not diminished by his having dropped out for a year: ". . . everybody still considers Bill important and indispensable." He roomed that year in 33 Vanderbilt with another Philadelphian, also originally of the class of 1912, Carroll Chevalier Carstairs, whose interests were similar to Bullitt's—Carstairs had written for the *Lit*, the *Record*, and the *Courant*, and he was a member of the Elizabethan Club and the Mince Pie Club—although he had not strived for social leadership. Bullitt had a reputation among his fellow students as an oddball—once at a party he pulled the whiskers of a distinguished professor, who was not at all amused—and his standing did not depend on popularity, which was just as well. "He would never call on you unless he wanted something," one classmate observed, and another noted that he was always in a hurry, always pushing himself: "He may have accepted the snobbery of his contemporaries in Philadelphia, but never their detached contentment—he was one of those for whom 'the world is not enough.' " Still another remembered Bullitt as "bullheaded—you could not tell him anything," and in later years Yalemen would meet him on the street and say hello, only to be dismissed with icy formality.

Bullitt's brusqueness was intended, for the disaffection was mutual: "I cannot remember a single distinguished figure among my contemporaries there," he said of Yale fifty years later; "most of them thought only of going to New York and making a lot of money." There were exceptions, of course. Bullitt and Cole Porter found each other stimulating, though they lost contact soon after graduation, and Bullitt corresponded over the years with Philip S. Platt, an unassuming and almost unnoticed member of the class of '12. Bullitt wrote Platt from London in 1919 of having seen Carroll Carstairs—Carstairs, a decorated officer of British artillery and a member of the Coldstream Guards, had been seriously wounded in France—and told how his former roommate was keeping company with beautiful women: "I don't know how he manages to keep his virginity. He must have kissed hundreds." But Bullitt's lasting regard was reserved for members of the university faculty, men like Chauncey Tinker, an authority on Samuel Johnson. It appears, though, that only one of them, Charles Seymour—a history instructor who became president of Yale in 1937—kept in touch, and that was because he and Bullitt worked together in Washington in 1918.

Dropout at Harvard

"I'M GOING TO BE a lawyer . . . ," Bullitt had announced as a child, and in his entry in the 1913 Yale yearbook he listed the law as his intended profession, indicating he still meant to follow in the footsteps of his forebears; family tradition, however, was the one and only reason. "Bullitt was never interested in studying law," said a law school classmate, Alfred Jaretski. "He loved the limelight," explained another, George H. Day, "and men like that are always unhappy with the law, because it is years before they come into the spectacular things." Actually Bullitt had dreamed in childhood of becoming a diplomat—his greatest ambition, he said once, having achieved it, was "to be . . . the ambassador of my country in Paris"—and as a senior at Yale, in an exception to his rule, he signed up for a difficult history course that was considered valuable preparation for an overseas post. The professor was Hiram Bingham, an explorer (in 1911 Bingham led an expedition to Peru and discovered the ruins of Machu Picchu), who later became the governor of Connecticut and a United States senator from that state. Bingham admired Bullitt and chose him as one of a small group to go to Washington to take a foreign service test, during which each student was asked to state his qualifications and intentions. Bullitt decided it was no time to be modest: he was fluent in several foreign languages, he said, and was a good speaker; members of his family were socially prominent in Paris and Rome; he had excellent connections throughout Europe; and if he was assigned to an embassy there, he could not fail to do well. (Another student, William Bates, was do dismayed by Bullitt's self-assurance that when his turn came, he said simply: "Gentlemen, I am not able to report qualifications such as you have just heard, but my intentions are easy to give. My intentions are to return to New Haven and go on with my studies.")

Bullitt did not then get a chance to prove himself as a diplomat, however, for he was the dutiful son of an insistent father; and in the fall of 1913 he was in Cambridge, Massachusetts, a first-year student at the Harvard Law School. The faculty at Harvard was composed of the pillars of legal academia, such figures as Roscoe Pound, Ezra R. Thayer, and Joseph H. Beale, who would not stand for antics of the sort that Bullitt had practiced at Yale—the classroom repartee and the diverting of a discussion in order to dominate it. These were no-nonsense men, Bullitt soon learned—exacting perfectionists and sticklers about precise thought; in particular, much to Bullitt's distress, there was Joey Beale. Beale, who taught at Harvard over a forty-year span—save for a two-year leave, 1902 to 1904, when he was the founder and first dean of the law school at the University of Chicago—was dynamic and demanding. Short, plump, and balding, he was quite a cheerful fellow, as he pedaled his bicycle across the campus, a green book bag dangling from his shoulder, greeting his many friends, mainly students who had made it through the first year. During that first year, though, Beale could be brutal in class, as he bullied, cajoled, and singled out for ridicule students who had missed the point: he was determined to weed out those who could not stand the pressure, and Bullitt was one who could not. Others composed doggerel about Beale's teaching methods:

> Oh Joey Beale, oh Joey Beale, . . .
> 'Tisn't right, 'tisn't fair
> To split cases by the hair.
> You will find, if you pause,
> You're the proximate cause
> Of every young lawyer's despair.

But Bullitt, the minute class had ended, stomped back to his room in anger, unable to accept the browbeating. When he was not tormented, he was bored by the law, which he deemed to be void of the finer elements of life—beauty, grace, style—and it was affecting him physically: his hair was falling out, and he often suffered indigestion from drinking wine and smoking cigarettes. He worried about his sexual potency—sex for pleasure was tawdry, he believed, so he would have nothing to do with streetwalkers in town—and when a roommate raised the question of his manhood, he became enraged and took a swing at him.

With the death of William C. Bullitt, Sr., on March 22, 1914, any inducement to pursue a legal career disappeared, and Bullitt was ready to leave Harvard at the earliest excuse, which Beale—happily, it must be assumed, for he no doubt sensed Bullitt's attitude—provided. Beale asked Bullitt in class if it was illegal for a woman to possess an unregistered firearm, and Bullitt answered, yes—if the woman had an unregistered weapon in her purse, she was breaking the law. Next question: if we slip a dollar into her purse, unknown to the woman, is she in possession of that dollar? Again Bullitt answered yes, but he was uneasy, aware that Beale was setting a trap. Question: if we slip an unregistered pistol into her purse, unknown to the woman, is she in possession of that pistol? Yes, said Bullitt again, but he was not so certain. Final question: is the woman breaking the law by carrying an unregistered firearm? No, said Bullitt, she was not. Gently for the moment, Beale retraced the steps of the case to show that the woman was carrying an unregistered firearm and that such possession was a criminal act; and Bullitt retreated uneasily, asserting that she was carrying an unregistered firearm, which usually constituted a criminal act, but her act was not criminal. Beale, feigning exasperation, swept a handkerchief across his brow and again presented Bullitt with the logic of his own argument, trying to convince him that the woman was guilty of a criminal act. "No!" Bullitt was unnerved. "It isn't just!" Beale simply smiled and advised that the divinity school was just three blocks down the street. Laughter rocked the classroom, and Bullitt stormed out, going directly to the railroad station, where he caught an express for Philadelphia, arriving home in time for dinner.

Newspaperman and Novelist

———

BULLITT'S AMBITIONS were not altered by his dismal experience at Harvard Law—if anything the death of his father brought a government career into sharper focus. Beyond relieving him of parental pressures it called attention to financial realities: his father had left the bulk of his estate to his widow—except the mining properties, which he willed to the employees of the Pocahontas Coal Company—and Bullitt's inheritance, like that of his two brothers, produced an income of $6,000 a year, enough to live on comfortably in 1914 but hardly enough to make him wealthy. Money was a secondary motive—as it always would be for Bullitt, who never bothered to balance his own checkbook—although it was not irrelevant: Bullitt would become a foreign correspondent as a stepping-stone to a diplomatic post. There were those family connections abroad: he had contacts in the governments of Europe, which would make him invaluable to a newspaper. Going a step further—Bullitt had already devised his scheme by the spring of 1914—the U.S. government would be grateful for intelligence from Europe, since there was no agency in Washington at the time responsible for espionage. Had there been one, it might have been a bit more clear that the first world war was just months away, given that hostilities had been simmering for two years: in 1912 there was the first war of the Balkans, with Serbia, Greece, Bulgaria, and Montenegro lined up against Turkey; and in 1913 Serbia formed a coalition with Rumania, Greece, and Turkey to defeat Bulgaria. It had occurred to Bullitt that he could exchange information obtained in the capitals of Europe for a job in the administration of President Wilson, probably in the Department of State; in keeping with his plan Bullitt, in June 1914, escorted his mother—she was still disconsolate over the death of her husband—on a tour of Russia and Germany. He carried a letter from an editor of *The New York Times* saying that he would like to receive articles from Bullitt.

———

Bullitt had also begun working on a novel, though it would not be finished for another ten years; he would call the book *It's Not Done*, as opposed to what *is* done for the sake of good form. (Much of what was not done *was* done, even on Sunday, in Bullitt's fictional Philadelphia—Chesterbridge, he called it—and the explicit allusions to sexual behavior, wrote Bullitt's brother Orville, "aroused considerable controversy.") The book was essentially autobiographical, and the point of view of the protagonist, John Corsey, can be presumed to reflect the author's attitudes as a young man: democracies do not work and do not really exist; what appear to be democracies are actually secret aristocracies with a few gentlemen making decisions for the benefit of the masses. "There are certain things no gentleman will do," a dowager observes; "practices quite within the law, which people who aren't gentlemen will countenance." Her dinner partner, a man who speaks with self-bestowed authority, agrees and adds: "A gentleman is a man one can be sure of. You may be able to break him, but you can't make him bend." Then the voice of another gentleman at the table: "It's a matter of private manners and morals: a code of conduct for the whole area that's outside the law. . . . And it's much stricter than the law, and finer. An aristocrat is a man who holds to that code." On the other hand there are upstarts and parvenus, who have achieved power in a society gone to hell: "The worst of it," Corsey laments,

is that men who ought to be street cleaners and grocers and dry goods clerks and butchers and mechanics, and would be in any other country, have millions and millions. They *are* the country today. We may have been here three hundred years, and they may have been here twenty or fifty, but the whole taste of the country has become their taste, and its standards have become their standards.

Bullitt had real people in mind, parvenus, he believed them to be, named Wanamaker and Widener (Roediger and Leather in the novel), who by 1914 had made millions and had become established—John Wanamaker was postmaster general of the United States when Bullitt was born—if not accepted by Old Philadelphia society. Bullitt also had envisioned his own future in the plot of his novel: John Corsey goes to work as a reporter for *The Chesterbridge Times* and soon becomes the editor, appointed by his brother, the publisher, whose wife had inherited the paper.

———————

Bullitt was closer than ever to his mother once she was widowed, and he lived with her in the house on Rittenhouse Square and at the country estate in Devon until she died of influenza in 1919, when he had been married for three years. Bill could do no wrong in Mama's eyes: when Orville, who was an infantry private in France during the war, wondered in a letter when his brother, by then with the State Department in Washington, was going to join the army, his mother wrote back sharply that anyone could carry a gun, but only a few could hold an important government position. (Her stepson, Jack, who had spent three unhappy years trying to settle on a career—one at law school and two in the bond business—moved out when his father died and took a room at the Rittenhouse Club with a convenient entrance to an apartment in the building next door, where he kept a mistress.) There was, though, a curious twist to the affection between Bullitt and his mother: when they were apart, they longed for each other; when they were together, there was constant emotional strain. Nevertheless, he was devoted to her: years later he recalled how she had refused to eat after the death of her husband, really wishing to join him in heaven. "The doctor said that the only thing that might make her eat again would be for her to go somewhere she had never seen before. The only two places . . . were Russia and China, and Russia rather appealed to her, so in 1914 we went to Moscow, and we were there when the war broke out."

On June 28, 1914, Archduke Francis Ferdinand of Austria-Hungary and the archduchess were assassinated by a Serbian nationalist at Sarajevo, but there seemed to be no reason to fear that a major war was in the making. The United States ambassador to Germany, James W. Gerard, a former New York judge and a friend of the Bullitt family, was at Kiel on the Baltic Sea for a weekend of sailboat racing, and on the night of Saturday, June 27, he and his wife went to dinner on the yacht of Emperor William II, the Kaiser. Gerard wrote an account of events the following day, when word was received from Sarajevo:

> There was much rushing to and fro in fast launches, the Emperor himself being summoned from the race . . . in progress. That night we dined on board the yacht of the Prince of Monaco. All the diplomats and notables whom I met during the afternoon and evening seemed to think that there was no chance that the tragedy at Sarajevo would lead to war. The next morning the Emperor left early for Berlin, but expressly directed that the festivities and races at Kiel should be carried out as arranged.

The Russia that Bullitt and his mother visited was a country in turmoil: there had been marked economic progress—from 14,733 industrial plants employing 1,832,783 workers in 1909 to 17,356 plants employing 2,151,191 workers in 1912. The seeds of revolution had been planted, nevertheless, as indicated by the number of cooperative societies, or unions—19,325 with over nine million members in 1914—and the existence of an outspoken Socialist press. The regime of Czar Nicholas II was doing what it could to stop the workers' movement: when gold miners struck in Siberia in April 1912, they were shot down by government troops. "In the middle of July 1914 the workers of Petersburg and many other industrial centers proclaimed a political strike," wrote Gregor Alexinsky in *Russia and the Great War*.

> The number of workers who took part . . . amounted to 250,000 in Petersburg alone. . . . The situation of the government had become all the more critical. . . . It was

on the brink of an inevitable fall. But then came the war, and the situation was suddenly transformed. The danger of foreign aggression forced the masses of the Russian people to check the remarkable impetus of its struggle for liberty and to occupy itself with the problems of national defense.

War had not been declared, but it was imminent: Germany announced its support of Austria-Hungary, while Russia lined up on the side of Serbia; France made ready, threatened by a German invasion; England joined the allied cause when German troops marched into Belgium. The Russian people were responding; they gathered at the palace in Moscow to hear the czar repeat the promise of his great uncle, Alexander I, during the invasion of Napoleon in 1812; he would make no peace with the enemy so long as one armed invader stood on Russian land. Bullitt and his mother, in their room at the National Hotel, were awakened by the shouting and the singing of the "Imperial Anthem" by Alexis Lvov, to the music of the 1812 Overture by Tchaikovsky: "God save the Czar; long may he reign. . . ."

"Suddenly the sleeping city was filled with a wild uproar," Bullitt later said. "I was young, and . . . I hated war, and I'll confess . . . that I was naive enough to make up my mind . . . that I was going to stop the war. . . . We retreated to Warsaw, . . . and arrived in time to find cossacks flogging peasants down the main thoroughfare. [They also watched the peasants being mobilized for a march to slaughter in the Masurian Lakes of east Prussia.] The ambassador . . . announced that Mrs. Bullitt and her son had just gotten off the last train to Berlin." This, he said, did not disturb his mother, "for she planned to visit the birthplace of Chopin on the following morning. And so she did, wearing a fashionable black silk dress in the oppressive heat. It turned out there was another train to Berlin. . . ." They stayed at the Adlon Hotel in Berlin—from their window they could see German troops marching on the day in August that war was declared—but they were soon advised by Ambassador Gerard to leave as soon as possible. They arrived in London in time to witness preparedness on the other side: His Majesty's First Expeditionary Corps passing in review.

In London Bullitt almost succeeded in becoming an accredited war correspondent: he had his letter from *The New York Times*, and he was introduced by his uncle, Colonel Ronald Brooke, to Sir Ian Hamilton, the commander of British home defense forces (in 1915 General Hamilton commanded the disastrous invasion of Turkey at Gallipoli); but the War Office refused the request. No reason was given, but it might have been that Bullitt was a suspected spy: he was detained for questioning because he had traveled from Russia via Germany, and he was not released until his credentials had been established by Colonel Brooke and Doctor Osler, who was at this time teaching at Oxford.

Bullitt turned his attention to a family matter: his grandmother, Maria Gross Horwitz, had recently died, and there was reason to fear that her possessions would be plundered, her jewels in particular, which were kept in a wall safe in her apartment in Paris. The first battle of the Marne would be fought in a few weeks, in early September 1914, and a German occupation of the city was a distinct possibility (avoided only by a last-minute decision by the Kaiser to alter the battle plan in the belief that reinforcements were required on the eastern front). The war casualties had been horrendous—more French soldiers killed in a few months than Americans lost in the four-year Civil War—but a full report of the slaughter had not reached Paris, and the mood of the people was buoyant. Bullitt's first reaction on arriving there was to cheer with them, and he went to a café, where he witnessed the triumphant arrival of a group of colonial troops, Wolof warriors from Senegal. They were waving small objects, undoubtedly war trophies, and Bullitt applauded until he realized what they were: the ears and fingers of dead Germans.

Bullitt's immediate problem was how to open the safe containing his grandmother's jewels: "It was simplicity itself," he later boasted. "I went to the chief of police and asked him if he did not have an expert cracksman in jail. . . . Of course he had one. . . ." Bullitt, in his usual resourceful way, had gone to the prefect of the city jail with a written introduction from the mayor of Paris, and the prefect agreed to lend the services of a jailed safecracker: ". . . in five hours he felt out the combination of the safe, while three guards watched over his shoulder." Bullitt opened a bottle of wine for the cracksman and his guards; he then buried the jewels in the garden of a friend, rather than take responsibility for returning them to Philadelphia. (The jewels were left to a cousin of Bullitt's, his grandmother's niece, who later married a German and moved to Germany. At the end of World War II, for some reason, she gave them to an American soldier, a sergeant from West Virginia, who mistook the priceless diamonds and pearls for cheap costume pieces, and when he got home he bestowed them indiscriminately on various lady friends. Eventually the FBI questioned the ex-serviceman's mother, who said that those gems he had not given away had been eaten by the chickens.)

Bullitt, before leaving Paris, made a rash move: he tried to join the French Army. It would have been a risky experience, with a no better than 20 percent chance of survival—to fight, perhaps to die, was what stirred Bullitt, who envied his former roommate Carstairs for having joined the British Army—but he was rejected owing to a law that prohibited foreigners from the armed forces of France. (The law had just been passed out of fear that foreign espionage agents would infiltrate French forces, but it was soon repealed.)

Back in Philadelphia Bullitt went to work for *The Public Ledger*, the best paper in the city (it was later merged with *The Inquirer*, as big-city newspapers consolidated), and while he landed the job through family ties—an owner of *The Public Ledger* had been Anthony J. Drexel, who had retained Bullitt's grandfather as his attorney in the 1870s—he started as a ten-dollar-a-week reporter, and his advancement, which was rapid, could be attributed entirely to his ability. His assignment was to cover an aspect of Philadelphia he had not known, the seamy side of life—gambling raids and murders; and he wrote a poignant story about the suicide of a youth too poor to afford a pair of dress shoes, unable therefore to take his girlfriend to an Easter promenade. (That night, as if to emphasize his detachment, Bullitt attended a ball at the home of Edward T. Stotesbury, the senior partner of Drexel, Morgan & Company.) Bullitt did not remain a police reporter for long: he submitted astute analyses of the war, which were published on the editorial page—he was deeply concerned about the war, certain he was watching the decimation of his generation—and he soon was named an associate editor.

Bumping the Bumps with Ford

BULLITT got a lucky break in late 1915, and by taking full advantage of it he proved to a national audience that he was a fine newspaperman: he was invited to cover a peace expedition to Europe sponsored by Henry Ford, the automobile manufacturer, who was a brilliant entrepreneur but utterly unsophisticated in affairs of state. If Bullitt's interest in the mission was based originally on his dedication to pacifism, it was not evident from his dispatches; for he was first a journalist, possibly the best of a group of some sixty men and women of the press. He was not among second-raters: the self-appointed dean of the corps was J. Jefferson O'Neill of *The New York World*, a debonair veteran, who commanded attention by rapping the floor with his ivory-handled cane; and Elmer Davis, later a well-known radio commentator and from 1942 to 1945 the director of the Office of War Information, was there for *The New York Times*. Yet Bullitt was signed by a syndicate representing 234 newspapers, and his account—he wrote a series called "Joy Riding to Peace: Bumping the Bumps with Ford"—was published nationwide. His own paper ran his picture, looking square-jawed and handsome and sartorially exquisite, and announced proudly: "Mr. Bullitt, who is the only representative of a Philadelphia newspaper on the expedition, is a member of the Public Ledger editorial staff and an experienced writer."

They sailed aboard the *Oscar II*, a Swedish liner chartered by Ford, on the damp, drizzly morning of December 4, 149 delegates in all. It was, as Bullitt described,

> one of the most picturesque, as well as noisy, demonstrations ever witnessed in New York. . . . On the liner the Ford pilgrims lined the rails and cheered and shouted and sang, while on the pier more than 3,000 peace devotees . . . joined in general jubilation. . . . Bands played national anthems, "God Save the King" and "Deutschland über Alles," and soap-opera box orators ranted, although one, a German, was pummeled to the ground when a translator called attention to the anti-British drift of his harangue.

On hand for the send-off was William Jennings Bryan—his pacifism had caused Bryan to resign as secretary of state six months earlier—who had likened the expedition to the voyage of Noah's Ark. "Beside Bryan," Bullitt wrote, "stood Thomas A. Edison and Mrs. Ford and her son Edsel. Behind these stood 10,000 howling men and women. And . . . one man . . . plunged into the river, . . . saying he would swim behind the ship to ward off torpedoes." Ford implored Edison to come along, Bullitt reported:

> Mr. Ford retained his clasp on Mr. Edison's hand and repeated again and again, "You must stay on board." Mr. Ford then leaned over until his mouth was hardly an inch from Mr. Edison's ear, and said with a quizzical smile, behind which there was intense seriousness, "I'll give you a million dollars if you'll come." . . . Mr. Edison smiled and shook his head.

Bullitt noted that the sixty-eight-year-old inventor was deaf and had difficulty hearing Ford; Mrs. Edison later denied that the million-dollar offer had been made by Ford.

The *Oscar II* had barely passed Sandy Hook at the entrance to the New York harbor when Bullitt realized that the peace pilgrimage was to be a tragic farce: tragic because the endeavor was well intentioned—"to get the boys out of the trenches by Christmas," as an ingenuous Ford proclaimed; a farce in that many of the principals behaved foolishly, their self-ennobling efforts thinly concealed. There had been little advance planning, as the spur-of-the-moment idea had been presented to Ford two weeks before: "On the whole," Bullitt wrote, "the expedition totally lacks organization, and the delegates may be said to be on their way, but don't know where they are going." Even Henry Ford was not consulted as to the conduct of the mission except when it was necessary for him to sign a check: "The trip has so far cost Mr. Ford $125,000, and if the schedule is followed, $500,000 will have been expended before the pilgrims set foot in America again." Bullitt reported that the bills were being settled by Ford's designated agent, Louis P. Lochner, "who, with Frau Schwimmer, is really running the expedition, so far as it is being run at all." Rosika Schwimmer was a mysterious, furtive woman, a gray eminence, who had gained Ford's confidence in the two weeks she had known him prior to departure, but who was disliked and distrusted by the others and was ultimately blamed for the failure of the delegation to win the confidence of people in Europe. "Frau Schwimmer is dominant," Bullitt noted, "as to all conference plans, invitations to neutrals and so forth, and is divulging none of the details. . . ." (In 1919 Schwimmer became the Hungarian ambassador to Switzerland, representing the Communist government of Bela Kun.) The expedition was also rent with dissension over U.S. policy, specifically a plan to make ready for war—the sinking of the British liner *Lusitania* by a German submarine on May 7, 1915, with the loss of over a thousand passengers, including 128 Americans, had stirred belligerence in the United States—as President Wilson had enunciated it in a recent message to Congress.

"The Ford pilgrims are still separated into two parties on the question of 'preparedness' . . . ," Bullitt wrote on December 15, 1915, "and the angry feeling has by no means died down. Mr. Ford is endeavoring to soothe the insurgents, . . . in order to prevent a secessionist movement when the *Oscar II* reaches Norway." The leaders of the disaffected included some prominent delegates: Samuel S. McClure, a social crusader, muckraking publisher, and the founder of *McClure's Magazine*; Benjamin B. Lindsey, a judge in Colorado widely known for juvenile court reform; and L. B. Hanna, the governor of North Dakota. "I came on board a pacifist," said an angry McClure, "but I am now converted to militarism. If we want to raise the greatest American army, we need only to march this bunch of pacifists through the country." Governor Hanna threw up his hands and simply exclaimed, according to Bullitt, "I haven't discovered yet why I am on board."

The peace ship arrived at Christiania, the capital of Norway (the name was changed to Oslo in 1925) on December 18, having been delayed by the British Navy for three days at Kirkwall, Scotland, much to the displeasure of the restive delegates: "Squabbles Split Peace Party as Pilgrims Land," ran a headline in *The Public Ledger*. Ford claimed he was still confident of ending the war—if not by Christmas, then by the end of winter—and he revealed to the Norwegian press his plan for curtailing the output of arms. He had invented a motor plow, he said, which would cost no more than one horse but would do the work of six; and he would permit arms and munitions makers in Europe and the United States to manufacture the plow without paying royalties, but subject to a condition that they stop producing war materials.

The people of Christiania were friendly to Ford "in a personal sort of way," Bullitt reported, but the peace pilgrimage was regarded with suspicion in neutral

Norway. "There is a general disposition to view Frau Rosika Schwimmer, a Hungarian by nationality, as a representative of a belligerent power. . . . There is no disguising the fact that Frau Schwimmer is disliked here. She spent thousands of dollars of Ford's money . . . trying to stir up a favorable reception . . . and made a complete failure of it." On December 24 it was announced that S. S. McClure and Governor Hanna would quit the party, and it was then learned that Ford himself was returning to New York, having sneaked off in the middle of the night to avoid an explanation to the delegates. "Before leaving," read a cable dispatch by the Associated Press in London, "Mr. Ford gave a check for 1,000,000 kroner (about $270,000) to finance the expedition. He left because he recognized it was impossible to make headway. His party was always at loggerheads and Scandinavian pacifists adopted an attitude of reserve. When Mr. Ford found all official doors closed, he broke down." Bullitt had this to add on December 25: "Although Mr. Ford has made financial arrangements for the continuance of the trip, his leaving . . . has caused such depression among the delegates, and even those who have been the most optimistic are now less hopeful that the expedition will achieve anything toward peace in Europe."

Only after the failure of the peace mission had been signaled by the sudden departure of Ford did Bullitt begin his "Bumping the Bumps" series, a daily log of events spiced with impressions—his satiric humor was applauded by most of his colleagues, though one critic wrote that he had "pilloried and defamed the peace pilgrims, mocked their motives and jeeringly condemned their intent"— that appeared in *The Public Ledger* starting on January 6, 1916.

Sunday, December 5: The ship's band struck a keynote at seven o'clock this morning, which depressed the pilgrims all day. After it had played a hymn to the tune of a funeral dirge most of the Oscarnauts decided that digestion was the better part of valor and remained in their bunks. The *Oscar* pitched amazingly, and when the pilgrims who are to stop the war assembled for afternoon service, . . . they did not look capable of stopping anything larger than a battle between pet Pomeranians. Dr. Aked [the Reverend Charles F. Aked of San Francisco] revived them by a sermon on small beginnings which have led to great endings. He convinced the roomful of people that something would come of the expedition, and there were cheers when he said, "Ford will rank with Washington and Lincoln. . . ."

Tuesday, December 7: This night S. S. McClure read the President's message to Congress to the Oscarnauts. He read it in the second-class smoking room, which serves the pilgrims as general assembly room. It is the most miraculously uncomfortable room in which I have had to sit. For the industrious steam heaters under its wall benches throw out continually such waves of heat that four or five portholes must be kept open continually. One smokes or listens in the midst of gusts from Iceland interrupted by Hades heat. Its dim electric lights are encased in paper shades the color of over-ripe grapefruit. Mr.

McClure . . . read the message of the President from end to end. The message seemed to impress on the pilgrims only a desire to sleep, but Ellis O. Jones, late of the staff of *Life*, cut the rest of the slumberers. "Only the armor trust wants preparedness," he shouted. "And it wants military profit not military preparedness. . . ." There were cheers. The reporters swarmed about Mr. Ford like a flock of ducks. What had Mr. Ford to say about the message? Mr. Ford was unable to give voice to his sentiments. He requested Mr. O'Neill to announce that he desired the passengers to deliberate over the message for two or three days and that a general convention of the ship would then answer specifically each recommendation of the President. Mr. O'Neill precipitated a verbal battle when he announced that the message would be debated by the various "bodies" of the ship. . . . This was considered little less than an ultimatum by the disembodied bodies of the ship. "Where do I come in?" roared Jenkin Lloyd Jones [a Unitarian clergyman]. "To what group do I belong?" queried May Wright Sewall [the National Suffrage Association chairman]. "Surely there will be some open forum in which my voice may be heard," barked Dr. Aked, who is known popularly as the "clean-up hitter of the nuts." In all quarters of the room verbal artillery unlimbered and fired. War on the peace ship seemed imminent.

Friday, December 10: The carnage began . . . when Louis P. Lochner, secretary of the Peace Expedition, . . . delivered an address on "World Federation," in which he advocated immediate and universal disarmament. Mr. Lochner never intends to offend anyone. He is a gentle soul. He looks like the rabbit in *Alice in Wonderland*. . . . But he has the ability to get on people's nerves. During the speech the more human members of the party stirred uneasily in their chairs. . . . When Mr. Lochner sat down, Doctor Aked popped up to read the "Declaration of Principles". . . . [The key principle was opposition to any increase by the United States of her military and naval forces.] S. S. McClure . . . sprang up and with great intensity said: "For years I have been working for international disarmament. I have visited the capitals of Europe time and again in its behalf. But I cannot impugn the course laid out by the President of the United States. . . ." At once nearly every peace pilgrim found invaluable words to contribute to the debate. The room buzzed with talk. . . . The knots of disputants became angry. Madame Schwimmer, the Hungarian skipper of the expedition, and Jenkin Lloyd Jones, the Chicago preacher who looks like the prophet Isaiah and talks like a Y.M.C.A. secretary, accused Mr. McClure of corrupting the youth by talking preparedness. . . . Then the newspapermen decided that it was unnecessary to rush about from group to group, and that the remainder of the fight had better be staged in the pressroom. The pilgrims submitted with amazing docility. The reporters sat on the benches around the walls like inquisitors. . . . S. S. McClure was the first. . . . "I believe in preparedness, . . ." he said. "By this futile protest about a matter entirely foreign to the purpose of the party, which is to stop the war in Europe, you will merely bring upon the expedition a great weight of ridicule and opposition. I cannot work with the party if it is necessary to sign this resolution." "Why," Dr. Aked snapped, "will you not accept the Declaration of Principles as you accepted the letter of invitation?" "Because," replied Mr. McClure, "your Declaration of Principles is like the . . . Westminster confession [a seventeenth-century pronouncement of Calvinist doctrine]." . . . Jenkin Lloyd Jones heaved himself to his feet. His eyes flashed from under his mane of white hair, which is six inches long, . . . above his beard, which is a foot long. "Sir," he bellowed, "I am not here to discuss this matter. I am here to tell you that we do not care what you do. . . . We will not take your judgment on any subject. . . ." McClure interrupted, "I do protest." "Go to bed," roared Jenkin Lloyd Jones, as he shook his fist at Mr. McClure.

Bullitt was an instigator of shenanigans among the press contingent, regarded as caustic and snobbish yet knowledgeable and hard-working. The Ancient and Honorable Order of the Vacillating Sons and Sisters of St. Vitus (St. Vitus is the patron saint of epileptics) was his idea—it was a drinking society formed by the correspondents, who had assumed mistakenly that liquor would be forbidden by Ford, a teetotaler, and had come well supplied—and he was a founding member of the Press Club. "At least it thought it organized itself," he wrote.

It didn't. Not for nothing did Jo O'Neill learn the ways of life at the knee of a father who was boss of the Twenty-ninth Ward of Philadelphia. He assembled five of us before the meeting and made out a slate. We bowed to the Twenty-ninth Ward as far as the presidency was concerned. The rest of us took the other places on the ticket. . . . Thereupon, as one of the gentle peace delegates . . . phrased it, "The dear boys and girls of the press closed their meeting by singing 'How Thirsty I Find Myself.' "

Wednesday, December 15: The battle line of the peace ship showed activity on another front today. Madame Schwimmer sent word to the Press Club that she would not have tea with the newspapermen because she would not sit at table with persons who had insulted her. We asked her to come and let us explain that we had done nothing of the sort and that we were quite ready to be good friends. When she entered the room we applauded her heartily, but she snapped, "Don't be hypocritical. . . ." The scene which followed is characteristic of the invariable fate of all attempts to harmonize the warring factions on the boat. . . . Madame Schwimmer then accused the newspapermen of saying to Mr. Ford that she listened at keyholes. This did not tend to produce any undue amount of good feeling. . . . Madame Schwimmer continued to make herself solid with everyone by classifying all the photographers on board under the head of "crooks."

Saturday, December 18: What is so rare as a day on which pacifists are pacific? The pilgrims had every excuse to be calm. They were filled with turkey and surrounded by beauty. The hills of snow and pine leaping out of the blue Christiansand Fjord under the pink fingers of the sunset would have made a dinosaur a household pet. . . . A meeting called by Judge Lindsey after dinner unanimously adopted a new peace platform. . . . Speeches redolent of the fatherhood of God and the brotherhood of man soared upward from every corner of the room. A general embrace seemed imminent. But there was just a tinge of disappointment on the faces of the pacifists. They all seemed to feel that something had been forgotten. What was it? Of course! They had overlooked the evening fight, and to be a pacifist and to forget one's evening fight is more serious than to be a baseball fan and miss the opening game of the World's Series. . . . Mr. McClure rose to defend the newspaper correspondents, who were threatened with dismissal. He asked that they should not be dismissed . . . until the matter had been discussed in an open meeting. . . . "Let us come together in the spirit of God," he begged. "Let us lift this expedition above the backbiting and chicanery in which it exists today." The fight was on. Governor Hanna put Mr. McClure's idea in the form of a motion. . . . Judge Lindsey, who was presiding, attempted to speak in favor of the newspapermen, but was howled at by the Lochner-Schwimmer supporters. Finally the calls of "question" grew so loud that he could not be heard. He put the question. The Lochner-Schwimmerites were in the majority. The pacifists sighed with content. They had had their evening fight. . . . At midnight Mr. Ford, who was ill in bed with grippe, announced that he would not permit any newspapermen to be sent home.

On the subject of Henry Ford Bullitt changed his tone—from acerbic and irreverent to respectful, though candid and incisive.

Monday, December 20: No one likes to say so because it sounds sentimental; but in looking for characters to compare to Mr. Ford inevitably one returns . . . to Christ. Mr. Ford is not an active member of any church. He is not quite an agnostic, but almost. Agnosticism implies philosophic thought, and Mr. Ford apparently cannot think vigorously in terms of anything but steel and human emotions. "Don't you think this is a holy cause?" a minister asked him. "No," replied Mr. Ford. "I don't know what you mean by holy. Instead of a holy cause I consider this expedition a people's affair." "Are you not sailing with faith?" asked the minister. "Yes," answered Mr. Ford, "but it is faith in people. I have absolute confidence in the better side of human nature." . . . The faith in people . . . is really plain human pity—pity, "the rebel passion," which cuts across all creeds and boundary lines, which dares ridicule and makes revolutions. . . . Mr. Ford is human, all too human. "There is no such thing as a bad man," he says. "Give a man a chance to lead a decent life, and he will do it. In the same way I believe that nations can be won by moral suasion. . . ." Before Mr. Ford was confined to his cabin by evidence of grippe, . . . he had made himself the personal friend of everyone on the ship. His tenderness is combined with a bashfulness that makes comparative strangers wish to protect him. . . . Under the hounding of sixty-odd newspaper people . . . he never lost his gentleness and sweetness of temper. . . . He reads little, but he likes to have near him either Emerson or Thoreau. . . . He doesn't like novels. . . . "All those fellows use too many words, . . ." he says. "I can get ideas quicker in other books." Literature is to him a mine from which to dig more ideas. And the best literature is that which returns the greatest number of moral ideas per square page of digging. He has no knowledge of history, biology, physiology or psychology. He has no desire to know them. . . . European history begins for him with August 1, 1914 [when World War I began].

Wednesday, December 22: Mr. Ford has not left his bed. . . . Norway is not cooperating with Ford in any way. The reason for the indifference . . . is . . . that the Ford expedition is considered a pro-German movement. The Norwegians seem to be, without exception, pro-Ally. . . . They believe that the Allies are sure to win if the war lasts much longer; therefore they look upon any attempt to bring about immediate peace as a pro-German move. . . . Mr. Ford sailed for home on December 24. . . .

Thursday, December 30: Now we are on our way to Copenhagen. So long as Mr.

Ford's bank account holds out, most of the pacifists are content to go with the party. . . . A number of the best brains in the expedition have left. . . . S. S. McClure resigned as a delegate on shipboard. . . . But the really important defections are those of Herman Bernstein [an editor and writer, he had reported on Russia for *The New York Times* until the war] and Inez Millholland Boissevain [a respected reformer and women's rights advocate]. They were the only persons among the delegates with any real understanding of international affairs.

Tuesday, January 4: One of Mme. Schwimmer's first acts on reaching Copenhagen had been to hire a steamer to carry the peacers to The Hague by way of the North Sea. The price for the ride was to be $50,000. When the delegates heard the price they quivered. They were not worried about the chunk to be bitten from Mr. Ford's pocketbook. But they discovered that nearly four-fifths of the price was to be paid for insurance because of the likelihood that a North Sea mine would send the boat to the locker of which the *Lusitania* is now the most distinguished occupant. [A train to Holland via Germany was arranged by Maurice F. Egan, the U.S. minister to Denmark, who called his German counterpart in Copenhagen.]

Saturday, January 15 (The Hague): To say that the Ford peace train ran over Germany like water over a duck's back would be a little unfair to Germany. For a duck probably has some sensation when water runs over its back; and Germany gave no sign whatever that it had noticed the passage of the men and women who left America to "bring the boys out of the trenches. . . ." During the twelve hours . . . from Warnemuende—a little port to the east of Kiel—to Bentheim, on the Dutch border, hardly one hundred Germans even gazed at the train. No curious crowds waited to see the Americans go through. . . . The pursuers of peace put their heads out of the windows . . . as they liked. . . . Germany seemed to be too busy about serious things to bother about peace pilgrims. . . . Holland treats the expedition with the same gentle disrespect as Denmark. "Dear children," all Europe seems to say, . . . "go on with your expedition so long as it makes you happy. You dear uplifters know nothing about the ways of men on this planet. But it is easier to talk than to study. So play your nice little game out to the end, make your speeches and dream your dreams."

Sunday, January 30 (The S.S. Rotterdam*)*:

> By bedlam's bats and bugs of yore,
> By Bellevue and by Matteawan,
> By all the mad paretic corps,
> With intellects entirely gone; . . .
> By vacuous and vacant domes,
> And all the world's nobody-homes;
> With gibberings and ghoulish squeaks,
> I swear that I've been nuts for weeks. . . .

When this bit of verse was adopted as the oath of the Vacillating Sons and Sisters of St. Vitus, while the *Oscar II* lay in Kirkwall harbor, not many of the peace delegates could have repeated it truthfully. They were moonstruck, but not mad, but by the time the expedition was nearing . . . The Hague each "peacer" could have sworn honestly that he was . . . at least a semilunatic. Gaston Plantiff, the unemotional Broadway businessman whom Mr. Ford had left in charge of the party, was stirred to such a pitch by the conflicting insanities of the "peacers" that he interrupted their final battle in The Hague with these words. "I wish I could get out of this insane atmosphere and back to sane America. Unless you peace delegates stop fighting, . . . everyone in the whole party will be crazy. Yesterday the automobile in which Judge Lindsey and I were motoring to Amsterdam broke down in front of an asylum. Every lunatic in the place ran out to greet us. They thought we belonged. . . . I'm not sure we don't. . . ."

Mr. Ford and his fellow uplifters set out to "save" Europe in the same spirit with which they would . . . save a fallen man. The *Oscar II* was rosy with human tenderness. But none of the delegates who remained as members of the exposition until its expiring hours in The Hague had any knowledge of the history or present condition of affairs in Europe. None of them understood the emotions of a people at war. They believed they could "bring the boys out of the trenches . . ." by pouring out affectionate words. They did not think it was necessary to hammer their vague tenderness into a coherent plan of action. . . . Mr. Ford was the tenderest of the tender and the vaguest of the vague; a charming child. In Mr. Ford human pity is exalted to a ruling passion.

On the same day it carried Bullitt's account of the peace train crossing Germany, *The New York Times* published a report from Washington on the prospect of the United States entering the war: "That there is a graver aspect to the *Lusitania* controversy . . .," it read, "was . . . confirmed semi-officially by a high officer of the Government today. . . . 'The situation is now graver than it has been for some time—and the country has a right to know it,' " the official was quoted as having said. It was also noted in the *Times* that Edward M. House, President Wilson's confidential agent, "is now in Berlin, conferring with high officers of the German Government."

Honeymoon at the War

FEBRUARY 1916 was a triumphant month for Bill Bullitt. Arriving in New York City from Europe, he helped organize a press banquet at Keens Chop House—copies of *The Scandihoovian Clarion* were passed around, with a banner headline: "Peace at All Prices Reigns at a Low Market in Stockholm"—and he returned to Philadelphia the star of the staff of *The Public Ledger*; later that month he was engaged to be married. His reward at the paper was to be assigned as a feature writer to the heavyweight title match between Jess Willard and Frank Moran, scheduled to be fought in New York on March 25. "A descriptive writer whose racy and distinctly humorous articles have recently given a hearty laugh to all Pennsylvania," it read beneath Bullitt's picture in a promotion piece March 8. "Bullitt's portion of the page will be written for the average man—not the fight fan alone—and will appeal to every one who understands the meaning of the phrase 'prize fight.' " He interviewed the two fighters and portrayed them as human individuals. "Willard and Moran are utterly different men," he wrote. "Only a blind man would class them together on the principle, 'All pugs look alike to me.' Willard is a typical product of the prairies of the West; Moran a son of the factories of the East." He proposed that Willard would make "a complete Jack London hero"—it was London, in fact, who had named Willard "the great white hope" when he defeated Jack Johnson, a black fighter, for the heavyweight championship in 1915—although Bullitt cast him as an Ernest Hemingway character in his way of talking. What did Willard want most in the world? "Why, to get through with this fighting business and out on a ranch of my own, where I can have good horses and the best black cattle that I can buy and go to bed when I ought to at night and get up early in the morning and feel fine all day." (London died in 1916; Hemingway was a teenager in Oak Park, Illinois, who that year, interestingly, wrote a short story on boxing for the high school magazine.) Bullitt found that Moran had an ambition to be an evangelist, a Roman Catholic Billy Sunday (Billy Sunday was a baseball player who became a Presbyterian minister, then turned to theatrical religion with astonishing success): "If he beats Willard he may carry out his dream. But if he loses—well, Moran is not so far removed from the fleshpots of Egypt as he imagines. He is likely to end his life as the very talkative, very belligerent, very popular proprietor of a corner saloon." Bullitt wrapped up his coverage on the day of the fight with a prediction:

Willard, like the Gauls who gave Caesar such a run for his money, has never come in contact with those things "which tend to effeminate the spirit" [shades of Mr. Ned at Camp Pasquaney]. Moran has spent his whole life in the tawdrier sections of tawdry American cities. . . . Moran is far more lithe, active, inventive and imaginative than Willard. By nature he is more of a fighter. He loves a fight. Willard regards a fight as a disagreeable but necessary way of earning money. But Willard possesses a huge reservoir of strength that Moran lacks. In his present perfect condition Moran does not show the results of the life he has led—the ordinary bat-about life of a butcher's son with a strong body, strong wit and strong passions. But he appears to have lost (if he ever possessed it) the enormous reserve of strength which makes Willard seem as irresistible as a landslide.

Willard won the fight.

The Public Ledger on March 19, 1916, made prominent note of Bullitt's marriage on its society page, omitting any mention of his professional position (newspaper writing was definitely not *de rigueur* in Old Philadelphia): "One of the most interesting weddings of the season took place yesterday when Miss A. Ernesta Drinker, daughter of Mr. and Mrs. Henry S. Drinker, of University Park, South Bethlehem, became the bride of William C. Bullitt, Jr." Aimée Ernesta Drinker, born a year later than Bullitt, was of a family whose arrival in America predated the founding of Philadelphia—according to legend an Edward Drinker was the first child born of European descent in the Quaker colony—a prominent family over the generations: an ancestor, Henry Drinker, was elected to the first common council of Philadelphia following the Revolution; Ernesta's father was the president of Lehigh University; and her older brother, another Henry, was to be a leading lawyer and the president of the Pennsylvania Academy of Fine Arts. *The Public Ledger* published a picture of Ernesta, a photograph of a portrait painted in 1914 by her aunt, the noted artist Cecilia Beaux; and her younger sister, Catherine—Catherine Drinker Bowen, who later became an accomplished violinist and noted biographer—wrote of the wedding in *Family Portrait*, remarking that the bishop of Bethlehem, Ethelbert Talbot, had presided "in all his magnificence."

The marriage would last only seven years, prompting Catherine Bowen to comment: "My sister's early ambition to marry a man who would let her argue with him did not materialize. With her first husband [Bullitt] I think no woman . . . could have held her own." Yale classmate Philip Platt, who was an usher in the wedding, claimed that Bullitt had known Ernesta forever, but it was a figurative sentiment, far from the actual fact, which was that he never really did know Ernesta. Henry S. Drinker, before he became the president of Lehigh, practiced law in Philadelphia—like William Bullitt, Sr., he was a railroad lawyer, representing the Lehigh Valley company—so presumably the Drinkers and the Bullitts were acquainted; but according to his close cousin, Orville Horwitz, Bullitt first noticed Ernesta when he was at Yale. They dated thereafter—Ernesta visited New Haven more than once, Phil Platt remembered—but evidently they did not get to know each other well. The evidence is circumstantial, albeit convincing: Bullitt failed to understand Ernesta—or any woman, for that matter—as a person. Women were objects: the good ones—proper ladies like Ernesta, from upstanding families—were to be regarded with respect, even reverence; the others were to be considered for what they were, temptresses and tramps. "Neither drink nor women will ever touch Willard," Bullitt wrote two weeks before he got married—he was hearing Mr. Ned again. "Jess Willard is more than champion of the world—he is a man."

Ernesta Drinker grew up in a rented house on the campus of Haverford College—it was just down the road from the Bullitt country home in Devon—as her father was a legal adviser to his friend Isaac Sharpless, the eminent president of the Quaker institution. She was thirteen when she heard they were moving to Bethlehem—settled in 1740, it was the site of Bethlehem Steel—and she sat in a cherry tree and sobbed for three days. Catherine Bowen later observed that Ernesta's life was "already established in suburban Philadelphia—her friends and her hopes and what I afterward learned were her ambitions," which were largely confined to social aspirations. It would not be too presumptuous to suggest that Ernesta's early desires had a lot to do with the man she would marry, and while Billy Bullitt was not in the picture as yet—she would always call him Billy, in slightly mocking endearment—her ideal was no doubt someone like him: intelligent, good looking, well-bred, a Philadelphian. Young men could not help but notice Ernesta, for she was so striking in appearance that at parties and concerts and in hotel lobbies on family trips eyes would turn and necks would crane. "It was in Europe that I first recognized the quality of Ernesta's beauty," Catherine Bowen wrote.

At home people took this for granted. . . . But abroad we were among strangers. . . . "Is that beautiful girl your *daughter*, Mrs. Drinker?" Ernesta said they sounded as if she were something in a zoo. . . . In my diary I wrote, "When people in the railroad cars stare at Ernesta it makes her so furious she can hardly stand up. She doesn't seem to realize how pretty she is. . . ." It is not easy to describe Ernesta. I have said she was black-haired, black-browed, with high cheekbones, and that her eyes were large and lustrous. To this day I am not sure of their color, if brown or green. I used to think her eyes changed with the clothes she wore, or that somehow her irises reflected the light, shifting suddenly from bright to shadow. There was no single feature to celebrate, such as noticeably fine skin, a beguiling mouth. . . . Actually it was the structure of her face that fascinated—the bones beneath, . . . the line of brow and chin. Whichever way my sister turned her head on that long neck there was enchantment. I have seen men catch their breath, looking at Ernesta. And immediately they want to talk about it—to tell her or even tell me of their discovery.

Ernesta was an active, high-spirited young woman: long-legged and nimble, she could beat her older brother at running or climbing a tree; and she excelled at sailing, riding, and ice skating. She also could be warm and compassionate, which she showed most distinctly in Bethlehem, having finally become reconciled to moving there. After taking a walk one day at age eighteen through an impoverished neighborhood of the city, she was determined to provide a milk station for the children of underpaid steelworkers. She proposed a plan for funding the project to her father, who refused to cooperate or to allow her to approach the Lehigh trustees, as it would be, he believed, an undue use of his influence. (It might also have interfered with President Drinker's remarkable building program, which included in the course of a decade two dormitories, a dining hall, two engineering laboratories, a gymnasium, and a football stadium.)

Ernesta persisted, however—she disobeyed her father and obtained university support—and the milk station was built.

For all her early academic exposure Ernesta was surprisingly resistant to a formal education. Except for what her sister called a "brief unhappy interval" at Baldwin, a private school for girls in Bryn Mawr on the Main Line, she was tutored at home until she was twenty and sent off to "that fancy school in Paris," as her brother Philip called it, where she took courses in languages and literature. Catherine Bowen was quite annoyed by her sister's neglect of learning, and in *Family Portrait*, published in 1970, she remarked that "the five of us"—referring to her four brothers and herself and pointedly excepting Ernesta—"possessed what were called active brains." It made no difference that she returned from France and embarked on a college career: "Somewhere between the Paris school and marriage," Catherine acknowledged, "Ernesta had a term at Radcliffe, studying sociology and economics. I don't know how the powers were persuaded to enroll a girl without degrees or academic credits, except that Felix Frankfurter, then teaching at the Harvard Law School, had something to do with it. He admired Ernesta." Frankfurter, who would become a confidant of Franklin D. Roosevelt and a justice of the Supreme Court, was not just an admirer, according to Phil Platt; he was a suitor, one of many. "When Ernesta was about twenty-two," her sister wrote, "she had kept count of the men who proposed marriage until it got to fifty, when she gave up." Ernesta was twenty-two in 1914, the year she and Bullitt were both in Cambridge, Massachusetts—she at Radcliffe and he at Harvard Law—and one day he stormed into her dormitory room and declared, "I'm not going to leave until you agree to marry me." It was a bold move, somewhat surprising in that Bullitt had not been a persistent pursuer: at least no letters or photographs were preserved indicating so. Yet it was a proposal Ernesta could not reject: she had promised herself she would never be bored, and Billy Bullitt certainly was not boring; besides, they were well-matched from the Old Philadelphia standpoint, and they made a very attractive couple.

Bullitt was on top of the world for good reason: professionally he was recognized for the considerable talent he brought to the newspaper trade; and socially he was the envy of all the lawyers, doctors, businessmen, and bankers who lunched daily at the Philadelphia or the Rittenhouse clubs. For Ernesta it was an escape from Bethlehem, which was not a trivial matter—she had decided to be married at the home of her brother Henry in Wynnewood, near Philadelphia, but her parents prevailed, and the ceremony was held at the Packer Memorial Church in South Bethlehem—and she and Billy, she thought, would sail through life in Philadelphia, living at 222 West Rittenhouse Square and at Oxmoor in Devon.

First, however, they would spend a honeymoon in Europe, watching the war from the side of the Central Empires: for Bullitt, who had valuable contacts in Germany and Austria-Hungary, it would be a chance to further his career; Ernesta would also travel as a journalist, keeping a diary, which would be published. "Billy is, fortunately, a newspaperman, and not a diplomat," she wrote in Copenhagen en route—not intending irony, as there was no way she could anticipate what was in store for her. "I can imagine nothing worse than being married to a man who only tells you things which he thinks he safely may, or the things he would tell anyone—which amounts to the same thing."

Touring Europe in the midst of hostilities was a dashing idea, made all the more dangerous by the *Lusitania* "crisis": sinking ships without warning by German submarines was pertinent to the issue of American neutrality. Two months before Bullitt and Ernesta were married, speaking in Cleveland, President Wilson had delivered a "solemn warning," as *The New York Times* reported, "of the need of prompt steps for national preparedness." Wilson said he was hearing two pleas from those who would guide him on the basis of public opinion: one was that the people were counting on him to keep them out of war; and in the next breath he was told that the people counted equally upon him to maintain the honor of the United States. Wilson said he had a ready response, which was quoted in the *Times*: "You can count on my part a resolution to keep you out of war, but you must be ready if it is necessary to maintain your honor. The real man believes his honor is dearer than his life." Bullitt expected the United States would eventually join the Allied side—he reasoned that large loans by the U.S. to England, France, Italy, and Russia made it a virtual certainty—hence his choice of Germany and Austria-Hungary for the wedding trip. Resolved to become the most informed American journalist on the political and military structure of the Central Powers—he was well-grounded in the history of the countries and of course fluent in German—he made meticulous preparations to assure access to important officials: he got letters of endorsement from the Department of State and the German legation in Washington; he asked influential Philadelphians to write letters of introduction; he even carried a Philadelphia police press pass, to prove to German authorities he was not a dangerous radical.

Ernesta called her book *An Uncensored Diary from the Central Empires*, although she contradicted her title in an entry on September 17, 1916, in Berlin: "Have to send my diary to the Foreign Office tomorrow to be censored, so I shall not be able to write any more." Nevertheless, it was a commendable, often amusing, and always informative piece of work, as she proved to be an able observer who was quite blunt in her criticism of a husband prone to moodiness and of boorish German authorities. "A young man got into our compartment . . .," she wrote of their first train trip across Germany.

[He] opened conversation by explaining how much he hated America, because she was selling munitions to the Allies. . . . Billy, being of a chameleon-like nature, had become solemn. He did little things as if they were important, and he began to order me around and look as if he expected me to carry my own suitcase. . . . At Warnemuende we became Number 36. . . . There were guards all about. . . . The officer in charge . . . came to superintend our unpacking. Billy presented our letters to the civil and military authorities from the German Ambassador and the Minister in Holland. The officer pocketed them. . . . "I am a military authority; therefore I shall keep the letters . . .," he said. "Don't you think that is a trifle idiotic?" asked Billy. Visions of a firing squad. . . . But the officer merely turned upon his heel, while Billy told me that Junkers always thumbed their noses at reason.

She would be a chronicler of the trip, but Ernesta was determined to be more than a passive bystander: she had come as a feminist, interested in women's suffrage and women's working conditions; and she was furious when, upon arriving in Berlin on May 29, she learned that representatives of the Foreign Office had been assigned to take her shopping. "I came away with a hat and a black-and-white dress chic enough to ruin my reputation in Berlin," she wrote, still irate. A trip to the Central Labour Exchange was more in line with her expectations: "Before the war they averaged two hundred applications a day in the women's department . . .," she noted. "In the first months of the war from three thousand to ten thousand women came every day. . . . In Germany, as in other warring countries, there is little the women are not doing."

On their second day in Berlin the Bullitts had lunch at the embassy with Ambassador and Mrs. James W. Gerard, and Ernesta recorded her impression of Judge Gerard: "brusque, frank, quick-witted," she wrote, with "a typically judicial mind and a typically undiplomatic manner," a man she was certain the Germans would not understand. "His dry, slangy American humor, his sudden lapses into the comic in moments of solemnity, his irreverence for the great" — these qualities, she was certain, would "shock the worthy German," and she supposed that he treated the Kaiser as a mere business acquaintance. She repeated Gerard's story of an encounter with Alfred Zimmermann, the foreign undersecretary. The United States could not go to war with Germany, Zimmermann had said, "because we have five hundred thousand trained Germans in the United States." "That may be," Gerard replied, "but we have five hundred thousand and one lampposts." Zimmermann was the first German official to be interviewed by Bullitt (a note sent by Zimmermann in January 1917 to the German ambassador in Mexico City, which was intercepted by British naval intelligence, would help draw the United States into the war). "He is genial, calm, and although the busiest man in the Empire, quite unhurried . . .," Ernesta wrote.

I told him he was like Disraeli, who said he was not "unusually busy today" but "usually busy." Billy asked if the U-boat war was likely to be resumed. "That depends on Wilson," answered Zimmermann. "If he pushes England into obeying international law, we will not resume it. If he goes on doing nothing [about the British naval blockade of Germany], . . . I cannot answer for what our military and naval authorities will do." . . . I asked him if he didn't think the war was going on and on because no one would speak frankly of peace; he agreed but insisted that Germany had done all she could. "All that is done if we mention peace is for everyone to shout: 'The Germans are beaten; they can't go on any longer.' "

The Bullitts were in contact with all sorts of Germans, not just officials of the government: an army officer, back from the Western front on leave, assured them that Verdun would fall in two weeks (the scene of the bloodiest battle of the war, in which one million men were killed, Verdun never was surrendered by the French, led by Marshal Henri Philippe Pétain); and a liberal leader of a growing peace movement, Kurt Hahn, stated a wish for an alliance of America, Germany, England, and France in order that Russia would not dominate all of them at some future date. The most productive interview, in terms of what Bullitt would later write about the future of Europe, was with Walter Rathenau, an industrial genius and discerning social philosopher, who would become a leader of postwar Germany. "He talked so frankly," Ernesta noted on July 17, the day of their meeting with Rathenau, "that I hesitate to write down his name." (Rathenau was a Jew, as was Kurt Hahn, and from them Bullitt got a sense of the anti-Semitism that was beginning to prevail in their country.) "When will the war end?" Bullitt asked straight off. "At the earliest in 1918," said Rathenau. "It might just as well end now, for Germany is ready to make peace, . . . but I think the English will have to become far more weary of the war . . . before they will be ready to talk sensibly. . . . One condition of the peace will have to be a return to the status quo before the war in an economic way." Bullitt proposed an alliance of Germany, Great Britain, and the United States: Germany would limit her fleet and allow Britain supremacy of the sea; Britain would lift the blockade; and the U.S. would guarantee the keeping of the agreements by vowing action against either nation, should it violate them. "That is perfectly possible," said Rathenau. "That is the peace Germany is ready to make today. England probably will not be ready for it until 1918. The great danger is that peace will be put off many years longer. . . . This danger springs from the even chance that Germany will recommence the U-boat war." Rathenau was fearful that the Kaiser would be influenced by his military commanders: General Erich von Falkenhayn, minister of war; and Admiral Alfred von Tirpitz, secretary of state for the navy. "Falkenhayn said . . . that he could crush the Russians, French, and English. . . . [He] explains: 'I would do it if the fleet gave me proper support.' Tirpitz said his fleet was to crush England. It has not, and his answer is that he is forbidden his most effective weapon, the submarine. . . . With the opening of the Reichstag [the German parliament] in the autumn, the fight will begin again. I do not think . . . then, but early in the spring, after the people have suffered another winter, . . . the submarine war party will be stronger. . . ."

They went to occupied Belgium, guests of the German government, arriving on July 21 in Brussels, "a gay and cheerful place," Ernesta wrote, although the Belgians did not conceal their hatred of the Germans nor had they lost confidence that the British would return. "They think the English are gods and tell you stories about their bravery," such as one about a single soldier hidden behind bushes, who kept shooting as the Germans advanced. "When all his ammunition was gone, he sat on a stump and lit his briar pipe, smoked awhile, and then . . . jumped into the river." Another was about a small squad behind a sandbag barricade, which kept the Germans at bay for twelve hours. "When all their shells had been fired, instead of surrendering, they started a cricket game and . . . played until they all were down. . . ."

Bullitt probably was not so impressed with such tales of valor, for his dislike of the British was pronounced, rooted in the patriotism that made him proud to be a descendent of Patrick Henry (at De Lancey in 1907 he argued in a debate that "the people of the United States should dislike the people of England," and won). He was presumably pleased to return to Berlin—they had lunch at the U.S. embassy August 4—where he could resume his campaign for peace, perhaps emboldened by an awareness that the Germans admired his arrogance. "Every time Billy has a new idea about the war," Ernesta noted patiently, "he gets a German and inflicts it on him.

This idea is that Germany's idea of peace is on the plan of a thermometer. The height of the mercury denotes Germany's military success—the higher the mercury, the more Germany will say she absolutely must have. Freezing point is territorial integrity. As the mercury sinks below that, she pays indemnities to Belgium and France; lower still, gives back Alsace-Lorraine; then Schleswig-Holstein, her portion of Poland, and so on. . . .

The Germans even allowed Bullitt to tour the war zone, providing him with a huge car, its hood, trunk, and doors decorated with a German coat of arms and driven by an army chauffeur. "Billy has gone to the eastern front," Ernesta wrote on August 13. "I am most wifely depressed at having him away." She went to a beach resort with a group of American diplomats—they included Ambassador Gerard and Christian Herter, an embassy aide who would one day be secretary of state—but she returned shortly to Berlin, anticipating Bullitt's return. "The next morning Billy got back," she wrote. "The trip to the front had been a great success. He went up in an aeroplane over the Russian lines and got shot at and had all sorts of a good time."

In late August the Bullitts went to Hungary, arriving in Budapest on the twenty-eighth: "One does not have to be here very long," Ernesta observed,

> to discover a decided bitterness toward Austria. They say that the Hungarian troops are always put in the front trenches and that the Hungarian losses are proportionately far greater than the Austrian losses. We find that here, as in Austria, there is no love for the Germans. They respect and admire them and trust them, but affection for them, they have none. Of their fondness for France they speak continually. They do not fight against her, and they worry continually over whether the French will hate them after the war. . . .

Bullitt also wrote about the trip to Austria-Hungary, and his story was published by *The Public Ledger*:

> Like all who strive to snatch the day and not to "heed the rumble of a distant drum" [Bullitt was quoting from the *Rubaiyat* of Omar Khayyam, the 1879 translation of the English poet Edward FitzGerald], the Austrians and the Hungarians can never clear the drumbeat from their ears. And the drum is beating retreat, failure, death. For Austria-Hungary is at the end of her human resources. Every boy and man between the ages of seventeen and fifty-five is under arms. There are no reserves left. . . . Because of this lack of manpower, . . . the Germans have not only taken over the higher command of the whole eastern front, but also have taken over the business of supplying gaps in the part of the line ostensibly held by the armies of the Dual Monarchy. . . . At the end of their resources of men, in swift economic decline, why do not the statesmen of the Hapsburg monarchy strive to make a separate peace? [Bullitt was showing his admiration for European nobility, which would affect his thinking throughout his diplomatic career.] Because they are gentlemen. . . . The Hapsburg monarchy is an aristocracy with all the vices of an aristocracy, but with all the virtues as well. . . . Not one of the great leaders of Austria-Hungary will consider separate peace. . . . Nearly everyone in Austria-Hungary would welcome peace on the status quo ante bellum. When one suggests to a German that the war is likely to go on for two more years, he replies, "Of course." When one suggests the same thing in Vienna or Budapest, the Austrian or Hungarian throws up his hands and cries, "Impossible."

Bullitt interviewed Count Stephen Tisza, the premier of Hungary—"startling but cannot be put down," Ernesta wrote in her diary on September 3—and while realizing it could not be published, Bullitt still had a use for it. "Tisza requested me neither to publish nor to repeat this conversation," he wrote at the end of the transcript. "I replied that I would not publish it but that I would repeat it in my office and in the State Department." In the session with the Hungarian chief of state, as in one two weeks later with the German secretary of state for foreign affairs, Gottlieb von Jagow, Bullitt proved to be a superb interviewer: well grounded on the issues, articulate and clever, and never one to be intimidated by the high station of his subject. He came right to the point with Tisza, whose threatening note to Serbia in 1914 had touched off the war (on July 23, 1914, following the assassination of Archduke Francis Ferdinand, Austria-Hungary had issued an ultimatum and five days later declared war, not satisfied with the Serbian response): "What do you wish to do with Serbia?" Tisza refused to answer, so Bullitt made an insertion: "Tisza's confidential secretary tells me that Tisza wishes to divide the northeastern corner of Serbia between Hungary and Bulgaria, so that the railroad from Budapest to Constantinople will be entirely under the control of the Central Powers." "You knew," Bullitt then said to Tisza, "that Serbia would not accept your note." "I knew that Serbia would have to accept it unless Russia supported her," Tisza replied. "We had endured injuries for years. We had to put an end to them. I hoped that Russia would see the justice of our case and would force Serbia to submit to our demands. I realized that if Russia urged Serbia to refuse our demands she would refuse them; and that Germany and ourselves would have war with Russia and France. I believed that England would not enter the war. I was soon undeceived." "Had the German government known in advance," Bullitt then asked, "of the note to Serbia?" Again Tisza declined to answer.

They were back in Berlin on September 17, and Ernesta made a final entry in her diary before sending it to the Foreign Office: she had told the censor that "if he cut a word out of it, I should come back and finish him with an axe. He promised that it should not be touched. Poor man. We do give him so much trouble, and he is so nice about it. . . . Billy has just had a second long talk with von Jagow."

Bullitt first wanted from the foreign secretary a clarification with respect to the note from Tisza to the Serbian government, though in phrasing the question he took it for granted that von Jagow had seen it in advance: it was a ruse, and it worked. "When Tisza wrote the note to Serbia, what you and he wanted was not land but control?" "I did not have a hand in preparing that note," von Jagow replied. "I saw the note for the first time at eight o'clock the night before it was presented in Belgrade [the capital of Serbia]. . . ." Bullitt sensed that the German statesman wished to lecture this young American, who obviously had connections in Washington and would take the message there, so he allowed him to ramble. "I do not see any way to peace now," von Jagow said with seemingly sincere sorrow. "We are in the midst of a terrible offensive on all sides. . . . People have talked a lot in the past three months about the possibility of peace with England; the possibility has always been remote. The thing I am afraid of is that President Wilson will allow himself to be drawn into an entente with England and France." He was a bit more optimistic about the immediate issue of submarine warfare: "I do not believe that we shall have to resume sinking without warning. . . . I am much opposed to it myself." Bullitt asked if the chancellor, Theobald von Bethmann-Hollweg, would resign if U-boat attacks were renewed. "Our cabinets do not resign because they are forced into a position in which they do not believe," von Jagow told him. (As a matter of historic fact, unrestricted submarine warfare was resumed by Germany at the end of 1916; von Jagow resigned and was replaced by Alfred Zimmermann; and von Bethmann-Hollweg was overthrown in 1917 for attempting to negotiate peace.)

At a point in the session von Jagow became aggressive and accusing: "Now be frank. The United States is in favor of England winning this war." Bullitt's response was thoughtfully pragmatic: "We do not want England to crush Germany, but if any nation except ourselves is to control the sea, we prefer that nation to be England. And this is not because we consider Germany our enemy and England our great and noble friend but because we have two clubs over England: Canada and exports. We have no clubs whatever over Germany." Von Jagow pressed: "Do you believe that Wilson is consciously neutral?" "No," said Bullitt—he was about to be very bold and presumptuous—"I believe he considers himself neutral." "What about Lansing?" von Jagow demanded, referring to the U.S. secretary of state. "I don't know anything about him." (It was an evasive answer. Bullitt knew that Robert Lansing was an ambitious lawyer, who had married the daughter of a former secretary of state, John W. Foster; he had succeeded William Jennings Bryan at the State Department and had advocated U.S. entry into the war on the Allied side; and he was the uncle of a Bullitt contemporary, also an ambitious lawyer, John Foster Dulles.) "Well, Lansing doesn't matter, . . ." said von Jagow. "He's only Wilson's office boy," which Bullitt knew to be the case but did not say so, as he let von Jagow talk. "I don't understand their point of view in Washington. . . . It is perfectly right that the United States take a stiff course with us and . . . insist that we come to terms; but why, then, does your government let England walk over you?" Bullitt's response was carefully worded: "So far as I know about the opinions of the President, that is quite untrue. I believe that the President hopes the war will end in more or less of a draw."

It was Bullitt's turn to be argumentative. "Are you ready," he demanded, "to make peace on these terms: the abandonment of the Allies' 'economic war'; an international agreement in regard to the unhindered passage of merchantmen in time of war; and otherwise the status quo ante bellum?" "Absolutely not!" Von Jagow's tone had changed from rueful to angry. "Do you think that would be a German victory?" Bullitt had a ready reply: "Tisza and everyone else in Austria-Hungary is ready to make peace on those terms." "I haven't talked to Tisza for some time," von Jagow admitted. Bullitt decided it was time to inflict, as Ernesta had put it, his theory on von Jagow. "Your peace terms, to put it graphically, are the degrees of a thermometer, in which the mercury is the military situation. As your military success rises and falls, your peace terms rise and fall." Von Jagow would easily concede that: "Yes, of course, the peace terms we want depend absolutely on the military situation." At the end Bullitt asked, "Do you see any end of the war?" "Everything has an end," von Jagow replied.

En route to America the Bullitts had dinner in Copenhagen at the home of the U.S. ambassador to Denmark, Maurice F. Egan—Bullitt was acquainted with Egan, a fellow Philadelphian—where they again met Ambassador Gerard, who was returning to Washington to report to President Wilson, stirring speculation that he was bearing an important message. Gerard was noncommittal, however, when he landed in New York aboard the Danish liner *Frederick VIII*, and it was reported in *The New York Times* on October 11, 1916, that he "brought no German peace proposals, nor did he bring any official note or other communication from the German Government relative to Germany's reported intention of resuming . . . ruthless submarine warfare. . . ." The source of the story was apparent, for on the same day the *Times* carried an article datelined Philadelphia, October 10. "*The Public Ledger* will print tomorrow morning," it read in a preceding note, "the following from its correspondent, William C. Bullitt, who was a fellow passenger with Ambassador Gerard on board the *Frederick VIII*":

I am able to state with absolute certainty that the Ambassador brings no statement of definite peace terms, either from the Kaiser or from the Chancellor. . . . Ambassador Gerard has not seen the Kaiser since his visit to the Great Headquarters last April. Moreover I am able to state from German sources that four weeks ago the Kaiser refused to grant to Ambassador Gerard another conference with the council at headquarters for the purpose of discussing Germany's peace terms. That council rules Germany, . . . and the fact that the American Ambassador was not granted a conference at headquarters is about proof positive that Germany is not considering a move for peace by way of the White House. . . . Indeed at the present moment Germany is thinking a great deal less about peace via the United States than about war with the United States. That is the true reason for the return of Mr. Gerard. The Ambassador's object is to discuss with the President the specific steps which may be taken . . . to keep Germany from beginning again to sink merchant ships without warning. In addition, his wish is to acquaint the President with the details of the inner political struggle between the supporters of Admiral von Tirpitz and the supporters of Chancellor Bethmann-Hollweg—a struggle whose outcome will determine whether or not the United States is to be drawn into the war. In Berlin one hears . . . the prediction that sinking without warning will be recommended. . . . The supporters of von Tirpitz are certain that they will win. . . .

"Sharpest of the Correspondents"

B ULLITT'S REPORTING on the war was page-one material for *The Public Ledger* for weeks to come: "HUNGARY ROUSES TO MEET MENACE FROM RUSSIA," read a headline October 19, "by William C. Bullitt, staff correspondent, . . . who recently returned after spending several months in the warring countries of Europe." He had been in Budapest on August 29, when Romania declared war on Austria-Hungary, and had interviewed "the three strong men of the Hapsburg monarchy": Count Albert Apponyi, "the splendid old aristocrat, who officially leads the opposition party in the Hungarian parliament"; Count Julius Andrassy, "perhaps the cleverest man in Austria-Hungary"; and Count Tisza, "who since the day he wrote the Austrian ultimatum to Serbia has guided the destinies of the dual monarchy." On October 22 Bullitt revealed—"for the first time," *The Public Ledger* boasted—the reaction in Germany and Austria-Hungary when Britain entered the war. "The foreign offices of the Central Empires were as astonished and enraged as the little people in the crowd which stormed the British Embassy in Berlin," he wrote.

> From throne to stable, Germany and Austria-Hungary believed that England would not enter the war. Why? . . . What was the . . . basis for their belief that England would not take up arms against them? This! Fifty days before England declared war on Germany, Sir Edward Grey [the British foreign secretary] and Prince Lichnowsky, the German Ambassador in London, initialed a secret treaty in regard to the Bagdad Railroad and other interests . . .; and shortly before, Germany and England initialed another secret treaty. . . . These treaties secured England's approval of a great German colonial empire, . . . and of a German economic empire. . . . They laid the basis for a permanent peace between England and Germany.

On October 30 Bullitt offered an explanation for a statement by David Lloyd George, the British prime minister, opposing a move for peace by the United States. "The fight must be to a finish—to a knockout . . .," Lloyd George had said. "Why cannot England, France and Russia accept intervention at this stage? Why must they talk of going 'to a knockout'? Because at the present moment Germany holds all the trumps . . .," said Bullitt. "There is a common saying in Europe: 'When the diplomats sit down at a table, they will never be able to get up until they have made peace.' This is true. And so long as they can fight, the leaders of the Allies will be unable to sit down at a table until they have cards as good as Germany's or until they have a definite statement as to what use the rulers of Germany intend to make of their trumps."

It was a first-rate job. Bullitt was a dogged reporter, adept interviewer, and a perceptive analyst, though perhaps inclined to the German position—a bias that was arguably understandable, as he had been a guest of the Central Powers for four months—and there was better work to come, articles based on the vast amount of information Bullitt had stored in his notebooks. He had achieved his goal: he had become the most informed American journalist on Germany and Austria-Hungary. "I have known Mr. Bullitt for a considerable time," wrote Walter Lippmann, a respected editor of *The New Republic*, recommending Bullitt for an Army intelligence assignment in 1917, "and I have examined with care the material he brought back from Germany when he visited that country in the summer of 1916. He is, in my opinion by all odds, the sharpest of the American correspondents. His intuitions as to coming events prove to be extraordinarily accurate."

Lippmann was sufficiently impressed to publish in *The New Republic* on October 28, 1916, an article, "Worse or Better Germany," in which Bullitt argued it was wrong to label Germans as Germans, as Americans were inclined to do, all with "a bloody red tag . . . on which is written Hun." There was, he maintained, a distinction between the officers of the army and the navy, the Junkers, on the one hand; the social democrats on the other: "the camps of conservatism and liberalism, of worse and better Germany." The difference between the two, he emphasized, was over objectives in the war: the conservatives were committed to military dominance of territory to the west, which would mean establishment of a German protectorate in Belgium, annexation of much of France, and annihilation of the British fleet; the liberals were dedicated to economic supremacy in the east—a German mercantile empire from Hamburg to Bagdad. It was a personal struggle as well, between Admiral von Tirpitz and Chancellor von Bethmann-Hollweg, and the issue of submarine warfare was at the forefront: the conservatives led by von Tirpitz held that with the U-boats they could "starve England into submission in a few months"; while von Bethmann-Hollweg's liberal faction opposed renewing the attacks for fear they would bring the United States and other countries into the war. "To a nation like our own . . .," Bullitt wrote,

there is a temptation to remark that to choose between worse or better Germany is "poor picking between rotten apples." And it is true that, except for the Socialist minority, every human being in Germany lives by the . . . "Deutschland über Alles" philosophy. It is true that lasting peace to liberal Germany is not an international conciliatory body, . . . but strong frontiers, a large army and navy, and good alliances. . . . [Why] should the United States bother about distinctions between Germans . . .? Because we cannot continue to enjoy our . . . neutrality unless Bethmann remains Chancellor. The day conservative Germany overcomes liberal Germany, sinking without warning will be recommenced, and we shall be drawn into war.

Bullitt was right, of course—as Walter Lippmann would say, his intuitions were "extraordinarily accurate"—and once that was so painfully clear, he put the submarine attacks in the context of the larger issue of hostility between Germany and Britain. "It lies . . .," he wrote in July 1917 in *The Public Ledger*, "in the thing which is usually at the bottom of a great hatred—fear. Fear on the part of Germany, that the British fleet will starve her to death; fear on the part of England, that the German submarines will starve her to death." The fear, he explained further, was "inherent in the economic life and geographical position of those two great industrial nations, cooped together in the same corner of Europe. Germany today, scarcely less than England, is dependent upon the sea for her life."

In November 1916 Bullitt was named to head the Washington bureau of *The Philadelphia Public Ledger*, a coveted assignment, especially in wartime, when government actions are vital—the decision of the U.S. government to enter the war was imminent—and his familiarity with the leaders in Berlin and elsewhere in Europe enhanced Bullitt's value as a capital correspondent. He was still too prone to accept the German line of reasoning, as events would demonstrate, but he was always careful to identify his sources. "The representatives of Germany," he wrote on December 1, "are certain that there has been no change in the policy of the Foreign Office in regard to sinking without warning. [Bullitt's sources were misleading him; sinking without warning was soon resumed.] It is pointed out that the Chancellor himself has said that the new Secretary of State for Foreign Affairs, Zimmermann, is to carry out the same policies as his predecessor, . . . von Jagow." On December 15 he reported that Washington would not intercede on behalf of a German peace proposal. "It is the opinion in official circles that the United States can only sit tight until Lloyd George gives the answer of the Allies. . . . It is believed that there is . . . an even chance that England will refuse the German offer . . .," which it did. Secretary of State Lansing said on the morning of December 21, "We have been drawing nearer to the verge of war . . .," and Bullitt wrote: "In spite of Secretary Lansing's statement this afternoon that the Government has no thought of abandoning its policy of neutrality, official circles believe that his morning statement . . . lies close to the truth."

The world of journalism was not enough for Bullitt. On October 20, 1916, he had written a letter to Frank L. Polk, the counselor and second in command of the Department of State: "We returned from our . . . trip in Germany and Austria-Hungary about ten days ago. I have a lot of information I cannot publish, including conversations with Tisza and von Jagow, which might interest you." The information was indeed of interest to the government—in late 1917 Bullitt would get what he wanted in return, a job with the State Department, writing reports on Germany and Austria-Hungary—but he was acting in flagrant violation of an ethical code, representing himself concurrently as a correspondent and as an agent of the United States. It was not just that Bullitt believed newspaper work to be beneath him, though his dignity *was* involved; it was more that he really pretended to a position of authority, which could only be realized as a government official. He was not pretending in the simple sense of playing a part—he enjoyed that, too, for acting was a talent not to be dismissed, as he had shown at Yale—but in the important sense of laying claim to the position. *"We* do not want England to crush Germany, but if any nation except *ourselves* is to control the sea, *we* prefer that nation to be England," he had said to von Jagow (emphasis added), and while the German foreign secretary might not have been fooled, Bullitt apparently was misleading himself into thinking he could speak for his government.

Then again Bullitt was probably compelled to divulge his discoveries in Europe because they were significant: he had perceived that Russia was finished as a military force—a view that was at variance with predominant beliefs in Europe and the United States—as he watched from his hotel window in Berlin Russian soldiers, who had preferred capture to fighting the Germans, coming to cart away garbage; he had learned that the armies of Austria-Hungary were crumbling at an even faster rate than Russia's; and he had discovered that the airplane, until then used only for observation, was being adapted as a fighting machine. The war would end in 1918, Bullitt had been told by a prophetic Walter Rathenau, who would become the German foreign minister in 1922 and then be assassinated by nationalist fanatics; and the nation to fear in the future was Russia, in the judgment of Kurt Hahn, a liberal idealist, so there ought to be an alliance of the United States, Germany, Britain, and France to prevent Moscow "from squeezing the life out of all of them at some future time."

On March 23, 1917, Bullitt wrote to Walter Lippmann, who had become a good friend, and told of a personal tragedy. "Ernesta is very ill just now. . . . She bore a son day before yesterday, and I buried him today. Ernesta is doing well physically, but the death of the baby has wrecked her emotionally." That Ernesta was never able to have more children was undoubtedly a factor in the unraveling of her marriage to Bullitt: he was obsessed with producing another, she confided years later. There were, however, other reasons for their breakup, which would occur in 1923, probably the most important being that Ernesta became an accouterment to Bullitt's existence, rather than a partner in his life.

Pipeline to the President

BULLITT'S SUCCESS as a Washington correspondent was noticed first by other newsmen, his rivals, and they even had him tailed by a private detective, hoping to learn—unsuccessfully, as it turned out—how he was able to beat them on story after story. The answer was simple enough: he was in touch with excellent sources—he even had a private telephone line to the office of President Wilson's intimate adviser, Edward M. House. ("Colonel" House—he was always called by his honorary title—had been active in Texas politics before coming to Washington to support Woodrow Wilson for president in 1912. He became Wilson's chief assistant, specializing in foreign policy, and prior to U.S. entry into World War I he was in charge of an advisory group on peace strategy.) House admired Bullitt—presumably the president did as well—for the quality of his insights, and as of early 1917 he was receiving from Bullitt advice on future events in Europe. "The German offensive can be stopped now only by arms," Bullitt wrote on January 22. "Germany is in that pre-offensive state of elation when all the jingo emotions of the common man well to the surface. . . . But the German liberals will hate the offensive. And all the more, if before it begins, they are assured . . . they can have peace the day they send to represent Germany one of themselves. If they can be convinced of the bona fides of American liberalism, they will seize the terrible depression which will follow the failure of the offensive to swing themselves into power. . . ."

Bullitt's prediction was on the mark: with the abdication in November 1918 of William II, followed by the armistice, Philipp Scheidemann, a Social Democrat supported by the liberals, became the first chancellor of the German republic. The objective of liberals in Germany and the United States—and Bullitt considered himself one of them—was permanent peace through world federation.

Bullitt was irrepressible when his emotions were stirred, as when war was declared on April 6, 1917. "I just want to tell you," he said, having been permitted a brief meeting with the president in his office, "that today you said the things which everyone in the world who cares about the future of humanity has been waiting for you to say. And you said them supremely well. You've made yourself the leader of everyone in the world who wants real peace." (Wilson, Bullitt later reported, called the members of Congress who had applauded his speech "mean-spirited fools," and he expressed his repugnance for "this war" and "all war," which was the theme of a speech Bullitt would draft for a future president, Franklin D. Roosevelt.)

Bullitt wanted to serve this president, whom he called in letters to friends "clean-hearted," "wise," and "pure," and he was bothered by the prospect of missing the war, of sitting it out in a suite at the Hotel Willard, where he and Ernesta lived in Washington. He thought about how his Yale classmates had signed up to fight—even the musically talented Cole Porter, who had joined the French Foreign Legion—and on July 5, 1917, he wrote a pleading letter to Colonel House: "The unhappy results of an appendicitis operation make it impossible for me to do active military service. It has occurred to me . . . that because of the war the President might need an additional personal secretary. . . . I have thought that he might need the services of a young man who is used to . . . dealing confidentially with all sorts of men from Foreign Ministers and Ambassadors to day laborers."

There was no opening for Bullitt at the White House, but in December 1917 his appointment as an assistant secretary of state, which had been engineered by Colonel House—although he officially reported to Joseph C. Grew, chief of the Division of Western European Affairs, Bullitt would send his reports to House— came through. Before long Bullitt was going beyond the scope of his assignment, as on February 3, 1918, when he proposed to House that the president address Congress with three purposes in mind: to impel the German people to take control of their government; to unite revolutionary Russia against Germany; and to place the war aims of the United States and the Allies "on the most liberal and lofty plane." He said in a letter to House:

> In the appended memorandum I have passed over the question of the Bolsheviki, because I know little at first hand of Russia. But it is obvious that no words could so effectively stamp the President's address with uncompromising liberalism as would the act of recognizing the Bolsheviki. . . . If we cannot recognize the Bolsheviki government, will it be possible to send to Russia an Ambassador who will not be an obvious target for radical attack [the U.S. ambassador until relations with Russia were broken in 1918 was David R. Francis, a former governor of Missouri, who was distinctly anti-radical], and will be able in at least some measure to understand what the Bolsheviki are about?

By his readiness to recognize Red Russia and his none-too-subtle disapproval of Ambassador Francis, Bullitt was marking himself as a radical, which would in time affect his credibility. An illustration of the official attitude toward the Bolsheviks was reflected in a memorandum written by Secretary of State Robert Lansing in November 1917, having just been informed by Ambassador Francis that the provisional premier, Aleksandr Kerensky, had fled Petrograd, his government having been overthrown by the followers of Lenin. "I believe," Lansing wrote,

> the Russian "Terror" will far surpass in brutality and destruction of life and property the Terror of the French Revolution. The latter at least possessed the semblance of government and made pretense of legality. Russia possesses neither. There is no authority,

no law. It is a seething caldron of anarchy and violence. I can conceive of no more frightful calamity for a people than that which seems about to fall upon Russia.

Bullitt was an astute political analyst and an accomplished propagandist, credited with devising a way to accentuate the internal divisions of the enemy: Austrian and Hungarian troops were told that the Americans had nothing against them and were fighting only the Germans; Bavarians were assured that the United States meant only to fight Prussians; and Prussians were promised it was the Kaiser who was the real villain. The messages were delivered by air-dropped leaflets, and the success of the campaign was attested to by Adolf Hitler, an Austrian army corporal in World War I, who wrote in his book, *Mein Kampf:* "The army gradually learned to think as the enemy wished it to." Bullitt also sought to destroy the confidence of the German people in their government, and he explained his method in a letter to President Roosevelt in June 1939, when he was ambassador to France. "I used to have telegraphed to me," he wrote, "every criticism of the Kaiser's regime that appeared in Germany. At that time there were about a dozen . . . Socialist and Radical papers . . . permitted to criticize. . . . The result was that the Left heard its own words . . . from President Wilson's mouth. . . ."

Bullitt indicated to House on May 20, 1918, that he had not yet decided to embrace the Russian Revolution. "I wish I could see Russia with as single an eye as Reed," he wrote, referring to John Reed, the radical writer, who had just returned from Petrograd, where he had observed and supported the Bolshevik victory. "I am unable to win through the welter of conflicting reports . . . anything like a solid conviction." Bullitt had not known Reed well, though he was fond of saying, "Jack Reed and I are of the same American strain," by which he meant that they had similar backgrounds: they both came from prominent families (Reed's mother was a cousin of the ambassador to Germany, James W. Gerard), and each attended one of the best universities—Reed was a graduate of Harvard, class of 1910. Their great mutual friend was Lincoln Steffens, the journalistic crusader, who suggested to Reed in 1917 that he visit Russia and who would go there with Bullitt in 1919. "The appended memorandum has been written for me by Jack Reed . . .," Bullitt said in his letter to House of May 20. "Reed knows Lenin and Trotsky so intimately that his recommendations . . . may be regarded, I think, as the recommendations they would make themselves." (When Reed returned to the United States from Russia in April 1917, his papers were confiscated, including the notes from which he would write his eyewitness account of the Russian Revolution, *Ten Days That Shook the World*. He sent a plea for help to Bullitt, who apparently relayed it to the right place, for in September the papers were returned after Colonel House had interceded on Reed's behalf.)

Bullitt was firm in his conviction about one aspect of U.S. policy toward Russia: he was strongly opposed to sending troops there, and in this he was at odds with his government. Anti-Bolshevik feeling soared in Washington with the signing in March 1918 of the Brest-Litovsk Treaty between Soviet Russia and the Central Powers, a perfidious separate peace; and American Army units—mostly volunteers from Michigan and Wisconsin, who called themselves "the polar bear expedition"—were soon to be dispatched to support the White Russian forces against the Reds. Bullitt wrote Colonel House on June 24 that he was

sick at heart because I feel that we are about to make one of the most tragic blunders in the history of mankind. . . . Ambassador Francis and others who urge intervention say that there has been formed in Moscow a strong combination of landed proprietors, bankers, professional men and commercial men, who, unless the Allies intervene at once, will appeal to the Germans for assistance to overthrow the Soviets. . . . Therefore, . . . we must get one step ahead of the Germans and intervene for the benefit of this crowd, which is ready to cooperate with the Kaiser as with us. . . . The Russian upper classes are about to appeal to Germany to overthrow the Soviets. Let them appeal. . . . Let us join the Soviets.

American troops were sent, however—they would hold the eastern ports of Archangel and Murmansk until 1919—and Bullitt did not conceal his anger. "One year ago today," he wrote House on September 20,

Russia was fighting by our side against Germany. . . . Today we are fighting Great Russia, and it is possible that before summer one million Russians will be acting as German depot and supply troops on the western front. This is the year's achievement of our Russian diplomacy. When the men charged with aircraft production failed, the President threw them out, and now we are beginning to produce aircraft. . . . If we are to avoid driving Russia into military alliance with Germany, *which is the only thing that can prevent our winning this war*, we must put our Russian policy in the hands of men who can weigh evidence and see Russia as it is. . . . What is our present Russian policy? We have sent small expeditions which are fighting Bolsheviki. But there has been no rush of Russians to support these expeditions. And the Bolsheviki are undisputed masters of Great Russia. . . . Unless we are to continue to blunder blindly to disaster in Russia, we must establish here in Washington an organization competent to interpret Russia and the Revolution. This requires men of deep wisdom and liberality.

Bullitt was remarkably assertive and arguably out of line for an assistant secretary of state with less than a year of service in the government, but Colonel House respected his wisdom; and he evidently took steps, such as controlling the distribution of Bullitt's communications, to see to it that no one was offended by his protégé's outspoken manner. There was a risk, though, that Woodrow Wilson himself, from whom House could not withhold the memos or conceal their authorship, would come to regard Bullitt as intemperate and unreliable. It had been foolish, as a case in point, for Bullitt to suggest the possibility that before summer a million Russian troops would be supporting Germany on the western front, since the defeat of Germany before the end of 1918 was a likelihood. Bullitt knew this, for he was counseling House on how Wilson should face the prospect of an armistice. "The time is rapidly approaching," he wrote in a long memo on September 12, "when it will be necessary for the President to go before Congress . . . to restate the war aims of the United States." He suggested thirty-three such aims—from a league of all free nations to home rule for Ireland—and he made proposals as to presentation: "When the President speaks, I feel that he should follow the general lines laid down in his address of January 8, 1918"—this was Wilson's memorable Fourteen Point declaration—"with the following exceptions. . . ." The important one was a rearrangement of the order of the Fourteen Points that would emphasize the importance of the league "by stating this aim at the beginning instead of the end. . . ." (Wilson did not heed the advice, preferring to leave his fourteenth point where it was: "a general association of nations to be formed under specific covenants for the purpose of affording mutual guarantees of political independence and territorial integrity to great and small states alike.") Bullitt also anticipated obstacles to the program, such as the opposition of powerful Senate Republicans to a league of nations. On September 27, 1918, Wilson did, before a Joint Session of Congress, restate his objectives, much along the lines recommended in the memo. "I have just read the President's address," Bullitt wrote House, "and I want to tell you how much new confidence and inspiration it has given me. By this act the President has gone far toward making himself the political leader of the Allies. . . . It is a great call to the peoples of the world."

III

Emissary
to the
Revolution

Yearnings of an Idealist

―――――

"W H A T am I going to get killed for?" Bullitt asked in a piece of fiction written in the final months of the war.

> I am going to get killed. I have no doubt of that. For years I have been sure that I should die in an aeroplane, and when we entered the war I said to myself, "Here it is!" and began to fly. I have counted myself out as a casualty already and don't worry about it anymore.· . . . But I'm naturally a coward. I shrink from unpleasantness. So I had to force myself to do the hardest things always. And flying was the hardest thing, so I had to do it. . . ."

Yet in this moment of dwelling on imminent death, Bullitt was cogently seeking for the meaning of human sacrifice.

> But what do I want to come out of the war? If I am going to die, I would like something worthwhile to come out of it. What do I want to come? I do not want particularly to kill Germans. And I do not want a great lot of Germans to be killed. I would like to finish off the Kaiser and some of the officers whose pictures I have seen. But you never get a crack at those people. The Germans you get a chance to kill are young fellows who look like your own friends. There was a picture . . . last week of a boy in a machine-gun crew who looked like my roommate in college. I know I would like him if I knew him. . . . And there isn't anything I want especially to die for in the President's list of fourteen peace terms or in the elaborate war statements of the Inter-Allied Labor and Socialist Conference. Those two statements of aims seem to me to be the fairest I have seen and to be the blueprints of the good machinery for building and repairing the peace of the world. But there is nothing in political machinery that warms me enough to make me want to die for it.
>
> Still there is something in the possibilities of this war that makes me glad to have a chance to serve. I suppose it is the sort of feeling that Wordsworth talks about in his poems on the French Revolution in which he says, "Bliss was it in that dawn to be alive, but to be young was very heaven!" I feel as if there might be a dawn after this war, if it comes out all right, a sort of spiritual conversion in the hearts of Americans and Englishmen and Frenchmen and Italians and Russians and Germans and all the worried peoples of Austria-Hungary. . . . No marching for bringing peace on earth can bring good will to men unless the hearts of the people of the world are changed. . . . No marching will do the trick. There has got to be a spirit of conversion. . . . I know a lot of men who have been to Russia since the Revolution began, and they have all suffered conversion. They are done with Emperors—political emperors, financial emperors and moral emperors. They have exiled the Czar, . . . taken over the banks and buried Mrs. Grundy. As a nation . . . [the Russian people] have become brotherly, open-hearted, free from convention and unafraid

of life. Is it impossible that the war may end in a similar state of grace in the rest of Europe and America? I believe it may end that way, and that is the thing I am ready to die for.

The war was about to end, and Bullitt would die only in his fantasy. The Germans had mounted an offensive in the spring of 1918—the "Great Battle," they called their all-out bid for victory. With reinforcements from the Russian front they had one hundred ninety-two divisions to send against the Allies; but the Allies were using tanks effectively for the first time, and they had gained control of the skies, which gave them a crucial observation advantage. The Allies, bolstered by the American Expeditionary Force of a million men, also were numerically superior: "Out of a billion five hundred sixty-five million people who . . . inhabit the earth," wrote a retired German general, Wilhelm von Blume, "a billion stand against us." Germany and Austria-Hungary had suffered about a million casualties in the 1918 offensive and had failed in their objectives: to drive the British from the European continent and to cross the Marne River and take Paris.

On August 8—General Erich Ludendorff, the chief of staff, called it a black day for the German Army—the British launched a massive armored attack at Amiens, seventy miles north of Paris, and overran a half dozen German divisions. It was just a matter of time: on September 27, the day President Wilson went before Congress to state his objectives, Field Marshal Paul von Hindenburg, the German commander, concluded that defeat was inevitable; on October 3 Prince Maximilian of Baden, the interim chancellor, requested that Wilson "take steps for the restoration of peace"; and on November 11 the armistice was signed at Compiègne, France.

Six days later, however, a new war started in Russia: Vladimir I. Lenin, the Bolshevik leader, seized power in the capital, Petrograd; and Aleksandr V. Kolchak, an admiral who had remained loyal to the deposed czar, Nicholas II—Kolchak had formed an anti-Bolshevik government in Siberia—declared himself the "supreme ruler of all Russia." Both sides, the Reds and the Whites, insisted they were fighting for peace, as they slaughtered each other, and the civil war would continue until 1920.

On December 4, 1918, Bullitt sailed from New York for Paris aboard the *George Washington* as a member of the staff of the American Commission to Negotiate Peace, and if there ever was an appropriate time for the United States to export its political system—to make the world "safe for democracy," as Wilson had said when the U.S. entered the war—this was it. With the German surrender largely to his credit—Germany's acceptance of the Fourteen Points was the basis for the armistice—Wilson was at the peak of his power abroad, and the stature of the nation was immense: foreign commerce had almost tripled during the war, from $3.9 billion to $9.2 billion, and the indebtedness to the U.S. by European governments was $10 billion. Bullitt worried about Wilson, nevertheless, for the president had barely glanced at reports on the civil war in Russia, a subject of urgent concern to Bullitt; and he had not revealed that he had any ideas about the structure of a league of nations—even Colonel House, whose confidence Bullitt enjoyed, appeared not to know of them. Bullitt was aware, adding to his misgivings, that the president's influence was in decline at home: he had asked the people in November for a mandate to achieve "peace without victory," which was Wilson's way of articulating the goal of international cooperation, and they had denied it by electing a Republican majority to Congress. With the indomitable Henry Cabot Lodge of Massachusetts as chairman of the Senate Foreign Relations Committee Wilson could expect, no matter how he fared with his European counterparts in negotiating a treaty, an uphill battle over ratification. Bullitt was more than idly curious about the president's intentions and the outlook for his program, as he was now the chief of the Division of Current Intelligence Summaries. It was his job each morning to brief the members of the American commission—they were, in addition to the President, Colonel House, Secretary of State Lansing, Henry White, a former ambassador to France, and General Tasker H. Bliss, who had just stepped down as chief of staff of the Army—on military and political intelligence, including news developments, relevant to the peace conference.

Bullitt's apprehension was shared by his colleagues on the commission staff, for there were hard questions begging answers. Would Germany be held accountable, as the British and French were certain to insist, for the cost of the war? William E. Dodd, a University of Chicago historian—Dodd would become ambassador to Germany in 1933—was concerned that no one had stopped to consider what it would be possible for the Germans to pay. As to the German colonies in Africa and elsewhere—would they be ceded to the conquering British and her dominions, or would Wilson's principle of self-determination be applied? What about colonies of other nations, such as French Indochina? (A young revolutionary from Annam—his name was Ho Chi Minh, and he had helped found the Communist Party in France—was in Paris arguing for independence.) What about Korea, which was held by Japan? And Japan's claim on former German concessions in Shantung, China? British control of Ireland? American hegemony in the Philippines? Largest of all the issues for Bullitt was Allied policy in Russia, and it weighted heavily with him as he wrote in his diary on the day of departure, noting an odd coincidence: "Three years ago exactly I sailed from New York with another gentleman who planned to bring eternal peace to the world," referring, of course, to Henry Ford. "I am sure that the Ford party was a more wonderful experience than this will ever be; and tonight I wonder if Wilson will be much more successful than Ford." (Bullitt was not a diarist in the sense that he kept a daily record of his life for any extended period, though he did on occasion write personal reflections in the form of memoranda, some of which were stored for posterity.) On December 7 he made another entry: "Everyone is entirely in the dark in regard to the President's intentions. . . . None of the specialists has any idea what he will be asked to do. . . . Altogether the prospects for unified, powerful, liberal action seem very slight."

Bullitt decided to take bold action as he found himself seated beside the President in the ship's theater just before the moving picture began on the evening of December 8.

> I . . . said to him that he ought to call together the . . . people on board and explain to them the spirit in which he was approaching the conference and so far as possible the policies he intended to pursue, particularly in regard to a league of nations. I explained that everyone on board was in a thoroughly skeptical . . . mood and that it would have a fatal effect if, when we reached Paris and met our British and French friends, we were ignorant . . . concerning his intentions. . . .

Startled at first, Wilson replied he would schedule a briefing for the very next day: he was obliged to Bullitt for the suggestion—"it simply had not occurred to him that it would be necessary." At noon on December 9 Wilson summoned the commission staff, most of whom were men in their twenties and early thirties, and Bullitt supposed that it reminded him of his days as a professor at Princeton. "I have never seen the President in a franker and more engaging mood," Bullitt wrote. "He was overflowing with warmth and good nature. He sat at his desk, and we grouped about in chairs. He explained his entire program in some detail." Wilson outlined his plan to establish in a neutral country—he mentioned Switzerland and the Netherlands as likely candidates—a council of a league of nations, which would report to the governments of each league member any world development that might lead to war. "War" he said, as Bullitt recorded it, "must no longer be considered an exclusive business. Any war must be considered as affecting the whole world. If any nation refuses to listen to the powers composing the league, . . . they should be boycotted absolutely, . . . cut off absolutely." He was asked about the treaty with Germany, and Wilson said he was opposed to indemnities except for specific damages—"no open-ended bills for the cost of the whole war." The revolution in Russia? Wilson shared with Secretary of State Lansing an abhorrence of the Soviet "terror," but he offered a novel interpretation: "The only way I can explain the susceptibility of the people of Europe to the poison of Bolshevism is that their governments have been run for the wrong purposes." He drew a lesson from the experience of those people with regard to the treaty about to be negotiated: "I am convinced that if this peace is not made on the highest principles of justice, it will be swept away by the peoples of the world in less than a generation."

Bullitt would stay his concerns about Russia, as he had been somewhat soothed by Wilson's words—his field of interest had been, after all, Western Europe, and he had questions about the apportioning of the Austro-Hungarian empire. What would become of Bohemia, for example? Wilson took a pencil and drew a line through a map of Europe. "Bohemia will be a part of Czechoslovakia," he declared. "But, Mr. President," Bullitt protested, "there are three million Germans in Bohemia." Wilson looked perplexed as he replied, "President Masaryk never told me that." (Thomas G. Masaryk, a founder of Czechoslovakia, had just returned from exile in the United States to be president of the new republic.) Bullitt was taken aback, and his misgivings about Wilson as a peace negotiator were revived.

The *George Washington* docked at Brest on the coast of Brittany on December 13, and the Wilson party rode to Paris on a special train sent by the president of France, Raymond Poincaré, an ardent nationalist who had resolved that Germany would be punished. Wilson would soon find himself at odds with the French leaders—compared with Poincaré, Premier Georges Clemenceau was a moderate on the German question, though he considered the Fourteen Points too conciliatory and therefore unacceptable—but the French people greeted him with unlimited enthusiasm. "An enormous crowd, dominated by passions never before shown for any . . . visitor, was waiting for Wilson," wrote the historian Claude Paillat. They had greeted King Albert of Belgium with tears in their eyes, Paillat wrote, "but the man who got the most widespread welcome . . . was Wilson, . . . the man . . . who tipped the scales of war in favor of France. . . ." Poincaré and Clemenceau were waiting at the railroad station, and there was a procession through the streets—it may have been the last of the great cavalcades—with French soldiers, 36,000 veterans of the war, standing in locked formation to hold back the cheering crowd. When Wilson's carriage reached the Arch of Triumph, it was led beneath it, and Bullitt realized that the president was being accorded a historic honor: until then it had been reserved for Napoleon, who passed under the arch on his return from war in Russia in 1812.

The ovations ceased, and when the Allied leaders got down to the business of negotiating, they realized that the civil war in Russia, as Bullitt and other young staff members had been insisting, was an explosive problem: there was not one stable government east of the Rhine River, and Bolshevism was rampant. There was even reason to fear that the revolution would spread westward and engulf Europe. "At all times," wrote Ray Stannard Baker, the press officer of the U.S. delegation and later Woodrow Wilson's authorized biographer, "there rose a specter of chaos like a black cloud out of the east, threatening to overwhelm and swallow up the world." As of January 1919 the specter consisted of the revolutionary forces of Lenin and Leon Trotsky—Trotsky had negotiated the Brest-Litovsk Treaty and had organized the Red Army—and although the Reds were badly outnumbered, they had the advantage of unity, while the White commanders, Admiral Kolchak and General Anton I. Denikin, were barely on speaking terms. Allied troops—comprising contingents from the United States, Britain, France, Italy, Japan, Czechoslovakia, Serbia, and Greece—were deployed at random with orders to lend encouragement to the White Army, but there was confusion over Allied aims. The French attitude was well known: Clemenceau had demanded persistently that an army be sent to destroy Bolshevism, and he had been joined by the ranking French general, Ferdinand Foch, who was the supreme Allied commander as well; however, both Clemenceau and Foch were reluctant to commit French troops to the effort, because, they said, the men were war-weary and disgusted, therefore probably prone to Communism themselves. (Clemenceau, a tough and tenacious warrior—he was called The Tiger—was adamant about the defense of France, and opposition to the Bolsheviks was based on a struggle for economic survival: nearly bankrupt in 1919, France was the largest creditor of czarist Russia, so Clemenceau had reason to believe that a victory by the White forces would mean solvency instead of fiscal disaster.) David Lloyd George, the British prime minister, was also in a quandary, for he feared that the cost of an intervention in Russia would bankrupt Britain's economy, which had been depleted by the war, and its failure could inspire a Communist revolution. But Lloyd George was being harassed by a conservative member of his coalition cabinet, the secretary for war, Winston Churchill, who saw Lenin as Antichrist, "the nameless beast so long foretold in Russian legend." So the French and British both were in a difficult spot, unable to go forward or to go back, and Wilson sympathized with their predicament: "To arrest revolutionary movement by means of deployed armies," he wrote, "is like trying to use a broom to sweep back a high tide."

Lloyd George was the most anxious of the Allied leaders to reach a solution on Russia, and he was the one who had paid the most attention to those that had been proposed, all of which he considered unthinkable: any strategy that depended on the armies claiming allegiance to the czar was bound to fail, he reasoned, so a negotiated peace was mandatory. (Lloyd George was known to be an impatient man: "I always feel like knocking down every fence I come across," he once said.) On January 2, 1919, he asked the chiefs of state of the other Allied powers to join him in a summons to each of the Russian factions, asking them to send representatives to a special conference in Paris. The French said immediately that they would have no part of such a meeting, contending that to invite the Bolsheviks to Paris was tantamount to recognizing them. "The

French government," said Stephen Pichon, the foreign minister, ". . . will make no contract with crime." Lloyd George argued that recognition of the Russian Reds was not what he had in mind; he merely wished to bring their leaders to Paris so they could explain themselves, much as disorderly tribal chiefs were brought to Rome by the Caesars. He found himself in a classic liberal dilemma, caught between extremes: the French and the conservatives of his own country, Winston Churchill in particular, were adamant in wanting nothing to do with the Bolsheviks, while supporters of the Revolution belittled his suggestion that Lenin and Trotsky be called to account to their actions. "Lloyd George omitted only one trifling circumstance," a Soviet historian commented in retrospect. "Russia had not entered into . . . the British Empire."

Churchill stated his case on January 14 and 19 before the Council of Ten (consisting of the four Allied leaders—Wilson, Lloyd George, Clemenceau, and Premier Vittorio Orlando of Italy—and the heads of state of six Associated Powers), denouncing the "baboonery of Bolshevism" and arguing for large-scale intervention. Wilson, having observed with seeming detachment, had a compromise to offer: why not invite the leaders of the warring factions in Russia to meet in a remote part of the world? On January 22 he personally typed a proposed truce; the site he had selected was the Prinkipos, islands belonging to Turkey in the Sea of Marmara. (Originally known in English as the Princess Islands, they were used in early times for the banishment of prostitutes and lepers and other outcasts, and their selection as a meeting site indicated the contempt of the Allied leaders, Wilson included, for the Bolsheviks.) There was immediate opposition at the French foreign office, which was echoed on the editorial pages of French and British newspapers, and anti-Soviet voices in Russia joined those of Russian émigrés in Paris in the chorus of denunciation. By February 4, when an acceptance by the Bolsheviks was received—Lenin viewed the meeting, which had been scheduled for February 15, as a way to buy time—the idea was already dead.

Wilson and House were becoming increasingly uneasy about the military situation in Siberia, their anxieties having been enhanced by Bullitt, who wrote to House on January 30, expressing the view that the American troops at Archangel and Murmansk—there were four thousand of them, along with six thousand British and two thousand French—"are no longer serving a useful purpose." In fact, Bullitt asserted, Allied presence in Russia "serves mainly to create cynicism in regard to all our proposals and to stimulate recruiting for the Red Army." He also warned that the troops were in danger of being slaughtered by the Bolsheviks: "Unless they are saved by prompt action, we shall have another Gallipoli," he wrote, no doubt intending to disparage Churchill, who as first lord of the admiralty in 1915 was discredited by the failure of the British campaign on the Dardanelles strait.

Bullitt had concluded there was little to be gained from trying to force the French to agree to a meeting of the opposing Russian factions—a circumstance made all the more certain on February 19, when Clemenceau was wounded by a gunshot in an assassination attempt—and he proposed instead, originally in a memo to House on January 19, that an American delegation be sent "to examine conditions in Russia with a view to recommending definite action." He even nominated three men to be sent on such a mission: Learned Hand, a distinguished jurist; William Allen White, a respected journalist from Kansas; and Raymond Fosdick, an aide to General John J. Pershing, the U.S. Army commander in Europe. "As soon as this policy has been agreed upon," Bullitt wrote, confident that his proposal would be accepted, a government official "should get in touch with Litvinov, . . ."—Maxim Litvinov was the assistant commissar for foreign affairs—"to ascertain whether or not the Soviet Government will consent to admit the mission to Great Russia." House approved of the idea and persuaded Wilson to okay it, though they agreed the operation would have to be carried out in secret—it was certain to arouse a loud protest by the French and the British conservatives, if they learned of it—and men as well known as Hand, White, and Fosdick would be too conspicuous. House thought finally of Bullitt himself, who had suggested in his memo that he go along "as general bootblack"; for with an unknown junior aide in charge, the mission could be disavowed if word of it leaked out. There was another reason for choosing Bullitt, who was getting a reputation as a liberal zealot: as Secretary of State Lansing noted in his diary on February 16, 1919, they were sending him "to cure him of his Bolshevism."

Off to See the Future

I T   W A S   a busy and exciting time for Bullitt, satisfying as well, for he was doing the sort of government work he deemed most important, and he was making a contribution to the cause of world peace. It was at this moment of accomplishment that he was hit by a personal tragedy, the death of his mother on January 20, 1919. Bullitt's schedule would not allow a trip to Philadelphia for the funeral, though he did wear a mourning band on his left suit-coat sleeve for the rest of the peace meeting. There was, for that matter, little opportunity for him to tend to his personal life—Ernesta came to Paris but hardly saw him from January to mid-

May—though it is safe to say that Bullitt endured the sacrifice, and a firsthand look at the Russian Revolution was what he had most hoped for. True, Bullitt was a liberal, perhaps even a radical, but he wore the labels with pride and defiance. He was one of several junior members of the American peace delegation—others were Adolf A. Berle, Jr., the youngest graduate of the Harvard Law School in its history, and Samuel Eliot Morison, the military historian—who counted themselves as liberal by basic definition, meaning they favored internationalism and individual freedom. Bullitt may have been a bit more so, however, for he was a natural leader and did not mind notoriety, if it served his purpose. In addition Bullitt had been greatly affected by his newspaper career, brief as it had been: he esteemed and considered himself of a piece with liberal magazine writers such as Lincoln Steffens, William Allen White, and Ray Stannard Baker, who had exposed corrupt politics and big-business misdeeds. By no coincidence all these men were a generation older than Bullitt, and therein lay another explanation of his attitudes: Bullitt was influenced by older men—especially Steffens, the famous muckraker, who was fifty-three in 1919, when Bullitt was 28.

Bullitt's instructions, issued by Lansing, were terse and to the point but unspecific and open to interpretation: "You are hereby directed to proceed to Russia for the purpose of studying conditions, political and economic, . . . for the benefit of the American commissioners plenipotentiary to negotiate peace. . . ." Lansing evidently had in mind a fact-finding trip, but Bullitt construed his assignment to be a preliminary negotiating effort—he was determined from the outset to face Lenin across a bargaining table—which according to Steffens, a reliable reporter if a bit biased, is what Colonel House had intended. Steffens, who was covering the Paris conference, claimed it was he who had suggested to House a secret mission to Russia, "to see if they understand what you are up to and so make sure that they will come in a desired state of mind to an official meeting with your full-powered delegates," as Steffens wrote in his *Autobiography*.

"That's right," said House thoughtfully. "That is the way to do it." . . . He looked at me aggressively, and he declared . . ., "But not you. You shan't be on it." I laughed. He knew that I ached to go to Russia then. Much had happened since I was last there. . . . "No. We'll not send you," he repeated. "I know whom to nominate." A few days later William C. Bullitt . . . came bouncing up to ask me how I'd like to go to Russia. It was a secret, but Colonel House had got him commissioned to . . . arrange some business there with Lenin. . . . Would I go as a sort of political observer and liaison man? I would.

As Steffens understood Bullitt's orders, he was to "negotiate a preliminary agreement with the Russians so that the United States and Great Britain could persuade France to join them in an invitation to a parley, reasonably sure of some results. Colonel House had proposed; Lloyd George had planned, the visit. . . ."

It was still to be a hush-hush exercise—in fact, with Steffens involved extra precautions were called for. "House, knowing I was regarded as a friend of Russia," wrote Steffens, "wanted me to go unofficially as a friend of Bullitt, capable of official repudiation."

Bullitt chose his party carefully, keeping it to a minimum number for security reasons and making sure that duties were clearly delineated (he would be criticized later for not having taken a seasoned diplomat, such as Joseph C. Grew, and accused of not wanting to share the principal responsibility): Steffens, apart from Bullitt's high regard for his journalistic talents, had returned from Petrograd in June 1917 and would be useful as a guide as well as an observer; Walter W. Pettit was an Army intelligence officer, fluent in Russian; and Robert E. Lynch was a government clerk. Steffens had joked that only spies and armies could enter Russia at the time, and in Pettit they had both; as for Lynch, Bullitt brought him along as a playmate. "On trains and boats they skylarked," Steffens recalled, "wrestling and tumbling like a couple of bear cubs. . . . A pretty noisy mission we were, but Bullitt knew just what he was about; nobody could suspect us of secrecy or importance; and at formal moments and in emergencies the head of our missions was all there with the form, the authority, and the—audacity." Bullitt was also thorough in his preparation, having obtained from Philip H. Kerr, Lloyd George's secretary—Bullitt had known Kerr, later Lord Lothian, having been introduced by his British relatives—a list of eight terms the Bolsheviks would be expected to accept: hostilities to cease on all fronts; all de facto governments to remain in control of territories they occupy; railways and ports to be subject to the same regulations as international railways and ports; Allied subjects to be given free right and full security to enable them to enter Soviet Russia; amnesty to political prisoners on both sides; trade relations to be restored; questions concerning Russia's debts to be considered independently after peace had been established; Russian armies above a quota to be defined to be demobilized and their surplus arms surrendered or destroyed as a precondition of a withdrawal of Allied troops from Russia. Bullitt was led to believe that acceptance of the terms by Lenin would ensure a peace agreement.

———————

On February 22, 1919, four furtive Americans slipped from Paris over to London—Bullitt enjoyed the clandestine aspect of the operation as much as anything—where they hitched a ride to Norway on a British naval vessel. It was not a pleasant trip, however: there was annoying red tape in the form of papers issued to them in London, to show in case they were stopped by ships of the Allied blockade of Russia; and there were long hours of anxiety crossing the storm-tossed North Sea, wondering as they lay strapped in their bunks—only

Bullitt was not seasick—if they would be sunk by a stray mine. Nevertheless, they arrived in Christiania without serious incident—for Bullitt here was another reminder of the hapless voyage for peace with Henry Ford—and then traveled across Sweden by train and sleigh, reaching Stockholm on March 1. "The sun-burned Swedes . . . let us pass at salute over their sunny winter snow," Steffens wrote; "we were the United States. There was something like a meeting of conspirators in Stockholm the beautiful, where U.S. Minister Morris"—Ira Morris, the minister to Sweden, was impressed with Bullitt and treated him deferentially—"put us in touch with Bolshevik agents. . . ." Morris introduced them to Karl Kilbom, a Swedish Communist—Kilbom was an important link, as he was a friend of Lenin's from their days of exile in Switzerland—who was dubious at first. When Morris assured him that the four Americans were not spies but simply wished to collect information, Kilbom laughed—he had already assumed that Pettit was a military man from the way he wore his heavy leather overcoat—and he demanded: "What differentiates spying from collecting information?" However, Kilbom agreed to lend a hand in the hope it would help end the fighting in Russia; he cautioned that without him to guide them—Kilbom had made the trip four times in the two years of war—the journey to Petrograd would be very risky. First, though, *he* had a problem: he did not know whether he could get a visa to cross Finland, where anti-Communist forces were in power and Reds were not welcome. (In the civil war of 1918, Red forces, supported by Russian Communists, were soundly defeated by the army of Marshal Carl Gustav Emil Mannerheim, the hero of Finnish liberation.) Bullitt remembered that Herbert Hoover, the war relief administrator, was in Helsinki, and through Hoover he put pressure on the Finnish foreign ministry, with the result that an amazed Kilbom was immediately issued a visa.

On arrival in Helsinki by boat, Kilbom bid his American friends *au revoir*. He had become fond of them: "They were so nice and open," Kilbom noted in his journal, "as only Americans can be when they are at their best"; he was going alone to Russia in the hope of convincing Lenin that Bullitt had come to engage in genuine peace negotiations. He told the Americans to remain in Helsinki for a few days, then go to Terijoki, a town on the Russian-Finnish border; and, provided he was able to persuade Lenin, he would meet them there and take them to Petrograd. The trip by sleigh from Helsinki to Terijoki was a depressing experience, since in the war the toll in human lives had been heavy; and along the way Finnish peasants warned that it would be worse in Russia, for there had been famine as a result of war and harsh weather, with the Allied blockade adding to the suffering from starvation. "You will have to eat rat soup," said a Finn seriously, and Bullitt was glad they had thought to pack their steamer trunks with canned rations. As they reached the border, there was almost a serious incident when an armed Finnish officer ordered them to stop and be searched. "Hands off, you," Bullitt commanded the officer, who was reaching for the reins of their horses. "Telephone for orders. We pass." As Steffens appropriately put it, "Bullitt outdid him in arrogance."

It was March 6, 1919, when they crossed into Russia, and Kilbom was waiting with an official Bolshevik delegation accompanied by a brass band and cavalry troops: "They no longer have the beaten-dog look that distinguished them under the Czar," Bullitt wrote in his diary, "but carry themselves like free men and curiously like Americans." Aboard a special train bound for Petrograd, Kilbom explained that he had met with Grigory Zinoviev, the head of the executive committee of the Communist International, and had spoken with Lenin by telephone; as a result they would be greeted by Georgi Chicherin, the commissar for foreign affairs of the revolutionary government, and his assistant, Maxim Litvinov. As it turned out, there was no such high-level reception party in Petrograd when Bullitt and his followers arrived on March 8—there was, in fact, no one at the railroad station, and the streets were cold and deserted—and it was due only to a chance encounter with a low-level official that they were able to make their way to a hotel. Kilbom was embarrassed—such slip-ups actually were a common occurrence, Bullitt would learn soon enough—but the Swede had done his job: he had escorted Bullitt, Pettit, and Steffens to Petrograd (they had left Lynch in Finland), and they would be able to fare for themselves, Bullitt assured him. The hotel they stumbled on had been a favorite of American tourists before the Revolution, but its bygone elegance was impossible to imagine, given its bleak and vacant state: frigid corridors led from a run-down lobby to a suite of unheated rooms that offered little protection from the March gales.

Sleep was the only escape for Bullitt and Pettit, who huddled together in a corner for warmth, while Steffens agreed to go with Kilbom to seek someone of authority. He found Zinoviev, who was having a midnight cup of tea in his quarters in another deserted hotel. Without any greeting Zinoviev demanded of Steffens, in German: "Are you empowered to negotiate?" Steffens answered that they were not and began to explain the preliminary nature of their mission. "He would not listen," Steffens wrote in his *Autobiography*. "When he heard that we were not plenipotentiaries he turned away abruptly, and we never saw him again." Bullitt refused to be discouraged by either the gloomy look of Petrograd or the news Steffens brought of his meeting with Zinoviev; he was in fact heartened in the morning by the sight from his hotel room window of Soviet soldiers, several thousand of them. "The men marched well," he wrote, "and their equipment . . .—rifles and machine guns and light artillery—was excellent." He soon discovered why his mission was getting a hot and cold response: there was a split in the ranks of Soviet officialdom. Zinoviev and Trotsky considered the Americans nothing but eavesdroppers, while Chicherin and Litvinov were favorably disposed, although they confided their mistrust of the French, who they feared, as

Bullitt recorded it, "would employ the period of the armistice to send large supplies to anti-Bolshevik armies and to raise forces to operate against . . . Soviet governments." Bullitt assured them that the United States, not France or Great Britain, was the dominant power at the peace conference, and if given sufficient compromise by the Bolsheviks he would be able to negotiate an end to the fighting. With Chicherin and Litvinov on his side and having been notified that Lenin would see him in Moscow, Bullitt was optimistic and said so in a message to Colonel House, for the eyes of the president, in Paris. "Journey easy," he cabled on March 10.

> Reports of frightful conditions here ridiculously exaggerated. Discussion yesterday with Chicherin and Litvinov. Leave today for Moscow for discussion with Lenin. Both Chicherin and Litvinov, speaking with authority, stated that the Soviet Government is most favorably disposed towards the cessation of hostilities and a peace conference. . . . Chicherin and Litvinov express full confidence in the good will of the American Government. . . . Suspend judgment on any action. . . . I am certain from conversation already held that the Soviet Government is disposed to be reasonable. . . .

"Shatov! That's Bill Shatov!" Lincoln Steffens had spotted an American friend, but Bill Bullitt and Walter Pettit were paying attention to a military parade: "Troops with religion in their feet, shoulders, and eyes will fight," said Captain Pettit, hardly noticing the burly, dark-haired man in uniform, who had Steffens in a bear hug. Shatov was a radical from Chicago, a member of the IWW, the Industrial Workers of the World. "He knew what I was there for," Steffens wrote. "I asked what he was doing. . . . 'I'll tell you if you won't give me away. . . . I am chief of police of Petrograd.' . . . Bill Shatov had had a command in the October revolution and been occupied ever since in holding the control over the city. He was a happy man." Shatov also was trained to recognize fellow professionals, and he proposed to Pettit a visit to the northern front to observe the American forces from Bolshevik trenches. Pettit thanked him but declined, laughing in an uneasy way, which confirmed Shatov's suspicion, and Bullitt realized it would be prudent to leave Pettit in Petrograd: just he and Steffens would go to Moscow, for it was better to do without an aide who knew Russia and spoke the language, if it meant being accused of having a military agent in his entourage.

Their first view of the new capital on the morning of March 11, as Bullitt and Steffens arrived on the Petrograd-to-Moscow express, was of a city that "glistened in the sun like a gigantic Christmas tree," Bullitt wrote in his diary. They were escorted to warm and comfortable quarters in what had been a luxury hotel, where their table was abundantly supplied, although the menu was limited: caviar, black bread, and tea for breakfast, lunch, and dinner. Bullitt suspected they were being shown a distorted picture of life in Moscow, for it contrasted sharply with the reports of harsh conditions that had reached Paris. He was right, of course, as there was virtually nothing to eat for the people of Russia, even the leaders of the Revolution, who predictably came to call at mealtime. "Yes, Mr. Secretary, supper is ready," Bullitt would say in greeting Commissar Chicherin, which would have been amusing had it not been tragic. Stories of death by starvation were commonplace and made all too real by streets littered with corpses—it was so bad that there was a black market in human flesh—and Bullitt, ever impressionable, blamed it entirely on the Allies: "The blockade . . . is the cause of this distress," he declared in an advisory to House. He also cabled a glowing assessment—superficial in that it was based on what he had been told, not seen for himself—of conditions fostered by the Revolution: "The red terror is over. . . . One feels as safe in the streets of Petrograd and Moscow as in the streets of Paris or New York. . . . Prostitutes have disappeared from sight, the economic reasons for their career having ceased to exist." To Steffens privately Bullitt was exuberant. "We have seen the future, and it works!" he said repeatedly, until it was a litany; and when Steffens upon returning to Paris adopted it in conversations, neglecting to give Bullitt credit—one was even recorded in his *Autobiography*—it became a memorable quotation. Bullitt also was favorably impressed by the chairman of the Council of People's Commissars. "There is already a Lenin legend," he wrote in a report to President Wilson in April after returning to Paris. "He is regarded as almost a prophet. His picture, usually accompanied with that of Karl Marx, hangs everywhere. In Russia one never hears Lenin and Trotsky spoken of in the same breath, as is usual in the western world. Lenin is regarded as in a class by himself. Trotsky is but one of the lower order of mortals."

At the Peace Table with Lenin

BULLITT met with Lenin on March 14—by his decision he went alone to the Kremlin, though he arranged a separate appointment a day later for Steffens, to ask "undiplomatic" questions—and as he sat in an anteroom his reporter's eye missed little. "I had to wait a few minutes until a delegation of peasants left his room," he wrote.

They had heard in their village that Comrade Lenin was hungry. And they had come hundreds of miles carrying eight hundred poods of bread [which would have been impossible, since eight-hundred poods is the equivalent of 28,888 pounds, over fourteen tons]. Just before them was another delegation of peasants to whom the report has come that Comrade Lenin was working in an unheated room. They came bearing a stove and enough firewood to heat it for three months. Lenin is the only leader who receives such gifts. And he turns them into the common fund.

Lenin was forty-nine years old in 1919, though he looked older. The hardening of brain tissue, which would kill him in five years, was not showing its effect, however; and a recent assassination attempt—he had been shot in the left arm, and the bullet penetrated his chest—had not caused serious disability. He was the same energetic Lenin who had led a victorious revolution of the proletariat: when he talked, his eyebrows twitched, and he was feared by underlings more for his mocking laugh than his angry tongue. He may have lacked certain qualities of greatness—he was not a towering politician or a renowned military tactician—but he had one magnificent talent: he could marshal all the forces of his mind on the issue at hand. This great Marxist monk, as he was often called for his power of concentration, was in a precarious position, threatened by the White Russian cossacks and the Allied armies and plagued by famine and disease. Lenin badly needed a pause, a cessation of hostilities, and when he had spoken by telephone with Karl Kilbom, finally agreeing to meet with Bullitt, he had been persuaded by Kilbom's assurance that the Americans wished to negotiate seriously. "There was no doubt," Kilbom wrote in his diary, "that Lenin was happy about the delegation"; he was mistaken perhaps in believing that Bullitt had the authority to agree to a treaty, but he was willing to accept any terms the Allies would offer, if it would buy him some time. Lenin was aware that Bullitt brought with him a list of eight terms that had been stipulated by Lloyd George of Britain—Bullitt had presented the terms to Commissar Chicherin in Petrograd—and he was familiar with them. When Lenin and Bullitt met shortly after three on the afternoon of March 14—face to face, Bullitt judged the Soviet leader to be "straightforward and direct, but also genial and with a large humor and serenity"—Lenin got right to the point: he " . . . seized upon the opportunity . . .," Bullitt wrote in his report to Wilson, "to make a definite statement on the position of the Soviet Government. He was opposed by Trotsky and the generals, but without much difficulty got the support of . . . the executive council, and the statement of the position of the Soviet Government, which was handed to me, was finally adopted unanimously." Trotsky the idealist had been opposed to it—as author of the credo of the Revolution he was uncompromising—and the generals were obedient to him, but Lenin the pragmatist insisted on a statement that was nearly identical to the one Bullitt had submitted to Chicherin. Some of the provisions were repeated word for word, as for example: "All de facto governments to remain in control of territories they occupy"; and while there were additional details, Bullitt could not find one important discrepancy between the list of terms he had received from Lloyd George's confidential secretary, Philip Kerr, and the one he was being offered by Lenin.

"Lenin's proposal meant," Bullitt wrote in retrospect, "that the Soviet Government offered to give up, at least temporarily, the whole of Siberia, the Urals, the Caucasus, the Archangel and Murmansk areas, Finland, the Baltic States and most of the Ukraine." In addition the Soviets offered, as the proposal stated, to "recognize . . . responsibility for the financial obligations of the former Russian Empire"—they included the huge war debt of the czarist regime—although according to the terms transmitted by Bullitt the debt was to be "considered independently after peace has been established." There was one Soviet term that Bullitt refused to accept—it asked for a commitment by the United States and Britain "to see to it that France lives up to the conditions of the armistice"— maintaining that the French would reject the entire treaty if they learned of it, though he assured Lenin that the U.S. was the dominant Allied power. He was then handed the formal document, which contained a final and ultimately crucial paragraph: "The Soviet Government of Russia undertakes to accept the foregoing proposal provided it is made not later than April 10, 1919." Bullitt had less than a month to obtain official Allied approval of the offer, precious little time, but he was elated: he believed his dreams of ending the war were soon to be a reality. "You must do your utmost for it," Bullitt said of the Soviet response in a cable to Colonel House from Helsinki on March 18, "for if you had seen the things I have seen during the past week and talked with the men I have talked with, I know that you would not rest until you had put through this peace." He also sent an official account of his progress to President Wilson, Secretary of State Lansing, and House, attesting to the sincerity of the Soviet officials, who were "absolutely bound to accept the proposals, . . . provided they were made on or before April 10, and under no conditions would they change their minds." Lenin, Chicherin, and Litvinov, he emphasized, were "full of the sense of Russia's need for peace."

Bullitt sent several cables to Paris, having prepared on the return journey to Helsinki a series of reports to the peace commission extolling revolutionary Russia. "The Soviet Government is firmly established, and the Communist Party is strong politically and morally," he observed, hardly cured of his Bolshevism, as Secretary Lansing no doubt noted. "There is order in Petrograd and Moscow. There have been no riots and no uprisings for many weeks. Prostitution has disappeared. Robberies have almost ceased. One feels as safe as in Paris. The opera, theaters and ballet are performing as in peace." There was but one serious problem, one "true cause of the miseries of Russia": that was the Allied blockade, which was the cause of widespread famine. He repeated his praise of Lenin, a man "of the quickest intelligence," and he described the Red Army as "high-spirited and well-equipped." He argued that, yes, the Communists could be overthrown, but at an unbearable cost. "If we are able to continue the blockade and intervention indefinitely," he wrote,

> We can produce such famine, such hunger riots and battles for bread that the anarchists and Left Social Revolutionaries will rule for a moment over the ruins of Russia, for starvation will drive Russia to the left, not to the right. We can destroy the Communists only by producing anarchy. Then we shall finally have to intervene over the dead bodies and dead hopes of the simple Russian people and set up a form of government they do not want and against which they will revolt whenever strength returns to them.

The other course? It was "to make an offer of peace along the lines of the proposal of the Soviet Government, transmitted in my foregoing cable," which would be responding to the will of the Russian people. "They received us," he wrote in the final lines of his eloquent plea, "because they had gathered the impression that President Wilson was beginning to see through the lies . . . to the very simple truth that a . . . young people were trying rudely but conscientiously and at the cost of great suffering to themselves to find a better way to live. . . ."

Lenin's reaction to the meeting, his "sense of Russia's need for peace," was contained in a memoir, published in 1920; in it he declared that the Bolsheviks were being forced by the Western powers to "repeat much of what we did at the time of Brest-Litovsk": we would be forced to sign "the most severe terms of peace. . . ." He made clear, however, that the agreement would have been only as durable as the White Russian governments he had sworn to destroy. "When we proposed a treaty to Bullitt a year ago," Lenin explained, "a treaty . . . which left tremendous amounts of territory to Deniken and Kolchak, we proposed this treaty with the knowledge that if peace was signed, those governments could never hold out."

Mission Repudiated

UPON THEIR RETURN to Paris Bullitt and Steffens were so bubbling with enthusiasm for what they had witnessed in Russia—William Allen White called them "bug-eyed with wonder" and "full of strange tales"—that they were bound to be questioned by skeptical friends. Herbert Bayard Swope, the famed war correspondent for *The New York World*—he had won a Pulitzer Prize in 1917 for reporting from Germany—was "dismayed" by Bullitt's avowal of the end of prostitution in Petrograd and Moscow. "My God, Steff," he demanded, "what did you do?" Jo Davidson, the American sculptor, wanted to know why they were pleased to be back in Paris—they had allowed that they were—if they had found Moscow so wonderful. "I thought," Steffens replied, "it was because, though we had been to heaven, we were so accustomed to our own civilization that we preferred hell." (It was in Davidson's studio that Steffens uttered Bullitt's memorable remark—to Bernard Baruch, the economic advisor to President Wilson, who inquired as he was sitting for a portrait bust: "So you've been over to Russia?" "I answered very literally," Steffens wrote, " 'I have been over into the future, and it works.' ") Bullitt did not remain in the background: he buttonholed James T. Shotwell, the eminent historian and peace activist, and lectured him on the compromises the Soviets had offered. "If Bolshevism is willing to make the compromises which Bullitt is sure it will," Shotwell wrote, "the situation is not so desperate." Bullitt was conducting himself commendably in a difficult diplomatic situation—he was perhaps too inclined to believe the crafty Lenin, though he was right about the blockade being the cause of famine in Russia—but, as Steffens would write in his *Autobiography*:

> It was a disappointing return. . . . Bullitt had set his heart on the acceptance of his report; House was enthusiastic; and Lloyd George received him . . . at breakfast the second day and listened and was interested. Of course, Bullitt had brought back all the prime minister had asked. . . . No action was taken on the proposal, . . . and after a few weeks of futile discussion the Bullitt mission was repudiated. . . . I have had it explained to me. . . . It was a political custom in British parliamentary practice to use young men for sounding or experimental purposes, and it was understood that if such a mission became embarrassing, . . . it was repudiated; the missionaries lay down and took the disgrace till later, when it was forgotten, they would get their reward. But Bullitt would not play this game.

Bullitt had arrived in Paris on March 25, late in the day, and that evening he went to see Colonel House, who was in bed but not asleep. He showed House the Lenin peace proposal—it had been officially presented to him by Chicherin and Litvinov a day after the meeting at the Kremlin—which bore the seal of the Soviet foreign office. House, who was more skilled in politics than in foreign policy, agreed that the offer merited consideration, and he supposed it could lead to peace, if. . . . "If what?" Bullitt wished to know. "If we can get action by the prime ministers," House replied—Lloyd George, Clemenceau, Orlando—and Bullitt felt a twinge of anxiety, with regard to the French in particular. House telephoned the president to ask if he would see Bullitt right away as it "was a matter of utmost importance." "No, I have a terrible headache," said Wilson. "Congratulate him, and tell him I'll see him tomorrow." Wilson was not feeling well the following morning either, so Bullitt reported instead to the other members of the American commission, Secretary Lansing, Ambassador White, and General Bliss. "We had a long discussion," Bullitt later recalled, "at the end of which it was the sense of the . . . meeting that it was highly desirable to attempt to bring about peace. . . ."

The president still was not available the next day, March 27—Wilson never did see Bullitt; he was occupied with other matters, specifically the peace treaty and such related issues as autonomy for the Saar—and at House's suggestion Bullitt presented the proposal to Prime Minister Lloyd George. They met at breakfast at Lloyd George's apartment, along with Philip Kerr, Maurice Hankey, the secretary of the British cabinet, and Jan Christiaan Smuts, the South African soldier and statesman. (It was a secret meeting, but Bullitt was not observing security rules: "Sorry I can't breakfast with you," he wrote in a note to Oswald Garrison Villard, editor of *The Nation*, "but I've got to breakfast with L. G.") Smuts favored immediate action, having scanned Bullitt's report, but Lloyd George was hesitant: he held a copy of *The London Daily Mail* and said, "As long as the British press is doing this kind of thing, how can you expect me to be sensible about Russia?"

The editor of the *Daily Mail*, Henry Wickham Steed, had been leaked word of Bullitt's mission and had written: "The issue is whether the Allied and Associated Governments shall, directly or indirectly, accredit an evil thing known as Bolshevism." Lloyd George was quick to acknowledge that Bullitt had made a strong case: the Communists were probably in Russia to stay, and inevitably it would be necessary to make peace with them; but given the fragile state of his Labor-Conservative coalition government, he was not in a position to dictate such a peace. He was concerned as well with the probable public reaction to the choice of the Allied emissary—Bullitt's youth and liberal attitudes would count against him—which led the prime minister to propose a second mission: ". . . we have got to send in somebody who is known . . . as a complete conservative," he declared, "in order to have the whole world believe that the report he brings out is not simply the utterance of a radical." Lloyd George listed a number of possibilities, British conservatives such as Robert Cecil of the foreign office, noting though that Cecil was needed in the league of nations debate; and then he turned to General Smuts: "It would be splendid if you could go, but, of course, you have got the other job," which was to go to Hungary to deal with the threat of a Communist dictatorship there. The meeting was terminated by Lloyd George, who urged Bullitt to make his report public, and Bullitt would ultimately take the prime minister's advice.

Bullitt became all the more persistent as he saw success slipping away. That afternoon he called on the British foreign secretary, Arthur J. Balfour—Balfour was committed, Bullitt knew, to the cause of peace—whose reaction was predictably favorable; Colonel House, meanwhile, visited Orlando, the Italian premier, and advised Bullitt he could depend on the support of Italy. So much for the good news; the rest was by and large bad: France could not be counted on—Clemenceau had not even been formally approached, though he had no doubt read reports of the mission (it later developed that French intelligence agents had monitored Bullitt's movements), and he was surely displeased—and Lenin's deadline of April 10 was less than two weeks away. On April 1, beginning to feel despondent, Bullitt wrote his friend Walter Lippmann about "this last beautiful fight on Russia"; and on April 2 a reporter for *The Times* (London) filed a story for the April 3 edition of his newspaper, which would assure the failure of the mission. "It is now generally known in Paris," it read, "that the idea of a shameful deal with the Bolshevists on the basis of some sort of Allied and American recognition of the Lenin-Trotsky government . . . very nearly found acceptance in influential quarters here last week." Reports had become so specific that a Conservative member of Parliament, Samuel Hoare, asked during debate in the House of Commons if it was true that an American named William Bulet had recently returned from Moscow, having negotiated with Lenin. The prime minister's office, taking advantage of a technicality, replied that it knew nothing of a trip by a man named "Bulet," but the disclaimer did little to quiet the furor. On April 5 *The London Daily News* carried a report of "a definite concrete proposal signed by Lenin," and on April 6 another Conservative member of Parliament, Clement Edwards, stated that an American—this time he was identified as "Bullit"—had been sent to Russia, had talked with Lenin, and had brought back a document that, if approved by the Allies, would ratify recognition of the Soviet government.

Enter Winston Churchill, who had become alarmed by the reports and had decided it was time to resort to anti-Bolshevik propaganda. "Surely the moment has come," he had said in a letter on March 28 to George Curzon, who was soon to replace Balfour as foreign secretary, "to publish the Bolshevik atrocity blue-book. I find a difficulty in supplying the necessary reinforcements for Archangel and Murmansk. Public opinion is not sufficiently instructed." Churchill pressed his demands on the information office, and they were met with publication by the government of an eighty-eight page pamphlet, *White Paper on Bolshevik Atrocities*—in it were alleged without attribution such inhuman deeds as turning churches into whorehouses, torturing priests, and sponsoring free-love commissariats—which was an immediate best-seller in Britain. It had an impact on members of Parliament, only one of whom, Josiah Wedgwood, a Liberal who had served in Siberia with the war office, was willing to question the authenticity of the pamphlet: "anonymous tittletattle," Wedgwood called it. A message signed by two hundred MPs—it was printed in *The Times* on April 10, Lenin's deadline day—was sent to Lloyd George: "We the undersigned learn with great concern that there is a proposal before the peace commission to recognize the Bolshevist government in Moscow, . . . and urge the British plenipotentiaries to decline to agree to any such recognition." Churchill prevailed upon the prime minister, directly: "I do trust that President Wilson will not be allowed to weaken our policy. . . . His negotiations have become widely known and very much resented." Lloyd George knew they were not Wilson's negotiations, but his, and he returned to London to cover his tracks: there was "no question of recognition," he promised in a speech in the House of Commons; it has never been "put forward." He was just hedging there, but he was lying when he declared, "No, we have made no approaches at all." He then resorted to "a political custom in British parliamentary practice," as Steffens called it:

Of course there are constantly men of all nationalities coming from and going to Russia, always back with their own tales. . . . But we have nothing authentic. . . . There was a suggestion that there was some American who had come back. All I can say about that is that it is not for me to judge the value of these communications. But if the President of the United States had attached any value to them, he would have brought them to the conference, and he certainly has not done so.

Bullitt was appalled and personally offended by what he later termed "a most egregious case of misleading the public," but there was little he could do. "I clipped his statement from a newspaper and sent it to the President," he explained to the Senate Foreign Relations Committee, "and I asked the President to inform me whether the statement . . . was true or untrue. He was unable to answer, inasmuch as he would have had to reply on paper that Mr. Lloyd George had made an untrue statement."

On April 6 Bullitt appealed in desperation to the president, asking for "fifteen minutes to discuss this matter with you," but he got no reply. (Bullitt and the world at large did not know it, but Wilson had been seriously ill since April 3, with a 103-degree fever and symptoms of the arteriosclerosis that would incapacitate him in less than six months.) By this time Wilson had received a report from Herbert Hoover, dated March 28, in which Hoover argued vehemently against making any settlement with Lenin: "The Bolsheviki resorted to terror, bloodshed and murder to a degree long since abandoned even amongst reactionary tyrannies . . .," Hoover wrote. "We cannot ever remotely recognize this murderous tyranny without stimulating actionist radicalism in every country in Europe and without transgressing . . . every national ideal of our own." Then there was an event in Russia that conclusively settled the issue (not for fourteen years would recognition of the Soviet government again be considered by the United States): czarist forces led by Aleksandr Kolchak went on the offensive, and it appeared to Western observers—actually the success of the White advance was being exaggerated in France—that they would overrun Moscow. "[T]he entire press of Paris was roaring and screaming on the subject," Bullitt testified, "announcing that Kolchak would be in Moscow within two weeks; and therefore everyone, . . . including, I regret to say, members of the American commission, began to grow very lukewarm about peace in Russia. . . ." Bullitt was authorized by the commission to send a cable to Petrograd—he and Chicherin had devised a message to indicate that negotiations had been stalled: "Action leading to food relief via neutrals likely within week—Bullitt." It was dated April 10, 1919.

Bullitt was also disturbed by many of the provisions of the pact between the Allies and Germany, having read a draft copy of the Treaty of Versailles. He called them "black inequities . . . in the name of justice and right": Germany would be divided in two, with Poland having dominion over the city of Danzig; three million Germans would be absorbed into the new state of Czechoslovakia; and thirty-six million Chinese in Shantung province would be subjected to Japanese rule. "This isn't a treaty of peace," he complained. "I can see at least eleven wars in it." There was a protest meeting of the commission staff at which Bullitt demanded a mass resignation, and while he was supported by a few colleagues—Adolf A. Berle and Samuel Eliot Morison were among the eight who also quit—most of them swallowed their objections and stayed with the State Department. Twenty years later in a letter to Upton Sinclair, the author, Berle remembered a dinner at the Crillon Hotel following the meeting. "Some of us had resigned, or decided to; others had not," he wrote. ". . . the table decorations . . . were yellow jonquils and red roses. Bullitt, over coffee, tossed the yellow jonquils to the people who had not resigned and the red roses to the people who had." Lincoln Steffens also wrote about the meeting, adding personal insight.

Bullitt was not to be mollified. . . . He was one of the group of aristocratic young American liberals who were so outraged by the treaty that they met to protest by some united action. . . . I was the only older man there to see that significant scene; all those conscientious, high-bred, mostly rich young gentlemen and their wives, who wanted to do right and had to decide then and there whether to sacrifice their careers . . . by an open challenge to the wrong done by their government, . . . or yield and play the game. They asked my advice, sure, I could see, that I would be for the heroic course. And I would have been in the old muckraking days. But, as I said, I had seen the Russian Revolution, the war, and this peace, and I was sure that it was useless—it was almost wrong—to fight for the right under our system. . . . Either they and we all should labor to change the foundation of society, as the Russians were doing, or go along with the resultant civilization we were part of. . . .

Bullitt's resignation was tendered to Secretary Lansing—and accepted without public comment—on May 17, and he explained his action in an emotional letter to President Wilson. "I was one of the millions who trusted confidently and implicitly in your leadership," he wrote,

> and believed that you would take nothing less than "a permanent peace" based upon "unselfish and unbiased justice." But our Government has consented now to deliver the suffering peoples of the world to new oppressions, subjections, and dismemberments—a new century of war. And I can convince myself no longer that effective labor for "a new world order" is possible as a servant of this Government. Russia, "the acid test of good will" [Bullitt was quoting Wilson, who on January 18, 1918, had applied the phrase to U.S. policy toward Russia] for me as for you, has not even been understood. Unjust decisions of the conference in regard to Shantung, the Tyrol, Thrace, Hungary, East Prussia, Danzig, the Saar Valley, and the abandonment of the principle of the freedom of the seas make new international conflicts certain. It is my conviction that the present league of nations will be powerless to prevent these wars, and that the United States will be involved in them. . . .

He was prophetic, as he had just foreseen the great conflict of twenty years hence, and Bullitt did not mind telling the president of the United States what to do about it. (Coming from an upstart just six years out of Yale, it must have galled Wilson, who had been named the president of Princeton when Bullitt was eleven years old.) "Therefore," Bullitt lectured, "the duty of the Government of the United States to its own people and to mankind is to refuse to sign or ratify this unjust treaty, to refuse to guarantee its settlements by entering the league of nations, to refuse to entangle the United States further. . . ." Also on May 17 Bullitt sent a note to Colonel House, who had shown him the draft of the treaty, and attached a copy of his letter to the president. "I hope you will bring it to his attention," he wrote, "not because he will care what I may think, but because I have expressed the thoughts which are in the minds of many young and old men in the commission—thoughts which the President will have to reckon with when the world begins to reap the crop of wars the seeds of which have here been sown. I feel sure that you will agree that I am right in acting on my conviction. . . ." House apparently did agree: he sent for Bullitt—it was "the only reply that I had," Bullitt later recalled—and "we thrashed it all out"; then in June 1919 House and President Wilson had a falling out over the conduct of negotiations, and their association was terminated irreparably. (Bullitt told his daughter years later that Henry White, the commission member and respected diplomat, came to him—Bullitt assumed that White had been sent by Wilson—and said if he did not resign, he would be named ambassador to the newly proclaimed republic of Poland; but Bullitt declined.)

———————

Bullitt was the host of a farewell dinner in his suite at the Crillon Hotel, and he left the next day with Ernesta—she had stood by his side dutifully—for the Riviera, where he intended, as he confided to friends, "to lie on the sand and watch the world go to hell." The future of Europe was all too apparent, he told them: the Red Army would overrun the continent, from Vienna to London; and when asked if he would be marching with Trotsky and his troops, Bullitt replied, "I would feel honored. . . ." His resignation caused hardly a flutter at the time: the Treaty of Versailles was such major news that the defection of a junior staff aide was barely noticed in the world press. That changed over the next four months, however, as Bullitt became a principal player—player or pawn, he was a principal—in the debate over ratification of the treaty and the League of Nations. When his letter of May 17 to President Wilson was made public, Thomas A. Bailey, author of *Woodrow Wilson and the Great Betrayal*, termed it "sensational," while William E. Dodd, the University of Chicago historian, called it "bombastic and unreasonable." (Dodd was never an admirer of Bullitt, writing in 1920 that his resignation "revealed a rare mind" and an arrogant attitude toward the president: "One would have supposed that he was the next ranking member of the American commission.") "I got my bullet at the conference . . .," commented Clemenceau of France, referring to the attempt on his life. "Wilson got his Bullitt when he returned home."

In September 1919 the issue had been brought back to America and was being aired by President Wilson, who carried his message to the people on a whistle-stop tour of the country—on July 10, two days after his return, he had presented documents proposing the treaty and the league to Congress—and by the Senate Foreign Relations Committee in hearings in Washington. The chairman of the committee, Henry Cabot Lodge, was an articulate critic of Wilson's program: "an evil thing with a holy name," he had called the league; however, compared with such "irreconcilable" Republican isolationists as Hiram W. Johnson of California and William E. Borah of Idaho, Lodge was a moderate, whose differences with the president were as political as they were ideological. He was, though, an imperious man, who had become impatient with witnesses who would not cooperate—Secretary of State Lansing, as one example, had testified that he knew of no draft copy of Wilson's peace plan—so Lodge issued a subpoena for Bullitt, who was on a canoe trip in Maine with Ernesta and was met by a subpoena-server at Ford Kent on the St. John River. Bullitt knew, as he discussed it with Ernesta, that he had a lot to tell—about Danzig and the Saar and other touchy points in the treaty—and he decided there could be but one result if he did: it would destroy the treaty and the league and possibly Wilson himself. Then again he had little choice: he would testify and tell what he knew and let the chips fall. "Maybe, after a dozen years or so," he said, "the United States would make peace with the Bolsheviks, and maybe people would understand that the league was a bad thing and that he was right to oppose it." As for his own immediate future, Bullitt saw his career in ruins.

On September 4 President Wilson began his 9,500-mile railroad tour of the West on which he would speak thirty-seven times in twenty-nine cities in support of ratification of the Treaty of Versailles and membership in the League of Nations. On September 10 Senators Johnson and Borah launched a tour of their own, an opposition campaign; and on September 12 the Foreign Relations Committee—the committee, six of whose ten members were "irreconcilables," had before it forty-five amendments and four reservations to the treaty "to protect traditional American policies"—heard the testimony of William C. Bullitt in Room 310 of the Senate Office Building in Washington. Following his account of his duties in Paris, his mission to Russia, and his resignation from the government, Bullitt was questioned, first by Philander C. Knox, a Pennsylvania Republican, who had been secretary of state in the administration of William H. Taft— Taft was defeated for reelection by Wilson in 1912—and was a leader of anti-treaty forces in Congress. Knox was interested in Bullitt's final meeting with Colonel House in Paris.

Senator Knox: Was anything said during this conversation which you feel . . . disposed to tell us, which will be important?

Mr. Bullitt: I made a record of the conversation. Inasmuch as the conversations which I had with various members of the commission on the occasion of my resignation touched on a number of important issues, I kept a record of those conversations. . . . They are the only conversations of which I made records, and I made them simply because we did deal more or less with the entire question of the peace treaty. On the other hand, they are personal conversations. . . .

Senator Knox: I would not press you on the personal conversations. . . . I should like to ask you this one question: I suppose your letter of resignation to Mr. Lansing was merely formal?

Mr. Bullitt: My letter of resignation to Mr. Lansing was a formal letter.

Senator Knox: You certainly got a reply to that.

Mr. Bullitt: I did, sir. I wrote a formal letter, and I got a formal reply, and the Secretary sent for me the same afternoon and explained that he only sent me a formal reply because it was necessary. . . . We then discussed various other matters in connection with the treaty."

Chairman Lodge: Are you through?

Senator Knox: Yes.

Chairman Lodge: Did any member of our delegation . . . express to you any opinions about . . . this treaty?

Mr. Bullitt: Well, Mr. Lansing, Colonel House, General Bliss, and Mr. White had all expressed to me very vigorously their opinions on the subject.

Chairman Lodge: Were they enthusiastically in favor of it?

Mr. Bullitt: I regret to say, not. . . . It is no secret that Mr. Lansing, General Bliss, and Mr. White objected very vigorously to . . . numerous provisions. . . ."

Chairman Lodge: It is known that they objected to Shantung. That, I think, is public information. I do not know that it is public information that they objected to anything else.

Mr. Bullitt: I do not think that Secretary Lansing is at all enthusiastic about the League of Nations as it stands at present. I have a note of a conversation with him, . . . which, if I may, I will just read. . . . This was a conversation . . . at 2:30 on May 19. . . . This is a note which I immediately dictated after the conversation. "Mr. Lansing then said that he, too, considered many parts of the treaty thoroughly bad, particularly those dealing with Shantung and the league of nations. He said: 'I consider that the league of nations at present is entirely useless. The great powers have simply gone ahead and arranged the world to suit themselves. England and France in particular have gotten out of the treaty everything that they wanted, and the league of nations can do nothing to alter any of the unjust clauses of the treaty. . . .' We then talked about the possibility of ratification by the Senate. Mr. Lansing said: 'I believe that if the Senate could understand what this treaty means, and if the American people could really understand, it would unquestionably be defeated. . . .' "

Wilson, aboard his train, *The Mayflower*, learned of Bullitt's disclosures from newspaper accounts on September 13, and he was deeply hurt, though his resentment was directed at Lansing, not a whippersnapper named Bullitt. "This is the man I raised to the great office of secretary of state of the United States," he lamented to his secretary, Joseph Tumulty. "I did not think it was possible for Lansing to act this way." On September 16 Lansing tried to explain his position in a lengthy telegram to the president, and he made a public statement in a book on the negotiations published in 1921.

It is very easy to see how by making a record of one side of this conversation without reference to the other side and by an omission here and there, possibly unintentionally, the sense was altered. Mr. Bullitt, by repeating only a part of my words and by omitting the context, entirely changed the meaning of what was said. My attitude was, and I intended to show it at the time, that the Treaty should be signed and ratified . . . because the restoration of peace was paramount. . . . Having submitted to the President the question of making a public explanation of my interview with Mr. Bullitt, . . . I could not do so until I received the President's approval. That was never received. The telegram . . . was never answered. It was not even acknowledged.

Lansing resigned on February 12, 1920.

Bullitt was castigated in newspaper editorials, in the United States and abroad: he was an "unmitigated liar" and an "impertinent Yankee," it was written in London; he was one of "that too numerous class of worshipers at the shrine of radicalism . . . who have been summoned to fill posts in Washington," in the opinion of *The New York Times*. The Bullitt of twenty years hence—by 1939 he had dealt closely with the Soviets as the U.S. ambassador to Moscow— might not have differed by any marked degree with the *Times*: a young man of intelligence and perception, as he was unquestionably, had been blinded by his adulation for a man like Lenin and by his own romantic rhetoric. He would not apologize, however, for his congressional testimony: "I felt sure," he wrote in retrospect,

> that I was right about . . . the Treaty of Versailles, . . . and I felt it was my duty . . . to inform American public opinion about the realities of the situation. . . . The Senate, when it is considering a peace treaty, . . . like a court has the right to subpoena anyone. . . . After my return to America, I was summoned by the Committee on Foreign Relations. . . . To lie to the constitutional representatives of the American people in a matter of great national importance is not my tradition. It never occurred to me not to tell the truth.

On September 25 in Pueblo, Colorado, President Wilson suffered a collapse. All public appearances were canceled, and he was rushed back to Washington; on October 2 a stroke left him seriously paralyzed. On November 6 the Foreign Relations Committee reported a resolution of ratification, which contained fourteen reservations but did retain a provision for the league; Wilson opposed the resolution: it "does not provide for ratification," he asserted in a letter to his supporters in the Senate, "but, rather for the nullification of the treaty." On November 19 the resolution was defeated by an alliance of Wilson loyalists and "irreconcilables," and the treaty and the league were dead issues—Wilson's "dream of the friends of humanity through all the ages" had been shattered— although they remained officially unresolved until July 1921, when Congress terminated war with Germany and Austria-Hungary by joint resolution and then ratified separate treaties with Germany, Austria, and Hungary.

As for Bullitt, he had been asked during his appearance before the committee what he planned to do, and he said simply: "I expect to return to Maine and fish for trout. . . ." He had become fond of remote corners, so he purchased an old farmhouse in Ashfield, Massachusetts, which he and Ernesta redecorated. "I now spend a good deal of my time at my farm," he wrote the alumni office at Yale, "and when I am not engaged in doctoring puppies or riding cross-country or picking apples, I write." He added that he was living a nineteenth-century existence, lighting the house by candles and cooking with wood: "The civilization to which I belong no longer exists. It's gone forever."

IV

Expatriate

At Home Abroad

THE ELECTION in November 1920 of Warren G. Harding as president of the United States confirmed for Bullitt that whether or not the world was "going to hell," the country was certainly headed there. As a Republican senator from Ohio, Harding had been a member of the Foreign Relations Committee—he was one of six who were present on the day of Bullitt's hearing—and his attitude toward the League of Nations, Bullitt believed, was indicative of the American malaise. As an "America First" advocate Harding had stood against international entanglements, but as an ambitious politician who heeded his party's position— former President Taft and Charles Evans Hughes, who lost to Wilson in 1916 by only twenty-three electoral votes, both approved of joining the league—he could not afford to join the "irreconcilables." In the campaign he straddled the issue— it was a successful strategy, for he won with 60 percent of the popular vote over the Democrat, James M. Cox, who stoutly supported the league—but once in office he permitted foreign policy to be dictated by isolationists in the Senate, even though Hughes was his secretary of state.

There was much more for a young romantic to dislike about America in 1921: an erosion of leadership (of the four major candidates in 1920, Harding and Cox and their running mates, Calvin Coolidge, the governor of Massachusetts, and Franklin D. Roosevelt, the assistant secretary of the navy, the only one Bullitt could admire was Roosevelt); and outright corruption for another (another senator at the hearing on September 12, 1919, was Albert B. Fall of New Mexico, who as secretary of the interior under Harding leased oil reserves in Wyoming and California in what would become known as the Teapot Dome scandal). America in 1921 was a land of the evangelism of Billy Sunday and Aimee Semple McPherson; it was a land of materialism and "boobism," as Sinclair Lewis captured it in the character of George Babbitt; it was Al Capone and bathing beauty contests and bootleg gin, the Chicago Black Sox and the Ku Klux Klan. It was not a land in which Bullitt could thrive, nor would it be for a decade or more, and he would join the expatriates of his generation in an exodus to Europe. "I see Bill Bullitt, in retrospect," wrote George Kennan in 1972—early in his long and distinguished diplomatic career Kennan served as an aide to Bullitt in Moscow—

as a member of that remarkable group of young Americans, born just before the turn of the century (it included such people as Cole Porter, Ernest Hemingway, John Reed, and Jim Forrestal—many of them his friends) for whom the First World War was the great electrifying experience of life. They were a striking generation, full of talent and exuberance, determined . . . to make life come alive. The mark they made on American culture will be there when many other marks have faded. But in most of them there seems to have been a touch of the fate, if not the person, of the Great Gatsby. . . . They knew achievement more often than they knew fulfillment; and their ends, like those of Bullitt himself, tended to be frustrating, disappointing, and sometimes tragic.

Political dissident, aspiring artist, expatriate Bullitt was a composite of his contemporaries, some of whom went abroad for political reasons: one did not have to be as radical as Jack Reed to reject the conservative policies—isolationism, reduced taxes, retrenched government spending—of Harding and Coolidge; others, who were writers and painters, went to escape the stultifying cultural atmosphere of America. Many Americans settled in Europe, France in particular, because the living was inexpensive—the exchange rate in 1921 was eight francs to the dollar, and a young family could get along well on about $5,000 a year—and the American colony in Paris and on the Riviera was known for its gaiety. (They denied it, but for most expatriates Prohibition, which went into effect in January 1920, was a factor in their decision to live abroad.) In the summer of 1922 Cole Porter introduced another friend from his days at Yale, Gerald Murphy—Murphy and Bullitt, both of the class of 1912, knew each other but not well—to Antibes, a Riviera resort. Murphy renovated an old chateau and named it Villa America, where he entertained many famous friends, including Hemingway and Fitzgerald and Archibald MacLeish, the poet. Bullitt was in his element in France, or as Kennan wrote of the Bullitt who later came to Moscow, he was "handsome, urbane, full of charm and enthusiasm, a product of Philadelphia society and Yale but with considerable European residence and with a flamboyance of personality that is right out of F. Scott Fitzgerald—a man of the world. . . ."

———————

Nineteen twenty-one was a year of personal loss for Bullitt, as two events affected him acutely: his half brother died and his marriage broke up. Jack Bullitt was thirty-five when he succumbed to Bright's disease, a kidney inflammation, and Bill Bullitt's distress was accentuated by the implications of his own mortality of a brother dying young. He also had a deep-felt affinity for his older brother, understandably, as there was much to admire about Jack: he was manly and attractive—he had a way with women that Bullitt envied and longed to emulate; he was adventurous in his quest of pleasure; and he was bold and independent, unconcerned, for example, if there was a fuss about his keeping a mistress. Bullitt also respected Jack for his so-called delinquency, his lack of ambition, which in part was another expression of independence; and it was a trait that Bill Bullitt shared, however committed he was to achievement as he defined it. Jack Bullitt spent a year at the University of Pennsylvania Law School and then quit, just as Bill Bullitt did some five years later at Harvard Law; Jack Bullitt went to work as a bond salesman and stuck it out for only two years, which is probably a lot longer than Bill Bullitt would have lasted. Orville Bullitt, the younger brother, was the businessman, a prosperous stockbroker to whom success and stability were important: "That's what Orville wanted," their cousin Orville Horwitz explained, "whereas Bill wanted places all over—apartments in Paris and so on." So Bullitt made a major decision in 1921: he would seek a job for the sake of his career, in Philadelphia or Washington; he would write—he had his novel to finish, and a nonfiction work, an analysis of the origin and consequences of World War I, was beginning to take shape—and he would live where it suited him, probably not in the United States (although he would always be a Philadelphian, listing the Rittenhouse Club as his legal address). The other major decision of 1921, the one to terminate the marriage, was not made by Bullitt. It was Ernesta who walked out on him, though Bullitt was held responsible, probably for two reasons: one, he did not like the idea of Ernesta walking out on him; and, two, he was too much of a gentleman not to say to her, "Okay, it was my fault." Bullitt severed his relations with Ernesta, although the divorce was not final until 1923; the only time he called her again was to ask for his golf clubs.

Bullitt moved to New York and became managing editor of the Paramount-Famous-Lasky Corporation, later Paramount Pictures, which was essentially a script-editing job that paid little; he was financially secure, however, for his mother had left an estate of $130,000, which went to her sons save two small bequests to charity. Editing scripts for silent films was not work that greatly stimulated Bullitt—certainly it was a step down from being an associate editor of *The Philadelphia Public Ledger*—but there was a particular advantage to living in New York: it enabled him to join a sociopolitical circle, the Greenwich Village intelligentsia. Bullitt's radicalism was singularly personal, based on instinctual reactions to individuals—"Think, if I only had a father like that," he had exclaimed to the Swedish Communist Karl Kilbom, as they talked about Lenin on the trip to Russia—and one American revolutionary who captured his interest was Louise Bryant, the widow of John Reed. The psychological implications of Bullitt's love for Bryant are all too easy to presume: "Strangely, . . . he was emotionally caught up in a *posthumous* idealization of John Reed," wrote Virginia Gardner, Bryant's biographer. Gardner also quoted George Biddle, a friend and Philadelphia contemporary of Bullitt: "Bill seemed to make Reed *his* love mystique too." Then again, Bullitt's infatuation for Louise Bryant might simply have been inspired by her charm, for she was, as Gardner noted, "an exhilarating and vital woman"; and he might also have been impressed—although it was not easy for Bullitt to hold a woman in professional esteem—by her journalistic talent. Bryant, herself the author of *Six Red Months in Russia*, had come to

Bullitt to discuss a film adaptation of Reed's book, *Ten Days That Shook the World*, and while there is no record of what became of the documentary, there is written evidence of a budding personal relationship. "Dear Miss Bryant," Bullitt wrote on September 29, 1921, and he then invited her to an evening at the theater.

The only account of Bullitt's feelings toward his two wives is contained in his *roman à clef*, *It's Not Done*, which was dedicated to "Louise Bryant, my wife"; but it was extremely revealing and ought to be regarded as personal history, given the fictional license Bullitt allowed himself (he treated the two relationships as having been concurrent, while they actually occurred sequentially). "I don't want you to get the wrong idea about my relationship with Nina [Nina Michaud was Louise Bryant]," John Corsey, the autobiographical hero, says to a friend. "She makes me happy, terribly happy. . . . I can't imagine not having her. But I can't imagine her living a life in the society you and I were born in. She doesn't know any of the people you and I know and wouldn't get along with them if she did know them. She's not our kind." So he marries Mildred Ashley (Ernesta), but within a year and after the birth of a son—years later the son is killed serving with British forces in World War I—Mildred turns frigid: "How can I sleep when you're so restless?" she complains. "Do go into the next room, dear. I'm so tired. It's silly anyhow for us to sleep in the same bed. Only peasants sleep in the same bed." Nina, who had gone to Paris to have Corsey's child, returns to Chesterbridge (Philadelphia), a successful sculptress, after his marriage to Mildred has failed. "He believes in things," Nina says of their son, Raoul, who has become a Communist (the character Raoul was patterned after John Reed): "convictions, principles, believes violently, ready to die for them. . . ." "Then, Nina, you've got to do it," he says. "What?" "Marry me." "Oh, John, you sweet old thing," she laughed, "don't be ridiculous."

Louise Bryant and John Reed

ANNA LOUISA MOHAN was born in San Francisco on December 5, 1885, and the only similarity of her background and Bullitt's was that they both had fathers whose livelihood had been in coal; but while William C. Bullitt, Sr., became a coal company owner, Hugh J. Mohan, who was born in 1858 in Minersville, Pennsylvania, worked as a boy in the mines. Mohan became a newspaperman and labor union official, as well as a father, but he did not remain with his family for long: by the time his daughter was three his wife, Anna Louisa Flick, had moved to California by way of Reno, Nevada, where she got a divorce. Louise was six when her mother married Sheridan Daniel Bryant, a railroad brakeman and conductor, and while she was willing to take her step-father's name, she lived with what she called in a memoir "all the resentment of having lost my own father." Her father had died, she pretended, and her fantasy became reality: "Coming from one of those broken homes where one of the parents is dead and the other grief-stricken beyond all recovery, I found myself a very, very lonely little child sitting for hours in a corner, listening to my mother play the piano." Louise attended the University of Nevada at Reno—she was on the staff of the *Student Record* and edited a literary magazine—and in September 1906 she enrolled in the University of Oregon at Eugene, listing her birth date as December 5, 1887, which was not the last time she lied about her age. In August 1908, not having graduated with her class, she was in San Francisco looking for a job on a newspaper—unsuccessfully, for the country was in a financial crisis, and editors were not hiring—so she taught school in the state of Washington for two semesters and returned to Eugene in the spring of 1909, determined to get her degree. She got married instead, however, to a Portland dentist, Paul A. Trullinger, whose grandfather was a prosperous lumberman, and they lived on a houseboat docked at the Oregon Yacht Club on the Willamette River.

In 1912 Louise Bryant—she retained her name, as she would in later marriages—was active in a successful campaign for women's suffrage in Oregon, and she became acquainted with Charles E. S. Wood, a Portland lawyer and anarchist. Wood wrote satirical pieces for *The Masses*, which was edited in New York by Max Eastman, a well-known author and a radical intellectual. Bryant sold subscriptions to *The Masses*, and did so well that Eastman took notice of her. Through Wood she met Emma Goldman, also an advocate of anarchy, and she came under the influence of Sara Bard Field, Wood's wife, who made her aware of the activism of American workers, in particular the so-called wobblies of the IWW. "She was sort of a protégée of mine," Sara Field said in an interview with Virginia Gardner, and it was Field who introduced Louise Bryant to John Reed. "I think I must have been searching for John Reed all my life," Bryant wrote.

I came to Portland, and there I bought a *Metropolitan Magazine* one day. I was going somewhere on a street car. I began to read a story by Jack. I sat on the street car, passed my station, not caring whether I ever reached my destination or not, and suddenly realized that I must have fallen in love with somebody—whoever wrote that story. . . . Then Jack came to Portland. It was during that great period of unemployment we had, and they had . . . asked him to lecture for the benefit of the unemployed. . . . Jack was there only for a little while. He had a cable to go to Europe, . . . where he was later in the Serbian retreat. . . . He had said to me when he left, "I'll be back in a year." He came back in a year. It is a very difficult thing to wait a year if you are young and very much in love. But I did wait and he did come back. And then he told me he wanted me to come to New York, and I said I would. He met me at Grand Central Station and took me to his house. . . . He had gotten me a room in another place, . . . but I never went there. . . . I began then for the first time to lead a life that was not unhappy and lonely. I had come in January 1916. . . .

Louise Bryant and John Reed were married in November 1916 four months after her divorce from Dr. Trullinger. The following June, Bryant went to France in an unsuccessful attempt to become a war correspondent; it was also a trial separation, as their relationship had been strained by his attention to other women and by her lingering affair with Eugene O'Neill, the playwright. "Sweetheart," Reed wrote Bryant on June 28, 1917, "I do hope you're going to get all over your awful feelings . . .," and when Lincoln Steffens, just back from Petrograd, asked how he was, Reed said he had been "a fool and a cad." Bryant decided to come home, "because I kept getting heartbreaking letters from Jack . . .," arriving in New York on a hot day in August: "Jack was standing on the dock waiting for me in a shantung silk suit and Panama hat. He said, 'You just got home in time. In four days we're going to Russia.' " For the next seven crucial months of the Revolution they were in Petrograd, living in a two-room suite in the Astoria, which had been a hotel for Russian officers, but there was no heating, and when it turned cold in the fall they slept in their overcoats. "We called on the American Ambassador, who was not interested in the Revolution," Bryant wrote.

Ambassador Francis was without doubt one of the crudest and stupidest ambassadors that was ever sent abroad. He never knew anything about Russia, he never tried to find out, and when Jack told him that this was a real revolution, he wouldn't believe it. . . . We called on Kerensky, who called John Reed "comrade" and said, "If they (the Allies) force us to make a new advance we are lost. The soldiers are tired. They won't fight any more." . . . Kerensky was quite a broken man by this time.

Bryant's reporting was superb, and it would be acclaimed in the United States when her articles were syndicated to four hundred newspapers and when her book was published. "The Bolsheviks took Petrograd, and Jack and I were part of it all," she wrote. "They gave me the first military pass issued and Jack the second. We were free to go where we pleased. . . . Out of those days he found his material to write *Ten Days That Shook the World.*" On November 19, 1917, just twelve days after the Bolshevik victory, she wrote friends in Paris: "Russia is wonderful now, in spite of all the sadness of so many lives lost this week, for the first snow is beginning to fall. . . . I suppose you will hear many wild tales of this . . . revolution. I have great sympathy for it. Russia was slowly starving, and no definite steps were being taken by the provisional government. . . ."

On Christmas Eve they went to a party at the American embassy, but Reed had a row with Ambassador Francis, who had suggested they have a glass of champagne. "Drink champagne! Drink champagne!" he cried. "When American boys that very moment will be dying in the trenches!" He strode out, followed by Bryant, and that night Reed recorded a single thought in a notebook, as Bryant looked over his shoulder. "Oh, America," it read, "if I only could have given you an easy love." In the morning Bryant wrote: "Christmas day found us then with certain clear decisions before us and certain things clarified. With Jack it was marching toward that Red horizon from which there is no returning."

On March 15, 1920, Bryant wrote to her friends John and Marguerite Storrs—Storrs was an American sculptor living in Paris; Marguerite was his French wife—from 1 Patchin Place, her Manhattan address: "I am exiled here, and so are all of us who have spoken against the terrible food blockade which has caused the death of so many dear little children. . . . We are not allowed passports anywhere. About five thousand are in prison for protesting. . . . Jack is not because he is too powerful. He had three trials and was always acquitted. The juries love him. . . . He has been away six months. I am very lonely. He did not wait for a passport. You can guess where he went, to the place we would all like to go, where there is new life and real freedom. If the blockade goes down, then I will go also."

Bryant did go to Russia, on a Swedish steamer, posing as the wife of a Swedish businessman. She traveled a roundabout route, arriving in Petrograd in late August or early September, only to discover that Reed was not there, although there was a letter from him, postmarked Moscow, August 26. He was on his way with the Communist Party executive committee to Baku in the Caucasus to attend the Oriental Congress; and he asked her to go to Moscow and wait for him at the Dielovoy Dvor Hotel. On the morning of September 15, she later said in a letter to Max Eastman, Reed ran shouting into her hotel room, and their passionate reunion was followed by days of excitement: he took her to meet Lenin—"John Reed was as near to his heart as any Russian," she wrote—and they celebrated the victory of the Red Army at Archangel. Then, one week after his return from Baku, Reed fell ill, complaining of headaches and dizziness; it was first diagnosed as influenza, then typhus, and Reed was taken to the hospital. Bryant sat at his bedside for three weeks, holding his hand and hoping. "Five days before he died," she wrote, "his right side was paralyzed. After that he could not speak. And so we watched through days and nights and days. . . . Even when he died I did not believe it. . . ." It was October 17, 1920, five days before John Reed's thirty-third birthday.

Retreat of the Bulut Pasha

ON THE FIRST ANNIVERSARY of her husband's death Louise Bryant was the principal speaker at a memorial gathering in New York City: "The splendid stand of Russia," she said, "caught the imagination and great heart of John Reed and sent him to Russia to fulfill the mission of the most humane government the world has ever seen." In June 1922 her four-part series of articles on Lenin and other top Bolsheviks—it was titled "Mirrors of Moscow"—was sent to hundreds of newspaper subscribers to King Features, the Hearst syndication service; and in October she was the first American reporter to interview Benito Mussolini of Italy, and the story also was carried by Hearst, although under Mussolini's byline. She returned to the United States in February 1923, "clearly a top Hearst writer of her time," in the words of an editor of the newspaper chain, but at this point she decided that her life with William Bullitt was more important than her career. She went with Bullitt to the Bosporus, the strait connecting European Turkey with Asian Turkey, and they rented a villa called Yali-Kuprili, which had been the residence of four grand viziers of the Kuprili family in the days of the Turkish empire and was described in tourist guidebooks as "one of the loveliest of the Bosporus houses." Bullitt leased it from a wealthy Turk, Kuprili Hussein Pasha, agreeing in lieu of rent to educate Hussein Pasha's son, Refik. For Bryant there was the practical advantage of being just a few miles from Constantinople, where she worked for the International News Service, though it was to be her last job, as she was soon to retire as a journalist. For Bullitt, who was progressing well on his novel, Yali-Kuprili was a small corner of heaven. "You may picture me," he wrote his brother, Orville, "as the lord of the old estate, . . . with the Bosporus under my window and a golden room with a marble fountain in the center, filled with goldfish—and all the Judas trees and wisteria . . . and roses in full bloom." Yali-Kuprili was an ideal place to work, its spacious living room extending on timber pilings over the Bosporus, which offered a commanding view in three directions through huge windows; his life with Louise Bryant was relaxed, their relationship passionate; and his Turkish neighbors called him Bulut Pasha, or Cloud General.

Virginia Gardner became convinced while writing her biography, *Friend and Lover*, that Bryant deserved credit for Bullitt being able finally to finish *It's Not Done*: "He had been trying to write that book for some time," Gardner explained. "When he found her she turned him on, and he was able to write." Lincoln Steffens, while he was not so direct about it, also believed, as reported by his biographer, Justin Kaplan, that Bullitt found his life as an expatriate in

Europe—that is, his running off to Turkey and France with Bryant—to be compatible with his writing effort. "He settled down to enjoy the wines, parties and a new life," Kaplan wrote, quoting Steffens, who was living in Paris and was one of the few people who had known both Bullitt and Bryant before they met. Kaplan elaborated:

In conclusion of an affair that had some of the super-heated quality of his mission to Moscow he had divorced his wife and married Louise Bryant. . . . In 1924 he was about to become a father for the first time, and this is what he and Steffens often talked about over their drinks and dinners. They also talked about what Bullitt was working on, a thinly disguised autobiographical novel. . . . In it he settled a number of old scores with Philadelphia society of Rittenhouse Square and the Main Line; with American responses to the Russian Revolution; . . . with post-war America. . . .

Bill Bullitt and Louise Bryant were married on December 5, 1923, five days after Bryant's thirty-eighth birthday (although Bullitt believed her to be twenty-nine, which would be an issue when Bullitt filed for divorce six years later). That Bryant was pregnant undoubtedly influenced their decision to wed, though it was probably less a matter of honor on Bullitt's part than his compulsion to beget a legal offspring. "I told you . . .," wrote Gussie Nobbes, an old ladylove of Lincoln Steffens's, to Laura Suggett, Steffens's sister "that this Bullitt who fell in love with Louise Bryant was crazy for a child. . . ."

A Useless Life in Paris

"ANNE MOËN REED, the widow of John Reed and daughter of Hugh Moën and Anne Fiennes Moën of San Francisco," was how Bryant was identified in the announcement of her marriage to Bullitt, with an explanation that Louise Bryant was her pen name: it may be that she was falsifying her name as well as her age, though it is more likely that it was Bullitt's idea. For all the scores he had to settle with Philadelphia society, he was still a highbrow when it came to the importance of a good name, and he preferred an Anglo-Saxon ancestry to immigrant Irish: her grandmother had married James R. Say, he pointed out, who was descended from English nobility; and more descendants of Lord Say—at least this was the explanation given to Virginia Gardner by Bullitt's brother, Orville—used the surname Fiennes than Say. Why Bryant assented to this name finagling is a mystery: when she married Reed, she had listed her maiden name as Say (her mother, as Bryant would too, had adopted her stepfather's name); but she was proud of her own name, which she retained professionally through three marriages. Her compliance certainly was out of character for a woman who had been active in equal rights activities, such as the campaign for suffrage in Oregon, and this undoubtedly occurred to her when she introduced Bullitt to her mentor and idol, Sara Bard Field, who visited them in 1924. (Sara Field disapproved of Bullitt: "After Jack Reed," she said, "to go to something so superficial, very rich and very society.") Nevertheless, Bryant not only permitted Bullitt to alter her identity; she agreed that their child, a daughter born February 24, 1924, would be named Anne Moën Bullitt.

Bullitt, living on his modest inheritance, was not as wealthy as he appeared to be; however, the exchange rate—Americans were still advantaged, even though the value of the franc almost doubled in 1925—made it possible to live handsomely at little cost. He rented a house near the Parc des Princes in Paris, which had been occupied by Elinor Glyn, the English novelist; and it was "perfect for its type," Bullitt wrote his brother—"soft gray curtains, green walls, curtained glass doors." Guests came often and found Bullitt in high spirits—"fastidiously dressed and a pleasant host," recalled, Kay Ehrgott, the daughter of Sara Bard Field; and they remembered Bryant as stylishly attired—wearing "a beautiful red velvet tea gown, a Poiret original," according to one account—but moody: sometimes serene and sometimes somber. "I live a useless life," she said to Charmion von Wiegand, later a well-known painter. (Five days before she was married Bryant mailed a story on the exiled king of Greece—it was to be her last assignment as a daily journalist—which appeared in *The New York American* on December 23, 1923.) She was not accustomed to the pampering she got from Bullitt, who waited on her every need, supervised her diet, and even tried to restrict her reading, lest it affect the well-being of the baby. "Billy hovered over her like a mother hen," said Ella Winter, who married Lincoln Steffens. Winter also recalled Bullitt returning one evening to find Steffens reading aloud from *Ulysses* by James Joyce, a novel judged by many to be indecent for its explicit sexual references and banned in the United States. "He was furious. He bellowed at Steff: 'Think of our baby, our child! What will it turn out to be if it hears language like that?' "

Anne was born at home, and an old friend from Philadelphia, George Biddle—Biddle, an artist, who had like Bullitt become disenchanted and had a studio in Paris—was her godfather. ("The most distinguished, and by far the most rebellious of all creative Biddles . . .," wrote Nathaniel Burt in *The Perennial Philadelphians*, "George Biddle . . . has never failed to indicate his rejection of Philadelphia and Philadelphia values.") Biddle, who was as good a friend of Bryant as of Bullitt, was on hand for the birth, which occurred at the second house Bullitt rented in Paris, on the rue Desbordes-Valmore. Bryant was enjoying "the ecstasy of motherhood," in the words of a friend—she apparently did share Bullitt's rapture over having a child—and Bullitt, a proud and adoring father, was absolutely in love with his wife. Vincent Sheean, an old friend and professional colleague of Bryant's, had just returned from assignment for *The Chicago Tribune* in Spain, and he found Bullitt "romantically dazzled by Louise." George Biddle had begun to notice, however, that Bullitt was restless and suggested, since he had completed his novel—*It's Not Done* was being readied for publication—that he write another. "Why should I?" Bullitt answered. "It was typical," Biddle commented to Virginia Gardner. "He had shown he could do it." (A more sympathetic reading would have attributed Bullitt's response to the agony of finding a publisher, one of whom, Horace Liveright, had told him the book would not sell three hundred copies.) Bryant, too, was troubled—hers were essentially financial worries, which she related to John Storrs: "The truth is," she wrote in the summer of 1924, "I have already sent away all I earned and haven't been earning any since the baby came. I'll begin writing soon, I hope. Then I'll be plush again. . . . I never ask Bill to go in on my personal ventures. . . ." She was also feeling a bit confined by the responsibility of raising a family, which included Refik, the son of Kuprili Hussein Pasha, in addition to Anne. "Our little Turk loves us so much," she wrote Storrs, "I don't believe we will send him away. . . . I'm weaning the baby in September. Then you can expect to see me . . . at any moment. I will feel wonderfully free when I can get out of the three-hour limit."

A Philadelphia Divorce

IN 1925 Bullitt went to see Sigmund Freud, and while he would deny that he became a patient of Freud's—he insisted that his frequent trips to Vienna were for the purpose of collaborating on a book, a psychological study of Woodrow Wilson, which at least by 1930 was the truth—friends in Paris contradicted him. George Biddle had no doubt about it when he talked with Virginia Gardner in 1970: "When Bill began his psychoanalysis with Freud, both Bill and Louise were trying to be very much in love." Biddle recalled an evening at their home when Bullitt explained his decision: there had been an incident on horseback—Bullitt's foot had slipped from the stirrup, almost causing an accident. "Can you even imagine my ever falling off a horse?" demanded Bullitt, who was an excellent rider. When Biddle did not seem to get the point, Bullitt explained further: "Then it dawned on me that I had wanted to fall off my horse. Frightening. Fortunately I've read a great deal about psychoanalysis. . . . And I knew, George, that there was only one man for me to see: Freud. Why not go to Vienna?" Word got around some years later that it had been Bryant who had been treated by Freud, and Vincent Sheean answered it directly: ". . . it was Bill, not Louise. . . . He had a very long analysis, with occasional brief returns to Paris; Louise went to Vienna a couple of times to talk to Dr. Freud as part of the analysis—that is, to help. . . . Freud never treated Louise at all, separately or with Bill." (Bullitt family records indicate that it was not Bullitt but Louise Bryant who was intermittently a patient of Freud while Bullitt and his daughter remained in France and Bryant was treated by Freud in Vienna.)

"Good Lord, how shocking our country is, John!" said Bryant in a letter to John Storrs in late May 1925. "New York . . . was enough to put one in an early grave. . . . We saw all the plays—awful! I could have wept at the new O'Neill play—so cheap. . . ." She and Bullitt and the baby, Anne, were spending five months in the United States, and she was writing to Storrs from the farm in Ashfield, Massachusetts, which she enjoyed with reservations, though in general her mood was more serene than somber. "Naturally it's a late spring this year—as cold as Christmas. . . . But it *is* beautiful! Bill's whole place here is as beautiful as New England ever gets, which is saying as much as we can say." (While horseback riding one day, Bryant noticed a farm for sale and told the MacLeishes, Archibald and Ada, who bought it and made it their lifelong family home.) They had stopped in Philadelphia—it was to be her only visit there with Bullitt—and she was favorably impressed. "Strangely enough we had a good time . . . ," Bryant wrote Storrs. "We went to see Orville, . . . then Francis Biddle, and a lot of people gave dinners—very gay. Francis is a lovely host—all that George isn't." (Francis B. Biddle, one year younger than his brother, was a lawyer—Harvard Law, 1911—who practiced in Philadelphia until he was called to Washington to serve as solicitor general and then attorney general of the United States.)

Not long after the Bullitts returned to Paris, in October 1925, *It's Not Done* was published by Harcourt Brace: the novel was a vast commercial success—

150,000 copies sold over twenty-four printings. As Bullitt no doubt had anticipated, it caused a furor in Philadelphia. "The book aroused considerable controversy," wrote his brother, Orville, in his understated way—Orville tried but
failed to buy up all copies on sale in his beloved city—"and Bill was criticized
by the social elements. . . . He did not accept the standards and conventions of
the environment in which he had been raised, and he was . . . branded a noncon-
formist." The reviews ranged from mixed to scathing: "Unusual talent is necessary to write a book that is so good at the same time it is so bad," read one in *The
Saturday Review of Literature.* A comment that appeared in the *International
Book Review* must have hurt Bullitt the most, however, for it was an unfavorable
judgment of the character of the protagonist, which Bullitt could not have helped
but take personally. John Corsey "is not in truth a decent human being," said the
reviewer, "much less the gentleman he is supposed to represent."

The relationship between Bullitt and Bryant was deteriorating at this time.
"She found him awfully hard to take," said Kitty Cannell, a close friend. "She
was a feminist and spoke up when she disagreed with him. . . . And at times he
was very edgy, and she couldn't always be tactful." Cannell, who had known
Bryant at the time she married John Reed—she had been trained as a dancer in
Paris and became a dance critic for *The Christian Science Monitor*—was
Bryant's confidante, she told Virginia Gardner. "She clung to me. . . . Almost
every night I had dinner at the Bullitt home, and later she and I would go dancing
in Montmartre with whatever attractive American was around. Most often it was
Jimmy Sheean." Vincent Sheean—his full name was James Vincent Sheean, and
friends called him Jimmy—reported an alarming incident on one occasion when
Bryant went to Vienna to see Bullitt, who for some reason "had barricaded the
door of his room at the Imperial Hotel with all its furniture so that she could not
get in." Sheean recalled in a letter to Virginia Gardner that Bryant had tended to
belittle psychoanalysis—which might have explained Bullitt's tantrum in
Vienna—and this he ascribed to the influence of Marxist dogmatists: she had
been indoctrinated with the idea that "there is no neurosis in the Soviet Union."
She had simply laughed when she heard from Bullitt that Freud had told him that
her problem with alcohol—it was a problem Bryant was only beginning to
acknowledge—was related to his first wife's being named Drinker.

It was by this time—late 1925, early 1926—that Bullitt had decided to be
unfaithful to Bryant: he had slipped off to the Riviera, where he had an affair
with Eleanor Medill Patterson. "I fell in love, . . . old fool that I am," wrote
"Cissy" Patterson of the Chicago newspaper publishing family, a divorcée, to a

friend, according to her biographer, Ralph G. Martin. "Ten years younger than she, William Bullitt was also divorced . . .," wrote Martin. "A dark-haired man with a lordly air that made him seem older than his years, Bullitt had been a member of Phi Beta Kappa at Yale; he had graduated from Harvard Law School and had worked as a war correspondent in Germany and Austria." (It is evident that Bullitt had not been entirely candid with Cissy Patterson about his marital status and his academic and professional background.)

Bullitt fascinated Cissy with his unbounded enthusiasm. He described American success as "futility on the upgrade," but Cissy sensed how much he wanted it. . . . Cissy listened to his story of being sent by President Wilson on a secret mission to sound out Lenin after the war. He said he had met a brilliant man in Vienna named Sigmund Freud, and they planned to write a book together about Wilson. . . . It was a memorable romantic interlude, but Cissy wrote . . . that she "left just in the nick of time." She was terribly vulnerable, and she did not want to be hurt.

The Bullitts arrived in New York again on September 11, 1926, aboard the French liner *Paris*, and Bryant was interviewed by *The New York American*, the Hearst paper for which she had been a regular contributor from overseas. Dictatorships dominated Europe, she declared: in Spain, Italy, Turkey, even Russia, where "Zinoviev and his crowd" had been replaced by "the Stalin group"—a choice of greater or lesser evils, she believed—as successors to the Lenin government. There is no way to determine the weight of Bullitt's opinions on Bryant's, but presumably they shared their thoughts, and allowing for a normal margin of discord there was ample room for agreement. He undoubtedly concurred in her view that the League of Nations had accomplished little—the league had done nothing, she reminded her interviewer from *The American*, to prevent the annexation of the Greek island of Corfu by Italy in 1923: it had "continued inactive while the Italian Navy put in force against Greece the imperialistic proclamations of Dictator Mussolini." She stated, moreover—and this had long been a point emphasized by Bullitt—that the League of Nations was dominated by Great Britain for the advancement of her interests.

Bullitt rented an apartment on East Eighty-second Street in Manhattan, and they spent a year there, going to parties and seeing old friends, which was just the sort of activity—lots of frivolity, nothing with a potential for accomplishment—that would be detrimental to their marriage. The parties were risky, because despite Prohibition the liquor flowed freely, giving rise to accounts—whether accurate or exaggerated, as witnesses had differing recollections—of Bryant's alcoholism; get-togethers with old friends, Bryant's by and large, were destructive, for they were an opportunity to revive a past highlighted by her romances and her marriage to John Reed. Andrew Dasburg, a painter then living in Mexico—Dasburg had been a lover of Louise Bryant's before her marriage to Reed—also was visiting New York, and he came for dinner one evening, just the three of them. "Louise seemed perfectly at ease," he said. "But there was something artificial about the whole thing. . . . Bullitt turned on the charm—but with a knowing smile, which didn't help. I felt he wanted me to know that he knew." Then they went for a weekend to Westchester County, where Bryant and Reed had lived—they were the guests of George Biddle, who had married a wealthy woman from Texas and settled in Croton-on-Hudson, as Bryant had suggested—and according to Floyd Dell, a former managing editor of *The Masses*, "Louise talked nonstop about Jack Reed and almost ignored Bill."

In December 1927 Ernest Hemingway, in a letter to F. Scott Fitzgerald that listed American expatriates currently in Europe, referred in an unkind way to Bullitt: "Also Bill Bullitt or Bull Billet," he wrote, "a big Jew from Yale and fellow novel writer." The Bullitts had returned to Paris in the fall—they were living in still another rented home, at 44 avenue Victor Hugo—and Louise Bryant was forced to confront her illness, which was painful and disfiguring. Bullitt and her friends both had noticed that she was drinking excessively, but that did not seem unusual at first, since most of the expatriates were heavy imbibers. "I have a feeling we were all rather desperate, and that's why we were drinking ourselves to death," Kitty Cannell said bluntly. But Bryant was attracting more and more attention as a problem drinker, though few of her friends were aware of her affliction, as she went from clinic to clinic seeking relief—it is suspected she was also taking painkilling drugs—and at times the alcohol only made her feel worse. "I have been quite ill again," she wrote Claude McKay in March 1928—McKay was a black American poet and novelist, whose book *Home to Harlem* was dedicated to Bryant—"and I went to London to see some specialists. They looked me over solemnly and then told me I had something called Dercum's disease and that it was incurable! So the trip was not much of a success." Named for a Philadelphia physician, Francis X. Dercum, who first described it, it was a very rare ailment, tending to strike women of menopausal age—Louise Bryant was forty-three at the time of the diagnosis—its symptoms being tumors, swelling of parts of the body, and emotional distress. On hearing the verdict Bullitt telephoned his brother, Orville, and asked him to consult with Dr. Dercum himself, and Dercum was in agreement with the London doctors: the disease was incurable. Bryant wrote McKay again in the summer from Bullitt's farm in Massachusetts, saying they were sailing for France on September 17 and would spend the winter at 44 avenue Victor Hugo, but she advised him to write her at

Dengler's Sanitarium in Baden-Baden in the Black Forest of Germany. "It's a lovely place," she said. "I mean to get well this time. I had a dreadful summer, full of collapses."

Bullitt by all accounts sympathized with his wife's suffering, but his patience was tried by her drinking, and he filed for divorce in December 1929 in Philadelphia. He was in good hands: his lawyer was Thomas Raeburn White, one of the best and a prominent Republican political leader; and the judge—it was customary in uncontested suits in Philadelphia for an arbiter called a "master" to preside at a preliminary hearing—was Francis B. Biddle, whom Bryant had thought "a lovely host" when she and Bullitt visited Philadelphia in the spring of 1925. Bullitt was the only witness except for a couple of servants he had brought with him from France—Bryant's exact whereabouts was a mystery, although a passport application indicated she sailed from New York on the *Paris* on November 29—and he testified that Bryant "invariably began drinking before breakfast, . . . hid liquor to drink at all hours of the day," and on several occasions had been drunk and disorderly in public. He charged in addition that she had engaged in a lesbian affair with the daughter of an English writer, and had run off with the woman and sent him a defiant letter, which he offered as evidence. "Dear Duck," she had written. "I want to say to you only one thing—I have lived too long with unconventional people to be suddenly made into a Bourgeoise." Bullitt added that following their return to Paris in the fall of 1927, "I had to manage the household entirely, . . . arranging the meals, etc." The divorce was granted on March 24, 1930, based on the recommendation of Francis Biddle, and Bullitt was awarded custody of six-year-old Anne. For Louise Bryant what remained of her life was steeped in sadness: "Emotionally she had gone to pieces because of this disease . . .," George Biddle told Virginia Gardner. "She became irresponsible, would get very angry. It was this disease that destroyed her." "I have not written you because I have been so ill . . .," Bryant wrote Marguerite and John Storrs in July 1930. "Bill is sending me Jack's belongings but does not say on what boat or when. . . . I never have news of Anne. It is difficult for me to work."

Just as Louise Bryant had as a child insisted that her father had died, not deserted her, Anne Bullitt refused to believe that her parents were not deeply in love throughout their lives. "Once I was playing the Eighth Symphony of Schubert," she remembered, "the 'Unfinished' Symphony, and I noticed my father was crying. I asked him what was the matter, and he said the piece reminded him of my mother, as it had been one of her favorites." Nevertheless, while Bullitt may have provided for Bryant's needs—Francis Biddle later commented that Bullitt had agreed to award her a "substantial sum"—he chose to erase any record of their marriage. "After his divorce from his first wife in 1923," read an entry in a thirty-year history of the Yale class of 1913, "Bill remarried, but gives no details."

Collaboration with Freud

THE EXTENT of Bullitt's material support for a dying Louise Bryant has remained, as has much about Bullitt's financial affairs, a subject of conjecture, made all the more confusing by a myth about his personal wealth. The fiction persisted until his death in February 1967: "he had a private fortune of about $9 million derived from his family," it was reported in his obituary in *The New York Times*, to explain how he had been able to live lavishly as ambassador to France, whereas it was revealed in probate court that his estate amounted to only $223,000, including the farm in Massachusetts. There even were rumors in Washington in 1942, when Bullitt was out of a job, that he was flat broke, although in 1930—and during most of his life—he was not near indigence: he had probably spent most of his inheritance during a decade of unemployment, but the royalty revenues from *It's Not Done* must have been considerable. How he weathered the stock market crisis of 1929 is another unknown, although there is evidence that he escaped unscathed, for he left his investment decisions to his brother, Orville, who was "very lucky or very smart" in the words of his son John C. Bullitt. As the younger Bullitt told it—John C. Bullitt returned to the traditional family profession, becoming a successful New York lawyer—Orville in the summer of 1929 "decided to sell all his stocks and go to Europe and sit on his money." He bought back into the market in 1932, so he was one of very few American stockholders to turn a profit on the Wall Street disaster, and it can be presumed that Bill Bullitt benefited from Orville's investment acumen. It was Orville, in fact, who summed up his brother's financial situation: "Bill was never rich . . .," he wrote in a foreword to *For the President, Personal and Confidential*, a collection of Bullitt's correspondence published in 1972,

but he was always comfortably off, which enabled him to travel and make many strong and valuable friendships all over the world. He took no interest in the acquisition of money and once wrote to me, "I don't know anything about investments, and I have no idea what you are holding now in the way of stocks or bonds or what is in my account."

Bullitt once made a terse observation to his cousin Orville Horwitz about his many valuable friendships. "He said," Horwitz recalled, "that if you deal with bright people, you'll know all the important people in the world. And Bill did know all the important people in the world—he knew everybody who was anybody. . . ." The point was emphasized in his obituary in *The New York Times*: "Few American diplomats of Mr. Bullitt's era had such a wide acquaintance. He knew every European statesman from Georges Clemenceau of France and Lenin of Russia to Winston Churchill of Britain. . . ." The list was much longer: it included Ramsay MacDonald, a founder of the Labor Party in Great Britain and the prime minister in 1931; Léon Blum, the French Socialist, who became premier in 1936; Thomas Masaryk, the president of Czechoslovakia until 1935; and Prince Maximilian of Baden, a former chancellor of Germany, whose widow allowed Bullitt to review private papers following the death of Prince Max in 1929. And there was Sigmund Freud: Bullitt had an intimate association with the eminent Austrian psychiatrist for several years, although questions were raised— from the one about the original nature of their relationship to a few surrounding their working agreement in the writing of *Thomas Woodrow Wilson—A Psychological Study*.

Bullitt's first encounter with Freud, in 1925, was unusual enough to defy belief—it was described by George Biddle, who could only have heard it from Bullitt himself—but even given a touch of exaggeration, which is fair to assume, it illustrated Bullitt's bold approach. He simply appeared at the door of Freud's home in Vienna, was told the doctor was ill, so he announced who he was and offered a card. Freud heard from upstairs, came down hurriedly, and said he had known of Bullitt and was very interested in his work; he was taking no new patients at the time, but he would be pleased to work with Bullitt, provided he would make a commitment to a long-standing association. Bullitt, while never willing to admit he was a patient, agreed to that association—they became close friends, so close that Bullitt was one of just three people permitted to call Freud by his surname and not by title (the others were H. G. Wells, the English novelist, and Yvette Guilbert, a French entertainer)—and it resulted in their decision to work together on the Wilson study. Bullitt even moved to Vienna after his divorce was final in 1930: he was a single parent, bringing up Anne with the help of a governess. (There would one day be heated controversy over the authorship of the book, which was not published until 1966, with disciples of Freud, including his daughter, Anna, insisting he had merely cooperated with Bullitt and advised him, and had written only an introduction. Ernest Jones, who was an assistant of Freud's and became his biographer—Jones, by his own account, was at the time the manuscript was completed "the only person privileged to read it"—claimed, however, that Freud was not a passive participant in the project. "It is a full study of Wilson's life," Jones wrote, "and contains some astonishing revelations. Although a joint work, it is not hard to distinguish the analytical contributions of the one author from the political contributions of the other.")

Not long after his first meeting with Freud, Bullitt had begun writing again, notwithstanding his remark to George Biddle about not intending to try another novel; but two attempts at fiction, a novel and a play, did not succeed. He decided then to return to factual analysis, not as a journalist, but as a historian, planning an epic study of war and peace, 1914 to 1919, for which he was uniquely qualified: he had witnessed the period from a number of advantageous positions; he would be able to interview political and military leaders of the United States and Europe; he had access to archives of the Allied governments as well as the papers of Prince Max of Baden, who was the chancellor at the time of the German surrender and whose papers included the minutes of German cabinet meetings from the end of September 1918 to the armistice. The working title of the history was *World Statesmanship*, as Bullitt informed Colonel House, who had remained his friend and mentor and who sent words of encouragement on July 31, 1930. "It is interesting to know that your plans are growing more definite. . . . I feel that you are going to write a book that will not only be a credit to yourself . . . but will be of benefit to the world." House added a piece of advice, perhaps aware that Bullitt would heed it lightly. "Let me say a word of caution," he wrote, "and that is to write with moderation and without bias, so that your influence may carry with those who disagree as well as those who agree with you."

In their frequent meetings Bullitt had outlined to Freud his project, and Freud had responded with enthusiasm, saying he was especially interested in the chapter on Woodrow Wilson and would be happy to collaborate on it. Bullitt was so taken with the idea of a coauthorship with the famous psychoanalyst that a Bullitt-Freud study of Wilson became *the* project, as Bullitt explained to House in August 1930; and he attempted in the letter to allay House's concern that the book's authority would be compromised by the authors' bias. "At least I shall try," he wrote, "to make moderation and understatement the chief features of anything I may write. After all, . . . nothing but understatement carries conviction." And as for Freud, Bullitt assured House, he "is as detached and scientific in his view of the whole human life as any man can be . . . ," adding, "I hope that I have acquired some of the same balance."

Bullitt was writing what House wanted to hear, but in truth he held Wilson in contempt, as did Freud, who stated in the introduction "that the figure of the American President, as it rose from the horizon of Europeans, was from the beginning unsympathetic to me. . . ." Nevertheless, House had made his point— he had made it for Bullitt's sake, not that of the late president, whom he had also opposed in the end—and from there on Bullitt sent him progress reports. "To-morrow F and I go to work," he wrote on October 26, 1930, from Vienna. He had been to Schloss Salem in Baden—Baden had become an independent re-public in 1918—to peruse the papers of Prince Max, but he had cut short his stay "because of the precarious condition of F's health," a reference to Freud's ill-ness, cancer of the mouth. Bullitt was visiting Philadelphia when he wrote on August 17, 1931: "F, after three operations, is in excellent health, and the first draft of the book is nearly completed. I shall have to go to Vienna again in November and hope to have a finished manuscript in May. It is an immense task but a fascinating one."

It was also a fascinating, if somewhat incongruous, collaboration: the seventy-five-year-old Freud, who had introduced psychoanalysis as a treatment of neurosis and whose influence had been felt by scientists, educators, and artists throughout the world; and the forty-year-old Bullitt, whose career as an Amer-ican diplomat was still before him and who was a relative unknown. "The book is at last finished," Bullitt wrote House on April 29, 1932, again from Vienna, "that is to say that the last chapter has been written, and it could be published if both Freud and I were to die tonight. Of course, it needs to be expanded, and every reference needs to be rechecked, and I should then like to put it in a vault and forget it for six months, so that I could really judge it and cut it with the detachment that is impossible now. But at least there is now a complete manu-script, and I am beginning to think about politics again."

The essential conclusion of the psychological analysis of Thomas Woodrow Wilson (Wilson dropped the Thomas in early life and would have been annoyed by the repeated references to "Tommy Wilson") was that the late president obsessively adored his father, Joseph Ruggles Wilson, a Presbyterian minister. "He never grew beyond this father identification," Bullitt and Freud wrote.

His qualities and defects remained the qualities and defects of his father. He could not imagine any more perfect man than his father. His father had found his supreme expres-sion in sermons from a pulpit. Tommy Wilson found his supreme expression in sermons from a pulpit which was the White House. His father was not in the habit of devising practical methods to compel the translation of the principles he expounded from the pulpit into reality. Wilson did not devise practical methods to compel the translation of his Fourteen Points into reality. His father sang, so did Tommy. His father read in the evenings to his family, so did Tommy. What his father had done was worth doing. What his father had not done was not worth doing.

Wilson's high regard for his father had been recognized by others: "His father was the greatest figure of his youth—perhaps the greatest of his whole life," wrote Ray Stannard Baker in his biography. Bullitt and Freud, however, explained it in terms of libido. (While use of the parallels between Wilson and his father to emphasize character flaws and failure was probably Bullitt's work, the sexual analysis was quite likely Freud's contribution, or at least a derivation of it.) "If the masculinity of the boy had been more powerful than his femininity," they observed, "he would have found the weight of that father intolerable; he would have hated his father. . . . But, in fact, Tommy Wilson's femininity was far stronger than his masculinity, at least in that period of his life." Bullitt and Freud determined there had been two important effects on Wilson's later relationships with men: his repressed hostility toward his father "broke out against father substitutes, driving him to violent and unreasonable hatreds. . . ." and he always needed an "affectionate relationship with a younger and physically smaller man"—John Grier Hibben, who succeeded Wilson as the president of Princeton, and Edward M. House were cited as examples—a relationship in which "Wilson clearly played the part of his own father, and his friend represented himself as a boy. . . ."

Coming Back to the Fold

MARIAN NEWHALL HORWITZ was a woman whose judgment Bullitt trusted implicitly; he had admired her since he was eight, in 1899, when she married his mother's cousin George Q. Horwitz (it was their son, Orville Horwitz, who became Bullitt's close friend and physician). The daughter of Daniel S. Newhall, a vice president of the Pennsylvania Railroad, she was intelligent and ambitious and sufficiently independent in 1916, the year her husband died, that she went to Florida and succeeded on her own. George Horwitz had been a successful Philadelphia lawyer (he was the attorney for the estate of William C. Bullitt, Sr.) who decided to become an investor in Florida real estate, acquiring thousands of acres along Lake Okeechobee, in the south central part of the state. Marian Horwitz went there in 1917 to manage the property—vegetable farming was the main activity—and she made a lasting impression: she introduced sugar cane, which became the major crop; she built a railroad along the fifteen-mile stretch between Clewiston and Moore Haven; she became the president of a bank; and she was elected mayor of Moore Haven.

When Bullitt was in Philadelphia in the summer of 1931, Marian Horwitz was there—she had since married John J. O'Brien, who had been George Horwitz's partner in the Florida land venture (O'Brien had once been Bullitt's boss, as city editor of *The Philadelphia Public Ledger*)—and he showed her the draft manuscript of the book he was writing with Freud. He also told her he intended to return to the United States the following year in the hope of obtaining a government appointment, for it appeared likely that a Democrat—the governor of New York, Franklin D. Roosevelt, had emerged as the favorite—would be elected president. Marian Horwitz was a Republican but first of all an astute politician, and she advised Bullitt that if he published a book critical of Wilson—the former president had been dead for only seven years—he could wave his political aspirations good-bye. Bullitt listened and decided to delay publication of the book indefinitely.

On January 9, 1932, Bullitt wrote Colonel House from Vienna about his interest in participating in the presidential campaign of Franklin Roosevelt: "I should, of course, be glad to have you show Roosevelt my letter, and I hope you will . . . let him know that I might not be altogether useless." He was referring to a letter to House the month before, also from Vienna, in which he reported what he had observed on a recent tour of Europe. "Never, even in the worst days of the war, has there been such a general pessimism on the continent," he had written.

In Paris I saw Aubert [Louis F. Aubert, the French premier] and various other politicians and was shocked by the hopelessness of everyone. They all felt sure that Hitler would replace Brüning [Heinrich Brüning, the German chancellor] before spring, and that it would be useless to go further along the road of . . . cooperation . . . since Hitler would upset any arrangements made. They had no other idea than to sit tight and await the deluge. Aubert, for example, said: "We shall do exactly what England and America did when they had the power to do something: That is to say, nothing!"

In London Bullitt had learned that his friend Ramsay MacDonald, who had become prime minister in a government dominated by Conservatives,

is fully aware of the difficulties he is going to have in controlling the wild horses he has to drive. . . . Neville Chamberlain is the motor in the government machine. . . . Churchill, supported by . . . most of the Tory reactionaries, wants to make a deal with Japan for the mutual exploitation of China and India. . . . I was so disturbed by various things I discovered . . . I wrote MacDonald more frankly than I should have dared to if I had not known him so intimately in the old days, and to my surprise and pleasure got a letter back at once thanking me for my "very wise advice" and saying that he intended to follow it. . . .

"I get many letters from abroad," House wrote Bullitt on December 28, 1931, "but I have not had a letter in a year that is comparable to yours in the light it sheds on conditions in Europe. I plan to let the governor read it, . . . so he may have the benefit of the information you give." Roosevelt had been assistant secretary of the navy when Bullitt was with the State Department in 1918, as he noted in his letter to House on January 9: "My acquaintance with him in Washington was so slight that I shall have to come into contact with him *de novo*, and I should of course rather come to him through you than anyone else in the world." Bullitt would have some negative impressions to overcome as he sought a post in a Roosevelt administration: William Phillips, an assistant secretary of state when Wilson was president and an intimate friend of Roosevelt's, resented Bullitt's disloyalty to Wilson in 1919; and Roosevelt himself had thought him affected, as he indicated in a letter in September 1919 to Herbert Bayard Swope of *The New York World*, who had just returned from Paris: "I really want to look you over to see for myself whether you are still the same good old Swope or have taken on the manners and customs of a Billy Bullitt."

Unaware of these mutterings, Bullitt was sounding confident in his letters to House. "How are the prospects for the election?" he asked on February 20, 1932. "There is going to be a chance to do something very great in international affairs during the next five years, and it will be a misfortune for more persons than ourselves if we cannot manage to get brother Hoover out of the White House." On April 29, in the letter to announce that his book was finished, he showed he was ready to be Roosevelt's unofficial emissary to the capitals of Europe: "Do you think it might be worthwhile for me to go to Berlin, Moscow, Warsaw, Prague, Budapest, Rome, Paris, and London before returning to the U.S. for the campaign, or will foreign policy play so slight a part . . . that intimate knowledge of the situation in Europe would be superfluous? I should like to be useful. Tell me how to be."

"Your idea . . . is excellent," House replied tactfully on May 11—he was quite possibly fearful that Bullitt would overstep his authority and embarrass Roosevelt—"but I believe it would be better to do it after November. If we do not win, there will be no need to go. However, things continue to go well with us politically, and when you get back we'll discuss the campaign and plan your activities. . . ."

Bullitt, unrestrained as always, went anyway on a tour of capitals, although he scaled down his itinerary: "Masaryk [Thomas Masaryk, the president of Czechoslovakia] has invited me to visit him at the chateau near Prague," he wrote House on May 27, "and I fly there tomorrow morning, and then . . . to Berlin and Moscow. . . . I am curious to know what Masaryk thinks about the present mess. In the days of the war he always seemed to be a very wise fellow, and I hope that he may now have some constructive idea in his head. No one else has." In Moscow he had a dinner engagement with Litvinov—Maxim Litvinov had replaced Georgi Chicherin as foreign commissar—but he had been called away suddenly, or so Bullitt was told. It was Bullitt's first visit to Russia since 1919, and it was a disappointment: he was ignored by Joseph Stalin and other Soviet officials—Stalin had succeeded to Lenin's leadership in 1927, having expelled Trotsky and Zinoviev from the Communist Party—and he was able to meet only with Karl Radek, a Trotskyite, who had become a propagandist under Stalin, to whom Bullitt asserted, gratuitously, that the Soviet Union was "marching manfully forward in the midst of world chaos and political disorganization."

It is safe to say that Bullitt misrepresented himself on his travels in the spring of 1932—he would claim outright years later that he had gone to Russia at Roosevelt's request—and while in Moscow he went so far as to speak for the next president on the subject of U.S.-Soviet relations. It was not idle conversation, for his listener—perhaps one of many—was Eugene Lyons, a correspondent for the United Press, who quoted Bullitt in his book, *Assignment in Utopia.* "The future American ambassador to the U.S.S.R., William C. Bullitt, came to Moscow . . . on an unofficial errand. . . . 'Franklin Roosevelt will be the next President,' he assured me at our first meeting, 'and American recognition of the Soviet government will be one of the first acts of his administration.' " Bullitt even implied that he would be the first ambassador, to which Lyons replied: "Bill, if you do come here as Roosevelt's ambassador, I guarantee that within six months you'll be as disgusted with this regime as I am." Lyons, a disillusioned American Marxist, was able to appraise Bullitt's attitude wisely:

His conception of the new Russia was deeply colored by the romanticism of the earliest period when he made his memorable trip to Moscow for President Wilson. . . . He was thoroughly informed, of course, about the *physical* changes that had taken place in the intervening thirteen years, but wholly innocent of the far greater changes in the mood of the Revolution—the hardening of the emotional arteries, its callousness and unromantic "realism." He was still seeing Russia through the ardors of a John Reed.

Bullitt went during his visit to place a floral wreath on Reed's grave, accompanied by Lyons, who noted that when he returned to the car, tears were streaming down his face.

———————

Bullitt returned to the United States in July 1932: Roosevelt had been nominated, promising a program of economic nationalism and social reconstruction, a "new deal for the American people"; and he was expected to defeat Herbert Hoover, the Republican incumbent, who was perceived as having done nothing to end the Depression. "If I can be of the slightest use, please command me," Bullitt wired House from his farm in Ashfield, Massachusetts. "I am entirely at the disposal of Roosevelt and yourself for any service you may wish in the campaign." He also sent a message to George Biddle, in which he was confident if a bit misleading, as he had been with Eugene Lyons. "Bill Bullitt writes from the Berkshires," Biddle noted. "He's been seeing something of Franklin this summer and thinks he's a swell guy. Bullitt has thrown his hat in the ring. I'm glad he's back in politics. Politics or diplomacy. All the same game. But he'll hardly want to publish just now . . . that life of Wilson. Rather too Freudian an angle for a party diplomat."

Bullitt immediately became impatient with House's inability to put him in touch with Roosevelt's campaign staff, so he contacted Louis B. Wehle, an influential New York lawyer and an old friend of Roosevelt's from their days together at Harvard. Wehle at first suggested that Bullitt wait for Colonel House to act on his behalf, as it would imply that he was still in the good graces of the Wilson wing of the Democratic Party; but Bullitt persisted, and Wehle agreed to meet with him. He meanwhile notified Roosevelt that Bullitt had returned from Europe—Wehle knew of his European connections and was impressed by them—and he supposed that Bullitt would be useful as a foreign affairs adviser. In their meeting Bullitt adapted his attitudes toward the Soviet Union to those generally accepted in America, as Wehle recalled in his book, *Hidden Threads of History*.

> I proposed . . . that he and I formulate the principles for an agreement of recognition between the U.S. and the U.S.S.R. In the course of doing so we ironed out such diffi-culties as there were between us. Whatever Bullitt's original thoughts may have been about the possibilities of the Soviet system, when it and Bullitt were both young, he had clearly become thoroughly disillusioned by the government of the U.S.S.R. under Stalin.

Bullitt wrote to House on September 3—he was not burning any bridges—to say he had met with Louis Howe, Roosevelt's campaign manager, and had ac-cepted an assignment as a researcher in the speech-writing section at campaign headquarters in New York City. "I should, of course, infinitely prefer to be with the Governor in Albany," he wrote, "but, as you said on the phone, there is no reason why, if he wants me, he should not lift me out of the New York organiza-tion." Always inclined to criticize, Bullitt assessed the campaign: "I liked Louis Howe," he wrote House. "He has a good eye. But the general organization is not impressive, and there seems to be scarcely a penny to elect Mr. Roosevelt." (By pledging to raise taxes on people of wealth, Roosevelt had lost many potential campaign contributors; Bullitt, not really a person of wealth, was able to donate only $1,000 to the 1932 campaign, far less than was expected of aspirants to ambassadorships.)

Bullitt's spirits were rising, his enthusiasm building, as he indicated in a letter to House on September 17. He had heard directly from Roosevelt, who had thanked him for his offer of service: "I am most anxious to avail myself of your help on my return from my western trip," the candidate had written. "In the

meantime may I ask that you get in touch with Professor Raymond Moley. . . ."
(Bullitt either failed to reach Moley, the economist who was a member of Roosevelt's "brains trust," or it slipped Moley's mind, for he later wrote that he met
Bullitt for the first time when he was introduced to him by Roosevelt in February
1933.) Bullitt was very impressed by a campaign address Roosevelt had made in
Topeka, Kansas, which he had listened to by radio at campaign headquarters.
"The Governor said the right things," Bullitt wrote House, "and he said them
with a 1776 spirit. There was a note of real leadership in the speech. . . . All of
the Patrick Henry blood in me applauded." Bullitt finally met with FDR—Wehle
had arranged the meeting and was present—in Albany on October 5, and by
Wehle's estimate it went well. "There was a certain community of social background," he wrote,

> as well as temperamental congeniality. . . . But there was also a difference: in the
> main Roosevelt was apt to absorb only what he could grasp quickly; Bullitt had the
> capacity for prodigious, sustained toil. . . . Yet he could swiftly and vividly make avail-
> able to Roosevelt his scholarship in history and also his familiarity with Europe and the
> current leaders. They made an ideal team.

Roosevelt won the election on November 8, 1932, by 472 electoral votes to
fifty-nine for Hoover; and three weeks later, at Louis Wehle's suggestion, Bullitt
was sent to Europe by Roosevelt—he was to go as a private citizen at his own
expense, since Roosevelt had no authority to send him officially—to investigate
the issue of war debts. (The debts to the U.S. of European nations were of some
consequence, as they amounted to billions of dollars: Great Britain, $4.5 billion;
France, $3.9 billion; Russia, variously put at between $75 million and $650
million.) The mission intrigued Bullitt for several reasons, not the least of which
being that it had to be kept a secret, for technically he was breaking the law: the
trip was not official, so Bullitt was acting in violation of the Logan Act, which
prohibited a private citizen from representing the United States in foreign affairs.
(Passed in 1799 and named for George Logan, a Philadelphia Quaker who had
traveled to France during an undeclared naval war of 1798–99, the law carried a
maximum penalty of three years in prison and a $5,000 fine.) Bullitt devised a
code by which he would send messages to Wehle, who would relay them to
Roosevelt: Ramsay MacDonald of Great Britain was "Philip"; Edouard Herriot,
who had succeeded Aubert as premier of France, was "Valentine"; and the debt-
payment issue would be referred to simply as "Bill." The mission also enabled
Bullitt to renew old contacts and establish new ones. He met with MacDonald
and Herriot and with Konstantin von Neurath, the German foreign minister, and
while nothing was settled—in fact, the debts were never paid—he extended his
understanding of European affairs, especially with respect to the devastating

effect of the worldwide depression on the economies of Britain and France. He did make some faulty observations, however, or at least one of major proportion: he became convinced from discussions in Germany that Adolf Hitler was nothing more than a rabble-rouser. (A month later—in January 1933—Hitler was named chancellor of Germany by President Paul von Hindenburg.)

Bullitt returned on December 23—he was credited by Senator Cordell Hull of Tennessee, who would be Roosevelt's secretary of state, with bringing "interesting and useful" information—and he met at dinner in Albany with the president-elect on December 27. Wehle was also there, and after dinner, when Bullitt was out of the room for a moment, he said to Roosevelt: "There is your man for Paris." No, said Roosevelt, for he had committed Paris to Jesse I. Straus, the president of R. H. Macy & Co., who had made a sizable campaign contribution. (There was no record that Bullitt made note of it, but Straus was of a kind with the Wanamakers and Wideners, successful entrepreneurs whom Bullitt castigated in his novel, *It's Not Done*. There was, however, an eerie coincidence that could not have escaped his attention: Straus's father and mother, Isidor and Ida Straus—Isidor Straus was the founder of Macy's—both perished in the sinking of the *Titanic*, as did George Widener and his son Harry.) "Well," said Wehle, "if we should recognize Russia, he would by all odds be your best man as our first ambassador," and with that Roosevelt concurred.

Roosevelt had come to value Bullitt for his sensitive eyes and ears, so he sent him in January 1933 on a second mission to Europe—the president-elect had been briefed by the outgoing secretary of state, Henry L. Stimson, but he wished to be updated—and this time Bullitt was ordered by Roosevelt to cable his coded reports directly to him. Bullitt went first to London, where he met with Mac-Donald on January 21; then to Paris for conversations with Premier Joseph Paul-Boncour, the successor to Herriot as the leader of the French government; and to Berlin for another meeting with von Neurath. He was eager to learn more about the new chancellor, so he looked up his old friend Putzi Hanfstaengl—Ernst (Putzi) Hanfstaengl was a German art publisher, who had become an intimate assistant of Hitler's and served in a liaison capacity with the American and British press (and later, having fled Nazi Germany, reportedly became a U.S. intelligence agent)—and put the question bluntly: "What kind of man is Hitler?" Hanfstaengl took him by the arm, and they walked to the window, which Hanfstaengl opened, so the din of traffic would prevent his reply from being picked up by listening devices: "He is a small, obscure Austrian house painter with the ability to speak to crowds."

Bullitt had made the mistake before departing of telling Colonel House about his mission, and House leaked it to the press; so on January 26, when Bullitt was in Paris, it was reported in *The New York Times* that he had been sent to Europe to discuss war debts. The story was promptly denied by Roosevelt's office—with some justification, since war debts were not the subject of this trip—but on February 3 Senator Arthur R. Robinson, a Republican from Indiana, asked in floor debate: "Who is this man Bullitt? I think the State Department should immediately apprehend him." Amid denials that the mission had been sanctioned—by the State Department, by embassy officials in Europe, and by Bullitt himself—Bullitt returned to New York on February 16 acting like a fugitive. Using an assumed name, "Mr. Williams," and in his most furtive manner—his coat collar turned up and the brim of his hat pulled down over his eyes—he appeared at Wehle's apartment and remained there in seclusion for five days. On February 21 he went to the Yale Club and sent Colonel House a note: "Just a line to ask you whether the recent publicity has in any way hindered my chances of obtaining the position you discussed with the governor." If House had spoken with Roosevelt, he was confused—House turned seventy-five in 1933—for he was apparently unaware that the Paris post was spoken for; and he replied to Bullitt's note, referring to "your appointment as ambassador to Paris," that the publicity would be "helpful rather than otherwise for the reason that it shows the American public how wide are your acquaintances in Europe and how many of the leading statesmen . . . are your friends." Bullitt soon learned he could not bank on House's words of encouragement—he realized he would not get an embassy posting right away—but the storm had passed; he would not be prosecuted under the Logan Act. At a cocktail party in Washington—Bullitt went to the capital in the spring of 1933 to seek a government appointment—he was confronted by Senator Huey Long of Louisiana: "Damn near sent you to jail for twenty years, hey, boy?"

Bullitt was hired, though not without opposition; his appointment at the Department of State was sustained ultimately by Roosevelt's high regard for him and the range of his European experience. "I did not know at the time how genuine was his jovial friendship with Roosevelt . . .," wrote Herbert Feis, a State Department economist.

I did not know whether his zestful accounts of talks with such heads of state as Prime Minister MacDonald and Premier Herriot . . . were imaginative or true, as they were. He was a fluorescent sort of fellow, to whom diplomacy was an incessant drama. . . . At first his jocund manners, his aura of habitual intimacy with great men and great events, his hasty rush to what seemed to me inadvertent conclusions, threw me off. But I came to respect his quick and incisive intelligence. . . .

Raymond Moley, who was named assistant secretary of state for international affairs after Roosevelt's inauguration in March, remembered meeting Bullitt at Roosevelt's Manhattan apartment in February: "He impressed me favorably,"

Moley later wrote, "and it seemed to me that simple justice called for his being given a chance to resume his career cut short twelve years before." In April, when Bullitt came to Moley's office in Washington seeking to "fit in somewhere," the former economics professor was more exacting in his appraisal, and it was not entirely positive. "He was pleasant, keen-minded, idealistic, and widely informed," Moley wrote. "On the other hand, he had a deep and somewhat disturbing strain of romanticism in him. Foreign affairs were, to his imaginative mind, full of lights and shadows, plots and counterplots, villains and a few heroes—a state of mind that seemed to me dangerous, if not constantly subjected to the quieting influence of some controlling authority." Moley noted that Felix Frankfurter had stopped by his office, and when he saw Bullitt, he asked, "Well, Bill, have you learned to keep your shirt on yet?" "Absolutely," answered Bullitt, "it is nailed down this time."

Despite his reservations Moley remained a supporter of Bullitt, and he prepared a memorandum designating him an assistant secretary of state and presented it to William Phillips, whom Roosevelt had appointed the under-secretary. Phillips balked, citing Bullitt's betrayal of Wilson, and Moley answered, as he later recalled, "that the years had shown that, on the point of difference between Wilson and Bullitt, Bullitt had been right: it seemed to me that loyalty to one's country superseded loyalty to a President; that it was a man's duty, under such circumstances, to pass up official position and take a public stand." Phillips finally agreed, according to Moley, although he decided that Bullitt would be a special assistant to the secretary of state, not an assistant secretary, "as the latter appointment, which required senatorial confirmation, might involve the raking up of old scores." (Phillips was one of several high-ranking officials in the Roosevelt administration who believed that Bullitt's appointment was actually a step by the president—Roosevelt had introduced Bullitt to Moley, after all—toward recognizing the government of the Soviet Union.)

Bullitt did not sever his ties with Colonel House, which contradicted an allegation by some in the government—Raymond Moley would be one of them—that Bullitt tended to snub his benefactors once he had achieved an objective. "I was delighted to hear from you again," he wrote House on May 13, 1933, on State Department letterhead. "We've been working about twenty hours a day with the visiting delegations, and while the work is in itself interesting, there is so much of it that enjoyment is out of the question. At least we have cleared the ground a bit and can see the difficulties in the situations, if not the solutions." House had asked Bullitt to assist a friend, Sarah Wambaugh, who was seeking a diplomatic appointment, and Bullitt had quickly complied. "I saw Miss Wambaugh yesterday. . . . She seems to be a most charming and intelligent person, but I felt compelled to tell her frankly that I could not support her for Vienna, as I must back my old friend George Earle." (George H. Earle—he and Bullitt had known each other since their days at the De Lancey School—had been a Republican whom Bullitt persuaded in 1932 to switch parties and to back Roosevelt; he raised money for the campaign and made a donation himself, one large enough to be named ambassador to Austria. Once in Vienna he loudly criticized the Nazis and warned that Americans would not abide anti-Semitism, causing U.S. isolationists to demand his recall; he did return and was then elected the first Democratic governor of Pennsylvania in sixty-six years.)

Bullitt went to London in June and July for an international economic conference, which ended with the American delegation, of which Bullitt was the executive director, in disarray and with Moley out of a job. In March the president had abandoned the gold standard and was therefore opposed to a program to stabilize currencies that was being pushed by the gold-bloc nations: France, Belgium, the Netherlands, Italy, and Switzerland. He specifically ordered Secretary of State Cordell Hull to limit U.S. participation at the conference to negotiating bilateral tariff treaties. When some of the U.S. delegates defied Hull and discussed stabilization—the European nations had insisted that stabilization come before tariff reduction on the agenda—they were rebuked by Roosevelt, leading one of them, New York banker James P. Warburg, to resign. Moley was accused by Hull of leading the defiant delegates and was dismissed, but Bullitt, while he had been a Moley associate, weathered the incident with his reputation intact. Bullitt was not interested in currency stabilization; he was in London for the principal purpose of meeting with Maxim Litvinov—Litvinov was the chief delegate of the U.S.S.R. at the conference—to discuss Soviet-American relations. On July 8 Bullitt wrote Roosevelt that Litvinov had asked how serious the new president was about renewed relations; he reported he had advised Litvinov that he could not speak for Roosevelt, but he did know that if there was to be any discussion, the first term his country would demand would be a commitment by the Soviets not to interfere in the internal affairs of the United States. Litvinov responded that Stalin was prepared to make such a commitment.

Talking Terms of Recognition

WHEN Bullitt returned from London in late July 1933, he was pleased to discover a receptivity in Washington to restoring relations with Russia, and he was gratified to note that his stature as a government official had been established. "In some respects we stood to gain more than Russia by restoration of diplomatic relations," Cordell Hull wrote in his *Memoirs*.

Without relations the Russians were probably much better informed about conditions in America than we were about the situation in Russia. . . . Moreover, it was easier for Russians to do business in the United States without diplomatic protection than it was for Americans to do business in Russia. . . . William C. Bullitt, an intimate friend of the president and my special assistant, was in close touch with the Soviet representatives. . . . A brilliant person, well versed in international affairs, he was particularly friendly toward Russia and was an ardent proponent of recognition.

Nor was the value of Bullitt stock in the State Department depreciated by the appointment in midsummer 1933 of R. Walton Moore as an assistant secretary of state, although there was an ironic twist to it. "A Virginian, with the amiable spirit and courteous manners of his region," Herbert Feis wrote of Moore,

he had served several terms in Congress and was a well-liked crony of the Secretary of State. He had friends and friendly associations on the Hill, mainly with conservative Democratic Southerners whose support Roosevelt and the State Department were to need. Another reason why he was favored by Hull and Phillips, many felt, was that they hoped to foreclose the possibility that the President might implant Bullitt permanently in the State Department. (They may not have known that Moore's and Bullitt's fathers had been roommates at the University of Virginia Law School and were lifelong friends.)

Feis was making certain important points, though he was incorrect on one key detail: Moore himself and Bullitt's father had been friends since rooming together at law school.

While Bullitt was meeting with Litvinov in London, Henry Morgenthau, Jr., who soon would be the secretary of the treasury, was attempting to establish a line of communication with Moscow through Amtorg, a Soviet government organization whose purpose was to purchase machinery in the United States (the name was an acronym for *Amerikanskia Torgovaia*, or American Trading Organization). When Bullitt immediately intruded, appearing at Morgenthau's office in Washington to offer advice and to be brought up to date, Roosevelt was annoyed, believing he was going over Hull's head; but he saw fit to handle him on "an easy rein," Morgenthau recalled, and before long Bullitt had taken charge. There were three main issues to be discussed, and the U.S. position was clear on each: Soviet propaganda in the United States—the undermining of U.S. institutions—had to be halted; Americans living or traveling in the Soviet Union would be guaranteed their religious rights; and the Soviets were to pay the czarist war debts and also make settlements on American property they had nationalized in Russia.

At 10:30 on the morning of October 11 Bullitt arrived at Morgenthau's office and was introduced to Boris E. Skvirsky, the head of Amtorg. He handed Skvirsky a copy of a draft proposal written by him and approved by Roosevelt, along with a set of conditions: there would be no publicity; if the Soviets agreed to the terms, a signed copy of the proposal would be delivered to Bullitt by Skvirsky; any announcement of an agreement would be made by President Roosevelt at a time and place of his choosing. "As I understand this," Skvirsky commented as he scanned the proposal, "there would be negotiations before recognition." "That's precisely what it says," Bullitt replied. "But you know," countered Skvirsky, "my government has refused several times to enter into preliminary negotiations." Bullitt said he was aware of that, as he reiterated the insistence of the U.S. government on negotiations prior to recognition; whereupon Skvirsky ended the discussion, saying he would transmit the proposed terms to Moscow at once. Skvirsky telephoned Bullitt at his apartment that evening to report that he had received a cable from Foreign Commissar Litvinov: "Draft letter entirely acceptable," it read. Bullitt asked for a written copy of the Soviet reply, to which Skvirsky agreed, and Skvirsky said Litvinov would represent his government in the negotiations; at eight that night Skvirsky cabled Moscow that everything was in order, and Bullitt so informed Secretary of State Hull at 9:55 P.M. The formal letters between President Roosevelt and Soviet President Mikhail Kalinin were signed and delivered.

Roosevelt's letter was dated October 10, 1933:

Since the beginning of my administration I have contemplated the desirability of an effort to end the present abnormal relations between the 125 million people of the United States and the 160 million people of Russia.

It is most regrettable that these great peoples, between whom a happy tradition of friendship existed for more than a century to their mutual advantage, should now be without a practical method of communicating with each other.

The difficulties that have created this anomalous situation are serious but not, in my opinion, insoluble; and difficulties between great nations can be removed only by frank, friendly conversations. If you are of a similar mind, I should be glad to receive any representatives you may desire to explore with me personally all questions outstanding between our countries.

Participation in such a discussion will, of course, not commit either nation to any future course of action, but would indicate a sincere desire to reach a satisfactory solution of the problems involved. It is my hope that such conversations might result in good to the people of both our countries.

Kalinin's letter was dated October 17, 1933:

I have always considered most abnormal and regrettable a situation wherein, during the past sixteen years, two great republics—the United States of America and the Union of Soviet Socialist Republics—have lacked the usual methods of communication and have been deprived of the benefits which such communication could give. I am glad to know that you have also reached the same conclusion.

There is no doubt that difficulties, present or arising, between the two countries, can be solved only when direct relations exist between them; and that, on the other hand, they can have no chance for solution in the absence of such relations. I shall take the liberty further to express the opinion that the abnormal situation, to which you correctly refer in your message, has an unfavorable effect not only on the interests of the two states concerned, but also on the general international situation, increasing the element of disquiet, complicating the process of consolidating world peace and encouraging forces tending to disturb that peace.

In accordance with the above, I gladly accept your proposal to send to the United States a representative of the Soviet government to discuss with you the questions of interest to our countries. The Soviet government will be represented by Mr. M. M. Litvinov, the people's commissar for foreign affairs, who will come to Washington at a time to be mutually agreed upon.

Maxim Maximovitch Litvinov was among the most able Soviet intellects, and while his appearance betrayed it—he was short and portly and might have been taken for an affable American storekeeper—he was a formidable negotiator. He was from an impoverished Jewish family and had grown up in the ghetto of Bialystok, a city in Russian Poland; he had joined the czarist army, but when he was degraded for being a Jew, he became a revolutionary. Litvinov lived in London for several years—it was there he traded for British currency the money obtained in a bank robbery in Tiflis in 1907, which had been engineered by Stalin—and the woman he married, Ivy Low, was the daughter of a former lord mayor. Lenin was fond of Litvinov and called him Papasha, or little Papa; Stalin tolerated him, for he found him useful. "Don't watch Russia, watch Litvinov," Western analysts of the Kremlin said to each other for many years, yet because he was a Jew he was never made a member of the Politburo. Bullitt found him inscrutable and capable of trickery: aboard ship en route to the United States in early November 1933 Litvinov told newspaper reporters he would hold out for establishing recognition before tackling the issues that the United States government had insisted be settled first. He knew that his government had agreed to the terms proposed by Bullitt to Skvirsky—he had signed the cable saying so—but he wished to keep the issue alive, while aware he had no choice but to back down: "Roosevelt and Bullitt . . . have . . . maneuvered Comrade Litvinov into a position of discussion before recognition," wrote Walter Duranty, the Moscow correspondent of *The New York Times*, who was on the ship with the foreign commissar.

When Litvinov arrived on November 7, elaborate security precautions were taken, for demonstrations by White Russian refugees were feared: at the entrance to New York harbor he was taken by Coast Guard cutter to Jersey City, New Jersey; he then boarded a private railroad train for Washington, where he was met by a delegation headed by Bullitt (they were pointedly not wearing the customary top hats of a diplomatic reception party). The talks began on November 8, and within three days, as Hull noted in his *Memoirs*, the issues of Communist propaganda and the religious rights of Americans in Russia were disposed of. The secretary neglected to mention it—he might not have known, for he said they were resolved "with relative ease"—but the propaganda and religious issues were the subject of behind-the-scenes debate, some of it heated. With Roosevelt's permission Bullitt met with Litvinov at Skvirsky's residence, where the commissar was staying, to discuss the propaganda point, the wording of which in the draft proposal was clear: the Soviets would refrain from any subversive activity that would affect the United States. Litvinov protested nevertheless, irritably pacing the floor, and Bullitt responded by handing him a schedule of ship sailings to Europe. "You are too hard on me, Bullitt," an annoyed Litvinov shouted in English, as he gave in. "I accept it! I accept it!" he said, aware that it was a meaningless pledge: it was nothing but a "scrap of paper," Litvinov told a meeting of the U.S. Communist Party before leaving for Moscow, as it was his position that Communist activities in America were not controlled by the Soviet Union. The religious question was settled in a meeting with Roosevelt at the White House. As he told it later, the president said to Litvinov, an atheist, that he was "willing to wager that five minutes before his time would come to die . . . that he would be . . . wanting to make his peace with God." The debt issue would be much more difficult to resolve, and as with Soviet subversion it would continue to be a subject of dispute for some time after diplomatic relations had been restored.

Robert F. Kelley, chief of the State Department Division of Eastern European Affairs, had advised in a memorandum in July that if the questions of the Russian debt and confiscated property "were not completely settled before recognition, there was little likelihood that subsequent negotiations would result in a settlement"; but Roosevelt decided that a statement of intent would be sufficient. (Roosevelt was by nature impatient: "Restless and mercurial in his thinking," Eric Goldman, a Princeton historian, later wrote, "he trusted no system except the system of endless experimentation.") He met at the White House with Bullitt and Litvinov on the morning of November 15, and then just Bullitt and Litvinov met at the State Department to fix a figure for the amount to be paid. Bullitt assured the commissar that an offer of $50 million would be rejected, for it would be up to Congress, and American estimates of total claims against Russia were over $500 million. "What sum do you think might be acceptable to Congress?" Litvinov asked. "I cannot predict what Congress will do," Bullitt answered, "but the president can predict very exactly what Congress will do, and you should address that question to him."

Bullitt wrote a memo to Roosevelt, indicating his belief that Litvinov was ready to come to terms. "I finally managed to shake him a bit," he said, "by telling him that the . . . bill forbidding loans to countries in default on their indebtedness to the Government of the United States, was certain to be passed in January and that if the Soviet Government should make any absurd offer of settlement, such an offer would surely be turned down by Congress, and the Soviet Government would be unable to obtain one penny of credit from either the Government or any private corporation or individual in the United States. . . ." He added a postscript: "I think we were a bit too gentle with him this morning," but when they met again with Litvinov that afternoon, a mood of geniality, at the president's insistence, continued to prevail. A compromise was reached—it was called a "gentleman's agreement"—and it was signed by Roosevelt and Litvinov: ". . . the Soviet Government will pay the Government of the United States . . . a sum to be no less than $75,000,000 in the form of a percentage above the ordinary rate of interest on a loan to be granted to it by the Government of the United States or its nationals. . . ."

Diplomatic relations between the U.S. and the U.S.S.R. were formally restored in the wee hours of the morning of November 17—a pleased President Roosevelt proposed a toast with a glass of 3.2 beer, the only alcoholic drink that was legal until the Twenty-first Amendment repealing Prohibition was ratified in December—and the documents were made public later in the day. However, the "gentleman's agreement" was missing from the package released to the press; it therefore remained a government secret until 1945, when it was inadvertently discovered by a researcher in the National Archives. In all likelihood it was deliberately withheld, for it could have been politically embarrassing: as a basis for settling the Soviet debt, it was determined in a State Department investigation, the agreement was ambiguous and misleading. "I don't think that Bullitt and some of the others were much interested in the financial aspects of recognition," Henry Morgenthau wrote in retrospect.

Roosevelt's Man for Moscow

ROOSEVELT had decided at the opening of negotiations that Bullitt would be his ambassador to the Soviet Union, and with Hull out of the country—he was attending a conference in Montevideo, Uruguay—he discussed the appointment with his old friend William Phillips, the acting secretary of state. Phillips had nothing but praise for Bullitt's ability, though he had not forgotten his disloyalty to President Wilson—and his betrayal of Secretary of State Lansing, for that matter—so he was arguably just as happy to see Bullitt out of Washington and in far-off Russia. There was scattered opposition to recognition around the country: the Daughters of the American Revolution was up in arms; and Archdeacon James F. Bullitt of Philadelphia, Bullitt's uncle, denounced dealing with the Soviets as a disgrace and called the Soviet Union "a country . . . beyond the pale, a pariah among nations." There was but one public criticism of Bullitt himself, a strongly worded statement by the British ambassador to Washington, Ronald Lindsay: "He may be regarded as thoroughly untrustworthy and completely unscrupulous whenever it is a question of taking his objective." Newspapers in the United States—a major exception was *The Los Angeles Times*, which opposed renewed relations—spoke in favor of the appointment; and in Moscow Karl Radek wrote in *Pravda* that Bullitt would be welcomed as an American who had long worked for a resumption of relations. American correspondents in Moscow, however—Eugene Lyons of the United Press was among them—predicted that Bullitt would run into difficulty with the Soviet leaders. "In fact, Bullitt was not ideal for the Russian post . . .," wrote Beatrice Farnsworth, a historian, in a carefully researched study, *William C. Bullitt and the Soviet Union*. "The nature of personality (combined with his emotional attachment to Soviet Russia) was to make him particularly susceptible to disappointment."

On November 18, 1933, Bullitt received a wire from Colonel House: "Loulie [Mrs. House], Miss Fanny [Frances B. Denton, House's secretary] and I send you our affectionate congratulations and felicitations." Bullitt, who had never wavered in his loyalty to House, replied in a note on November 22: "Of all the telegrams I have received there is one at least which is deeply sincere and that is yours. I have counted for years and shall count for the future on your friendship. You are the wisest counselor I know and I shall want your advice constantly." Bullitt spent a couple of days with Roosevelt at the president's retreat in Warm Springs, Georgia, and he then went to New York to prepare for a preliminary visit to Moscow—to present his credentials and establish his embassy.

V

Ambassador to
the Soviet Union:
1933–1936

To Moscow in Triumph

BULLITT sailed for Europe on November 29, 1933, with his nine-year-old daughter, Anne, and their dog, a West Highland terrier named Pie-Pie. His several steamer trunks were packed with what surely would be the best wardrobe in Moscow—business suits, cutaways, and white tie and tails, all finely tailored in London—for he had no intention of dressing drably, as other ambassadors did, to please the plainly clothed Russians: he was to be the representative of the leading capitalist nation, and he would look the part. Besides, he might be forgiven for a little preening, pleased with himself as he was: "I think you know what a joy it is to be able to work with you . . .," he wrote Roosevelt on December 6 while still at sea. "It has occurred to me that I have never thanked you properly for this assignment to Russia." Quite a number of old hands at the Department of State were miffed that Bullitt had been picked for the post, for they had expected it to go to John Van A. MacMurray, a Foreign Service veteran and an expert on the Far East. (Extending north of Manchuria to Vladivostok on the Sea of Japan, Russia was in part regarded as geographically Far Eastern and politically so as well, owing to her history of conflict with Japan.) Roosevelt, however, had little esteem for career diplomats, and he had been known to equate their work with the mating of elephants: a lot of noise and motion, but it took eighteen months to produce anything. Furthermore, Bullitt had earned the job by his persistent efforts in negotiations with the Soviets, and Roosevelt believed—it would turn out that he was wrong—that Bullitt was just the man for the task of hard bargaining that remained to be done.

As he passed through Paris on December 8, Bullitt was joined by George F. Kennan—not quite thirty, Kennan was a specialist on Russia, and he spoke Russian—whom Bullitt had hired as an interpreter and diplomatic secretary; and they proceeded by train to Moscow. "Bullitt is a striking man . . .," Kennan noted, "confident in himself, confident of the President's support, confident that he will have no difficulty in cracking the nut of Communist suspicion and hostility. . . . He is not a radical, but he is not afraid of radicals. He was once a friend of John Reed, and he was later married, for a time, to Reed's widow." (Kennan observed someone else, as their train pulled out of Paris: a woman standing alone on the platform was, he was told, Louise Bryant, presumably attempting unsuccessfully to have a moment with her daughter.) They arrived on December 10 at Negoreloye, a Russian village on the border with Poland—it was bitterly cold, Bullitt wrote Roosevelt, and "the air stank of sheepskin coats, sawdust, disinfectant, tobacco and human sweat"—where they were met by a delegation from the Soviet Foreign Office headed by Litvinov; and in Moscow there was an even larger reception committee: it was, wrote Walter Duranty in *The New York Times* on December 11, the first time a foreign envoy had received such attention.

They were taken to the National Hotel, where the suite reserved for the ambassador and his daughter was the one he had occupied with his mother in August 1914: "Imagine my feelings," said Bullitt in an interview with *The New York Times* a few years later, "when Anne and I entered the identical rooms in which . . . I had heard the first outcries of the great war." (Also staying at the National in December 1933 was Harpo Marx of the famed comedy family, who was asked by Bullitt to carry a packet of letters to the United States covertly. Marx agreed: he made the long voyage with the letters strapped to his leg, daring to remove them only on arrival in New York, where he was met by Secret Service agents.) It was Bullitt's moment of triumph in Moscow: "As the old American friend of New Russia," wrote Janet Flanner of *The New Yorker*, "he was received with fantastic acclaim. When he rode in the streets he was cheered, at the Opera the Muscovites rose to shout his name, the Ballet basked in his favor; . . . he moved in an atmosphere of hysterical Slavic emotion. . . ."

On December 19 Bullitt went to Alexandrovsky Palace to present his credentials to President Kalinin: "I do not come to your country as a stranger," he said, vowing to help create "genuine friendly relations" and "strong and enduring ties"; for their part the Russians kept reminding Bullitt that Lenin had spoken highly of him following his visit in 1919. "In recognizing as the central task the 'close collaboration of our government in the cause of preserving peace,' " read an editorial in *Isvestia* the next day, "William Bullitt has once again shown his understanding for the spirit animating the popular masses of the U.S.S.R." The highlight of Bullitt's stay in Moscow occurred on December 20: he had been invited by the senior Soviet military officer, Marshal Klementi Voroshilov, to a dinner at his residence in the Kremlin, which was attended by the leaders of the government, including Stalin. As Litvinov put it, having learned the English idiom during his years in London: "This is the whole gang that runs things." (Bullitt had asked in advance how he might express his gratitude for this welcome, and he was told that Stalin had been unable to get good American pipe tobacco; so Bullitt immediately sent an order to North Carolina for a case of Prince Albert.) Bullitt was greeted first by President Kalinin; then Vyacheslav Molotov, the chairman of the Council of People's Commissars; then by Stalin himself; then Alexander Yegorov, the chief of staff; Grigori Piatokov, assistant commissar for heavy industries; Alexander Troyanovsky, ambassador-designate to the United States; and so on. It was a formal event, and except for a cordial handshake and a stiff hello there was no exchange at first between Bullitt and Stalin. "I made no effort to continue conversing with him before dinner," Bullitt explained in a report to Washington, "considering it best to let him come to me in his own good time."

Bullitt drifted to one side of the room, Stalin to the other: "I noticed that from time to time he looked in my direction out of the corner of his eye, as if he were sizing me up before coming to close quarters," Bullitt reported. It was an interesting encounter: the handsome American aristocrat, not quite forty-three, almost six feet tall and trim at 170 pounds, who radiated well-being and health; and the shoemaker's son from Gori in the Soviet republic of Georgia, eleven years older than Bullitt, standing only five feet three inches, who smiled through bad teeth and a shaggy mustache and looked altogether unimpressive. (Bullitt did not find Stalin frightening, though he had heard stories about violence in his background: how his father had been stabbed to death in a drunken brawl, how his wife had committed suicide.) By Bullitt's account Stalin was "rather short, the top of his head coming to my eye level, and of ordinary physique, wiry rather than powerful." He was fascinated by Stalin's dark brown eyes: "They are small, intensely shrewd, and continuously smiling. The impression of shrewd humor is increased by the fact that the crow's feet . . . do not branch up and down in the usual manner, but all curve upward in long crescents." Bullitt was able— uniquely for an American—to compare Stalin with Lenin: "With Lenin one felt at once . . . in the presence of a great man. With Stalin I felt I was talking to a wiry Gypsy with roots and emotions beyond my experience."

Bullitt was reminded as the banquet began—lavish hors d'oeuvres of caviar and crab were being served—of reports of famine in Russia: some five million peasants (or possibly over seven million, according to more recent estimates), who had refused to join collectives, had died of starvation. But then there were toasts to numb his senses—vodka, glass after glass—and Bullitt, feeling the effect on about the tenth, started to sip, only to be nudged by Litvinov, who whispered that a toaster would be insulted if he did not drink to the bottom: "Whereupon," he wrote, "I continued to drink bottoms-up." Stalin drank to Roosevelt; Bullitt responded by drinking to the health of Kalinin; and Molotov drank to Bullitt, "who comes to us as a new ambassador but as an old friend." Stalin drank to the "health and prosperity and happiness and triumph of the American Army and Navy and the President of the United States"; Bullitt raised his glass "to the memory of Lenin and the continued success of the Soviet Union." As Bullitt could best remember, there were fifty toasts in all: "And I have never before so thanked God," he wrote in his report, "for the possession of a head impervious to any quantity of liquor. Everyone at the table got into the mood of a college fraternity banquet, and discretion was conspicuous by its absence." It also would be the high point of his friendship with Litvinov: "You told me you wouldn't stay here if you were going to be treated as an outsider," said the foreign commissar with a wide grin. "Don't you realize that everyone at this table has completely forgotten that anyone is here except members of the inner gang?"

The Soviets were in a mood to offer Bullitt about anything. "If you want to see me at any time, day or night," said Stalin when they finally sat down after the toasting, "you have only to let me know, and I will see you at once." Then, later, the chief of central administration offered to place at the disposal of the U.S. embassy all available economic statistics; and the commissar of finance, Gregory Grinko, assured Bullitt that he and members of his staff would be able to obtain rubles at a fair rate of exchange. "Please understand," as Bullitt recalled Stalin saying as they parted at the end of the evening, "that we should have received politely any ambassador who might have been sent us by the government of the United States, but we should have received no one but yourself in this particular way." Bullitt decided it was an opportune moment to ask a favor of Stalin: he had seen a piece of land up on the bluff overlooking the Moscow River—it was a vacant tract known as Lenin Hills—that would be ideal as a new U.S. embassy site, so he asked Stalin if it might be available. "You shall have it," Stalin declared. Then came a surprise farewell, which Bullitt reported graphically: "Stalin took my head in his two hands and gave me a large kiss! I swallowed my astonishment, and when he turned up his face for a return kiss, I delivered it."

When he got back to the hotel, Bullitt was so excited that he awoke George Kennan and dictated an account of the evening while perched on the edge of Kennan's bed. "This evening with Stalin and the inner circle of the Soviet Government seems almost unbelievable in retrospect," he exclaimed, "and I should have difficulty convincing myself it was a reality. . . ." Stalin appeared to be equally enthusiastic: "I and my comrades liked Bullitt very, very much," he told Walter Duranty. "I had never met him before, but I had heard a great deal about him from Lenin, who liked him too. . . . He is straightforward and says what he means. He made a very good impression here." There was cold logic behind the warm welcome—not to mention the elaborate flattery, which Bullitt mistakenly took to heart—of the new U.S. ambassador: it had to do with the Russians' fear of Japan, for they well remembered the staggering defeats of the Russo-Japanese War of 1904–1905. In his remarks at the dinner for Bullitt, while predicting victory in a war with Japan, Stalin had a request of the United States. "The second line of our railroad to Vladivostok is not completed," he said. "To complete it quickly we need 250,000 tons of steel rails at once." (There was good reason for the Soviets to fear an attack by Japan, for in the early 1930s Japanese military leaders were divided as to where to direct their aggression: one faction, dominated by the navy—it was the one that prevailed—favored further moves into China and then southward to Indochina, followed by a strike against the

United States in the Pacific; another, led by Sadao Araki, a formidable army general, argued for an invasion of the U.S.S.R. by way of Siberia. ". . . [T]he Army expounds a policy of hostility toward Russia," wrote Koichi Kido, the lord of the privy seal and a confidant of Emperor Hirohito, "while the Navy calls for commencement of war between Japan and America.")

Litvinov had proposed an alliance against Japan during the negotiations in Washington in November, and he had received a brusque rejection from William Phillips, the undersecretary of state; but he raised the matter again with Bullitt on December 21. Bullitt explained, as Phillips had, that the United States did not wish to jeopardize its relations with Japan, to which Litvinov countered: "Anything that could be done to make the Japanese believe that the United States was ready to cooperate with Russia, even though there might be no basis for the belief, would be valuable."

The Soviets were trying rather crudely to use Bullitt, whom they considered their personal connection to Roosevelt—they considered him a closer friend of the president's than he really was—and Bullitt was aware of their motive, as he reported to Washington on December 24. He assured Roosevelt and Phillips that he had emphatically explained that the American people, speaking through Congress, would not approve a nonaggression pact against Japan, although perhaps he had not been heard clearly in the Kremlin. He had failed to make his point because he actually had taken a sympathetic position: "Litvinov's entire preoccupation . . . is the preservation of peace in the Far East," Bullitt wrote in a report dated January 1, 1934. "I am convinced that there is almost nothing that the Soviet Union will not give us in the way of commercial agreements, or anything else, in return for our moral support in preserving peace." He added one more social note, referring to his last day in Moscow, December 21: "Litvinov gave a tremendous reception for me, . . . and that evening we left for Paris. . . ."

Bullitt was visibly impressed by the attention he had received, which well might have led the Soviets to believe he was susceptible to flattery: Stalin's offer to see him at any time was, Bullitt wrote, an "extraordinary gesture," one that had not been offered to any foreign emissary. It was with ill-concealed pride that he advised Washington that he and Litvinov had concocted the story that Stalin had simply dropped in on the Voroshilov dinner: ". . . it is desirable to have the inside track," he wrote, "but it seems to me not desirable to emphasize the fact to the world." Bullitt ought to have been alert to the deceptive way his ego was being exploited: why, for example, was so much being made of Lenin's high regard for him, when there had not been a hint of it on his visit to Moscow as a private citizen in June 1932? "From the beginning," Beatrice Farnsworth observed, "the Russians divined the nature of Bullitt's personality and played upon his weakness." Bullitt arrived in the United States on January 7, fully convinced that his trip had been a triumph: "Until we resumed diplomatic relations with the

Soviet Union," he declared in an address to the Philadelphia Chamber of Commerce on January 19, "it was impossible for the two nations to work together intimately for the preservation of peace. We can now work together. . . ."

Return to Reality

ON MAY 14, 1952, George F. Kennan presented his credentials as ambassador to the Soviet Union, and in his *Memoirs* he wrote of his thoughts that day: "My mind naturally went back to the occasion . . . when I had accompanied our first ambassador, . . . Bill Bullitt, on a similar errand to this same room." What struck Kennan was the contrast: "Bullitt . . . had come with high hopes and enormous enthusiasm. I came, now, only with misgivings and premonitions. So much had we learned in two decades of contact with the Soviet government." Kennan remembered Bullitt with admiration: "charming, brilliant, . . . imaginative, a man of the world capable of holding his own intellectually with anyone. . . ."; but he was also impatient and wanted his hopes realized immediately. "These hopes," Kennan wrote,

> were not the result of any ideological sympathy for the Soviet regime; they reflected, rather, . . . a certain overoptimism concerning the impressionableness of the Soviet leaders. Here Bullitt was no doubt betrayed by his earlier experience with Lenin. . . . On returning to Russia in 1933 . . . he had hoped, I suspect, that the approach of the Roosevelt administration, free of the prejudices of 1919, free of the rigidities of the Republican regimes that had intervened over the preceding twelve years, . . . would evoke a favorable response on the Soviet side. These hopes were quickly disappointed. This was, after all, the day of Stalin, not of Lenin.

Kennan, while doing an intensive study of Russia at the University of Berlin and then serving in the legation in Riga, the capital of Latvia (Latvia was not annexed by the Soviet Union until 1940), had come to doubt the wisdom of renewing relations with Russia. Before returning to Washington, where he was hired by Bullitt in 1933, he was asked by the U.S. minister in Riga, Robert P. Skinner, to offer his opinion of the negotiations. It was Kennan's view "that the Russians would not be willing to make significant concessions" on either of the key points at issue: encouragement by the Soviet Union of revolutionary activity in other countries, the United States in particular; and settlement of the Russian war debt. Kennan's analysis was sent to Washington, but he had reason to doubt it was brought to the attention of Roosevelt. "He attached little importance to these particular issues for their own sake," Kennan wrote.

He was concerned with them insofar as they meant things to influence sectors of American opinion; but here his concern was primarily to reassure, to allay apprehension, to give the impression that things were being taken care of—not really to solve the issues. He obviously considered the resumption of relations with Russia to be desirable for the sobering influence it might exercise on the German Nazis and on the Japanese militarists. . . .

If Kennan was right—his observations, published in 1967, were based on years of reflection and experience—Bullitt would have had good reason to be disillusioned by the detached attitude of the president toward the terms of the recognition agreement; even more so than he would be upon discovering, as he did in 1934, that the Soviets had no intention of abiding by them.

While Bullitt was in the United States, Kennan stayed in Moscow to "tend the store," living at the National Hotel, and right next door, still under construction, was the Mokhavaya Building, which was to be the embassy chancery and staff quarters. Kennan had two assistants: Charles W. Thayer, a young Philadelphian who had come to Moscow for the express purpose of working in the embassy and had learned Russian well enough to be hired by Bullitt as an interpreter; and a Muscovite named Grisha, whom Thayer had recommended because he owned a motorcycle with a sidecar. In Washington Bullitt was recruiting the rest of his staff—Roosevelt had told him he could have the pick of the crop—and he signed up two men who would be professional associates for just a few years but friends for much longer (until he died in 1967 Bullitt was "the boss" to his Moscow staff): Elbridge Durbrow, a self-taught expert on passport law; and Charles E. Bohlen, who had studied Russian in Paris and had spent two summers in Tallinn, the capital of Estonia (having gained independence from Russia in 1918, Estonia was absorbed by the Soviet Union in 1940). Bohlen accompanied Bullitt on the trip back to Moscow—they left Paris on February 27, 1934, stopped over in Warsaw, and arrived at the Russian capital on March 7— and having heard Bullitt tell of his grand welcome just three months before, Bohlen knew that this time something was wrong. There was no delegation from the foreign office at Negoreloye, just a lone assistant chief of protocol; and in Moscow Bullitt discovered to his embarrassment that a band at the railroad station was waiting, not for him, but for delegates to Red International Woman's Day. He was greeted by George Andreytchine, an official of the government tourism agency, Intourist, whom Bullitt had known for many years, and the chief of protocol.

The signs that relations had abruptly cooled were too clear, and the immediate reason was the disagreement over a stance against Japan. "Litvinov, who is still ill, received me in his bedroom this afternoon," Bullitt cabled Washington on March 14. "He asked if the President might be inclined to propose a pact of non-aggression between the United States, the Soviet Union, Japan and China. I replied that I had no intimation that the President had any such intention." Louis Fischer, an authority on the Soviet Union—Fischer wrote a biography of Lenin and was a correspondent in Moscow for *The Nation*—summed up Bullitt's situation in a few words, granted with the advantage of hindsight, in a book published in 1969:

> Soviet partnership with America against Japan was Stalin's hope. It can scarcely have been Roosevelt's intention. He recognized Russia because he was at the beginning of a long tenure in the White House and thought it a proper and easy thing to do. Moscow, however, could never accept such an uncomplicated explanation. Stalin expected a loan, more business, and partnership in the Far East. Roosevelt could not fulfill these hopes. Bullitt's mission to Moscow was consequently ruined in advance.

Bullitt was a perfectionist, and the very idea of failure made him livid. He wanted his embassy to be a model, Bohlen said in retrospect—in a memoir, *Witness to History*, Chip Bohlen looked back over a forty-year diplomatic career—and in several respects it was: it was the first U.S. embassy to post a Marine security guard; and it was Bullitt's original idea to assign a military officer, who was trained as an observer, to the inter-embassy courier route. (Bullitt's "spy" was Roscoe Hillenkoetter, a navy lieutenant in 1934, who as an admiral thirteen years later would be appointed director of the Central Intelligence Agency.) Bullitt was also a thoughtful administrator, concerned about the welfare of his handpicked staff—he had filled forty positions, all with men ("There is absolutely nothing for a woman to do here," he wrote R. Walton Moore)—and was "a man of great appeal," as Bohlen put it. "His brilliant smile and his eloquence, coupled with his wide knowledge, usually succeeded in charming even the dubious." Bullitt was also a taskmaster, hard to please and quick to criticize, as Bohlen found out when he was transferred at the pleasure of the ambassador. "The most likely explanation," wrote Bohlen—he would return to Moscow, first as an assistant to Bullitt's successor, Joseph E. Davies, and in 1953 as the ambassador there—"is that I was part of a cut in the embassy staff ordered by Bullitt as a result of the breakdown in negotiations with the Russians." But Bohlen candidly attributed his transfer also to his not measuring up to Bullitt's demands: "Ambassador Bullitt was a . . . man with very sharply developed personal likes and dislikes, and he insisted that his staff should give him . . . blind obedience and support in everything he did—which perhaps I was incapable of." Bullitt eventually removed his senior aide as well, the embassy counselor, John C. Wiley, but he usually saw to it that the careers of the men he rebuked were not permanently damaged (Wiley later became the ambassador to Latvia, Portugal, Iran, Colombia, and Panama).

Bullitt was a strict disciplinarian, swift to punish, as Charles Thayer learned when he was demoted for a personal indiscretion; but he appreciated steady performance: "Durbrow is an excellent boy," he wrote Moore with only slight reservation, ". . . slow and thorough in his work." He had questioned why Durbrow, who was in charge of the consulate, "required an extraordinary amount of time in the preparation of every citizenship case," and he was satisfied with the explanation that Durbrow had another demanding boss, the chief of the passport office in Washington, Ruth Shipley. "Mrs. Shipley takes the attitude," Bullitt wrote Moore, "that every error in a citizenship report is cause for decapitation." Bullitt was equally demanding of the clerical personnel, in particular his own secretary: "Please send secretary who can stand Moscow and me," he cabled Washington after one embassy clerk, whose wife had refused to move to Moscow, had departed, and the first few replacements had not worked out. The one who did was Carmel Offie, who came from an Italian immigrant family in Portage, Pennsylvania; had worked his way through business college; then entered government service as a stenographer, working at the Interstate Commerce Commission in Washington and at the American embassy in Tegucigalpa, Honduras. In response to Bullitt's plea he had arrived at the embassy in Moscow on June 11, 1934. Offie was superb at shorthand and typing, he was clever and discreet, and he was totally loyal: Offie literally stayed at Bullitt's side, in and out of government, for the rest of the ambassador's life. He was always available when Bullitt needed him: as a British embassy official in Moscow noted, ". . . this wretched young man puts up with being at his beck and call all day and all night. . . ." Bullitt made a daily habit of arising at about five in the morning and dictating messages to Roosevelt and the State Department, or if an idea occurred to him in the middle of the night, he would summon his secretary to take it down; however, for serving beyond the call Offie was rewarded by Bullitt in December 1934 with a promotion to vice-consul.

———————

The population of Moscow had doubled since 1919, but there had been little new construction; consequently housing was at a premium, and the embassy staff lived at the National Hotel until the Mokhavaya Building was ready. Bullitt's residence was a thirty-room mansion, Spaso House—he had been given a choice between Spaso House and an old Supreme Court building, which Bullitt considered suitable only as a prison—so named because it stood on Spasopeskovskaya Ploshchad, the Square of the Sacred Sands. Spaso House, which had been built during the reign of the last of the czars, Nicholas II, by a wealthy merchant—he reportedly had been an intimate of the sinister yet influential monk, Grigori Rasputin, and was murdered by his illegitimate son—was Florentine in appearance, with rounded balconies and giant columns. "It was a Russian Victorian pomposity," Anne Bullitt later wrote, "badly proportioned and cold, enormous with no room for anything." It was built around a large central hall, two stories high with a glass dome, and there was a music room off to one side, which Bohlen found to be quite suitable for Christmas parties and other social events as well as games of badminton. There was little about Spaso House, for which the rent was an exorbitant $20,500 a year, that pleased Bullitt: the rooms were cold and drafty; the decor was tasteless; the plumbing was in bad repair; the run-down condition of the kitchen never ceased to irritate the cook, Louise Mijoin, one of two servants Bullitt had brought from Paris; and furnishings were in short supply (Bullitt appealed to Roosevelt, who ordered the U.S. Navy to provide blankets, bed linen, towels, tableware, and kitchen utensils, and Bullitt went himself to the marketplace to purchase czarist-era furniture). Only the dog seemed satisfied with the residence: "Pie-Pie took one look at the white marble walls and went off scampering for rats," Bullitt wrote his friend Moore.

There was another inconvenience: a single telephone line linked Spaso House with Washington and the rest of the world—Bullitt was a heavy telephone user, with no regard for long-distance charges—and it rang constantly, although often there was apparently no one on the other end. It turned out that the mansion had once been occupied by Georgi Chicherin, the former commissar for foreign affairs, who in 1934 was ill and in disfavor. Chicherin lived alone in a nearby apartment, and the only person he would see—or was permitted to see—was a furnace maintenance man named Seryosha; Chicherin's way of signaling Seryosha that it was time for a visit was to ring the phone at Spaso House. Bullitt had one final complaint about the residence: there was a caretaker named Sergei, who lived in a basement apartment with his wife, and it was generally assumed that Sergei was a Soviet security agent.

While Bullitt's staff was topflight in most respects, it lacked a man of administrative talent: "For this reason," Kennan wrote, "the first months witnessed a confusion in our official and personal lives for which one would probably have to reach back to the voyage of the Ford Peace Ship . . . to find a parallel." He knew that Bullitt would understand—and no doubt resent—his allusion to the peace ship, though Kennan had come to remember the Moscow experience with amusement, as he hoped Bullitt would as well. "The struggle continued through most of the year, and left little time for anything else. It was, however, a struggle full of hilarity and good spirits. . . ." Bohlen, too, tried to accept his tasks with a shrug and a chuckle, though it was difficult at times, as when he, a third secretary, was assigned to search for clothes hangers. "Bullitt's two French servants insisted that hangers for the Ambassador's clothes must be obtained at all cost," Bohlen wrote, and he went on to tell how he and Thayer and Grisha had "careened around the muddy streets of Moscow all one day" in their search. "I had to look up the Russian word—*veselka*—in the dictionary. Eventually, we discovered a limited number of wooden hangers and took them back in triumph to Spaso." Bohlen explained that administrative responsibilities were relegated to Loy W. Henderson, also a third secretary, "since neither Bullitt nor Wiley was particularly gifted in that field"; and he expressed the relief that was felt because "two of the chores that consume so much of the time of our missions in Western Europe" were eliminated in Moscow: there were few American travelers in Russia, who might have required the services of the embassy; and with the secret police watching everyone who came to the U.S. embassy, there were almost no attempts by Russians to emigrate to the United States.

Charlie Thayer appreciated amusing incidents, which he recorded in a book; two of them occurred in the spring and summer of 1934. First, there was the delivery to Spaso House of a huge steel safe, which was left on a doorstep one afternoon, as it was time for Russian workers to quit for the day. "We held a council of war," Thayer wrote, "and took the only decision available: the Ambassador, the Counselor, three Third Secretaries and the Private Secretary put their shoulders to the safe and shoved. Bit by bit we got it moved to a point where only half the door was blocked." The following day the protocol office was advised of the situation, but no suggestions were forthcoming; then someone remembered that the Russians were prodigious weight lifters, and it developed there was in Moscow a Heavy-Weight-Lifting Trust. The weight lifters were hired, and it was an ingenious solution, as Thayer described it: "The safe rose like a feather and swayed precariously as they shuffled up the stairs and across the ballroom. In ten minutes it was in place."

The second incident disrupted embassy operations at the Mokhavaya Building soon after it was opened. It began with a notification from the office of the chief of protocol that at noon a week hence there would be dynamite blasts downtown, and, as Thayer recalled: "Would we therefore mind opening our windows so as to avoid smashing all the glass in the building?" The windows were opened, and the blasting caused only noise and tremors; then, a week later, it was repeated, only this time the notice was not received until about ten minutes before the blast. "Some fast footwork on the part of embassy messengers," Thayer wrote, "got the word around before it was too late, . . . and all the windows were open." The next week, though, there was a no-notice blast: "A few windows happened to be open . . .," Thayer recounted, "but the rest were blown to atoms. . . . About three days later the Chief of Protocol sent us a note asking us to be sure to have our windows open three days ago. Our reply was a . . . bit tart."

In the Moscow diplomatic community Bullitt was known for his resourcefulness: they ran out of razor blades, so he sent an order for several cases to the General Blade Corporation in New York; then it was alarm clocks that were needed, then fountain pens, and each time the item was requisitioned, though it took at least seventy-five days for it to be delivered. Bullitt was more than a little annoyed by the time required for mail delivery between him and Washington: "I have just received your letter of April 10," he wrote R. Walton Moore on May 4; but he tended to see the brighter side of things, at least for a while, and his embassy came to be called "Bill Bullitt's Circus." During his visit in December 1933 fawning officials had voiced the hope that the ambassador would get to know the whole of the Soviet Union; and when Bullitt observed that their country was so immense, they proposed that he bring an airplane. He took them seriously, and his pilot—officially the Army attaché for air—was a young lieutenant, Thomas D. White, who twenty-three years later would become chief of staff of the U.S. Air Force.

Conditions in much of rural Russia were bleak in 1934, and it was impossible for the Americans to ignore them: entire villages had been wiped out by famine. Thayer made an inadvertent tour of a devastated area: he was on his way to Sochi, a resort on the Black Sea, and was to change trains in Armavir, in the Kuban region; but he missed his connection, so he decided to take a ride to surrounding villages. He hired a droshky, a four-wheel carriage, driven by a bearded old peasant, who vowed to show him villages "the like of which you have never seen in your life." When they reached a cluster of about thirty huts—only a third of them were occupied, the rest either burned down or abandoned—the driver said: "This is my village, only I took my horse and went to town before the collectivization started." He spat out the word in disgust: "Collectivization, hell! It's hunger they gave us." At another village Thayer found an old woman sitting at the door of a dilapidated hut, eating a mush of water and chaff from an earthenware mug. "Where is everyone?" asked Thayer. "Gone," she answered. "Everyone's gone. My man they shot. They took my two boys. I'm too old to work, and this"—she was holding up the mug—"is my three meals for today." Other towns had been abandoned completely, a black flag hanging over one of the empty huts, and Thayer asked the driver to take him back to Armavir, for he had seen enough.

There were hardly any American tourists to worry about in Russia, as Bohlen noted, but there were U.S. nationals in the country—workers who had lost their jobs in the Depression and had been lured to the Soviet Union by the offer of work—and they were the concern of Elbridge Durbrow, the consular officer. "They had come from the soup lines," Durbrow recalled. "The Russians were saying, 'Bring your family. We'll give you good housing, and we'll pay you $500-a-month.' Some of them had even been talked into throwing their passports overboard on the boat from London to Leningrad." In his first year in Moscow Durbrow interviewed about three hundred Americans who had renounced their U.S. citizenship and wanted it back, and the one he best remembered was an agronomist from Iowa. "He had been in the Ukraine during collectivization, the winter of 1932–1933, and he said that literally millions of people had been allowed to starve . . . because they would not join a collective farm. He even showed pictures of bodies stacked like cordwood." (Of the five to seven million people who died of starvation, more than half were Ukrainians.)

End of a Rapport

O N E W A Y Bullitt coped with the less pleasant aspects of life in the Soviet Union was to get away, which he did during about half of his time there, fifteen of the thirty months: he went to Vienna and Paris for the treatment of various ailments (they were not serious, as Bullitt was never healthier, according to Orville Horwitz, his doctor); he took vacations, though they were seldom and brief; and he returned to the United States at least once a year for an extended period of consultation and leave. More than he disliked being in Moscow—he would mind it increasingly, however, as relations with the Russians worsened—he was disturbed by his absence from his own capital: "I miss Washington more than I could have imagined," he wrote Moore on March 29, 1934. "To be able to see you and the President each day was a joy which I find difficult to forego." Roosevelt was to make a sea voyage that summer—naval tours were a favorite form of relaxation for the president, who remembered with relish his days as assistant secretary of the navy—and he had proposed that Bullitt meet him in Hawaii; but he abandoned the plan, having been advised by the State Department that he would have to include as well Joseph C. Grew, the ambassador to Japan, and Nelson T. Johnson, the minister to China. "With much reluctance I yielded," Roosevelt cabled Bullitt on May 14, "though I am not in a happy frame of mind about it and still believe that you and I could have had our little party in Hawaii without bringing on a World War!" Bullitt wrote back on May 18: "I am deeply sorry that I shall not see you. I should like to hear the sound of your voice and be with you for a few days. I don't like being so far away from you."

There was a peculiar affection in Bullitt's tone, a longing for someone loved, although the ambassador and the president were professional associates who were not all that well acquainted. Was Bullitt showing signs of the same trait he and Freud had attributed to Woodrow Wilson—a father fixation, which led to unusual attachments to other men? While such an interpretation merited consideration, there was more to it than filial devotion, for Bullitt entered into an association with a man he admired, regardless of age—he saw Roosevelt, who was nine years older, as a contemporary—with boundless enthusiasm. If Bullitt had needed a father figure, it more likely would have been R. Walton Moore, who had been a friend and contemporary of William C. Bullitt, Sr.; he was a bachelor and felt a close kinship with Bullitt as well as his daughter, Anne. Bullitt corresponded regularly with Moore, whom he addressed as "Judge," the title having been acquired when Moore was a member of the House of Representatives, from 1919 to 1931, although he had never served on the bench. (Moore was called "Judge" by everyone but Franklin Roosevelt, to whom he was related and who called him "Cousin.") But Moore was a friend, not a father: when Bullitt moved into Spaso House, Moore sent him a portrait of George Washington, which Bullitt hung in his bedroom, and he wrote Moore, it "reminds me daily that I have a real friend . . . in the Department. . . ."; and he was a mentor with the wisdom of experience, as Colonel House had been.

It was to Moore that Bullitt confided his misgivings about the "general atmosphere" in Moscow upon his return in March 1934. "It is difficult to describe," he wrote. "Perhaps the easiest way . . . is to say that . . . I have found the outward official friendliness undiminished but the greatest difficulty in getting anything done." Bullitt knew the reason: "In December the Soviet Government was so fearful of an immediate attack by Japan that cooperation with us was eager and immediate. The Soviet Government now is convinced that Japan will not attack, and we are therefore simply one among the other capitalist nations." Moore concurred and added a theory of his own. "It is now quite apparent," he wrote Bullitt on April 10,

that Litvinov when he was here was not serious about any phase of the negotiation except recognition, and that he is now indifferent to all the assurances he gave. . . . It seems to me the only thing that would incline him to take a more reasonable attitude is the possibility of Japan knowing that the relations between our government and his have become strained. . . .

On July 2 Bullitt reported to the State Department that relations had further deteriorated: the Soviet government was not willing to provide embassy personnel with rubles at a reasonable rate of exchange, as had been promised by Grinko, the commissar of finance; there were indications the government would renege on Stalin's assent to Bullitt's request for an embassy site at Lenin Hills; and the Soviets were saying the war debt agreement—by far the most serious of the points at issue—was open to interpretation. Bullitt had been rudely awakened to the disturbing realization that "oral promises of members of the Soviet Government are not to be taken seriously."

Bullitt and Litvinov had come to grips over the ruble exchange on March 8, the day after the ambassador arrived back in Moscow, at a meeting in which Litvinov announced that his government could not fix a special rate for the American embassy and not for other embassies. To Bullitt's astonishment he suggested obtaining rubles on the black market, at two cents to the dollar, as opposed to the official rate of eighty-eight cents. Bullitt had prohibited his staff from buying black market rubles: "He was bending over backwards," Durbrow explained, "to show the Soviets that we capitalists were not trying to do them in and were willing to live by the rules." Bullitt wrestled with the problem for three months, pleading with the foreign office—his staff, meanwhile, was paying $35 for a pound of meat—until Litvinov finally suggested that he learn how other ambassadors were solving it. It was an open secret that the Soviet intelligence agency—the OGPU and then the NKVD, predecessors of the KGB—was sending rubles by the bundle to European capitals, such as Warsaw, where they could be bought for forty-to-fifty to the dollar and brought back to Moscow via diplomatic pouch. Bullitt unhappily accepted the suggestion.

The matter of relocating the embassy was not so easily resolved, and it meant a lot more to Bullitt than the price of rubles: "We have managed to obtain the best site in the entire Soviet Union," he wrote Moore on May 4, "and living conditions are so disagreeable for members of the staff . . . that life in the long run will be tolerable only if we have a first-rate American installation. . . ." But in June Bullitt was sounding anxious, mainly over impatience in Washington: "I feel absolutely certain of the desirability of pushing construction as fast as possible," he wrote Moore on June 14. "If we should drop the project after insisting so vigorously on obtaining the site, I feel the Russians would believe that they could not rely on our Government. . . ." Bullitt had conceived a building modeled on Monticello, the Virginia home of Thomas Jefferson, with an appropriate quotation of Jefferson carved on the main portal: "God forbid we should ever be twenty years without . . . a rebellion." Roosevelt approved: "I like the idea of planting Thomas Jefferson in Moscow," he wrote Bullitt, and even with the Depression he did not seem bothered by the cost, which was an estimated $1.25 million. Nor did anyone appear to be disturbed by the thought that a Monticello-like structure—architecturally a revival of classic Greek and Italian styles—would be quite impractical in Moscow, where heavy snow would put enormous stress on its flat roof. Bullitt hired a New York architect—he was Harrie T. Lindberg, who had designed homes for the Armours of Illinois, the Pillsburys of Minnesota, and the du Ponts of Delaware—who came to Moscow in May with blueprints and sketches.

Bullitt soon realized it was a long leap—in itself not insurmountable, though the Russians would make it so—between the planning and the building of a new embassy. First, it would be all but impossible, an engineering consultant advised, to establish a foundation in an area riddled by underground rivers and streams; second, an American inspector found fault with building methods in Russia: "Brick, mortar, and plaster are conveyed as they were 2,000 years ago," he said in his report. Lindberg discovered additional problems: there was "no seasoned lumber in Russia, no good mill work, no decent window glass, no rolled steel of standard sizes, no good metal work of any kind." Bullitt went ahead, nevertheless, and he submitted to the Soviet government a list of basic materials he wished to import from the United States: twelve hundred tons of cement, four hundred tons of lime, three thousand five hundred cubic meters of sand, five thousand cubic meters of gravel, and four million bricks. The answer was no: he would buy the materials from Russian suppliers and at the official exchange rate, which added up to price of $1.25 million, the entire estimate. Bullitt's request to bring in American foremen was denied as well, and in a last bit of red-tape strangulation he was ordered to seek authorization to clear the trees—for each tree, he was told, a permit would be required. Would the United States go ahead with its plan? Bullitt was being pressured in mid-1934 by Soviet officials, who had their eyes on the land as a campus for the University of Moscow, but he stood firm: Stalin had said he could have the land—Bullitt realized by this time that Stalin's promises, too, were not to be taken seriously—and he would have it. A year later, however, Bullitt did relent—the university eventually occupied the site—and he listed in his report to the State Department each of the instances of his inability to receive assurances of cooperation. "Therefore," he wrote, "the categorical refusal of the Soviet Government to give these written assurances renders the construction of the new Embassy in Moscow technically impossible." Spaso House was made the permanent residence of the ambassador, and the chancery would remain in the Mokhavaya Building, which was already beginning to crumble due to faulty construction.

Litvinov's insistence that only Russian workmen be hired for the construction of a U.S. embassy was for but one purpose, which Bullitt understood: eavesdropping devices would have been planted in the building, as they had been in Spaso House; it was apparent that the basement apartment of Sergei the caretaker, which was kept locked, was a listening post. Charlie Thayer, in his book, told of actually finding a microphone in a wall of Bullitt's office, and Chip Bohlen was so annoyed by the bugging that he eventually did something about it. "Years later, when I was ambassador and Sergei was still caretaker," Bohlen wrote, "I insisted on having a key. After a delay of several weeks, one was produced, but the apartment had been cleaned out. Sergei and his wife soon went into retirement." Bullitt was observed constantly by plainclothes police, and he was aware that every Russian he spoke to was a likely Soviet spy, yet he welcomed at the embassy those he found congenial—such as Karl Radek, the propagandist, who had become the editor of *Pravda*, and George Andreytchine, whom he had met in the United States when Andreytchine was working as an organizer for the Industrial Workers of the World. (Andreytchine, who grew up in Bulgaria, had attracted the attention of the king and was educated at court expense; he then pursued his ideals, despite the king's warning that he was on a path to destruction.)

Bullitt also entertained the dancers of the Moscow Ballet, who gave a private performance in return, and from then on, according to Bohlen, "there were usually two or three ballerinas running around the embassy." A prima ballerina, Lolya Lepishinkaya, fell in love with Bullitt, or so she said—she called him "her sun, her moon, and her stars," which amused the ambassador—and she was a regular guest at Spaso House in 1934. She was what Durbrow called a "tame Russian," one who had permission to socialize with the Americans: "We knew they were agents, reporting to the secret police, and they knew we knew." One evening after dinner Bullitt, Durbrow, Bohlen, and Thayer took Lepishinkaya for a boat ride on the Moscow River; as expected, they were being followed, so they decided to give the Soviet agents a run for it. "Chip had done a lot of rowing at Harvard," Durbrow explained, "and when we got to the boat, we rowed like hell. They were in another boat and were frantically trying to keep up, as it was their duty to follow the ambassador everywhere he went. I think we could have lost them, but we decided after a while to let them catch up." Bullitt was sympathetic with the detail assigned to watch him, for he had learned that police who allowed him to elude their surveillance were severely punished—stripped of their authority and probably sent to a work camp. He had taken Anne to a park for a picnic, and in what he believed was an innocent game of hide-and-seek he gave his followers the slip. A few weeks later, when Bullitt and Anne were walking in the same park, a Russian approached him and asked that they please not do it again. "You may notice," he said, "we are not the same police you ran away from."

"We are staggering along here," Bullitt wrote Judge Moore on June 14, 1934, "not only meeting disappointments in major matters but having to endure a thousand petty vexations each month. I fear that my telegrams must often give you the feeling that we are complaining unduly about conditions in Moscow, but I assure you that life is not easy. My own house, for example, still resembles the Grand Central Station more than a private residence." One of the "petty vexations" was a series of incidents involving the embassy first secretary: "It is quite true that he is drinking too much," Bullitt reported to Moore on July 13,

and from time to time he talks and acts wildly. About three weeks ago, . . . he became so wild that he . . . smashed his chauffeur in the eye, . . . knocking him to the pavement, and then proceeded to beat his Chinese servant. . . . The truth I think is this: he has run his own show for years, he was deeply disappointed by the living conditions he found in Moscow, and he found it intensely distressful to be subordinated to anyone else. He therefore started drinking too much. . . . He naturally desires when somewhat intoxicated to show that he is the real man in Moscow, and therefore belittles me as much as possible. I have tried to make him feel as important and independent as possible and have gone out of my way to be friendly, but without success.

Bullitt added that he would recommend a transfer but that his first secretary would probably apply for it himself, which he did the following November. Bullitt did not wish to replace his first secretary, as he explained to Moore, for there was no one he could depend on to take executive responsibility; and he was pointedly critical of his counselor, John Wiley. "Wiley has a most unusual character," Bullitt wrote Moore. "He has much political wisdom and an intimate knowledge of European affairs. Moreover, he can be counted upon during my absence to make no mistake of any kind. . . . On the other hand he is the most selfish man with whom I have ever worked and considers life purely from the point of view of his own ego. As a result, . . . I have learned . . . that I must control his decisions with great care. . . ." Bullitt was, for the moment at least, pleased with the performance of his third secretaries; Kennan, Bohlen, and Bertel T. Kuniholm, who all were "working admirably, and . . . we could run the embassy with the assistance of these three boys and no superior officers whatsoever."

There were other incidents, minor but irksome nevertheless. The six members of the Marine guard detail had little to keep them occupied, so they did as red-blooded young men are prone to do, which was okay by Bullitt except as it presented a security risk. Bohlen recalled that he was sitting in the lobby of the

Savoy Hotel one day when a "highly painted Russian woman" walked up to the desk and asked for a U.S. Marine sergeant by name; and when she was asked by the clerk the nature of her business with the sergeant, she replied brazenly, "I am his Russian teacher." (Bullitt considered sending the detail home—it would have been more a gesture of his annoyance with the Soviets than punishment of the Marines—but he thought better of it.) And then there was the memorable visit to Moscow of Evalyn Walsh McLean, the wife of Edward B. McLean, a former newspaper publisher—McLean had inherited *The Cincinnati Enquirer* and *The Washington Post* from his father—and a crony of Warren G. Harding's when Harding was president. Evalyn Walsh McLean, the heiress to a Colorado mining fortune, was among the wealthiest women in the world, and in 1910, on a trip to Paris with McLean shortly after their marriage, she purchased the Hope diamond for $154,000, then an enormous sum of money. When she came to Moscow in the summer of 1934, she had the diamond with her—or at least she said so—and she announced she intended to wear it in public as an act of capitalist defiance. In response to Bullitt's pleas, however—he had already assigned his toughest Marine guard to Mrs. McLean—she decided against it.

Bullitt's greatest pleasures in an otherwise dreary day-to-day existence were the excursions with his air attaché, Thomas White. "My first long flight in the airplane was highly successful," he said in the letter to Moore on June 14. "I visited Kharkov, Yalta, Odessa, and Kiev, and heard later . . . that the trip had made not only a profound impression throughout the Ukraine but also in the Kremlin. . . . Lieutenant White is not only an admirable aviator but also a delightful traveling companion." A week or so later, on a flight from Moscow to Leningrad to meet Anne—Anne Bullitt, age ten, was in school in the United States and was coming to spend the summer—there was a mishap, which Bullitt reported to the President on June 24: "Plane landed upside down but we emerged rightside up." On June 29 he described the accident in greater detail—he actually made it sound all the more harrowing by his matter-of-fact manner—to Judge Moore. "The plane accident was very terrifying to the people on the ground watching us alight," Bullitt wrote,

but I . . . was unable to get a single accelerated heartbeat out of it. The engine behaved as if the gasoline supply had been exhausted, but examination showed that there were thirty gallons left in the tank, and the only explanation either White or I can contrive is that the feed-pipe was stopped by dirty gasoline. . . . White made an extraordinarily skillful landing. We were just at the edge of a hummocky marsh cut across by deep ditches. He had to land between the ditches, on a tiny patch of marshy land, with only a hundred feet of altitude in which to maneuver. He did a quick side-slip, straightened the plane out and brought her down . . . in the marsh. The landing speed of the plane is about sixty miles an hour, and we had the good fortune to roll a short distance before the wheels got . . . caught in the marsh and we went over. The Soviet officials who were waiting to receive me got a magnificent scare. . . . They came racing across the marsh, falling on their noses, to pick out the dead man, but by the time they arrived we had loosed our belts and climbed out and received them as if we were quite in the habit of landing upside down.

Roosevelt did not regard the accident quite so lightly. "I am a little late in telling you," he wrote Bullitt on August 14, 1934, "but I was glad that you and Lieutenant White landed right side up in the plane. That was a very close call."

Tilting with Litvinov on the Debt

B ULLITT dealt with World War I debts from time to time throughout his diplomatic career—they had been the subject of his trip to Europe following Roosevelt's election in 1932, and the French debt to the United States, still owed in 1939, would hinder his efforts as ambassador to Paris to obtain aid for France in the war against Germany—but never would they be for him an issue so perplexing as in 1934, when the Russian debt to the United States was a topic of heated dispute. As far as the Department of State was concerned, it was *the* issue between the two governments—Soviet subversion would not be raised significantly until the following year—and in a volume of correspondence published by the department, *Foreign Relations of the United States: Soviet Union*, a section on 1934 contains an almost daily exchange of dispatches on debt negotiations.

The issue appeared to be cut-and-dried—it stemmed from claims of about $600 million in czarist bonds held by American citizens and in obligations of the Kerensky government—but it had become snagged on the ambiguous wording of the "gentleman's agreement" signed by Roosevelt and Litvinov on November 15, 1933. This document was crucial to the argument (it was the one not published in 1933, and its whereabouts in 1934 was a mystery, at least to Bullitt: "I have no copy here," he wrote Moore on June 19), because the Russians were insisting on a literal interpretation: ". . . the Soviet Government will pay . . . a sum to be not less than $75,000,000 in the form of a percentage above the ordinary rate of interest on a loan to be granted to it by the Government of the United States. . . ." Roosevelt's casual attitude had been that the financial details would fall into place, as Bullitt explained in a dispatch to the State Department on July 17, advising that he and the president had discussed whether to hold up recognition until the debt issue had been settled: "The President felt that this was not necessary, as he thought his understanding with Litvinov was clear, and . . . as a result of changes of personnel at the Treasury Department"—he was referring to the appointment of Henry Morgenthau as secretary of the treasury—"it was somewhat difficult for us to go into details on any financial matters." Litvinov had demanded, however, that the United States make a "straight cash loan" to the U.S.S.R., as Moore put it in a department memorandum on July 19, or as an alternative "uncontrolled credit, enabling it to make purchases in this country at will." Roosevelt, once aware of the implications of such an arrangement—for one, it would have allowed the Russians to procure war materials from American manufacturers—had ruled it out absolutely, while probably realizing the validity of Litvinov's point.

As if the president's decision was not enough to place Bullitt in an inflexible bargaining position, the Johnson bill had been passed by Congress in April—introduced by Senator Hiram Johnson of California, it prohibited loans to any government in debt default to the United States—and the newly formed Export-Import Bank controlled credit granted the Soviet government for purchases in the U.S.; the bank had resolved that transactions with the Soviet Union would be deferred pending settlement of the debt. "There was a complete breakdown of the negotiations at Moscow," Judge Moore wrote in his memorandum of July 19.

On March 21, 1934, as he had advised the State Department, Bullitt was unequivocal in announcing to Litvinov Roosevelt's decision: there would be no loan. "I added," he wrote, "that if his position should be unalterable, I should wish to cable the President immediately so that the Export-Import Bank might be liquidated at once and all thought of trade with the Soviet Union abandoned." Bullitt was not merely bluffing—he added quickly that he hoped friendly relations would continue in the absence of trade—although he did not expect Litvinov would break off the debt talks. He was relying on a hopeful hunch: at moments when he would have been forgiven for a feeling of despair, Bullitt had an ability to be optimistic—his critics viewed it as a tendency to blow hot and cold, to shift abruptly from high expectation to dejection—and he still held to the opinion, at least occasionally, that Litvinov could be persuaded. "Previous negotiations with Litvinov," he wrote on March 21, "have led me to observe that his decisive negations are often followed by acquiescence, and I do not consider the present problem insoluble." Even in May, when Bullitt was fully aware of the fundamental differences of the two governments, he was predicting that they would bridge "the big water jump," as he called it in a letter to Moore on May 4: "My guess is that . . . we shall be able to get Litvinov to offer at least a hundred million dollars . . . with a basic interest rate of five per cent and an additional interest rate of five per cent." Bullitt's hopes were hinged significantly on the influence of the military and its fear of an invasion by Japan, and he was speaking

directly with Marshal Voroshilov, the defense commander. Voroshilov was press-
ing him on the 250,000 tons of steel rails for the railroad to Vladivostok, which
Stalin had requested urgently in December, and Bullitt had replied that delivery
of the rails would depend on a debt settlement. "The nub of the matter is this,"
he cabled on May 21. "If the Soviet Government should again become convinced
that an attack by Japan was likely, . . . we should probably find Litvinov willing
to reach an agreement on the basis of our proposals." Bullitt had made a misjudgment, however, as he realized in June: "Litvinov apparently feels . . . that Japan
will not attack," he reported, "and that the United States, no matter how the
Soviet Union behaves, will attempt to prevent war between the Soviet Union and
Japan and will support the Soviet Union in case of war."

The U.S. proposal, which had been presented in February to Alexander
Troyanovsky, the Soviet ambassador in Washington, set the debt at $150 million;
it called for an interest rate of 5 percent a year and an additional 10 percent for the
purpose of reducing the principal; and it was stipulated that credits would be
tightly controlled by the Export-Import Bank. On April 2 Litvinov handed Bullitt
a counteroffer, which had been approved by the People's Council of Commissars:
a twenty-year line of credit would be extended by the Export-Import Bank, "to
be drawn upon by the Soviet Union . . . to pay for purchases made in the United
States"; the credit would come to double the amount of a war claims settlement—
$200 million, hypothetically, on a settlement of $100 million; and interest on the
credit would be 4 percent annually with an additional 3 percent, beginning in the
fifth year, to liquidate the debt. The response from Washington was quick and
blunt: the Soviet offer was "wholly unacceptable," Hull cabled Bullitt on April
5. "It substitutes for a loan, which the President heretofore declined to consider,
a credit, which is the equivalent of a loan. . . . Were the credit extended and
the other details of the proposal approved, the indebtedness . . . at the end of the
twenty-year period would . . . be about twice what it was at the beginning of the
period."

On April 8, 1934, Bullitt wrote to Washington:

I had a completely unsatisfactory discussion with Litvinov this afternoon. He was
angry and adamant. He refused to take the State Department draft as a basis of discussion,
. . . alleging that it was in absolute contravention of his understanding with the President.
I replied that our belief . . . was that it was in accordance with his understanding with the
President. He said . . . that the State Department contemplated not a loan or a credit but a
taxation on Soviet trade. . . .

He asked me what reply the Department had made to his proposal. I told him that his
proposal was entirely unacceptable even as a basis of discussion and asked him if he had
anything to add to it. He said he had nothing to add. . . .

I asked Litvinov if he had considered the consequences of his attitude, pointing out that the credit markets of the United States would be open to nations not in default and would remain closed to the Soviet Union until an agreement had been reached. He said he was fully aware of this and was not disturbed. He added that the Johnson bill presumably applied to England, France, and Italy, as well as the Soviet Union, and said, "We shall be in very good company."

Troyanovsky met on April 30 with Roosevelt, who sensed that the ambassador was attempting to transfer the debt debate to Washington, and FDR rejected the idea brusquely. "The President made it very clear . . .," Judge Moore reported to Bullitt, "that the best course is . . . to let the representatives of both Governments in Moscow understand the desirability for them to proceed. . . ." Roosevelt was opposed to moving the negotiations to Washington mainly because Bullitt and Litvinov had been principal participants in the discussions that led to a resumption of relations. (In July, after negotiations in Moscow had reached an impasse, Moore did begin meetings with Troyanovsky, but they were concluded in disagreement over the Soviet demand for a loan or credit, and Moore wrote Bullitt: "We can only for the present let the matter ride.") Roosevelt did, however, argue a few specific points with Troyanovsky: he reminded the ambassador, for example, that the amount the U.S. was proposing, $150 million, had been reduced by devaluation of the dollar to about $90 million. Troyanovsky raised the possibility of counter-claims by his government, since American forces had fought against the Bolsheviks at Archangel and Murmansk in 1918 and 1919. "If the U.S.S.R. asserted counter-claims," Roosevelt replied, smiling—he knew that Troyanovsky had been the Russian ambassador to Tokyo and would understand he was not joking—the U.S. would do likewise, for "our troops in Russia saved Siberia from being taken over by the Japanese."

Bullitt was somewhat bothered by the report from Moore, for it indicated that Roosevelt was still not giving serious attention to the problem: "Was the basic disagreement touched upon in the President's conversation with Troyanovsky?" he asked in a cable to the State Department on May 2. "Did Troyanovsky indicate that Litvinov was prepared to negotiate on the basis of the Department's draft agreement? If not, did the President state that he felt that Litvinov had agreed to negotiate on that basis?" "The answer to each of your three questions," he was told the following day in a message signed by Hull, "is in the negative."

Bullitt was authorized by Hull on May 11 to decrease the debt demand to $125 million but ordered not to accept $100 million before clearing it with the department. Hull also explained the U.S. stand on credit and why a twenty-year line was out of the question: each transaction must be liquidated in "not more than five years," he wrote, "as this would have the effect of creating a revolving fund that would place the bank in a position to . . . engage in transactions probably totaling several times the amount of debt." The U.S. government would grant credit to the Soviet government, which through its New York trading company, Amtorg, would do business with American exporters; and the Export-Import Bank would assist in financing Soviet purchases by discounting Amtorg acceptances received by American exporters "in connection with specific transactions approved by the Bank and for that part of the credit . . . the exporter would not be expected itself to carry." Hull added that the Export-Import Bank "must reserve its right to approve any and all transactions, since otherwise it would be placing the business of this country with the Soviet Union under the control and direction of the Soviet Government."

In Litvinov's absence in May 1934—Litvinov was spending a month on the French Riviera—Bullitt made a bold assumption, which if accurate, might well have been the basis for resolution of the debt issue. It was that the foreign commissar, in his insistence on a twenty-year credit, was acting on his own—that is, in defiance of Stalin, whose authority as secretary general of the Communist Party was absolute—and that agreement could be reached by outmaneuvering Litvinov. "I have direct information from the Kremlin," Bullitt cabled on June 15—Litvinov was due back in Moscow the next day—"that Stalin recently ordered everyone in the Soviet Government to be extremely cordial to the American Embassy and feel that the cooperation of the United States is not a thing to throw away lightly."

On June 16, 1934, Bullitt wrote to Washington:

I have just spent a most unsatisfactory hour with Litvinov. He began by refusing in the most categorical manner to alter his position on payment of indebtedness. I told him I thought it was our duty to attempt to overcome the "misunderstanding." . . . He replied, "There is no misunderstanding" and asserted that the Government of the United States was attempting to back out of the agreement. . . .

We had a long argument, . . . the upshot of which was that Litvinov said that he and his Government were entirely ready to let the matter drop immediately and permanently, . . . that the agreement was clear and the Soviet Government would not change its position. I told him that I felt this attitude . . . might terminate any possibility of close collaboration between our nations. He replied, "I do not take the matter so tragically. No nation today pays its debts. . . . And no one will be able to make propaganda against the Soviet Union if we do not pay one dollar on a debt we did not contract."

On July 9 Litvinov offered an explanation of his government's position, which Bullitt would find fairly reasonable: "The claims against the Soviet Union of England, France, Germany, and various other nations are far larger," he reminded Bullitt, than the U.S. claim. "Those claims have now been shelved and forgotten, but the moment we make any settlement with the United States all other nations will demand immediate settlements." So it was necessary for the settlement with the United States to be one that no other nation could accept, such as the proposed loan: it would be impossible, said Litvinov, "for . . . the British, French, or Germans to lend us double the amount of their claims." While he accepted Litvinov's obvious logic, Bullitt preferred to be noncommittal—he wished to "fertilize his disquiet," as he wrote in his report—for he sensed an ulterior motive for the sudden softening of Litvinov's approach and he was right: fear of a Japanese invasion of Russia was again a factor. Had the State Department officially announced, Litvinov wanted to know, that the U.S. had refused a bilateral nonaggression agreement with the U.S.S.R.? Again Bullitt was noncommittal: "I intimated that our relations with Japan showed improvement," Bullitt advised, "and asked him if there had been a great improvement recently in the relations of the Soviet Union with Japan. He laughed and replied, 'The only improvement is that we are not yet at war.' "

On September 13, 1934, Bullitt wrote to Washington, "I venture to suggest that we should exercise whatever ingenuity we may possess in attempting to devise a basis of settlement, which while acceptable to us could not be acceptable to France, Great Britain and other claimants."

Bullitt had not been persuaded by Litvinov but by Boris Skvirsky, with whom he had negotiated a basis for recognition of the Soviet Union and who had become the counselor of the Soviet embassy in Washington. Skvirsky was on leave in Moscow in September when he visited the U.S. embassy, "obviously under orders from the Foreign Office," Bullitt noted, and he explained "the exact point of view of the Soviet Government with regard to debts and claims." The point was no different from the one stressed by Litvinov in July, but Bullitt seemed more willing to accept it: no deal that would incite a revival of claims by Britain, France, Germany, or other claimants was acceptable, said Skvirsky. "He argued," Bullitt reported, "that the payment of extra interest on credits from American exporters, even though the Government should carry a large part of the credit risk, would produce immediate revival of the claims of the other nations." On September 15 Bullitt cabled that the same argument had been put to him by Evgeny V. Rubinin, an assistant commissar for foreign affairs, who said further that "the French had recently attempted to revive discussion of their claims . . . and that the Soviet Union had refused flatly to discuss the matter." Secretary of State Hull, however, was not inclined to accommodate the Soviet logic: "Considering that Litvinov when here made no objection to added or extra interest feature," he cabled Bullitt on September 17, "and further that we are not responsible for the Soviet's relations with England and France, it would seem now obligatory on the Soviet to propose some plan that may conceivably be acceptable, but of course not including a loan or an open credit."

In the summer of 1934—it was for Bullitt a period of unusual, if superficial, rapport between him and the Kremlin leaders—the ambassador decided to try to deal with the Russians on horseback, rather than at the bargaining table. "Litvinov lunched with me yesterday . . . and accompanied me to the first polo match ever played in the Soviet Union . . .," he told Washington on July 27. Polo, a game of aristocrats, was all Bullitt's idea, although he enlisted his fellow Philadelphian and embassy aide, Charlie Thayer—Thayer had played on the polo team when he was a cadet at West Point—to handle the details. "I had personally imported the necessary equipment and taught the Red Army cavalrymen how to play," Bullitt advised. (It might not have been all that wise for Bullitt to introduce American games to the Soviets—before polo it was baseball, and Bullitt played first base and hit a home run for the winning team—for as Louis Fischer mentioned in his book, *Men and Politics*, he came to be regarded by Litvinov and others as not serious, even though he was extremely hard-working.) Thayer, in his book, described "the first experiment in Soviet polo":

> . . . a crack cavalry regiment . . . had been selected, and twenty of its best horsemen were detailed for the course. . . . They watched as we demonstrated the various strokes. . . . After a while they were each given a ball and a mallet and allowed to try for themselves. They were all superb horsemen; before very long, polo balls were flying in all directions. After one ball had hit him sharply on the shin, the Ambassador decided they had practiced enough. He sorted them into groups of ten. Then he pointed to a church steeple . . . and told one group to hit in that general direction. To the other group he indicated a factory chimney. . . . He went on to explain a few of the rules of the game and told them that when he blew the whistle the game was over. . . . He tossed the ball between the two teams, and the fun began. . . . For several minutes the scuffle continued; then the ball popped out of the melee, and all twenty horsemen went into mad pursuit. . . . At first the Ambassador galloped along beside the mob warning them of fouls, but it soon was obvious that no one was paying attention to anything but the ball. . . . "That was a foul," I said to the Ambassador. . . . "Foul, hell," said the Ambassador. "That was murder."

Bullitt was still persuaded that Litvinov was out of step with Stalin, or possibly he was deceiving Stalin by withholding crucial details of the debt negotiations. To understand how wrong Bullitt was, it is helpful to look ahead, into the career of Maxim Litvinov from 1934 forward, beginning with the Stalin purges. Litvinov fully expected to be shot, as were many senior Soviet officials, including his two assistants, Lev Karakhan and Nikolay Krestinsky; but he would live to be seventy-five. He was replaced as foreign commissar by Vyacheslav Molotov in 1939 and sent as ambassador to Washington in 1941. There was speculation that Litvinov survived because Stalin was grateful for his early support, but this was disputed by Roy Medvedev, a respected Soviet historian. "Stalin was not sincere," wrote Medvedev. "Gratitude was never one of his characteristics, but he realized he needed Litvinov . . . as a diplomat. Litvinov could not be easily replaced," although he probably would have been, had he been as treacherous as Bullitt believed him to be.

After the polo match Marshal Voroshilov and an aide returned with Bullitt to Spaso House, "where they remained until the early hours of the morning," Bullitt wrote in his July 27 report to Washington. "In the course of a very long and intimate conversation with Voroshilov I found, as I had suspected, that Litvinov had not given Stalin and Voroshilov an altogether accurate version of our discussions with regard to claims and indebtedness. . . . I feel sure that Voroshilov will use his influence with Stalin, which is very great, to soften Litvinov's obduracy." Bullitt was overlooking the fact that Voroshilov was not highly esteemed as an intellect and probably had little effect as a foreign policy adviser to Stalin.

Bullitt then turned to his friend Karl Radek, the editor of *Pravda* (Radek, originally a follower of Trotsky, was later convicted of treason, and he died in prison), who urged him to have a talk with Stalin and ventured the opinion, as Bullitt reported on September 9, that "Stalin would not support Litvinov's refusal to settle on the basis of participation by the Export-Import Bank in credits extended by American exporters." Radek offered to intercede in the matter when he visited Stalin, who was on vacation in the Caucasus, Bullitt wrote, "and if I should have word from him that Stalin would like to talk . . . personally, it might be advisable for me to make an airplane tour of the Caucasus and drop in casually on the boss." There would be no dropping in on the Red ruler, however, for Radek told Bullitt on September 15 that he had read the file on debts and credits, and "insofar as he could judge, Litvinov had reported the facts . . . without noteworthy distortions. . . . Radek added that Stalin's position was so clear that he believed the present moment was one to be employed in working out a new formula which though satisfactory to us would be unacceptable to France and England." Stalin had agreed, Radek advised Bullitt, that it was important in the interest of peace in the Far East to remove all obstacles to close cooperation with the United States, but it was more important for the moment to be on amiable terms with Britain and France. If an agreement was reached to meet the claims of the United States by paying extra interest on commercial credits, Stalin had declared, a similar agreement with Britain and France could not be refused "without greatly angering them and jeopardizing the relationship of the Soviet Union with them."

Hull was observing the Moscow scene with detached interest, perhaps even satisfaction, as his feathers were still ruffled for not having been consulted on restoring relations with Russia. "There can be no objection to your talking with

Stalin," he cabled Bullitt on September 15. "Personally I have little idea that the Soviet officials will come to any reasonable agreement. Litvinov won his victory when he obtained recognition, and he regards everything else as of minor importance." Only Roosevelt shared what little optimism Bullitt could still summon. Asked at a press conference on September 26, 1934, if he had been disappointed by what had transpired in Moscow, the president replied, "Oh, it will be worked out some way."

October 10, 1934, Bullitt wrote to Washington:

I then got up to leave, and Litvinov said that he had something . . . to say to me before my departure. He then embarked upon a series of declarations . . . obviously intended to impress me with the determination of the Soviet Government to make no concessions whatever. . . . He alleged that he had heard that officials of the Department of State were spreading the report that he had broken his agreement with the President. He said that his position was that the President had broken the agreement. A discussion then followed in which I thought it advisable to preserve equanimity but which became extremely acrimonious on the part of Litvinov. He finally grew purple and said that if there was any more talk of this sort, he would publish the memorandum of his conversation with the President. I replied that it was obvious that he had no wish for friendly relations with the United States. . . .

I called his attention to the fact that a loan was impossible. . . . He replied that the Soviet Government had no desire even for a loan except at a very low interest rate; that it desired to let the matter drop; that if the question of payment of debts and claims were settled in any way whatsoever he would have grave difficulties in his relations with England and France. . . .

Bullitt left Moscow on October 10, the first year of his ambassadorship at an end on a decidedly less than hopeful note: if not a shambles, relations between the U.S. and the U.S.S.R. were in a state of dire strain, of which the personal animosity between Bullitt and Litvinov was both a symptom and a symbol. Had it not been the dispute over the debt settlement, there would have been—and would be in time—other reasons for dissonance: the two nations were destined not to get along, owing to ideological and geopolitical conflict.

There is often a temptation to explain world tensions—it is seldom justified—as a dramatic contest of wills between individuals; but in the case of Bullitt and Litvinov it *was* an elemental factor: an American idealist to whom life, even if tragic, was a ballet to be enjoyed; and a Bolshevik cynic, who viewed his existence as a constant struggle for survival. Litvinov slept with a loaded pistol at his bedside, preferring death to prison, if he were to be a victim of the purges, which began on December 1, 1934. That day Sergei M. Kirov, the Communist first secretary in Leningrad—although apparently loyal to Stalin, Kirov was considered a rival of the secretary general—was shot and killed; and while the assassin was immediately arrested, it was clear he had not acted on his own. The official Soviet verdict was that Trotsky, in exile in France, was behind the murder, although a feeling lingered that Stalin had ordered it: "Kirov's growing popularity and influence could not to fail to arouse Stalin's envy and suspicion . . .," Roy Medvedev wrote. In an official history of the Soviet Union, published in 1962 during the period of de-Stalinization, there is but one reference to the killing of Kirov: "Stalin seized upon it to begin dealing summarily with people who did not suit him."

Home via Japan and China

ACCOMPANIED by his personal secretary, Carmel Offie, Bullitt returned to the United States by way of the Far East: it was a multipurpose intelligence mission, which Bullitt and Roosevelt had planned together. His assignment was to assess the Japanese threat to Russia and the rest of the region, although China was of equivalent if not greater interest—1934 was the year of the Long March to Yenan by the Chinese Communists, led by Mao Tse-tung—and Bullitt's visits to Shanghai and Nanking were as illuminating as his stop in Tokyo. First, though, there was a long journey by train to Vladivostok—recalling Stalin's plea for steel rails, Bullitt noted that the second track of the Trans-Siberian Railroad did not extend beyond a point well short of Vladivostok—much of which was spent putting up with lice. When he arrived in Tokyo on October 23, Bullitt was ill with a streptococcus infection, and Ambassador Joseph C. Grew—the same Joseph Grew to whom Bullitt reported when he first worked at the State Department in 1918—had him housed in the quarters of J. Graham Parsons, a junior embassy officer, who wrote in his diary that Bullitt received two "get-well" cables from Roosevelt. "My first impression of Bullitt," Parsons added, "was tremendously favorable—young, good looking, a born diplomat, . . . and very much the gentleman." Parsons also recorded an observation of his Japanese housekeeper, who was somewhat astounded by Bullitt's alcohol capacity, which by American standards was not unusual. "I asked Tomi-san how Mr. Bullitt was," Parsons wrote on October 29, "and she said very well indeed. 'He drinks all the time, cocktails every day, . . . and the other day he and Mr. Offie drank a whole big bottle of champagne in one meal.' . . . I told her Bullitt was a great friend of President Roosevelt, which thrilled her."

Bullitt was not too sick to do his job: he met with the Soviet ambassador to Japan, Constantin Yurenev, who cautioned him, prophetically, not to underestimate the quality of the Japanese Navy; in Shanghai he conferred with several Chinese officials, including T. V. Soong, the Harvard-educated economist who ranked second in the government to his brother-in-law, Chiang Kai-shek; and in Nanking he talked at length with the Generalissimo himself, as Madame Chiang acted as interpreter. He left Nanking on November 23; on December 2 he and Offie departed by ship for the final leg of the trip, across the Pacific, with Bullitt feeling worse than ever physically, the infection having lodged in his jaw.

On December 14 Bullitt gave Roosevelt a detailed report of his meetings with Chiang Kai-shek, the main topics of which had been Chinese-Russian relations and the danger of Japanese aggression. Cooperation with the Soviet Union had been hindered, said Chiang, by Soviet support of the Communist movement in China; as for the Japanese threat, Chiang had only to point to the invasion of Manchuria as evidence that it existed, and he assured Bullitt that Japanese moves into Mongolia or North China would provoke a declaration of war. (War between China and Japan was declared in 1937.) For the moment, however, Bullitt was more concerned with an impending economic crisis in China—for a man so detached from money matters personally, Bullitt had a sound knowledge of international economics—which he discussed by telephone with Secretary of the Treasury Morgenthau on December 21. Bullitt said he had talked with ten or fifteen people he had known for years—that Bullitt had that many contacts in China was in itself extraordinary and useful—and one of them, the director of the Bank of China, had expressed to him a position that was disturbing:

He said that the foreign banks in Shanghai and throughout China were withdrawing from all commitments, . . . throwing an unprecedented strain on the Chinese banks; that the flow of silver out of the country was beginning to make everyone extremely nervous—that there was already a flight of capital from the country, and it was impossible to say when a panic might start.

Bullitt told Morgenthau he had suggested a remedy: "I said that . . . it might be advisable to have one man come unofficially and . . . explain the situation. . . ." Morgenthau replied, "Well, I've asked for one man from the Central Bank of China." "Well, that's interesting," said Bullitt. "That's a coincidence of a great mind." Morgenthau asked to what extent Roosevelt was aware of the situation. "I wish I could remember accurately," Bullitt answered—he obviously relished being asked by a cabinet member what the president was thinking. "I talked to him so much about so many different things that I don't remember to what extent I've had a chance to emphasize this particular one."

———————

Bullitt had lunch in Washington on January 30, 1935, with Ambassador Troyanovsky, who raised the question of claims and credits, and Bullitt said there would be an opportunity to discuss the subject with Secretary of State Hull the following day. "He laughed nervously and said that he was afraid to discuss the question with the Secretary of State," Bullitt reported,

> that he feared their conversation might result disastrously, that it might end the possibility of close friendship between the Soviet Union and the United States. He said, "Could I not, instead of going to the Department of State, just have a private conversation with you here?" I replied that private conversations with me were absolutely out of the question and that he would have to come to the Department of State and take the consequences of Litvinov's policy.

The Russian ambassador did meet with Hull, who cabled John Wiley, the chargé d'affaires in Moscow, on January 31: "Troyanovsky this afternoon rejected my proposal . . . for settlement of the question of debts, claims, and credits and made no new proposal. I am issuing a statement for publication . . . this evening. . . . It is anticipated that the Export-Import Bank will be abolished immediately, that the Naval and Air Attachés will be withdrawn. . . ."

Hull also advised Wiley of Bullitt's plans. "The Ambassador will return to Moscow as soon as he has recovered from his present illness, which is not a diplomatic invention but a streptococcus infection." The Export-Import Bank was not abolished, but the air and naval attachés, Lieutenant White and Captain David R. Nimmer, were relieved, having been ordered to inform Marshal Voroshilov that unnecessary obstacles to the development of Soviet-American friendship had been created by Litvinov. The falling out was the subject of newspaper headlines the world over, and editorial writers tended to agree that Litvinov had behaved shabbily, although the U.S. government was not absolved altogether. *The New York Times*, for example, suggested that the Soviets had simply sat back, going through the motions of negotiations, while "laughing in their sleeves at American simplicity." John Wiley reported that Litvinov had shown Walter Duranty of the *Times* a copy of the memorandum "initialed by the President relative to settlement of debts and claims," the so-called gentleman's agreement, but the foreign commissar had "rejected Duranty's suggestion to permit publication of memorandum. . . ." Wiley also advised that Karl Radek of *Pravda* and Yakov Doletski, the chief of the Soviet news service, Tass, had agreed to refrain from placing blame on the United States; however, the Soviet press, said Wiley, "is almost daily quoting American newspaper articles criticizing American Government and officials." *Isvestia* had quoted an editorial in *The New York Post*, attributing the failure of negotiations to an anti-Soviet stance at the State Department, and one in *The Baltimore Sun* in which the U.S. government was accused of "acting like a spoiled child."

Finally, Wiley told of a meeting at the foreign office. "Litvinov said that he had long since accepted the rupture of the negotiations for a settlement of debts and claims as a foregone conclusion . . .," he cabled Washington on February 5. "He claimed that when the American government decided to abandon the 'letter of the agreement,' namely a loan, he had 'capitulated' just as far as possible. . . ." The foreign commissar "gave no indication of perturbation," Wiley reported: "Indeed, Mr. Litvinov calmly stated that he thought it was a good thing for the negotiations to be 'put on ice' for a while. . . ."

Moscow, 1935: The Year of the Comintern

BULLITT passed through Paris on his way to Moscow in April 1935, and he was at pains not to encroach on the realm of Jesse Straus, the ambassador to France, even though the foreign minister, Pierre Laval, had asked that they meet. "I have carefully avoided going to the Quai d'Orsay," Bullitt wrote Judge Moore on April 7—the foreign ministry was often referred to as the quay on the Left Bank of the Seine, where it was located—"and have regretted three times suggestions that Monsieur Laval wished to see me, as I have not wished to trespass on Jesse's preserves. Apparently as Laval is coming to Moscow the end of the month"—Laval was coming to discuss a mutual assistance pact with Stalin and Litvinov—"he wants to ask me some questions about the Soviet Union, and I suppose I may be leaning over backwards in discouraging the idea, . . . but I feel acutely that traveling ambassadors should not make a nuisance of themselves by seeing the highest government officials." Bullitt could still observe, however— his skill as a journalist was an asset throughout his diplomatic career—and there were midrank officials who were quite candid; so Bullitt was able to send Moore a detailed report, albeit a disturbing one. "I have never known a more disagreeable atmosphere in Paris," he wrote.

The German rearmament is throwing into pretended friendships men and nations who cordially distrust and detest each other. . . . Europe is superficially . . . united by fear of Germany. . . . There is a small group in France that believes this temporary cohesion should be taken advantage of and that France should move actively against Germany; but the French people have never been more completely pacifist than they are today, and any aggressive action by France is out of the question.

Bullitt predicted that a Franco-Russian alliance, under the aegis of the League of Nations, would be arranged, even though "Laval distrusts and dislikes the Russians and is wriggling as hard as he can . . .," and "Flandin, I am told"—Pierre-Étienne Flandin was the French premier in 1935—"is opposed to the Pact and would be ready to allow Germany to carry out any aggressive designs she may have in the East." Bullitt explained to Moore what he expected to be the provisions of the pact: in the event of German aggression against either nation—and following a decision at the League of Nations that Germany was the aggressor—France or the Soviet Union, whichever had not been attacked, would place its armed forces at the disposal of the other. Bullitt reflected the attitude of his friends in France, who

have no illusions about the Russians and do not expect any real help from the Soviet Union. If they make the alliance, they will make it merely because they are afraid that, if they do not, the Soviet Government will turn to Germany. . . . My own feeling is that the Soviet Government will make the mutual assistance pact with the French and then begin to flirt with Germany . . . and succeed in getting Germany and France bidding against one another for Soviet support. . . . Thank God we are standing aloof. We can do absolutely nothing to help. Any action of ours would, I believe, merely tend to make it certain that we would be involved . . . in the conflict which is coming. . . . The present nationalist movement in Germany has, in my opinion, been inevitable since the terms of the Treaty of Versailles were imposed. Only a nation without courage could have endured that Treaty, and the Germans, whatever their other shortcomings, have courage.

Bullitt did meet with Foreign Minister Laval, as he informed the president on April 8:

It was indeed Laval who phoned last night, and I saw him this morning. I reported at once to Jesse Straus, and you will unquestionably have seen the telegram which Jesse dictated. . . . Laval said he would reach Moscow on the 25th and would sign the mutual assistance pact. . . . [The Franco-Soviet alliance was signed in Moscow on May 2, 1935.] He then asked me what policy I thought the Russians would follow. . . . I replied that the Russians would doubtless . . . attempt to develop close relations with Germany. He said that he thought the agreement would place the Soviet Union in a very favorable position.

. . . My own opinion is that the Soviet Union will be the single great beneficiary of the agreement. . . . It is obvious, of course, from all these maneuvers and counter maneuvers that no one in Europe is any longer thinking of peace but that everyone is thinking furiously about obtaining as many allies as possible for the next war.

Litvinov, when he conferred with Bullitt in mid-May, was thoroughly pleased about his meetings with Laval, which in his view "had done much to start Franco-Soviet collaboration in a friendly atmosphere." Unable to resist one final try on a well-worn question, Bullitt asked if the subject of czarist debts to France had come up, which angered the foreign commissar. "Exactly the opposite is true," Litvinov asserted. "Stalin flatly refused to discuss the matter," as he had with Anthony Eden of Great Britain (the foreign secretary as of October 1935). "Litvinov then said," Bullitt reported,

> that while . . . not averse to reopening the question, . . . he could see no point in . . . it unless there was some possibility of agreement. He added that as the difference between our Governments was one of principle—that the Soviet Government insisted on a loan and we refused to give a loan—he felt that . . . the difficulties were insurmountable.

Back in Moscow Bullitt scrutinized the work of John Wiley, who, he allowed, had been "a dignified and imperturbable chief of mission" during his extended absence. "However, he does only an irreducible minimum of work," Bullitt wrote Moore on April 25—it was not a private communication, but written on embassy letterhead and addressed to R. Walton Moore, assistant secretary of state—

> and his laziness, selfishness and snobbery have had a most unfortunate effect on some of the youths on the staff. He has adopted a little clique of those whom he considers gentlemen and has made those outside this royal family feel comparative outcasts. Those he favors with his friendship are Bohlen, Durbrow and Thayer. . . . His general attitude may be illustrated by the fact that on my arrival he informed me that he considered it highly improper for me to invite any of the clerks or their wives to the ball I gave on the 23rd of the month, with the single exception of Thayer. There is, as you know, nothing that moves me to greater anger than snobbery. . . . In a word Wiley has great talents and great defects. When I am in Moscow he is almost entirely useless. When I am not in Moscow he is perhaps more distinguished than the Russians deserve.

Wiley soon was transferred to the legation in Antwerp.

The ball mentioned in the letter to Moore was a memorable social event, and although it was too extravagant for some proletarian tastes—Ivy Litvinov, the wife of the foreign minister, was disgusted and stayed but a short while—Bullitt reported to Roosevelt on May 1, 1935, it had been "an astonishingly successful party, thoroughly dignified yet gay. . . . In fact," Bullitt boasted, "it was the best party in Moscow since the Revolution. We got a thousand tulips from Helsingfors [Helsinki] and forced a lot of birch trees into premature leafage and arranged one end of the dining room as a collective farm with peasant accordion players, dancers, and all sorts of baby things, such as birds, goats, and a couple of infant bears. . . ."

The ball had been scheduled for months, and when Bullitt left Moscow in October, he told Charlie Thayer, whom he had put in charge of it, "The sky's the limit, just so long as it's good and different." Thayer took the ambassador at his word—the bill came to over $7,000, which Bullit paid personally—and planned a spectacular "spring festival," the theme having been the idea of Irena Wiley, the counselor's wife. She was also the one who insisted on live animals— mountain goats, white roosters, one hundred zebra finches, and the baby bears— all borrowed from the Moscow zoo. As Thayer in his book, *Bears in the Caviar*, described the scene at Spaso House, the animals caused the sort of trouble that might have been anticipated: a rooster kicked out the bottom of its cage and flew into a platter of pâté de foie gras; the finches escaped through the mesh of a fish net that contained them (Thayer first glimpsed the ambassador that evening, on his hands and knees in white tie and tails, trying to catch a landed bird); and one of the bears, having been fed champagne by Karl Radek, vomited on the dress uniform of General Yegorov, the chief of staff.

There were an estimated five hundred guests at the embassy, including all of the top Soviet leaders except Stalin, some of whom would survive the purges (Litvinov and Voroshilov) and some who would not (Radek and Yegorov). The party lasted through the night, and the final scene of Thayer's account was at nine in the morning: Marshal Mikhail Tukhachevsky, the commissar for defense, was doing a Georgian dance with Lolya Lepishinkaya, the ballerina. "It was," Thayer wrote of the man they called the "Red Napoleon"—Tukhachevsky was given credit for having modernized the Red Army—"[his] last appearance in the Embassy before he was shot."

"The Russians still dare to come to my house for large entertainments when there can be no possibility of private conversation," Bullitt wrote Roosevelt, referring to the ball on April 23. "The terror . . . has risen to such a pitch," he explained, "that the least of the Muscovites, as well as the greatest, is in fear. Almost no one dares have any contact with foreigners, and this is not unbased fear but a proper sense of reality. . . . The only real friend of this Embassy, George Andreytchine, . . . is in Lyublianka prison awaiting either death or exile,

. . ." (Andreytchine had served for a time as a secretary to Trotsky—it was this association that marked him as a purge victim—and he had been arrested in the United States for union organizing activities. Sentenced in 1918 to the federal penitentiary at Fort Leavenworth, Kansas, he was released on bail, pending appeal; his twenty-year term was upheld by the Supreme Court in 1921, whereupon he jumped bail and fled to Russia. In 1934 Andreytchine was appointed the Soviet liaison officer to the U.S. embassy, and Bullitt requested a presidential pardon for him, which Roosevelt denied, saying: "Sorry we cannot accommodate him for the moment!") He had been arrested by the secret police in January 1935: "I can, of course, do nothing to save anyone," Bullitt wrote Roosevelt. "In fact, strictly between ourselves, I got a message from Andreytchine, sent by grapevine [it had been written on toilet paper and slipped under his door], . . . asking me for God's sake to do nothing to try to save him, . . . [as] he would certainly be shot." George Andreytchine was not shot, but he later died in a prison in Bulgaria; and his successor in the liaison job, Boris Steiger—Steiger, according to Thayer, was "a cultured man of Baltic background with an excellent sense of humor and a fund of stories"—was arrested and sent before a firing squad.

Bullitt's health was still a cause for concern: Carmel Offie wrote to Judge Moore on May 11 that the ambassador was "not at all well, but as long as he gets plenty of rest he manages to go through his regular work"; Offie revealed that Bullitt had acquired the dangerous habit of using strychnine "to keep him going, but he hasn't taken any since April 25, which is somewhat encouraging." Bullitt himself wrote to Moore on June 2 to allay his concern: "So many wild stories are flying around about my illness that I fear some of them may have reached you . . .," although he did admit he had been suffering from exhaustion so severe that he had been taking a nap each afternoon and going to bed at seven-thirty in the evening. When he had gone to Warsaw for the funeral of the Polish head of state, Joseph Pilsudski, he was on the verge of collapse several times during the procession from the cathedral. Bullitt had considered seeing a doctor in Moscow, but his confidence in Russian medicine had been shaken by the death of the Turkish ambassador, who had suffered a heart attack at age thirty-nine following an operation for a misdiagnosed case of appendicitis. Instead he went to Vienna, where it was found that the streptococcus infection "had been eliminated entirely from my body, but it had left a bit of devastation. In the first place it had reduced so greatly the sugar content of my blood that my blood pressure was down to one hundred. . . . In order to get more sugar into my blood I simply have to take a slight stimulant for a short time for the adrenal glands and consume quantities of sugar and a certain amount of alcohol. . . . In four days in Vienna my blood pressure was raised . . . to one hundred and thirty, and I already feel so much better that it is no longer necessary . . . to take naps in the afternoon, and I can sit up without undue fatigue until eleven in the evening."

In the letter to Moore, drawing on his trip to Poland for an updated outlook, Bullitt sounded anything but optimistic: "Unless the states of Europe stop fighting each other or the Soviet Union is defeated in war within the next fifteen years, it will be a juggernaut that will be able to sweep the continent." He observed that "the countries of Europe are rapidly falling into the situation of the squabbling city states of Greece with respect to Macedonia. Athens and Sparta—France and Germany; Philip of Macedon—Stalin. I don't like the comparison, but I cannot get it out of my mind." Bullitt may well have been alerted to the allusion to Philip of Macedon by a letter George Kennan had discovered in the embassy files and had sent to Washington, as though it were an up-to-date dispatch, demonstrating that history repeats itself. The letter had been sent originally by Neill S. Brown, the American minister in Moscow from 1850 to 1853, and it was a report on the regime of "his Majesty the Emperor of all the Russias," Nicholas I. Brown wrote of a

strange superstition . . . among the Russians that they are destined to conquer the world. . . . The motive power is . . . the Emperor of Russia. . . . He is the modern Philip of Macedon, strong in resources, both mental and physical, but still more powerful in his position, and impelled by a hostility to free institutions, that admits of no compromise and yields to no relaxation.

In his heated exchange with Litvinov just before leaving Moscow in October 1934, Bullitt anticipated a serious point of contention in the year ahead: Communist interference in the internal affairs of the United States. "I went on to say," Bullitt reported to Washington,

that if a negative attitude with regard to a settlement of debts and claims should be followed by activities of the Comintern [Communist International], . . . our relations would become so difficult as to be almost impossible. He replied, "No nation ever starts talking about the activities of the Comintern unless it wishes to have as bad relations as possible with us. The activities of the Comintern are merely an excuse for breaking diplomatic relations." I told him that the people of the United States as well as the Government of the United States were extremely sensitive about any interference in our internal affairs and that he might expect the most drastic reaction in case the Comintern Congress should take place. . . .

In May 1935 it was evident that the Seventh Congress of the Communist International would be convened in Moscow that summer: on May 13 Moore sent to Bullitt an article from *The Daily Worker* telling of a send-off dinner to be held

June 8 in New York for the American delegation. On July 2 Bullitt advised that he had been contacted by Louis Fischer, "obviously under the instructions of some agency of the Soviet Government," who said the Comintern Congress would open at the end of July; and Fischer had asked if the appearance of American Communists at the meeting—as it turned out, William Z. Foster, the chairman of the U.S. Communist Party, and Earl Browder, the secretary general, were already in Moscow—would constitute a violation of Litvinov's pledge with regard to interference and if the United States would protest. Bullitt well knew the answers were affirmative, but he refused to reply to hypothetical questions, wishing to await an official response from Washington. Secretary Hull cabled: ". . . the American Government expects that the Soviet Government will take appropriate means to prevent acts in disregard of the solemn pledges given by Mr. Litvinov. . . ."

"At this moment, when we do not know if we shall have an Embassy in Moscow because of the impending Congress of the Communist International," Bullitt wrote Moore on July 15, "it is almost superfluous to write about the staff," though he did anyway, "in case everything blows over." He urged the transfer of Wiley—he was, however, no longer provoked, calling the counselor "much too valuable a man to waste on an unimportant post"—and the reassignment of Bohlen; and he requested a raise for Offie, who was "more useful to this mission than any man here." Then Bullitt shared his personal plans, as he often did with Moore: "My daughter will reach Odessa toward the end of this month, and as Litvinov and almost everyone else of any importance will be away from Moscow, I think that the work of the mission will not suffer . . . if I go down to meet Anne and remain for a couple of weeks of sunlight on the Black Sea. There is a daily airplane, . . . and Offie will fly back and forth bringing me . . . any important papers or telegrams. . . . At Odessa, where we have no one to take the dictaphones out of the hotel walls, we do our work in a small rowboat. . . ."

Bullitt did not get to Odessa to meet Anne, who was coming, accompanied by a governess, from the United States via Italy, Greece, and Turkey, for the Comintern Congress did convene, on July 25, and Foster and Browder were present. "It really grieves me to disappoint my little girl," Bullitt wrote Moore. (It was on a later jaunt to Odessa that Thayer made a pass one evening at Anne Bullitt's governess, who also happened to be a close friend of the ambassador's; and when the lady rejected him, Thayer drove back to the hotel in a fury—he had borrowed Bullitt's automobile, a prized Essex roadster—and hit a pothole, breaking a spring. Thayer was demoted to the post of receptionist in the consulate section.)

Bullitt (*left*) with his half brother, Jack, his younger brother, Orville, and their father.

Bullitt and his brothers with their mother, Louisa Horwitz Bullitt, circa 1900.

As a counselor at Camp Pasquaney, 1910, Bullitt (*middle row, left*) is seated next to Edward S. Wilson, "Mr. Ned," who founded the camp.

Bullitt (*front row, center*) as chief of the Division of Current Intelligence Summaries, Department of State, in Paris, 1919. Christian A. Herter, secretary of state under Eisenhower (*seated, second from left*), and Allen W. Dulles, director of the CIA in the 1950s (*seated, right*), were assigned to the division. Bullitt is wearing a mourning band in observance of the death of his mother. (*U.S. Signal Corps*)

Bullitt as Katherina in an undergraduate production of *The Taming of the Shrew* when he was at Yale. (*Yale Picture Collection*)

Ernesta Drinker Bullitt in a portrait by her aunt, Cecilia Beaux. (*The Metropolitan Museum of Art*)

Louise Bryant in Provincetown, Massachusetts. (*By the permission of the Houghton Library, Harvard University*)

Bullitt in Moscow, December 1933, being greeted by the commander of the Kremlin guard. George F. Kennan, the ambassador's aide, stands in the doorway. (*National Archives*)

Bullitt and Roosevelt, Washington, D.C., 1933. (*National Archives*)

Ambassador to France with daughter, Anne, and their West Highland terrier, Pie-Pie, at the Château de St. Firmin, Chantilly. (*National Archives*)

At his embassy office in Paris. (*National Archives*)

Bullitt meeting Freud at the Gare Saint-Lazare, Paris, June 1938, as Freud was on his way from Vienna to London. The woman on Freud's arm is Princess Mathilde Bonaparte, who had been a patient, and at right is Carmel Offie, the ambassador's aide-de-camp. (*National Archives*)

Greeting Howard Hughes at Le Bourget, July 1938. Hughes was on a record-breaking round-the-world flight. (*National Archives*)

The crash of the Douglas DB-7, Los Angeles, January 23, 1939. (*McDonnell Douglas Photo*)

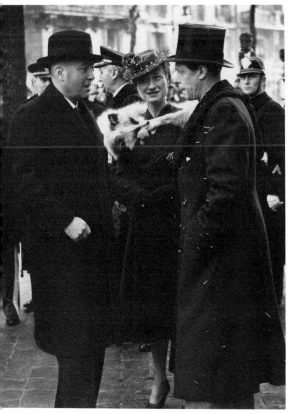

The ambassador and the Duke and Duchess of Windsor celebrating the twentieth anniversary of the American Legion, March 1939. (*National Archives*)

Bullitt and Sumner Welles in their cordial days. (*National Archives*)

Commandant Bullitt of the Free French Army is greeted by General Eisenhower (General Bradley is on Eisenhower's left), France, 1944. (*U.S. Army Signal Corps*)

Bullitt had advised Judge Moore on July 15 that his Soviet contacts—the few he considered his intimates—were adamant on the subject of the Comintern. "A few evenings ago," he wrote,

Karl Radek was at my house for a dinner and dance that I was giving in honor of the Italian Ambassador. . . . I said to Radek in a most friendly way that I hoped that he and his friends . . . would not raise such hell at the Communist Congress that they would compel us to break relations. I never saw a man grow more instantaneously and violently angry. He sprang up and said, "We have lived without the United States, and we can continue to live without the United States. We shall never allow you to dictate to us what we may do or what we may not do in Moscow." I replied that Litvinov had made certain formal promises on the subject, whereupon Radek stalked away. Mikhailsky [Pavel Mikhailsky, a Russian writer, who like Radek would be arrested in the purges], . . . who overheard Radek's remarks, said, "You must understand that world revolution is our religion, and there is not one of us who would not in the final analysis oppose even Stalin himself if we should feel that he was abandoning the cause. . . ."

Bullitt offered tentative recommendations, depending on the extent of the affront posed by the Comintern Congress. "It seems to me that if the Soviet Government should lean over backwards to avoid offending the United States, . . ." he suggested to Moore—by which he meant the presence of the American Communists would be obscured—

we shall probably wish to ignore the Congress altogether. If the violation of Litvinov's pledge should be merely technical, . . . I think we should confine our action to an oral protest by me . . . and a tightening of our liberal policy of giving visas to Soviet officials. . . . If the violation should be not technical but gross and insulting, I think we shall all feel that we are obliged to break relations. . . . The results of a break in relations would, I think, be (1) a reduction of Soviet purchases in the United States; (2) a long period without relations; . . . (3) the loss of an observation post in Moscow; (4) an increased chance that Japan will attack the Soviet Union; (5) a considerable decrease in the prestige of the Soviet Union. . . .

The American presence at the Comintern Congress was not obscured but given prominent billing, especially Earl Browder's report on the progress of Communism in the United States, which Bullitt relayed to Washington on July 29, 1935. "The party has increased its membership by more than three times and numbers more than thirty thousand members . . .," Browder told the delegates.

In 1930 native American-born citizens constituted less than ten percent of the party; now they constitute more than forty percent. In 1930 there were less than 100 Negroes in the ranks of our party; now there are over 2,500. . . . The party took upon itself the responsibility of directing the creation of mass organization of the unemployed. . . . We adopted the revolutionary traditions of 1776 and 1863 and came forward as the successors of those revolutionary movements. . . .

It was plain to Hull that the Soviets were meddling in U.S. affairs, but he waited until he had seen the proceedings of the complete meeting, then cabled Bullitt on August 19: ". . . would like to have your recommendations and suggestions . . . by Wednesday the 21st if possible."

Bullitt recognized there had been a serious breach of Litvinov's pledge to the president, but he had shifted from the position he stated to Moore on July 15, "that we are obliged to break relations. . . ." Such a break, he wrote Hull on August 21, "would satisfy the indignation we all feel and would be juridically correct; but . . . this question should be decided neither on emotional nor juridical grounds, but on the basis of a cold appraisal of the wisest course to pursue. . . ." His appraisal was pragmatic and had less to do with relations with Russia than with the importance of the U.S.S.R. in terms of international realities: "In this decade the Soviet Union either will be the center of attack from Europe and the Far East or will develop rapidly into one of the greatest physical forces in the world. In either event an official observation post . . . in Moscow will be desirable." Bullitt also opposed submitting a written protest to the Soviet government, recommending instead an address by Roosevelt, which would "make clear to the American people the aims of the Soviet Government . . ." and would state the official U.S. reaction. "The main point," he said in a letter directly to the President, "is to handle the matter from the domestic, not the foreign, political viewpoint. . . . Whatever you do, the Bolsheviks will make it hot for us. But, as Judge Moore says, we are already accustomed to Hades and acclimated." His idea was rejected, however, as Hull informed him tersely on August 23: "The President and I feel that it is necessary to make a formal written protest. . . . Accordingly there is quoted below the text of a draft note which the President has approved and which it is desired you present to the Acting Commissar for Foreign Affairs"—the protest was to be addressed to Nikolay Krestinsky in Litvinov's absence—"at earliest possible date." It read in part:

The Government of the United States would be lacking in candor if it failed to state frankly that it anticipates the most serious consequences if the Government of the Soviet Union . . . is unwilling, or unable, to take appropriate measures to prevent further acts in disregard of the solemn pledge given by it to the Government of the United States.

On August 25, 1935, Bullitt wrote to Washington:

I handed our note of protest to Krestinsky this afternoon . . . without comment, except the statement that we should make it public at once. Krestinsky replied: "If your note is a protest with regard to the Congress of the Communist International I can tell you . . . that it will be rejected."

As he was leaving the Narkomindel, the Soviet foreign office, Bullitt told newspapermen that the note was an "emphatic protest" of a "flagrant violation" of Soviet-American agreements, and there was no hint to the press that his recommendation had been vetoed in Washington. But Judge Moore, afraid that Bullitt's pride had been bruised, sent an explanation on August 27:

Touching the suggested protest to the Soviet, our thought is that should be the first step, and what, if any, action should follow to depend upon the reaction of the Soviet authorities to the protest. If you knew how many questions are now troubling the President, I think you would understand that it is undesirable for him to single out for specific treatment in an address the violation of Litvinov's pledge. The public reaction to the protest, as shown by the newspaper comments and talk in Congress, is altogether favorable.

The troubling questions Moore referred to were both domestic and foreign. The U.S. still struggled with its economic crisis—in August 1935 the president signed the Social Security Act and the Banking Act, revising the Federal Reserve; and with Hitler and Mussolini both menacing the peace and with civil war threatened in Spain, he approved the Neutrality Act, prohibiting arms shipments to nations at war.

Bullitt wrote Moore on August 30 that one thing was certain about Soviet-American relations: they "inevitably will be extremely distant and frigid"; and he reported that since publication of the protest in *Pravda*, on August 28, he had not met with a single Soviet citizen. "Perhaps I should say no one has *dared* see me. Henceforth I expect to be as completely isolated as the other Ambassadors." He admitted he was in "somewhat of a quandary" as to how to approach the Soviet foreign office; and that he was inclined to omit visits there entirely unless invited by Litvinov, "and then to restrain my conversation, . . . whatever my emotions may be and however much I should like to speak out." He predicted that the Soviet propagandists would do their best to smear him and were contriving the story that the protest had been his idea, "for the purpose of breaking relations, so that I might return to America as a popular hero and compel the President to appoint me to a more important post." Bullitt was anxious to come home, if only for a visit: "I have wished a thousand times that I could be with you in Washington," he wrote Moore. "If this situation continues to be complicated, and if by chance you or the President or the Secretary wishes to have me come to Washington for a consultation, please do not hesitate to send me the orders. . . . I shall, of course, be home to spend Christmas with Anne, but if you want me before that time, just say the word, and I shall be on the first steamer."

Still suffering from the aftereffects of the strep infection—a doctor in Berlin had prescribed "careful living and plenty of rest"—Bullitt went on a vacation in September, accompanied by Offie, to Ragusa, an ancient city in Sicily, and then to Capri. "Ragusa remains surrounded by its medieval city walls, . . ." Bullitt wrote Moore on October 2, "and inhabited by a population that might have stepped off a Greek vase. . . . We spent all our time in Ragusa taking sun baths, and I shall do the same . . . here in Capri. Offie has proved himself just as good a doctor as he is a secretary. He has made me follow rigidly my doctor's orders and sees to it that I take my different medicines to the minute."

Bullitt added that he had stopped smoking completely: "I have actually done it, thus breaking all family traditions. I think I told you how my great grandfather, William C. Bullitt, being confronted by the choice of giving up smoking or giving up work, at once gave up work; and how my father, being forbidden absolutely to smoke, lay for some weeks on his deathbed drawing alternate puffs from a tube of oxygen, which he held in his right hand, and a cigarette, which he held in his left." (Bullitt remained a heavy cigarette smoker throughout his life, though he would quit on occasion, to prove he could.)

"I have, of course, not yet seen Kelley but have talked to him over the telephone," Bullitt wrote Moore from Capri, alluding to an imminent trip to Russia by Robert F. Kelley, the chief of the Eastern European Division in Washington. Bullitt liked and admired Kelley and welcomed his assistance in the ever more difficult task of dealing with the irascible Litvinov. (". . . [D]o have Kelly in on all drafting," he urged Roosevelt, when he recommended that the president address the nation on the Comintern Congress. "The technical complexities of Soviet organization are so great that his encyclopedic knowledge will be indispensable.") Bullitt said in the letter to Moore that he planned to meet Kelley in Riga, Latvia, on his return from vacation and travel with him to Moscow, where he would do what he would not otherwise do: ". . . that is . . . attempt to entertain some high Soviet dignitaries in his honor. . . . I hate false human relationships, and any cordiality at the present time will be so forced that I do not feel that it will do any good. Kelley, on the other hand, should meet as many people as possible while he is in the Soviet Union."

That Bullitt was accurate in his prediction that such cordiality would do little good was reflected in his report to the State Department on November 9, 1935.

Kelley and I lunched with Litvinov alone today. . . . Both Kelley and I had told him that the United States had desired really friendly relations with the Soviet Union but now felt that the direction of the activities of the Communist International by Stalin was incompatible with really friendly relations. . . . [Litvinov] implied that . . . really friendly relations with the United States were of small importance to the Soviet Union.

Homeward in Anger

I N W H A T appeared to be an abrupt turn—in fact, his rancor had been growing for many months—Bullitt became outspokenly critical of the Soviet leadership. "He met the American correspondents every day," Louis Fischer wrote in *Men and Politics*, "and urged them . . . to fan the flames of anti-Sovietism." Further, he attempted to influence correspondents of other nations in a similar way, and he pressed fellow diplomats to persuade their governments to protest the Comintern Congress. En route home in November 1935, Bullitt stopped in Berlin and told startled German officials that Japan would be justified in a conquest of Siberia; and the U.S. ambassador, William E. Dodd, showed no less surprise when he noted Bullitt's visit in his journal:

His remarks about Russia were directly contrary to the attitude he held when he passed this way last year. Then he was to all intents and purposes enthusiastic. . . . Bullitt said [now] Russia has no business trying to hold the peninsula which projects into the Japanese sea at Vladivostok. That is all going to be taken by Japan. . . . I was amazed at this kind of talk from a responsible diplomat who had done so much to get Russia recognized in 1933.

"I was delighted to know that you are as confident as I am about the President's re-election," Bullitt wrote to Judge Moore from Moscow on November 9, a full year before the 1936 election.

I have always felt that . . . he might be able to establish the same ascendancy that Jefferson had. I only wish I could see a Madison and a Monroe on the horizon. The next twenty years will be as filled with horror, I believe, as any that the world has traversed, and we shall need not one F.D.R. but a succession of Presidents of his quality to keep us out of the shambles.

It was a global prediction without specific meaning, but in an earlier dispatch to Washington Bullitt had viewed the future of the Soviet Union in the perspective of the next twenty years. On July 19, 1935, Bullitt wrote:

War in Europe is regarded as inevitable and ultimately desirable from the Communist point of view. The Soviet Government fears war . . . at the present time because the Soviet Union is unprepared, and it is feared that war this year or next in Europe would grow into world war with simultaneous attacks on the Soviet Union by Germany, Poland and Japan. . . . It is, of course, the heartiest hope of the Soviet Government that the United States will become involved in a war with Japan. . . . To think of the Soviet Union as a possible ally of the United States in case of war with Japan is to allow the wish to be the father of the thought. . . . To summarize: the aim of the Soviet Government is, and will remain, to produce world revolution. The leaders of the Soviet Union believe that the first step toward this revolution must be to strengthen the defensive and offensive power of the Soviet Union. . . . To maintain peace for the present, to keep the nations of Europe divided, to foster enmity between Japan and the United States, and to gain the blind devotion and obedience of the Communists of all countries . . . is the sum of Stalin's policy.

"I think I told you, . . ." Bullitt said to Moore in his letter of November 9, "that I had engaged a house at Jupiter Island, Florida"—Jupiter Island was a resort, reserved for the rich, north of Palm Beach—"for the Christmas holidays. I should be back in Washington with Anne about the seventh of January. At that time I shall ask you to do me the favor of taking us out to visit . . . the charming lady who runs Foxcroft School [an exclusive boarding school for young women in Middleburg, Virginia]. I entered Anne for that school many years ago. . . . I have never yet made her walk into anything blindfolded and do not wish to begin now."

On January 6, 1936, Louise Bryant, Anne's mother, collapsed in her hotel room in Paris and died later that day of a cerebral hemorrhage. Bullitt arranged for her burial in a Paris cemetery, and he marked her grave with a granite cross, a replica of those on Bullitt family graves in Philadelphia.

Bullitt returned to Moscow in February 1936, aware that he could no longer be an effective emissary, and he was ready to get out: "I saw Litvinov . . . yesterday," he wrote Judge Moore on February 22, "and he made no remarks whatever about Soviet-American relations and showed no interest in the subject. . . ." He found little solace in knowing he was not alone in his frustration—to be like the other ambassadors was what Bullitt had tried to avoid—but he was more willing to listen sympathetically to their grievances, which he shared. "I feel like a prisoner pacing my garden between banks of snow, unable to escape," he wrote, quoting his British counterpart in the letter to Moore, and added that the Polish ambassador had suffered a nervous breakdown. (Bullitt reported that his own health was excellent: "I find . . . that my strength and ability to work have returned almost to the point where they were before I got that infernal streptococcus infection.") On March 1 Bullitt took Roy Howard, the Scripps-Howard newspaper editor, to see Stalin, who "clearly evaded the issue of his direction of the Communist Party of the United States"; Howard's reaction was that a break in relations was in order, and he said so to Stalin.

On April 20, 1936, Bullitt wrote to Washington:

. . . Stalin considers it sound strategy to support democratic forms of government in countries in which communism is still weak. . . . The problem of relations with the

Government of the Soviet Union is, therefore, a subordinate part of the problem presented by communism as a militant faith determined to produce world revolution and the "liquidation" . . . of all non-believers.

Bullitt said further in the dispatch that he did not favor a break in relations with Moscow, but in his letters to Moore he had been pessimistic. Konstantin Umansky, Litvinov's press aide and the chief government censor—Bullitt called Umansky "an astonishingly loathsome Jew, capable of any baseness"—had been sent to replace Skvirsky as counselor of the Soviet embassy in Washington. "I am concerned," Bullitt wrote Moore, "because I suspect that there is a further purpose in sending Umansky to America. He is extremely able as a Bolshevik propagandist. . . . The program and propaganda of the Communist Party in the United States is now under consideration. I suspect that he is being sent to control that propaganda. . . ."

Bullitt let Judge Moore know how homesick he was in a letter on March 30: "Russia is a good country for pine trees, St. Bernard dogs, and polar bears, and I must say that I long to be at home again." On April 8 he wrote his reaction to the prospect of reassignment, as Moore had outlined it to him: "Of course, I am ready to go anywhere and do anything that the President wants me to do; but I would honestly prefer to take a leave of absence without pay . . . and work in the campaign, rather than be appointed Ambassador to Italy. . . . I know Italy well. . . . There are no negotiations of importance, and there is a great deal of the sort of social life that I participated in with pleasure at the age of seventeen. . . . London and Paris are the only two posts in Europe at which one can make one's human contacts mean something. . . . At the present time I feel that there is important work to be done in America. . . ." Bullitt heard from the president himself on April 21: "I know how anxious you are to have some definite work, and I hope to Heaven you will have it by the middle of May. You know, without my telling you, that these things move very slowly, and this particular bit of work involves several changes. I can tell you this, however, that when the change is made, you will pack up your furniture, the dog and the servants—where you will deposit them, we will have to tell you later."

"I have just received your telegram saying that the President wants me to come home quickly . . .," Bullitt wrote Moore on May 9. "I shall plan to leave here on May 15 and travel by way of Warsaw, Berlin, Brussels, Paris and London. I shall make one-night stops in all those cities except in Paris, where I have a number of matters in connection with the belongings of my late wife to attend to, and in London. I cannot resist spending a few days with the Astors" [Nancy Astor, a cousin of Bullitt's, was born in Virginia, married Waldorf Astor and became a British citizen, and was the first woman to sit in Parliament] "and accompanying them to the Derby. . . . Probably I shall sail on the *Europa* on

May 30 and arrive in Washington about June 5." His desire to come home was being realized, but Bullitt knew that he was returning with his status in doubt. "I have assumed from your telegram," he wrote Moore, "that the President wants me to ask for home leave and not to resign. I am, therefore, in somewhat of a dilemma with regard to my household. . . . I shall pack my personal belongings but shall ship to the United States only those which I must have if I am to open my house in Massachusetts this summer. . . ."

On July 15, 1936, as Roosevelt's personal representative at the bicentennial of Patrick Henry's birth in Hanover, Virginia, Bullitt made a speech in which he denounced the Soviet Union and other totalitarian states. "Dictatorships, based on secret police and firing squads," he said, "have been set up in many lands. The noblest words that can issue from the mouth of man have been prostituted, and the noblest sentiments in the heart of man have been played upon by propaganda to conceal a simple truth: that those dictatorships are tyrannies imposing their dogmas on an enslaved people." He then reported to Washington, where he was assigned to room 201 of the Navy Building—the office assigned to Bullitt had become known as the "death cell"—to write a history of the Department of State. He remained in oblivion only briefly, however, for Roosevelt responded to his plea to work in the presidential campaign: he became a speech writer, a very useful one. "I have seen war," Roosevelt said in Chautauqua, New York, on August 14, 1936. "I have seen war on land and sea. I have seen the blood running from the wounded. I have seen men coughing out their gassed lungs. I have seen the dead in the mud. . . . I hate war." A memorable address, it had been inspired by Woodrow Wilson, who expressed his feelings to Bullitt on April 6, 1917, the day he declared the United States would enter World War I. "How hard it is!" said a fictional President Wilson in Bullitt's novel, *It's Not Done*. "Did you see those congressmen . . .? Applauding every wretched little warlike word I had to speak, ignoring all the things for which I really care. . . . They can't understand . . . that I hate this war, that I hate all war. . . ."

On September 14, 1936, Bullitt met with Attorney General Homer S. Cummings and FBI Director J. Edgar Hoover to discuss the Communist menace. "Mr. Bullitt told me," Hoover wrote in a memorandum, "that the Communist leaders in Russia make every effort to put spies in all foreign government agencies. . . ." As a result of this meeting the FBI began checking on the activities of Communists in the United States, starting with Umansky, the Soviet embassy counselor, thereby initiating an internal security program that eventually would become a subject of heated controversy.

VI

Ambassador to
France:
1936–1940

To Paris with Aplomb

"BILL," said his old friend, William Adams Delano, the architect who had been commissioned to remodel the embassy in Paris, "if we had stood at a window in the Crillon in 1919, and someone had said to you, 'You'll be Ambassador to France,' and to me, 'You'll design a building on the Place de la Concorde,' we'd have laughed in his face. . . ." "Not I," William C. Bullitt replied. "I always expected to be Ambassador to France."

Jesse I. Straus, the ambassador to Paris, was in failing health: he suffered from cancer and had collapsed at the Bastille Day parade on July 14, 1936; he returned in August and sent his son, Robert K. Straus, to Roosevelt's home in Hyde Park, New York, to announce his resignation. The president was prepared for the news, Robert Straus recalled; he summoned his personal secretary, Missy LeHand, and said, "Tell Bill Bullitt he is going to Paris." The appointment was announced on August 25; Bullitt sailed on September 24; and he presented his credentials to President Albert Lebrun on October 2. "I come to France not as a stranger," he said—his words were reminiscent of those he had spoken in Moscow in December 1933—"but as one who for many years has known the magnificent achievements of French civilization." On October 5 he wrote Judge Moore: "I was, of course, distressed by the news of Jesse Straus's death. I saw him on the morning of my departure from New York. Thanks to opiates he was not suffering in any way, and he was confident that in three weeks he would be well again. That is a happy way to die." He also wrote to Roosevelt, to report that he had phoned from Straus's bedroom but had not got through: "I didn't have anything to say except . . . good luck," referring to the election a month hence. "I have nothing to say now except that my reception was extraordinarily friendly, and that a series of conversations with old friends inclines me to believe that in Washington we have been much too pessimistic about the situation in France." He added immodestly that members of the French government "seem to be greatly pleased by my appointment," and he repeated a statement of Alexis Léger, the secretary-general of the French foreign office. "The best indication of the President's special friendliness for France," Léger had said to Bullitt, "is that he sent you here. . . ." The approval of the French was genuine. "Bullitt will be popular in Paris," it was declared in an editorial in *L'Europe Nouvelle*. "He has youth, finesse, cosmopolitan experience and vast knowledge of European affairs—and these are rare qualities . . . in American civil servants." There was but one voice of opposition: a journal of the arch-right with anti-Semitic leanings, *L'Action Francaise*, whose editor, Charles Maurras, tried to make issues of Bullitt's marriage to the widow of an American Communist and his Jewish heritage, for which Bullitt received an official apology.

Not everyone in Washington was enthusiastic, however: Secretary of State Cordell Hull was uneasy with an ambassador who regularly went over his head to the president; Undersecretary William Phillips still had not forgiven Bullitt for his defiance of Wilson in 1919 (Phillips was sent to Rome as ambassador in August 1936—he was evidently being put out to pasture by his old friend the president—and he would have bristled at Bullitt's disdain for that post, as he had expressed it in his letter to Moore in April); and the man who was named undersecretary of state in 1937, Sumner Welles, had the good sense to recognize Bullitt for what he was, a rival. Aware of the president's esteem for Bullitt, State Department officials kept their sentiments to themselves, but Eleanor Roosevelt was not so restrained. Upon learning that Bullitt was going to Paris instead of James A. Farley, the chairman of the Democratic National Committee, the First Lady said to Farley: "Damnit! That's just like Franklin." Moreover, Bullitt's glowing report to Roosevelt from Paris aroused skepticism, because there was good reason for the pessimism in Washington about the situation in France. The country was in a sorry state: its population growth was zero; it had been eclipsed industrially by Germany; and it was divided politically into incompatible factions, over fifty of them—Monarchists, Fascists, Socialists, Communists, and so on. Most Frenchmen had feared German aggression since the armistice of 1918, but a system of fortifications along the German frontier, the idea of André Maginot, the minister of war in 1929–1930, had instilled a sense of security: "They shall not pass," vowed the troops who manned the Maginot Line, and the vow became their motto. When, in March 1936, the German army marched into the Rhineland in a bold challenge to the terms of the Versailles treaty—at a time when French military forces far outnumbered Germany's—the caretaker government of Albert Sarraut did nothing but send its foreign minister, Pierre-Étienne Flandin, to London to confer with his British counterpart, Anthony Eden. France and Great Britain were showing their unwillingness to stand up to Adolf Hitler.

A coalition government, the Popular Front, came to power amid turmoil in June 1936, led by Léon Blum, a Socialist, who had been beaten nearly to death by a gang of rightists and vilified for being a Jew by Maurras, who was sentenced to four months in prison for incitement to murder. In May, during the final days of the Sarraut government, industrial workers walked off the job en masse, and by mid-June the strike had spread to the farms and to the department stores, hotels, and restaurants of Paris, with an estimated two million workers having joined the "revolution." Blum ended the strike by pushing labor legislation through Parliament—collective bargaining, a forty-hour week, paid vacations—and on Bastille Day he was triumphant as he addressed an enormous gathering: "Every effort, every advance toward social justice attaches the workers of France to the Republic. . . ." Four days later civil war broke out in Spain, and on July 23, with his foreign minister, Yvon Delbos, Blum went to London for a meeting on the Locarno Pact of 1925, which Hitler had abrogated by taking the Rhineland. "Are you going to send arms to the Spanish Republicans?" Blum was asked anxiously by Foreign Secretary Eden—the Tory government of Britain feared that aid to the Republic of Spain would lead to German and Italian support of the insurgent forces of Francisco Franco and in turn to general European war—and Blum affirmed his intent to do so. "It's your affair," Eden said to Blum, "but . . . I beg you: be prudent." On his return to Paris Blum realized he was opposed by the Radical Socialist bloc in his cabinet—it consisted of Delbos, Camille Chautemps, who would succeed Blum as premier, and Edouard Daladier, the minister of war—and arms shipments to Spain were canceled.

"I got away to a good start with Blum," Bullitt wrote Roosevelt on October 24. "We lunched together, . . . and I had a most intimate conversation with him. He . . . has the sort of quicksilver intelligence and the little fluttery gestures of the hyper-intellectual queer ones. . . . He has taken the position that if the Communists refuse to support him, he will not attempt to make a deal with the right but will ask . . . new elections. The Communists know . . . that new elections would mean an immense reduction in their vote, and unless they get orders from Moscow to raise hell, . . . they will, I think, continue to support him. . . . The whole of France has been shocked by the civil war in Spain. The lower middle class, which in the last election in considerable measure voted Communist, doesn't want that sort of thing in France." (Blum may not have known it, but Bullitt had had a hand in thwarting his plan to send military aid to the Spanish Republicans. When passing through Paris and London in May, on his way to Washington, he had stressed that the real threat to Spain was Moscow, warning of the widespread penetration of Communist propaganda and asserting that Spanish revolutionaries had been trained in Russia.)

With Blum and the other French leaders Bullitt achieved an immediate intimacy, which was not difficult due to his affinity for French people and his inclination to adopt their tastes and habits. "Bullitt practically sleeps with the French cabinet," noted Harold L. Ickes, a Roosevelt confidant and the secretary of the interior, in his diary; and Robert D. Murphy, who was named counselor of the embassy in Paris in 1937, later wrote: "If he erred, it was on the side of yielding to a subjective approach, which carried him inside the French Government to an unheard-of degree." The willingness of the French to befriend Bullitt was also stimulated by his close association with Roosevelt, as they perceived it:

they did believe, as Léger had said, that Bullitt had been sent to Paris as a token of the president's esteem. (It was not only the French who remarked at the bond between Bullitt and Roosevelt: "Bullitt was closer than anyone in the diplomatic service to the President," Jim Farley wrote.) So, with Roosevelt's landslide reelection on November 3, 1936, the ambassador was all the more highly regarded by the premier and his cabinet and courted accordingly. "Blum came personally to express his congratulations," Bullitt wrote Roosevelt on November 8. "He entered the front door, flung his broad-brimmed hat to the butler, his coat to a footman, leaped three steps to the point where I was standing, seized me and kissed me violently! I staggered slightly; but having been kissed by Stalin, I am now immune to any form of osculation."

That Roosevelt did hold Bullitt in high professional regard—FDR clearly considered his man in Paris number-one among foreign emissaries—was to a degree the result of the president's disdain for career diplomats. The Foreign Service, he believed, was laden with dead wood: "You can get to be a minister," he once supposedly said, "if you are loyal to the service, do nothing to offend people, [and] if you are not intoxicated at public functions." But Bullitt was also extremely effective: he was, Roosevelt had decided, a cut above the other non-career ambassadors, too—by and large generous political donators, such as Joseph E. Davies, who succeeded Bullitt in Moscow—and he became a de facto ambassador-at-large. "Bullitt dispatched couriers throughout Europe . . .," Farley wrote. "The embassy had a direct wire to Washington through which Roosevelt and Bullitt maintained constant communication."

Bullitt used his influence with Roosevelt to establish in the European capitals a network of American envoys loyal to him, such as John C. Wiley, the former counselor of the embassy in Moscow (whom Bullitt had castigated but now regarded as a friend and ally). "I wish you would . . . get Ray Atherton moved out of London," he wrote Roosevelt on October 24, "and John Wiley placed in his boots. . . . Wiley is much the best man for the job, and it would help me in Paris a lot to have him there. I can, of course, keep in close touch with Bill Phillips, with Hugh Wilson in Switzerland, and with Dodd, but there is no one in the London Embassy who will play ball." Wiley preferred to stay at his post in Antwerp, rather than replace Atherton as the counselor in London; the ambassador to Great Britain, Robert Worth Bingham (Bingham was a newspaper publisher in Louisville, Kentucky), died in 1937 and would be replaced by Joseph P. Kennedy, to Bullitt's satisfaction at least at first; Dodd in Berlin—William E. Dodd, the University of Chicago history professor who had been ambassador to Germany since 1933—would be recalled in another year at Bullitt's persistent urging; and it is questionable how well Bullitt got along with Phillips in Rome. Bullitt also tried to have a say about high-level appointments at the State Department, but with less success: "Please don't forget," he wrote Roosevelt, "that

. . . you must give Judge Moore the authority which he can have only if he is Under Secretary of State"; nevertheless, Sumner Welles became the undersecretary, and Moore was made the counselor of the department.

The Inevitability of War

———

THE DOMINANT CONCERN of Bullitt's four years in Paris was French-German relations, and Bullitt himself made a marked shift, from espousing conciliation—he arrived in France predisposed to sympathize with German objectives, as he had disagreed so vehemently with the terms of the Versailles Treaty—to accepting the inevitability of war. "Blum wants really to reach an understanding with Germany," he advised Roosevelt in the letter of October 24, 1936, although it was apparent he was writing as much from predilection as from observation; for Bullitt at this point was so resolute—his position was also based on his loathing of the Soviets—that he considered anti-German diplomats to be dangerous. Eric Phipps, the British ambassador to Paris, declared that Hitler was a fanatic, who would only be satisfied with domination of Europe, and Bullitt was enraged; and when André François-Poncet, the French ambassador to Germany, expressed a belief that there would be war, Bullitt accused him of dereliction. For Bullitt it was not the Hitler threat that counted, for the greater danger was a European war, which would so exhaust the combatant nations that they would be forced to bow to Soviet supremacy. "There is no feeling of crisis because no one believes that war is imminent," he wrote Roosevelt on November 8, "but there is a universal belief that Europe is drifting toward war and that no man on the continent has imagination enough to devise any method of reconciliation."

What Bullitt called "the nub of the problem" was French-German relations: "Ever since Hitler came to power," he wrote, "everyone in France has assumed that reconciliation is impossible," an attitude he conceded was shared by high-ranking Germans, including the foreign minister, Konstantin von Neurath. Bullitt differed, nevertheless: "I don't believe this is true. The essential thing the Germans must have is the development of their economic relations with Central Europe and the Balkans." It was "the logic of economic facts," he said, that there would be trade between Germany and countries like Rumania, Yugoslavia, Hungary, Bulgaria, and Turkey. "The French (or at least Blum and Delbos) have no objection to this . . .," he wrote. "The reason why so many people are afraid of it is because they fear that economic domination will lead to political domination and the realization of the old Berlin-to-Bagdad bloc." Bullitt understood very well both the designs of the Germans and the fears of the French—he had written an astute analysis of German military objectives in World War I, and they had not changed measurably—but he was hopeful that there would be "a general revival of . . . European unity. . . . It is a large order," he acknowledged, "but the events in Spain have made most people in most European countries realize that there is such a thing as European civilization, which reposes on certain very old civilized principles that may be destroyed by war or Bolshevism."

Von Neurath urged Bullitt to tell his French friends "that we are quite ready to establish the best possible relations with them," and Hermann Goering, the air minister and president of the Reichstag, assured him there was no conflict between France and Germany, since the French economy was agricultural and the German economy was industrial. Bullitt was so taken by the assertions of von Neurath and Goering that he made arrangements for Marcel Knecht, a French-Alsatian—Knecht was the editor of *Le Matin*, a pro-Nazi newspaper in Paris—to confer with them and with Hjalmar Schacht, the minister of economics and president of the Reichsbank. Knecht, while in Berlin in December 1936, attempted also to meet with Ambassador Dodd—on Bullitt's recommendation, by telegram—but Dodd declined and wrote in his journal: "Does this mean . . . that Bullitt is moving . . . without official instructions?" When the Knecht mission became public—an account of it was published in *The Times* (London)—Bullitt denied in a letter to Roosevelt that it had been his idea: it was a French initiative, he asserted, "to find out if Germany might be in a mood to negotiate. . . ."

If French-German rapprochement was to fail, as it would in 1937, Bullitt would not hesitate to name the responsible third parties. One was Ambassador Dodd, whose opposition to Hitler made it impossible, in Bullitt's view, to negotiate with the Third Reich. "When Dodd leaves Berlin," he advised Roosevelt, "I think you should select your man for that post with extreme care"; and he proposed Hugh Wilson, the minister to Switzerland. "His German is perfect," Bullitt wrote, "and in spite of the fact that his connections are largely Republican, . . . I cannot think of anyone else who could begin to establish the . . . intimate . . . relationship we need with the bosses in Berlin. . . ." Another was Phipps, the British envoy in Paris and a former ambassador to Germany, who "exhibited a hostility to Germany . . . surprising to me," Bullitt later said in a letter to Hull, remarking that Phipps had contended that all negotiations "would end in failure unless France and England should be prepared to accord Germany absolute domination of the international situation." Bullitt was aware that Phipps was merely taking orders from London. "I gather . . .," he wrote Hull, "that the policy of Great Britain is to keep the continent of Europe divided," as indeed it was, to gain time to prepare for war; but Bullitt, from conversations with Goering and with Pierre Cot, the French air minister, had decided that air power had made war unthinkable. "In all this intellectual chaos and impending doom," he wrote Roosevelt on November 24,

> the underlying truth is that the development of the airplane has made Europe an absurdity. . . . These dinky little European states cannot live in an airplane civilization. Today they have the alternative of submerging their national hatreds and national prides sufficiently to unify the continent or of destroying themselves completely and handing Europe over to the Bolsheviks.

Bullitt's mistrust of the British and the Germans alike made him unusually wary of espionage—he would learn, however, that as in Moscow it was the host nation that eavesdropped on the embassy, and France was no exception—and within days of arriving in Paris he asked that a U.S. Navy security expert be sent from Washington to inspect his residence and the chancery. He was just beginning to make the code room "air-tight," he reported to Moore on October 26; and he had taken the extra precaution of devising a code for his telephone conversations with Roosevelt, knowing the president shared his delight in stealth. The code was based on random information they shared, such as the score of the Harvard-Yale football game of a given year, which could be used to convey a statistic; and world leaders were known by aliases: Mussolini was Al Capone, and Hitler was Berle, for Adolf A. Berle, Jr. (Berle, who had resigned from the government with Bullitt in 1919 and returned in 1932 as a member of Roosevelt's brains trust, was displeased and said he was going to punch Bullitt's head. "I rather agree, . . ." said Roosevelt, "but why not punch your namesake's head instead of Bullitt's?") Secretary of State Hull disapproved quite definitely of the coded communications. "Liking the dramatic side of foreign affairs," Hull wrote in his *Memoirs*, "Mr. Roosevelt did not discourage the practice. . . . The result was that at times the State Department remained in the dark as to what Bullitt was thinking and doing."

Bullitt did keep Judge Moore abreast, mainly of day-to-day troubles: the inadequacy of the embassy residence, a "rather dreadful dwelling"; the inefficiency of the embassy staff; the incessancy of ceremonial burdens. The residence had been erected in 1886 and was, Bullitt wrote, "the sort of house that was built in America by the *nouveaux riches* [the Wanamakers and the Wideners, although he did not name them] about that time. . . . It is filled with every conceivable kind of marble known to man and is as cozy as a first-rate mausoleum." As he was in Moscow, Bullitt was brutal in his criticism of his subordinates, one of whom, he wrote Moore, "should be retired at once in the interests of the Service. He has reached the point of almost total incompetence." There were a few who pleased him: Robert Murphy, Bullitt advised, was suited to "handle the Consulate General perfectly and . . . the administration of both the Consulate General and the Embassy"; and Carmel Offie, whom he had brought along from Moscow, rated high praise. (Offie reverted to the rank of clerk in order to come to Paris, but in November 1936 he was named a vice consul and third secretary.)

"We shall . . . have to stop spending three fourths of our time entertaining visiting firemen," Bullitt insisted in a letter to Moore on November 8, and on the same day he told Roosevelt about the last of "the obligatory speeches that I have to make." He had addressed a church congregation in the Latin Quarter of Paris and had taken Offie along, so there would be a friendly face in the audience. "Offie was seated next to a very strange looking lady," he wrote, "who kept pulling out of her pocket a quart bottle of Pernod and taking enormous swigs, while announcing to the lady on her right that when I had finished speaking, she intended to brain me with the bottle. The lady on her right, in whispers, argued . . . that this would not be seemly. Finally, the absinthe-draining lady screeched out, 'Can't you see I'm in love with him?' "

———————

In the last weeks of 1936 Bullitt sent a series of warnings to Roosevelt and to Moore, who was the acting secretary of state, of the prospect of hostilities: "Everyone in France, including Blum, . . . is convinced that war is about to arrive," he wrote Roosevelt on November 24, either in the spring or summer of 1937 or a year hence. The French cabinet ministers and representatives of other European nations were of like mind, he reported, "as if they had within them the same phonograph record, playing the same theme: 'War is inevitable, and Europe is doomed to destruction unless President Roosevelt intervenes.' Invariably I reply by asking how you can intervene effectively. Invariably the reply is, 'We don't know, but the President must have some idea.' " Bullitt said he was reminded of the ending of a Greek tragedy,

> when the difficulties become too vast to be handled by man, and the *deus ex machina* appears to set everything right. I then remark that you are not a *deus* and that you have no authority to bend the rulers of Europe to your will, and that you are not going to send the American Navy and American soldiers to Europe. Invariably the reply is, "That is quite right. There is no reason why you should send your armed forces again to Europe; but . . ."

Bullitt expanded on how he had reasoned with the French in a letter to Moore on November 29:

> I . . . say that, after all, the President is not a god and has no godlike power to bend Hitler, Mussolini, and Stalin. . . . I add that he has but one power, which is the power of the American fleet, the American Army, and American economic and financial resources,

and that those . . . will not, so long as he is in the White House, be placed at the disposal of European peoples by involving the United States in a war. The answer at this point . . . is that the President . . . has great "moral authority." My reply . . . is that I am reminded of the great moral authority which Woodrow Wilson enjoyed before the Armistice. After the Armistice it became immediately evident what that moral authority consisted of. His moral authority did not avail one whit to turn Clemenceau, Lloyd George and the other vultures at the peace conference. . . .

"Czechoslovakia, clearly, is the next item on Hitler's menu," Bullitt advised Roosevelt, and he was essentially right, although the *Anschluss*, the annexation of Austria, would precede by six months the German occupation of the Czech Sudetenland. "If Hitler should send forces into Czechoslovakia, the position of France, as well as Czechoslovakia, would become tragic. . . . The tragic fact is that no one in Europe today is putting any constructive energy whatsoever behind the idea of preserving peace. Everyone is spending every ounce of energy on preparing the instruments of war." On December 7, however, Bullitt was able to report with some optimism that Premier Blum, "lunching with me alone a few days ago, said that he hoped to be able to inaugurate soon a movement for reconciliation with Germany based on the reduction of economic barriers, financial and economic collaboration and reduction of armaments." He wrote with pride that he had been able to develop "entirely confidential relations with Blum and Delbos," and it was no idle boast, for he cited his familiarity with the French leaders in an effort to disparage Ambassador Dodd. "It should be possible," he told the president, "for our ambassador in Berlin to establish the same sort of relationship with the heads of the Nazi Government. . . . If we had an ambassador who could do that, . . . he and I could at least be of some assistance in bringing France and Germany together. . . . Dodd has many admirable . . . qualities, but he is . . . ill-equipped for his present job. He hates the Nazis too much."

On December 20, 1936, Bullitt restated to Roosevelt—it was his final letter of the year, a summing-up—his view that a secure peace in Europe depended on a French-German entente. The "new element," as he called it, that had made this so was aerial bombardment: ". . . the French Government knows the Germans can destroy the city of Paris in twenty-four hours, and the German Government knows the French can destroy Essen and all the towns of the Ruhr in twenty-four hours."

Accepting a Crisis Agenda

B ULLITT was in Washington in March 1937 for conferences on events in Europe, which were occurring with no set direction: Joachim von Ribbentrop, the German ambassador to London, was attempting to appease the British with regard to Hitler's intentions—sincerely, Bullitt believed, but the British were still stalling for time, and Hitler would become impatient; relations between France and Poland had improved markedly, which Bullitt regarded as a deterrent to German aggression; and France had resolved to march in support of Czechoslovakia in the event of a German attack. Bullitt then spent a week with Roosevelt in Warm Springs, Georgia, where they conferred on Europe but also found time to enjoy each other's company. They did get along well, which is not surprising, as they shared similar backgrounds and had many mutual friends; and the president, who enjoyed a hearty laugh, no doubt appreciated the ambassador's clever mind and quick wit. Bullitt never missed an opportunity to cultivate the friendship, it must be said: he was very careful to attend to the needs of Roosevelt's many relatives, as they traveled in France, always noting their presence in his letters. One was Elsie Hooper, "aged seventy and looking fifty," Bullitt wrote the president, "having lost 250 of her 500 pounds." "Do I remember Elsie Hooper!" Roosevelt wrote back. "A cousin of mine, by Jove. In fact, several cousins of mine." Another was Franklin D. Roosevelt, Jr., for whom Bullitt gave "a little luncheon," which was attended by the three ranking French leaders: Blum, Delbos, and Chautemps. And when Sara Delano Roosevelt was in Paris in September 1937, Bullitt was especially attentive. "Your mother is in tremendous form," he wrote the president. "You might as well have asked me to stop the flow of Niagara as to have asked me to see to it that she did not accept a vast number of invitations. . . . She is, of course, having an immense personal success. All the French love her."

Bullitt's impatience with the government of Great Britain was more discernible in 1937: "There is increasing evidence," he wrote Judge Moore in January, "the British will use every means possible to prevent direct negotiations between France and Germany." He chose unusual ways to display his irritation. "I have been disgusted for many years," he had written Roosevelt in December 1936, "by the spectacle of American girls crawling on the ground . . . to be presented at Court," and he proposed to Roosevelt that he "instruct our Ambassador in London that in future no Americans except those attached to the Embassy are to be presented at the Court of St. James." (It was not the first time Bullitt had taken an interest in the presentation of young American women at Buckingham Palace, a practice that was continued in spite of his objections. In 1933, while he was in London for the economic conference, the daughter of Samuel D. McReynolds, an influential congressman from Tennessee and a delegate to the conference, wished to be presented and was denied; so Bullitt interceded with Prime Minister MacDonald on behalf of Margaret McReynolds.) Bullitt later was critical of Belgium for being "the little brother of England," and he withdrew the name of an American newspaperman, Edgar A. Mowrer, whom he had proposed as minister to Czechoslovakia, because Mowrer had a British wife.

In a letter to Roosevelt in May 1937 Bullitt summed up his understanding of the British strategy: Anthony Eden, he wrote, would tell Jozef Beck, the foreign minister of Poland, "that Great Britain desires nothing so much as to reach understanding with Germany," knowing Beck would repeat it to the Germans; but in reality both Eden and Prime Minister Neville Chamberlain

were convinced that it was absolutely impossible to come to any understanding with Germany and that the great problem was to gain time by pretending that reconciliation . . . was possible. In other words, while the British do not want war on the continent of Europe, they remain just as anxious as they have been all through their history to keep France and Germany from reaching any real understanding. So long as the British remain in that state of mind, . . . there is nothing that we can do to bring the continent together.

In mid-1937 the Popular Front government of Léon Blum would be defeated as a result of its inability to cope with an economic crisis caused by the flight of capital from France. When Blum became premier, the rich began withdrawing their money and investing it abroad, generating a loss of billions of francs by the Bank of France. Blum had been urged to regulate by law the export of gold or foreign exchange, as Hitler had done, but he feared that prohibitions would destroy faith in a free economy, so he would only appeal to the patriotism of holders of capital. His pleas were ignored, and when the cabinet decided on September 7, 1936, to allot a fourteen-billion-franc credit to urgent rearmament—an unavoidable step in view of massive war preparedness in Germany— there was panic and a further flight of capital, which depleted the value of the gold reserves of the Bank of France to fifty billion francs, the minimum necessary to keep the country afloat. On September 26 the franc was devalued, despite a promise by Blum that he would not resort to anything so drastic, and while there was momentary stimulation of the economy—industrial production rose twelve index points by March 1937—there was no significant improvement. A main purpose of devaluation had been to attract capital back to France, but due to a requirement that returning francs be exchanged at the rate before devaluation there was no profit incentive, and the money stayed abroad. Speculation against the franc and raids on the gold reserves of the Bank of France began anew; prices rose, and workers insisted on salary increases to meet them; strikes broke out; and by the end of 1936 the government's deficit amounted to sixteen billion francs.

Blum's difficulties multiplied: demonstrations by left and right factions led to riots in a Paris suburb in March 1937, during which police fired on supporters of the Popular Front, killing five and wounding one hundred fifty; as a result Blum was derided by his own working-class followers, to the satisfaction of French Fascists. International problems were even more serious, as France was becoming isolated: while nonintervention remained the policy of Britain and France toward the civil war in Spain, German and Italian aid was assuring the establishment of a Fascist regime under Franco; Mussolini had left little doubt as to Italy's future course by announcing in November 1936 a "Rome-Berlin axis"; Belgium, also in the fall of 1936, had withdrawn from an alliance with France; and both Poland and Czechoslovakia were hinting at a willingness to accommodate Hitler's ambitions. As for Great Britain, where self-preservation in the face of the Hitler threat was foremost, there was not the wherewithal to come to the aid of France; and the United States had no intention of becoming involved in a European War, as Bullitt had said repeatedly. He went so far as to believe it was prudent not to press the issue of World War I debts, not that France was in any position to make a payment. "It is my honest opinion . . .," he wrote Moore on November 29, 1936, "that unless we can prevent the flooding of enormous foreign loans, it is better for us to remain protected from them by the provisions of the Johnson Act—that is to say, to have the debts remain in default." He explained that every day he was hearing regrets of politicians that France had defaulted on her debt, "and the hope is expressed that it may be possible to reach a debt settlement soon. The object of a debt settlement will be double: in the first place, to open the American money market to the French Government; . . . in the second place . . . is the hope that . . . the ground could be laid for a gradual campaign, . . . which would slowly build up the same emotional sense of 'a duty to civilization,' . . . [as] in 1914, 1915, and 1916." By a "series of small steps," Bullitt warned, the French hope "we may finally become involved. . . ."

Blum was inclined, Bullitt's objections notwithstanding, to appeal to Moscow, but he was confronted with insuperable obstacles to a French-Soviet alliance: the Red Army was inferior to the Polish Army, the French military high command had concluded, and, in order to engage the Germans, Russian troops would be required to pass through Polish territory; however, Marshal Edward Smigly-Rydz, the commander of the Polish Army, had warned General Maurice Gamelin, the French commander-in-chief, that if the Bolsheviks entered Poland, they would never leave. There was also a fear, which Foreign Minister Delbos had expressed to Robert Coulondre, the French ambassador to the U.S.S.R., that the Soviets would try to "push France into a war with Germany." (There was a mysterious development late in 1936 that may have settled a decision in Paris to terminate negotiations with Moscow: Eduard Beneš, the president of Czechoslovakia, informed Blum that Czech intelligence had discovered that Russian military leaders were plotting with Hitler to overthrow Stalin; and the story seemed to stand up when, in 1937, several Soviet generals, including Marshal Mikhail Tukhachevsky, the commissar for defense, were arrested, tried, and executed. While there was evidence, later all but verified, that the Soviet generals had been framed in a clever German plot, the suspicions caused overwhelming opposition in the French Parliament to a pact with Stalin.)

Bullitt took a subtle approach in his effort to dissuade Blum from signing a pact with the Soviets, suggesting there was little to be gained from it. "Blum said that Litvinov had assured him categorically," Bullitt reported to Hull on May 20, 1937,

that if Germany should attack Czechoslovakia and if France should go to war with Germany to defend Czechoslovakia, the Soviet Union would make war on Germany at once. I commented that I did not see how the aid of the Soviet Union could be very effective in view of the condition of Soviet roads and railroads leading to the west and in view of the fact that Soviet planes and armies could not cross Poland. . . .

The condition of the French economy steadily worsened in 1937: from March to June industrial production dropped five index points; by June 15 there was a critically low 2.5 billion franc balance in the national treasury; and the gold supply of the Bank of France was depleted in the first three weeks of June by another eight billion francs. "French capital has gone on strike," Blum told the Chamber of Deputies, and Vincent Auriol, the minister of finance, said that the flight of capital was like "desertion in wartime." Following an emergency meeting of the cabinet on June 15 Blum asked Parliament for plenary power to take the measures necessary to deal with the crisis, and while it was approved in the Chamber of Deputies, it was voted down in the Senate. "I have had enough," Blum told Bullitt. "Everything . . . I have attempted to do has been blocked." On June 22, 1937, he resigned.

"Champagne Ambassador"

BULLITT had accepted an awesome assignment in Paris, at the center of a deepening crisis, and he was up to it because he was a tireless worker, always arising early in the morning so he could begin dictating to Offie the day's outflow of correspondence, most of it consisting of lengthy reports to Washington. But there was another aspect of his ambassadorship, which reflected his personal style: at age forty-six Bullitt was impressive in physical appearance—jaunty and physically trim—and always splendidly turned out in a homburg and one of thirty London-made suits, a fresh red carnation fixed to the left lapel. He gave fine parties, serving vintage French wines he himself had selected and Beluga caviar flown from Iran, and offering cigarettes imported from Virginia as a patriotic touch. (Bullitt's salary was $17,500 a year, and he received an entertainment allowance of only $4,800, so much of his hospitality was charged to personal funds. "No one except ambassadors knows how or why ambassadors manage," wrote Janet Flanner in a profile of Bullitt in *The New Yorker* in December 1938.) The French found Bullitt "witty, ingratiating and genuinely friendly," wrote Jack Alexander in *The Saturday Evening Post*, and they compared him favorably to Benjamin Franklin for his sensitivity to French attitudes. For his part Bullitt was overjoyed at being away from the oppressive atmosphere of Moscow, and any European capital would have been a relief—on his last train trip out of Russia, while passing through Poland, he remarked in some surprise that people actually displayed flowers—but Paris with its gaiety and sophisticated company was most to his liking.

"I have found the pleasantest country place in France to live in," Bullitt wrote Roosevelt on May 28, 1937, "a little chateau in the Park of the Great Chateau of Chantilly. The magnificent joker is that by renting the little chateau, I become the sole proprietor of the Park of Chantilly!" The estate had been there since the eleventh century, and the "little" white-stone chateau had been built in 1776 by the last of the line of great Condés, a royal family of Bourbon origins. Called the Château de St. Fermin, it briefly continued to be occupied by nobility: first, the Duke d'Enghien, who was executed on orders of Napoleon; then, the Duke d'Aumale, who willed the property to the Institute of France. Marshal Henri Pétain, the World War I Army commander, was the president of the institute, and Bullitt had approached him, offering to renovate the chateau—it was rundown and had no plumbing—if he could rent it for a nominal $1,000 a year. "I even had it stipulated in the lease," he wrote Roosevelt, "that I can swim in all the lake ponds and rivers, and can place an American Indian canoe on the great waterway. . . ." Roosevelt was impressed and amused: "The latest inside information," he wrote back, "is that not content with having leased Chantilly for the summer of 1937, you are negotiating with the French Government for . . . Versailles. . . ."

"If it were not for Chantilly, I would never be able to go on as I do," Bullitt confided to a friend. "I would go insane." The estate was near two of the best racetracks in France, and Bullitt kept horses for his own pleasure at nearby stables; he had installed a tennis court and a swimming pool on the grounds; and there was a golf course adjoining (a superb golfer as a youth, Bullitt had taken up the game again and was scoring in the mid-seventies). He reveled in the role of host during the summer season and would invite hundreds of friends to a champagne reception or forty or so to a sit-down dinner, with a chef, three cooks, four butlers, and two maids in attendance. (Bullitt's dinners at Chantilly and in Paris were acclaimed all over Europe, prompting King Zog, the monarch of Albania, to ask to borrow the chef for his wedding banquet; Bullitt happily complied.) Ernest Hemingway was a guest at Chantilly, and he sulked for an entire evening after being beaten at skeet shooting by Refik Kuprili, the young Turk whose education was still Bullitt's responsibility; and it was at Chantilly in July 1937 that Bullitt had Roosevelt's son Franklin for lunch along with Blum, Delbos, and Chautemps. It had been just a month since Chautemps had formed a government, succeeding Blum, and Bullitt reported to Roosevelt that the new premier "was so pleased to escape for a moment from his duties . . . that even before a cocktail, he turned somersaults on the lawn!"

Chautemps was an able politician—when first in Paris as ambassador Bullitt had described him in a letter to Roosevelt as "a jellyfish with lots of common sense," an accurate appraisal—who had rallied the support of the Popular Front by inducing Blum to serve as vice premier. "I had a conversation with Chautemps this afternoon," Bullitt wrote in a report to Hull on July 2, 1937; they had talked about the civil war in Spain and had agreed that Franco might well triumph over the Loyalists: a hostile Fascist regime in Spain "would place France in an extraordinarily dangerous position," Bullitt wrote, noting that war with Germany might also mean war with Italy and Spain. The prospect for Britain was equally perilous, Chautemps had observed; however, "all his information from London indicated that Chamberlain was still inclined to adopt a policy of 'wait and see. . . .' " Bullitt offered his analysis of a vexing dilemma for which he was partly responsible, having fostered fears of Communist designs on Spain: "France could not act without the full support of Great Britain, and [Chautemps] had little hope that such support would be forthcoming." There was, however, an impending crisis of more immediate concern, which Bullitt had addressed in a letter to Roosevelt on May 10: "Delbos and Blum are more or less in despair," he wrote, "with regard to the possibility of keeping Austria and Czechoslovakia out of the hands of Germany. Hitler has the ball and can run with it in any direction he chooses."

"Paris has become a madhouse," Bullitt had written Roosevelt—it was late May, the start of the tourist season—"and each day about fifty persons appear with letters of introduction from the Secretary of State and Senators. . . . I admit that I still give them champagne and caviar, as my self-respect continues to be more Virginian than the Whitelaw Reids, who, if I remember correctly your description, served their guests pink lemonade. . . ." (Reid, an Ohio newspaperman who became the editor and publisher of *The New York Tribune*, was the minister to France in 1889–92, during the presidency of Benjamin Harrison.) Feeling overworked, Bullitt was irritated with his staff, and he complained to the president about "the young men in the Embassy [who] think they have fulfilled the whole duty of man when they have entertained each other at luncheon and dinner. . . . I would have a lot of them transferred if there were any one better in the Service to bring here; but as Mr. Shakespeare remarked, 'It's poor picking between rotten apples.' " He elaborated on the burdens of his post in a letter to Judge Moore, June 2, calling them "almost intolerable": the embassy counselor, Edwin Wilson, and the first secretary for treasury affairs, H. Merle Cochran, were on trips, "and the other boys . . . are so useless . . ."—Bullitt apparently was even annoyed with Robert Murphy, who soon would be promoted to counselor—"that the Paris staff consists in reality of Offie and myself. We keep going about eighteen hours a day, and I do not know how long I can hold the pace." He could report, however, that he was in "incredibly good health," which he attributed to his being "intensely interested in everything that I have to do"; and he had been pleased to learn that Roscoe Hillenkoetter, the naval officer who had been his courier in Moscow, was to be his assistant naval attaché. "Hillenkoetter is one of the most remarkable young men that I know," Bullitt said in a letter to Moore July 5.

"I have just come to the decision that I will accept no invitations from organizations which desire to have the presence of the American Ambassador simply as a flower in their caps," Bullitt wrote Moore. "You will doubtless hear that I have become a hermit. The fact will be that instead of attending some function given by the Daughters of the American Revolution, I am having supper quietly with Chautemps or whoever happens to be Prime Minister . . . at the time." He might also have been entertaining royalty, such as the Duke and Duchess of Windsor, who were married in 1937, the duke having abdicated as Edward VIII of England in order to marry a divorced American woman, Wallis

Simpson. "I had the curious impression that while the marriage has been very good for the boy, it has been very bad for the girl," Bullitt commented in a letter to Roosevelt in November 1937, having spent an evening with the couple.

He is much calmer and much more self-confident. . . . Incidentally, he drank almost nothing and is obviously intensely in love with his wife. The girl, on the other hand, behaved like a person whose insides have been taken out and replaced by an idea of what a king's wife should be like. She has gone English in a big way so far as her accent is concerned. . . . She has lost that spontaneous wit and twinkle which used to make her very attractive; instead she is "gracious."

Bullitt's admiration for the Windsors was not inconsistent with his anti-British bias, as the dethroned king was at odds with his government and tending to sympathize with Hitler; in fact the duke and duchess had recently met with the German dictator, and Bullitt reported to Roosevelt the duchess had remarked, "in describing Hitler's intense interest in architecture, that the Fuhrer had said to her: 'Our buildings will make more magnificent ruins than the Greeks.' That seemed to me to be about as revealing psychologically as anything. . . ." (British officials were so concerned about a rumored romance between Bullitt and the Duchess of Windsor—they were worried mainly that the duke would learn of it—that they indirectly informed Roosevelt of the rumors, hoping the ambassador would be recalled.)

Viceroy of Europe

THE OLD-BOY NETWORK was expanding—Bullitt was better informed on prospective embassy appointments in Europe than he was, said Judge Moore—and communication lines between Paris and the various capitals were being tightened. "I am delighted with my appointment to Yugoslavia," wrote Arthur Bliss Lane to Bullitt, "and have reason to believe that I have you to thank for recommending it to the President." Lane proved his gratitude by sending Bullitt copies of his cables to Washington, as did Anthony J. D. Biddle, Jr., a Philadelphian, who was named ambassador to Warsaw in 1937, replacing another friend of Bullitt's, John Cudahy, who happily accepted a transfer to Dublin. Bullitt persistently proposed his Moscow counselor John Wiley, first for Austria—Wiley served in Vienna as counselor—then for Latvia, and Wiley was named ambassador to Riga in 1938. Bullitt was still bothered about London, however: "It is high time we were represented by a gentleman in that post," he wrote Moore on November 24, 1937. "If you go, . . . I'll send you Offie for alternate weekends just to straighten out the work of your office." Bullitt had not been informed, but the appointment of Joseph P. Kennedy as ambassador to Britain had already been made; nevertheless, the Boston Irishman and the Philadelphia aristocrat got along well until they had an angry falling-out in 1940.

There remained in Europe only two ambassadors whom Bullitt could not abide: Joseph Davies in Moscow, for kowtowing to the Kremlin; and William Dodd in Berlin, for his hostility toward the German government. "I have heard," Bullitt wrote Moore, "that Mrs. Davies' husband"—Davies had married Marjorie Merriweather Post, the heiress to a breakfast cereal fortune—"is to be on his way to the United States . . . in order to find himself a job which will carry enough prestige to enable him to continue being Mrs. Davies' husband. . . . I was also told that some months ago he had offered a million and a half for my job. . . ." (Bullitt may have had good reason to view Davies as a threat, for he was a popular figure in Washington. A Wisconsin lawyer of humble origin, Davies had come to the capital in 1912 to serve as the first chairman of the Federal Trade Commission and had left the government in 1919 to establish a law practice. He was an old friend of Roosevelt's and a heavy campaign contributor.) Davies was seeking reassignment, and Bullitt was correct in his spiteful comment about his wanting to impress his wealthy wife, but he was not angling for Paris. His wife, a woman of privilege who had loathed Moscow, was insisting on the capital of a monarchy, where there would be a royal court: London was her first choice, of course, but Davies had been married before, and his divorce disqualified him as ambassador to Great Britain, leaving Belgium as a suitable alternative. "Davies to Brussels was a stroke of genius," Bullitt wrote Roosevelt. "He cannot do much harm there. And as there is almost no work to do he will be able to survive physically."

As for Dodd, Bullitt finally prevailed—Hugh R. Wilson, the former minister to Switzerland, was named to replace him—by citing the criticism of André François-Poncet, the French ambassador to Germany, and Hermann Goering, the second-ranking Nazi leader. In a letter to Roosevelt on November 23, 1937, he quoted François-Poncet as having said, "Bullitt, for heaven's sake, get Dodd moved out of Berlin. He used to be bad as an Ambassador, but now he is impossible. . . . He is conducting a personal crusade against the Nazi Government. . . ." Goering's comment came as he was being interviewed by Bullitt in Berlin, and it was paraphrased in the same letter to Roosevelt. ". . . [H]e desired to say something . . . which he hoped I would not resent. The matter was a delicate one. But he considered it simply disastrous that there should be no American Ambassador in Berlin. Neither he nor anyone else in the German

Government could recognize Dodd as an American Ambassador. Dodd was too filled with venomous hatred of Germany. . . ." Bullitt wrote Roosevelt again two weeks later: "I cannot tell you how delighted I was to get the news of Hugh Wilson's appointment to Berlin. I have felt like singing a *TE DEUM LAUDAMUS.*"

Bullitt was not so pleased about the fortunes of his friend R. Walton Moore, who as counselor of the State Department had been removed from the line of authority, and at age seventy-eight was being eased out, or so Bullitt believed. "I am convinced," he wrote Roosevelt in November 1937, "that you won't have Moore long in Washington, or indeed on this earth, unless he is given something to do. . . ." Two months later Bullitt wrote, "He seems to have been shelved completely and feels it terribly." Bullitt's efforts were of no avail: Moore remained the counselor of the department until shortly before his death in February 1941.

———————

Bullitt spent two weeks in Washington in October 1937, and on returning to France he went to Nîmes, the city of his Huguenot ancestors, where he was welcomed at a festival and made a *chevalier du tastevin*, a knight of the wine cup. He was also presented with a sonnet, "À *Monsieur Bullitt*," written by a local poet, a copy of which he sent to Roosevelt:

> You are the predestined example
> Of what can be produced
> When American stock is grafted
> Onto old native vines. . . .

"The three days at Nîmes were really grand," Bullitt wrote, "all the way from the black bulls to the girls who danced the *Farandole* in the old Roman arena. . . . I have also to add that on my return from Nîmes this morning, Chautemps phoned me to ask if I would accept the vacant post of French Ambassador to the United States! I told him that I feared the American Government would refuse the *agrément*." "It is a good sonnet," Roosevelt replied on November 11, making no mention of the *agrément*—even in jest the offer by Chautemps was a mark of his high regard for Bullitt—"but it does not hold a candle to the sonnet recently written to me by my fellow Americans, the Eskimos of Alaska." It was the sort of lighthearted exchange between the ambassador and the president that would occur less often as Europe moved toward war, for Bullitt's mood turned somber, and his tone became admonitory and patronizing. "I talked with Norman Davis . . . on his arrival, . . ." Bullitt wrote Roosevelt on November 2—Bullitt was leery of Davis, the chief U.S. delegate to the Geneva Disarmament Conference and an avid supporter of the League of Nations—"and he was kind enough to inform me or, I hope, misinform me with regard to your own point of view. He made it sound as if you thought God had laid Woodrow Wilson's mantle upon you, and [you] were about to take on your shoulders, or rather those of the people of the United States, all the pains of the world. I don't believe this is so; but for Gawd's sake remember that Woodrow Wilson, as a collapsed ex-President, used to lie in bed thinking of the text, 'By their fruits ye shall know them'; and recalling that the fruits he could report to St. Peter were war and the Treaty of Versailles. [Bullitt was resorting to presumption to make his point, as he had no way of knowing the dying president's thoughts.] There are a lot of people in America . . . who are beginning to be ashamed of the idea of keeping the United States at peace. A number of times in Washington I heard the statement, 'Well, I'd rather not be in the Government if the United States won't intervene in . . . the war which is coming in Europe.' That sort of thinking seems to me the product of nothing but overgrown egotism on the part of men who are so old that they know they won't have to go out and die."

Bullitt was not content just to sit in Paris and read the reports of others in key spots—Tony Biddle in Warsaw and Hugh Wilson in Berlin—so he traveled to those capitals to meet with Polish and German leaders, and the reports he sent to Washington were incisive and elucidating, allowing for his belief that German dominance was destined. He arrived in Warsaw on November 14 and talked with Foreign Minister Beck.

Colonel Beck stated to me that he believed that Germany in the near future would take some action against Czechoslovakia. . . . I asked Beck what Poland would do in case France should become involved in a war with Germany because of a German attack on Czechoslovakia. Beck replied that in the hypothetical case I had presented, . . . Poland positively would not march. He went on to explain that Poland would fulfill the direct obligations of her alliance with France completely, and in case of German aggression against France, Poland would march at once; but that under no circumstances would Poland become involved in protecting French satellites in Central Europe, especially Czechoslovakia.

Bullitt wrote Roosevelt of his Berlin visit, which began on November 18. "You will remember," he said in a letter from Paris dated November 23, "that when I was representing you at the funeral of Marshal Pilsudski [the Polish chief of state, who died in May 1935], I had to sit and walk next to General Goering for three days and found him so repellent that I literally could not address a word to him. When I reached Berlin last Thursday, I was horrified to discover that . . . Attolico [Bernardo Attolico, the Italian ambassador to Germany], . . . without obtaining my consent, had gotten in touch with Goering and told him that I was coming through Berlin and that Goering had said that he would like to see me.

. . . I went to see Goering in his private residence. . . . His office is a big room with a huge oak table at one end. . . . There were three chairs, all built in mammoth proportions and covered with cerise velvet, trimmed with gold. The chairs were so big that Goering looked rather less than the size of a normal man, and, as you know, he strongly resembles the hind end of an elephant. In my chair I must have looked like some sort of animated flea."

He sent the State Department a memorandum of his conversation with the German air minister:

Goering said that there was no direct conflict . . . between Germany and France. Germany has given up entirely . . . the idea of regaining Alsace-Lorraine. . . . In addition, the economic systems of France and Germany were completely complementary. . . . Furthermore, the French had contributed so much to the culture of Germany, and the Germans had contributed so much to the culture of France, that as two civilized peoples who lived side by side they had a deep underlying esteem for each other. . . . The sole source of friction between Germany and France was the refusal of France to permit Germany to achieve certain vital national necessities.

I asked Goering what aims especially he had in mind. He replied, "We are determined to join to the German Reich all Germans who are contiguous to the Reich and are divided from the great body of the German race merely by the artificial barriers imposed by the Treaty of Versailles." I asked Goering if he meant that Germany was absolutely determined to annex Austria. . . . He replied that this was an absolute determination of the German government. . . . I asked Goering if the German Government was as decided . . . with regard to the Germans in Bohemia [western Czechoslovakia]. . . . He replied that there could be only one final solution to this question. The Sudeten Germans must enter the German Reich as all other Germans who lived contiguous to the Reich.

. . . He then asked me why I believed there was such hostility to Germany in the United States. I replied that there were many sources of this hostility. There had been a democratic government in Germany, or at least the semblance of a democratic government, which had been destroyed and replaced by a Nazi dictatorship. . . . He thought that the reaction . . . in the United States was probably due to the Jews.

In his letter to Roosevelt of November 23 Bullitt offered an analysis of the situation in Europe, which was astute and largely accurate, as events would prove, although defective due to his tendency to make his wish the father of the thought, as he might have put it: he was by and large in awe of the Germans; scornful of the Russians; suspicious of the British; and enamored of the French. "The atmosphere in Berlin today is singularly like the atmosphere before 1914," he wrote. "The Germans are confident and cocky; sure that time is working for them; sure that they can get exactly what they want and determined to get it. The Poles are convinced that this German estimate . . . is absolutely correct. . . . The Italians, fully aware that when Hitler has cleaned up Austria and Czechoslovakia, they will become mere German satellites, nevertheless are ready to accept this position." (Bullitt had talked at length in Berlin with Attolico, who had been the

Italian ambassador to Moscow and whom Bullitt knew well.) It was "not a promising picture" overall, Bullitt interjected, but "there is one element in it that is not altogether dreadful": the Russians "have now apparently retired behind their swamps, and the fact is beginning to be recognized even in France that the eastern boundary of Europe is not the Ural Mountains but the swamps which extend from Finland, past Poland, to Rumania. . . . The Russians . . . are completely out of the picture so far as Europe is concerned. . . . The British . . . are at the moment on the following line: they will finally, deviously, by silences and tacit approvals, as the lesser evil, permit Hitler to take Austria; take the Germans of Czechoslovakia and dominate Central Europe and the Balkans. . . . Furthermore, I believe the British are prepared to offer Hitler a colonial domain but no portion of their colonial domain. The colonial domain they will offer will be first that of Portugal; then that of Belgium; and finally, if necessary, that of France. . . . The French are at their wit's end, divided between the belief that it is better to have war now . . . and their fear that they will be defeated in such a war. . . . I should not be surprised to find Chautemps . . . swinging to the view that it is better to make a spectacular effort to reach terms with Germany."

That was the option preferred by Bullitt, who anticipated the reaction of the French foreign office: "He will unquestionably be opposed by the Quai d'Orsay, whose only policy since 1919 has been to question German violations of the Treaty of Versailles in order to prepare a beautiful White Book to be published at the outbreak of the next war." Bullitt then ceased to be an observer and became an outright advocate of reconciliation, if not appeasement: "To give up the Russian Alliance and admit that Germany, having lost the war, has won the final victory and will be henceforth the dominant factor in Europe would be . . . today regarded as the part of wisdom by the vast majority of the people of France who think about international affairs. . . . The only way that I can see that the growth of German strength, which I regard as inevitable, can be used for constructive . . . purposes is by a general effort to make the giving of these concessions to Germany a part of a general plan of unification for Europe."

Bullitt also saw fit to advise the president on Far East policy, taking as a point of departure a proposal Norman Davis had put to him: ". . . that the United States, Great Britain and France should never agree to recognize any territorial conquests of Japan in China and never . . . to make any loans to Japan so long as Japan should remain in occupation of Chinese territory." Bullitt wrote Roosevelt that he had said to Davis, "I should want to lie on my back and look at the ceiling for a number of hours while imagining all the possible consequences of such action." He did have an opinion, however, which he stated to Roosevelt: ". . . we have large emotional interests in China, small economic interests, and no vital interests." He noted that in 1905 Theodore Roosevelt, then the president, had been persuaded by the German Kaiser to urge the French to agree to a conference on Morocco by the argument that the destruction of the German Navy would allow France and Great Britain to partition China. "By 1914," Bullitt wrote,

T.R. must have thought that his fears about destruction of the German Navy . . . had been a rather lousy basis on which to determine policy. There is no basis of policy more unreal or disastrous than the apprehension of remote future dangers. . . . The far-off bugaboo of complete Japanese domination of Asia and an eventual attack on us seems to me no basis whatsoever for present-day policy. The Japanese will have their hands full with China and the Soviet Union, and their one hope will be to avoid war with us.

Ironically, the letter was dated December 7, 1937, four years to the day before the Japanese attack on Pearl Harbor.

Offie wrote to Missy LeHand on December 3 to warn that Bullitt was pushing himself too hard and was "completely run down and should have a vacation. . . . He is extremely popular here and is doing a swell job. . . . In order to live up to his reputation he is kept constantly on the go from fourteen to eighteen hours a day, and it's too much." Offie asked LeHand to "persuade your Chief to mention this subject to him sometime," which Roosevelt did, insisting that Bullitt take a rest. "Orders duly received and contents noted," Bullitt replied. "Obedience, however, impossible due to absence of second in command who is in Switzerland. . . . Don't worry about me. There is lots of life in the old carcass yet. . . . As you know, I am going to take a long holiday . . . beginning about the first of March." Bullitt then took the liberty of giving Roosevelt his marching orders. "Henceforth, your chief job is going to be to maintain our national honor while avoiding involvement in war. The best way to do that, I think, is to be as wise as the serpent *before* the event, not after."

Groping for the Meaning of Munich

B ULLITT was on home leave in mid-March 1938—he briefed the president and State Department officials in Washington and went to Philadelphia for the removal of an infected tooth—so he missed a succession of events in Europe. On March 12 Hitler declared the annexation of Austria, the *Anschluss*, at a time when the French government was in one of its periodic reshuffles: Chautemps had quit, rather than face the decision of whether to oppose the latest German aggression, and on March 13—it was on this day that Hitler proclaimed Austria "a province of the German Reich"—Léon Blum took over again, backed by center and right factions and the Communists. The Blum coalition lasted less than a month, however, and on April 8 Edouard Daladier, a Radical Socialist, became premier with the support of a moderate conservative, Paul Reynaud. Daladier met immediately with Joseph Paul-Boncour, the foreign minister, who stood for an unwavering defense of Czechoslovakia: an admirable policy, said Daladier, but he doubted that France was strong enough to back it up, so he replaced Paul-Boncour with Georges Bonnet, also a Radical Socialist and a clever politician of a peace-at-any-price persuasion. The foreign office was on the side of Paul-Boncour and "was prepared to go to any limit, even to the extreme of war, to defend Austria, provided that France did not find herself alone," Edwin Wilson, the chargé d'affaires, cabled Washington on March 14, having spoken with Secretary-General Léger. Léger said the French had "on four separate occasions proposed to the British . . . strong representations in Berlin," but Britain had instead notified the Austrian chancellor, Kurt von Schuschnigg, it "was not in a position to go to his assistance." Léger told Wilson that in view of the British attitude "the French Government had merely made the same formal representations after the event as had the British," though he vowed that with regard to Czechoslovakia "the case is very different."

It was not only in France that there was top-level realignment: in Germany Hitler replaced von Neurath with von Ribbentrop as foreign minister; and in Britain, Eden, who had lost patience with the willingness of Prime Minister Chamberlain to appease the Nazis, resigned as foreign secretary and was replaced by Edward F. L. Wood, Lord Halifax. On March 10, 1938, the day Hitler decided to march into Austria, von Ribbentrop met with Halifax in London, and that evening he cabled Berlin that England would do nothing. Von Ribbentrop elaborated: ". . . if a reasonable attitude was assumed by both parties, a final and lasting understanding between the two countries would be entirely possible."

Bullitt had made clear that he took issue with Léger and the other Quai d'Orsay career officers, one of whom was René Saint-Quentin, the newly appointed ambassador to the United States. "When I asked [Saint-Quentin] if he saw any possibility of preserving peace," Bullitt had written Roosevelt on January 10, "he said that he saw none. I said to him that this seemed to me not the policy of a statesman but the policy of an undertaker."

Roosevelt, at least before the *Anschluss*, seemingly had failed to sense the gravity of the European crisis, and he was urging Bullitt to run for governor of

Pennsylvania. "I could scarcely hear what you said on the telephone last night," Bullitt cabled Roosevelt on February 25, as he was about to sail from Le Havre. "I tried to express to you my profound conviction that for me to leave the field of foreign affairs at this critical moment . . . would be an abandonment of duty. . . . My entire interest at the present time is in devising ways and means to keep the United States out of the series of wars that are on the horizon." (Democratic leaders in Pennsylvania decided to try to draft Bullitt anyway, but his candidacy was vetoed by two influential Philadelphia bosses, Matthew H. McCloskey and John B. Kelly, reportedly because Bullitt had been twice divorced and married the second time to the widow of a Communist.)

It was clear to Bullitt upon his return to Paris that Sigmund Freud had to be rescued from Vienna, for Nazi persecution of Austrian Jews had begun, and Freud's life was in immediate danger. He received a cable from Freud, asking that the U.S. government intervene with the Germans in securing his release, and Bullitt relayed the message to Roosevelt. John Wiley was the chargé d'affaires in Vienna, and he was directed by the State Department to proceed via official channels; not satisfied that this was sufficient, Bullitt went to the German ambassador to France, Graf von Welczeck, who happened to be an Austrian himself, and warned of a worldwide uproar if any harm came to Freud. Freud was released in early June 1938, and on his way to London, his home for the final year of his life, he stopped in Paris, where he was met by Bullitt at the railroad station.

"We may have a complete blow-up within the next few hours," Bullitt cabled the State Department on April 24, 1938, which was an alarmist reaction, though he was only a bit less apprehensive when he sounded another alert on May 17: "The Czechoslovakian situation is so critical that . . . I . . . believe the Department should be prepared to face a major European war before August 15. . . ." On May 20 he analyzed that situation—with discernment but his antiwar sentiments were reflected—in a lengthy letter to Roosevelt.

. . . it looks to me as if the Czechs had decided that . . . it would be better for them to have general war rather than give the Sudeten a sufficient autonomy to satisfy . . . Hitler. . . . It is becoming a question of whether or not France will march when the Germans cross the Czech frontier. . . . I feel that it would be an unspeakable tragedy if France, to support Czechoslovakia, should attack the Siegfried Line. . . . The slaughter of the entire younger generation of France would be certain, and every city in France could be leveled to the ground by German planes. . . . [Bullitt was mistaken about the invulnerability of the Siegfried Line, which was lightly manned by German troops, and he overestimated German air power.] There could be only one possible result: the complete destruction of western Europe and Bolshevism from one end of the Continent to the other.

Bullitt believed an effort should be made to free the French of their moral commitment to the Czechs, and he offered a recommendation:

Call to the White House the Ambassadors of England, France, Germany and Italy. Ask them to transmit to Chamberlain, Daladier, Hitler and Mussolini your urgent invitation to send representatives at once to the Hague to attempt to work out a peaceful settlement of the dispute. . . . Add that, if the four governments desire, a representative of the United States will sit with them. . . . The conference in the Hague would probably have to recommend that a plebiscite be held in Czechoslovakia to determine the will of the different peoples of that country. If the Czechs should refuse to hold such a plebiscite, the French would have an escape from their desperate . . . dilemma, and general European war would be avoided. You would be accused . . . of selling out a small nation in order to produce another Hitler triumph. I should not hesitate to take that brick on my head, and I don't think you should either. . . .

Bullitt further advised on May 21—his cable was delivered to Roosevelt aboard the yacht *Potomac*—that the Soviet Union could not be counted on to support Czechoslovakia, as Litvinov had promised it would. His friend Juliusz Lukasiewicz, the Polish ambassador to France, had told Bullitt that his country "would immediately declare war on the Soviet Union, should that country attempt to send troops across Poland. . . ."

Bullitt's greatest fears for France were based on his impression of German air superiority: "The French General Staff estimates," he reported to Roosevelt, "that at the present moment France must have for war with Germany a minimum of 2,600 first-line planes. At the moment France has 1,500. [At that, Bullitt was overstating French air strength—a few hundred operating airplanes was more like it—evidently unaware of the extent to which industrial production had been affected by the economic disaster.] The present French rate of production is about forty-five a month. . . . Meanwhile the Germans are producing between three hundred and five hundred planes per month. . . . I asked La Chambre"—Guy La Chambre had been appointed air minister of France by Premier Daladier—"if he did not feel that the Germans were so superior . . . that they might be able to drive the French completely out of the air after a few weeks of fighting. He admitted that this was a possibility. . . ." (Bullitt was aware that the French air commander, General Joseph Vuillemin, had said at a meeting of the Permanent Committee on National Defense on March 15 that, given the strength of the *Luftwaffe*, "the French Air Force would be wiped out in fifteen days.") La Chambre, nevertheless, asserted that if Germany should invade Czechoslovakia, "the blow to French honor would be so great, . . . that France would declare war." Bullitt wrote that he replied with a question he had heard Daladier ask: "With what?"

"Here at Chantilly, . . . with the nightingales singing and the river pouring its white cascade below the still woods," Bullitt wrote Roosevelt on June 13, 1938, "I feel like a participant in the last days of Pompeii." He had that week conferred with two top French Army generals, Maurice Gamelin, the commander-in-chief, and Edouard Réquin, the commander "in the single area where attack on Germany remains possible—the Siegfried Line"; and they assured him "that if the German Army should cross the Czech frontier, France would mobilize at once. . . ." Réquin, wrote Bullitt, "looks upon a frontal attack on the Siegfried Line with absolute horror," and he had predicted it would resemble the Battle of the Somme (an Allied offensive in 1916, the memory of which haunted French and British military men for its enormous casualty rate) "on a much larger scale. . . . The casualties on the attacking side, . . . the French, would be three to four times the casualties on the German side. 'It means,' he said, 'the death of a race.' " Roosevelt replied on June 25: "Ever so many thanks for yours of the thirteenth. May God in his infinite wisdom prove that you are wrong."

As he often was on military matters—first, because he lacked experience; second, because he relied on the word of French generals of inferior ability (Gamelin suffered from mentally debilitating syphilis, and Réquin was a brooding pessimist); and third, because he let his emotions get the better of him—Bullitt was quite wrong as to the effectiveness of the French, though not about the imminence of a world war. "The chief advantage of the French," he wrote—this would be a major misjudgment—"would be the possession of tanks which are far superior to the German tanks." (He was referring to the heavy and slow Saumur, which would prove to be no match for the speedy German panzers, already assembled by Heinz Guderian, the German armored commander, into a fully mechanized division.) Further, Bullitt was impressed by the worthiness of French defenses. "They both feel," he wrote, still referring to his conversation with Gamelin and Réquin, "that the French would continue to hold out on the Maginot Line and would wait for the pressure of the blockade—since they both assume that England would be in the war from almost the first day—to strangle Germany."

The French were sublimely unaware in June 1938 that their failure to appreciate the value of fast tanks would be their undoing within two years. It was the belief of French generals that tanks were simply for the purpose of infantry support, as Marshal Pétain wrote in 1921 when he was supreme commander: "Tanks assist the advance of the infantry, by breaking static obstacles and active resistance put up by the enemy." A noted British military historian, Basil Lidell Hart—Hart was a veteran of the Battle of the Somme—became an early advocate of using the tank to lead an attack, plunging into enemy territory and opening the way for foot soldiers; and ranking German officers, such as Hans von Seeckt, agreed with Hart. "The whole future of warfare," von Seeckt wrote, also in

1921, "appears to me to be in the employment of mobile armies, relatively small but of high quality." Von Seeckt's theory was developed by Guderian, who wrote the definitive work on tank warfare, *Achtung-Panzer!* in 1937, and Adolf Hitler was already convinced: "That's what I need!" said Hitler after viewing an armored demonstration in 1933. But the French persisted in their outdated conviction: ". . . the primary role of the tank," wrote the inspector-general of tanks, François Keller, in 1940, "will be the same as in the past: to assist the infantry in reaching successive objectives." Keller was responding to a memorandum from Colonel Charles de Gaulle, who had been arguing for an armored division since 1933 and had written a book, *The Army of the Future, 1932–1934*, which had been studied closely by the German commanders.

Bullitt also made nonmilitary judgments that were questionable: for example, he placed the blame for the Sudeten crisis on the Czechs, as he indicated in a report to Hull following a meeting with Stefen Osusky, the Czech minister to Paris. "The impression I gathered . . . was that the Czechs prefer to see their nation succumb in a conflagration which will destroy all Europe, rather than make the large concessions which alone would satisfy Hitler. . . ." He was impatient with President Eduard Beneš, calling him an adventurer. "He knows that if he grants autonomy now to the Sudeten Germans," Bullitt said in his letter of June 13 to Roosevelt, "the Sudeten some day will vote themselves out of Czechoslovakia and into Germany, and he will go down in history as the man who began the disintegration of the Czechoslovak state. On the other hand, if he refuses to grant autonomy and makes only concessions which the Sudeten will reject and war comes, he will be the hero who resisted against great odds, and he will be able to fly at the last moment to the Soviet Union." (When Beneš resigned in October 1938 after Britain and France had yielded to Hitler's demands—he found refuge in London, not Moscow—he accused Bullitt of duplicity, saying he had claimed he was speaking for Washington as he argued for concession.) Bullitt personally respected Beneš, a founder of the Czech republic with Thomas Masaryk, whom he succeeded as president in 1935; but Bullitt's first concern was peace in Europe and, failing that, American neutrality. "There is beginning to be a general conviction throughout Europe," he wrote Roosevelt, "that the United States will be drawn into the war, if it starts. . . . Day in and day out, I say to the French that . . . the United States would declare immediate neutrality, and the Neutrality Act would come into force at once. The answer invariably is, 'Yes, we know that; but the Germans will behave in such a way that you will soon be drawn in.' "

Bullitt had a reputation, undoubtedly well deserved, for absolute incorruptibility: he never even gave much thought to personal finances, much less to ways of earning money that could be called into question. He was probably aware that others were not so principled; he might have known that, for one, Joseph P. Kennedy, the new ambassador to London, had with the repeal of Prohibition in 1933 made a killing by arranging to become the U.S. distributor for certain British distillers. Kennedy arrived in London in the company of James Roosevelt, the president's eldest son, which helped influence the decision of the British to award the liquor distributorships to him; Kennedy then refused to share his profits with James Roosevelt. Certain members of the Roosevelt family were impressed by their influence and not above using it, and Bullitt was anxious to please Roosevelt family members, in order to curry favor with the president. It was this combination of circumstances that might have caused a scandal in the summer of 1938, had Bullitt not blown the whistle.

G. Hall Roosevelt was born in 1891, the younger brother of Eleanor Roosevelt, the wife of the president, who was his surrogate mother following the death of their parents, and she called him "Brudie." Hall Roosevelt was tall, handsome, and energetic, and following his graduation from Harvard with an engineering degree he went to work for General Electric; he spent fifteen years with the company except during the first world war, when he was an Army flying instructor. By 1937, however, he was out of a job, twice divorced and "drinking himself to death," according to Joseph P. Lash, Mrs. Roosevelt's biographer, and it was at this point that he became involved in procuring aircraft for the Spanish Republican government. The Department of State had curtailed licenses to export aircraft to Spain; the president had called the selling of arms to a nation in civil war "thoroughly unpatriotic"; and as of January 1937 the practice was prohibited by an embargo. Nevertheless the exporters—beset by the Depression, they were desperate for business—continued their efforts to obtain the planes, claiming they were being sold to nations other than Spain. Douglas Aircraft of California in June 1938 received an order for two hundred DC-2s and DC-3s, which were ostensibly slated for delivery to France, Sweden, and Greece; but realizing that so many aircraft could only be headed for Spain, Douglas declined the bid and reported it to Joseph C. Green, the chief of the Office of Arms and Munitions Control in Washington, saying that it had been made by an "unnamed businessman."

In June 1938—the timing of his visit was not a coincidence—Hall Roosevelt arrived in Paris. In March, during the brief tenure of Léon Blum as premier, the French frontier had been opened to aircraft exports to the Spanish Republic, but on June 13, amid rumors of a large shipment on the way from the United States, Premier Daladier halted the exports again. On June 21 Bullitt reported to the State Department that Foreign Minister Bonnet had said "he was being pressed extremely hard by the Spanish government to reopen . . . the frontier. . . . I replied that I had received no intimations whatsoever that our government had altered its policy. . . . Bonnet answered that it would be most valuable to him to have authoritative information on this point immediately." Bullitt received a prompt reply from Undersecretary Welles: "The Department has received information indicating that an attempt is being made to purchase large numbers of used planes for immediate shipment to Spain. . . . There is no foundation for the statement that this government has approved the proposed transaction." Also on June 21 Bullitt sent Roosevelt a "very private letter, which requires no answer" about the visit of his brother-in-law:

> Some days ago I received a telegram from Mrs. Roosevelt informing me that Hall was coming to Paris and asking me to do anything that I could for him. . . . When Hall came in . . . this afternoon, he said that he, acting through Harold Talbott of Cleveland, had managed to gather for the Spanish Government approximately 150 new and second-hand planes of various makes. . . . [Harold E. Talbott of Dayton, Ohio, had been with the Chrysler Corporation and was chairman of the board of North American Aviation in 1931–32.] He said that he had discussed this transaction fully with you and that it had your entire approval. He stated that you and Jimmy had discussed all the details and that you had agreed to wink at the evasion of the Neutrality Act involved, . . . and had sent for Joseph Green and had ordered him to permit the export of these planes and to accept such falsified papers as might be presented. . . ."

Bullitt wrote that he had been noncommittal, but he had advised Hall Roosevelt that he had been instructed to "oppose absolutely the giving of licenses for shipments of planes to Spain," and he reminded him "that the French Government had closed the frontier to Spain absolutely." He then lectured Hall Roosevelt, saying that the French "had a real hope" that all volunteers—the international brigades from the United States, Germany, and elsewhere—might be withdrawn, and there was the prospect of an armistice. "I told him that I could not imagine a moment more unpropitious for an attempt to organize the shipment of planes to Spain. . . ."

If Bullitt betrayed a tone of moral superiority in the Hall Roosevelt matter— he had caught the president in an indiscretion, and he knew it—he was downright indignant over an attempt by someone to have John Wiley's appointment to Riga rescinded by alleging he was a drunkard. "I have never been much angrier in my life," he wrote Roosevelt on June 14, following a phone conversation in which the president had told him the question had been raised. "As you know, I worked intimately with Wiley from the time of the [London] Economic Conference in 1933 until 1936 when he left Moscow for Antwerp. . . . I have never . . . seen Wiley drunk or anything like drunk. The allegation is an outrageous lie. . . . I hope you will have sent Wiley's appointment to the Senate before this letter reaches you. . . . Incidentally, if you want any political support for Wiley, I can guarantee to have twenty Senators storming your office in twenty-four hours. . . ." Having heard from Missy LeHand before mailing the letter that "Papa will attend to the appointment," Bullitt wrote a postscript: "My profound thanks! Bless you!" The question appeared to have been settled, but it had not, for on June 15 Bullitt heard again from Roosevelt, who said he had not yet talked with Hull, "but Sumner [Welles] tells me that the secretary believes that our friend in Vienna worked with the crowd that was against him in London . . . in 1933. . . . This is just for your information, and I suggest that you do nothing . . . until I have talked with the Secretary."

Bullitt did do something: on June 30 he sent letters to both Secretary Hull and President Roosevelt. "The President has now let me know," he wrote Hull, "that you feel somewhat doubtful about Wiley because you were told at the time of the Economic Conference that he worked with Moley and his associates, who were hostile to you. . . . I recall that Wiley had to see Moley . . . twice in the line of his official duty, but I know that there was never any personal social contact between them. . . . I am absolutely certain that Wiley was never a member of any group that was working against you." While deferential to Hull, Bullitt was still angry and defiant in his letter to Roosevelt. "I don't know whose diseased brain invented the idea that Wiley was an associate of Moley's and hostile to the Secretary," he wrote. "I hope the Secretary will have no more doubts about Wiley and that you will announce his appointment forthwith. But if such doubts should remain, I feel that . . . Wiley should be informed of the allegations . . . and should demand an immediate inquiry. . . . I should, of course, accompany Wiley, and the result might be a very healthy purge of rats. A career officer can have his life ruined by lies whispered in secret. . . ."

Wiley's appointment to Riga was approved probably because Bullitt was commendably unafraid to make a fuss, but there must have been those in the Department of State—Judge Moore, for one—who were a bit bewildered, as they recalled Bullitt's harsh disapproval of Wiley when he was the counselor in Moscow. As for ruining the lives of career officers, Bullitt did not permit this concern to quiet him when he believed that criticism was warranted, as he did when he wrote to Roosevelt on November 23, 1937, about Philip R. Faymonville, the military attaché in Moscow, who was seeking an extension of his tour of duty. Faymonville was "the greatest Bolshevik lover at large," Bullitt wrote, "the most unsatisfactory member of the staff, as he constantly went behind the back of the Embassy to assure the Bolshies that they were loved by our Government. . . ."

For Bullitt the Sudeten crisis had begun on December 9, 1918, when President Wilson, briefing members of the peace commission staff while en route to

Paris, drew a line through a map of Europe and said that Bohemia would be part of Czechoslovakia. Bullitt had protested, noting that there were three million Germans in Bohemia—the term "Sudeten German" designated Germans living in parts of Czechoslovakia that bordered on Germany—and Wilson had simply replied that Masaryk had not told him that. The ceding of the Sudetenland to Czechoslovakia was a provision of the Versailles Treaty that Bullitt had particularly objected to in 1919, which is a reason—in addition to his fear of the horrible consequences of a European war—why he applauded the conciliatory position on the Czech issue of Daladier and Bonnet, who happened to agree with him about the treaty. "Both Daladier and Bonnet fought the Treaty of Versailles," Bullitt wrote in a report to Washington, "and wrecked their careers temporarily by telling the truth . . . when the truth was unpopular." The French leaders were also of like mind with Bullitt on the dim prospect of preserving peace in Europe: "Daladier said to me yesterday that he considered the present appearance of an improvement in the general . . . situation a mirage," Bullitt wrote on June 23, 1938. "Nothing had yet been settled, and he was not optimistic that any settlement could be achieved." Bullitt was further discouraged after talking with his friend Walter Lippmann, the author and syndicated columnist, who had been to Prague, "where he had a conversation of two hours with Beneš." Lippmann, Bullitt reported on July 18, was also pessimistic: "He is inclined to believe that the dispute is unsolvable, since the Czechs will not offer the Sudeten anything but a permanent status as an inferior minority, and the Sudeten will not accept any such status."

"I am living at Chantilly altogether," Bullitt wrote Moore on July 19, "and only open the town house when I have to give some sort of official dinner or other function," such as a ball he held for four hundred midshipmen of the Naval Academy at Annapolis, who were on a training cruise. "The ball . . . was really jolly . . . ," he wrote (Bullitt did not mention that he had caused a minor scandal by inviting several hundred Parisian lasses and failing to provide chaperones); it had been a brief bright moment in a period of gloom. "To say that peace is at the mercy of an incident was never more true than today, and the question of whether the incident will come or not is on the knees of the gods. As a result, I don't expect to leave . . . at all this summer except perhaps for a two-day visit to John Cudahy in Dublin." He was going to Ireland, he explained to Moore, because "Mr. William Nelson Cromwell has offered to give Anne a really good riding horse, and Cudahy has discovered one that he thinks she will like." (A contemporary of Judge Moore and a Bullitt family friend, William Nelson Cromwell was a New York lawyer noted for his astute counseling of business enterprises; a Republican, he was instrumental in negotiating the Panama Canal treaty in 1903, and his firm, Sullivan and Cromwell, would represent the Fascist government of

Spain.) Bullitt was fearful of an imminent outbreak but hedging his bets—the odds, he wrote Moore, "were sixty against and forty in favor of a general war this year"—but by mid-August he was reflecting a dire anxiety that had swept Paris. "The French Government is now convinced," he wrote Roosevelt on August 17, "that there will be another crisis during the first weeks of September," and he repeated his proposal that the president initiate a four-power conference at the Hague. "As you know," Bullitt wrote Roosevelt on August 31, 1938, "the Germans have one million eight hundred thousand men mobilized. . . . If we intend to . . . try to stop the holocaust, we shall have an almost impossibly brief period in which to work. . . . I am convinced more than ever that we should attempt to stay out and be ready to reconstruct whatever pieces may be left of European civilization."

Repeating a vow uttered by Daladier on September 8, Bullitt cabled Washington that the French "would order immediate mobilization and attack . . . at once, if the boot of a German soldier should cross the Czechoslovak frontier"; and the premier had intended to have his position understood, "however England might wobble or vacillate." Still, Bullitt was convinced the French would be at the mercy of the German air force, the *Luftwaffe*, all the more so after having listened to Charles A. Lindbergh, the American aviation pioneer, who had come for lunch at Chantilly with Air Minister La Chambre on September 9: German air power was greater than that of all other European nations combined, Lindbergh asserted—Germany had ten thousand warplanes, he estimated, and was building five hundred to eight hundred per month—and France would not be able to catch up for years. (Lindbergh, who had been decorated by Hitler, was so at odds with anti-German militarism in the U.S.—he was also embittered with America, owing to the kidnapping and murder of his infant son in 1932—that he resigned his Army commission and in 1935 became a resident of Britain.)

Hitler and Chamberlain conferred on September 15 at Berchtesgaden, Hitler's Alpine retreat, and Bullitt reported that news of the meeting "has been received by all circles in France except the Communists . . . with intense satisfaction. . . ." He then jotted a note to Roosevelt, which summed it all up for the moment: "If you have enough airplanes, you don't have to go to Berchtesgaden." The two leaders met again on September 22 at Godesberg on the Rhine River, and it was quickly apparent that the détente was momentary: what the British prime minister had to offer—and notwithstanding a provision for the transfer of the Sudetenland from Czechoslovakia to Germany—did not suit the German dictator. Dated September 23, a confidential memo was handed to Roosevelt during a cabinet meeting: "Bill Bullitt just telephoned the following. . . . He has just been informed

. . . that Chamberlain . . . is returning to London. The news is very bad. . . . It is said that Hitler wishes his troops to occupy the Sudeten. Resistance and war will follow."

Bullitt again called for a European conference, urging in a cable to Hull on September 24 that the president "issue an appeal to the Chiefs of State of England, France, Germany, Italy and Poland . . . to send representatives at once to the Hague to discuss ways and means to preserve European peace. . . . I believe we should offer to send a representative to such a conference." "My own thought was," Hull wrote in his *Memoirs*,

> that while I did not oppose the making of these appeals, I was not convinced that the results would justify them. . . . I feared lest too ardent steps by the President should throw us into the same appeasement camp with Chamberlain. . . . Moreover, I had no confidence whatever in any pledge by Hitler. . . . The President, however, believed with Bullitt that something should be done. . . . He said to me: "It can't do any harm."

Roosevelt had listened to Hull, however, and it was decided that the president would instead send Hitler a message, which he did on September 26: "On behalf of 130 millions of people of the United States of America and for the sake of humanity everywhere I most earnestly appeal to you not to break off negotiations looking to a peaceful, fair, and constructive settlement of the questions at issue." Bullitt was angered by the decision at the White House, insisting in an early-morning telephone call on September 27 to Jay Pierrepont Moffat, the chief of the European Division at the State Department, that the only hope for peace was a conference such as the one he had proposed. He had enlisted the support of Sumner Welles, who had just visited him in Paris, and the undersecretary was given a go-ahead to determine the sentiments of Chamberlain and Daladier. Events outpaced any American effort to convene a conference, however, and when Roosevelt learned on September 28 that Chamberlain had agreed to meet with Hitler at Munich, he sent the British prime minister a cable, which simply read: "Good man." Bullitt was elated by news of the Munich meeting—it would also be attended by Daladier and Mussolini—for it was what he had been proposing, only at the summit. "I am so relieved this evening that I feel like embracing everyone," he wrote Roosevelt on September 28, "and I wish I were in the White House to give you a large kiss on your bald spot."

"In itself the Munich Agreement covered only the procedures by which the territorial claims against Czechoslovakia of Germany . . . should be determined," wrote Telford Taylor, an attorney and the author of an exhaustive account, *Munich: The Price of Peace*. "But the scope and significance of the Munich crisis far transcended the document's bare provisions." On October 1

Bullitt appeared at the home of Georges Bonnet—the foreign minister had just returned to Paris from Munich—with an armful of roses, tears in his eyes, and a "fraternal and joyous salutation of America" on his lips, for it was not until he met with Daladier for lunch on October 3 that he realized the meeting had been "an immense diplomatic defeat for France and England." Bullitt added in a report to Washington: "Daladier recognizes that unless France can recover a united national spirit to confront the future, a fatal situation will arise within the next year."

Bullitt the Belligerent

BULLITT was on the first boat, literally—it was the *Normandie*, sailing on October 5, 1938—for the United States, bearing details of the message he had received at the luncheon meeting with Daladier, which also was attended by Jean Monnet, an economic planner and financial adviser to the French government, and Guy La Chambre, the air minister. Monnet had been called in by Daladier for the express purpose of negotiating the purchase of American airplanes: "If I had had three or four thousand aircraft," Daladier had said to Monnet, "Munich would never have happened." Bullitt would be their accomplice. "Munich threw Bullitt and Daladier more closely together," wrote Gordon Wright, a history professor at Stanford University and the author of a thoughtful study of Bullitt as ambassador to France, "for it aroused in them both a desperate sense of impending disaster. Daladier, who lacked real confidence both in his own foreign minister and his British allies, found that he could safely unburden himself to Bullitt, . . . and he proceeded to do so. . . ." As for Bullitt, who had sensed disaster for some time, it was a turning point, which he had reached with the help of the warnings of the French premier. "Until Munich," Wright wrote, "Bullitt was on the whole an appeaser and an isolationist; after Munich, he shifted ground, and eventually became one of the most vigorous advocates of outright American intervention."

In the early morning of September 28 Bullitt had dictated an urgent cable to the president, which began: "If war should begin on the first of October, the French would have six hundred battle planes"; but upon hearing that Hitler had invited Chamberlain, Daladier, and Mussolini to Munich, he mailed the report

instead. "It is just as vital," he said in an attached note, "to have this information
. . . now as it was when it seemed that war was certain; because it remains vital
for France to start building planes . . . at once." Otherwise, he warned, "the
time will soon come again when Hitler will issue a ukase and make war when it is
not obeyed. . . ." French military intelligence estimated, said Bullitt, that "the
Germans have ready for battle at this moment six thousand five hundred planes,
. . . two-thirds bombers and one-third pursuit planes"; and according to Air
Minister La Chambre, "French pursuit planes were so insufficient in numbers,
. . ." and "anti-aircraft artillery . . . inadequate in quantity, . . ." that

> the German planes would be able to bomb Paris at will. . . . The Minister for Air felt
> certain that the destruction in Paris would pass all imagination. He said that he had sent his
> wife and child to Brittany, . . . and he believed that every woman and child who could
> leave Paris should do so at once. . . . I have accordingly today given instructions to
> Murphy to inform each member of the staff . . . that I believe he should send his wife and
> children out of Paris. . . .

Bullitt had discussed with La Chambre "the problem of producing a sufficient number of planes to overcome German and Italian superiority," and he
submitted the opinion of the air minister "that such planes could only be produced on the continent of North America and by American manufacturers. Since
the Neutrality Act would prevent the manufacture of such planes in the United
States, he proposed . . . huge factories for planes in Canada, possibly just
opposite Detroit and Buffalo, so that American workmen . . . could be utilized
readily." Bullitt also reported that La Chambre had asked his opinion as to who
was "best qualified to organize this effort on behalf of France," and he had
suggested Jean Monnet, "who . . . has been an intimate friend of mine for many
years, whom I trust as a brother." (He was the same Jean Monnet who after the
war would produce a plan for modernizing French industry and would be a
principal founder of the European Common Market.)

————————

Bullitt arrived in Washington late in the day on October 13 and went straight
to the White House, where he huddled with Roosevelt until the early hours of the
following day, supplementing his written report with details and making a personal plea for an emergency air power buildup. The effect of his argument was
such that, according to an official history of the United States Army in World War
II, the president ordered an immediate preparedness program, which he outlined
at a press conference that very morning: he intended to seek a $500 million
supplemental appropriation; he would order the Army Air Corps to initiate an
extensive expansion; he would direct the State Department to study ways to
remove the arms embargo from the Neutrality Act; and he would order that

Monnet be given official cooperation on his forthcoming visit to the United States. Roosevelt then went to his Hyde Park home for a round of preparedness meetings—with Bullitt; Harry L. Hopkins, his special assistant, who was being sent on a tour of aircraft factories; and Henry Morgenthau, the secretary of the treasury.

Morgenthau voiced opposition of the measures Bullitt was urging: he was troubled by the thought of France purchasing American airplanes, which was an alternative—it was the one Bullitt favored—to building them in Canada. "They'll have to do it the way the Germans do it, inside of France, to help their unemployment situation," Morgenthau later told a meeting of his staff. "For every million dollars you take out of France," he wrote in a memo to the president, "it just makes their foreign exchange that much worse." But Bullitt had already prevailed with the president, who revealed his intentions to an unofficial British representative at Hyde Park, Arthur C. Murray, first pointing out that Germany had the capacity to produce forty thousand airplanes, while Britain and Canada together could turn out only twenty-five thousand and France fifteen thousand. Roosevelt told Murray that "the twenty or thirty thousand planes to give the necessary superiority over Germany and Italy" would come from the United States. Europe could not be permitted to burn, he said, for the fire would inevitably spread; if France and Britain fell, the United States would fall as well.

Monnet arrived in New York on October 18 and hurried to Hyde Park for an appointment with the president: "In Roosevelt's view," Monnet later wrote, "Munich had opened the way to war. He had decided to spare his country from ever having to give in under threats, as France and Britain had had to do." The meeting was kept a secret from Secretary of State Hull, Harry H. Woodring, the secretary of war, and General Henry H. "Hap" Arnold, the Air Corps chief of staff, each of whom had disapproved of military aid to Britain and France; but Morgenthau, who was Jewish and could be trusted to endorse any effort to contain Nazi Germany, was informed by Bullitt that Roosevelt had been "most frank and honest with Monnet."

Bullitt and Monnet went to Washington to meet with Morgenthau. Over dinner at Morgenthau's home on October 22, the treasury chief sternly observed that in four years "at least $4 billion of gold has left France"; there was little to be gained from "talking about building airplanes or anything else," he insisted, until the drain of gold had been halted and the French treasury replenished. Morgenthau then softened his tone and suggested a simple plan: Daladier could issue a decree making it an offense, punishable by a jail sentence, not to restore money to France—such a law had been authorized by a tripartite agreement, engineered by Morgenthau in 1936, by which the U.S., Great Britain, and France stabilized their currencies—and Monnet and Bullitt were "beside themselves with joy," Morgenthau noted in his diary afterward. Then, on October 26, Morgenthau wrote to Merle Cochran, the first secretary for treasury affairs in Paris, directing him to meet with Daladier "alone . . . without letting any French or British official know. . . . Monnet has seen the President and myself and is carrying a . . . secret message relating to the French financial situation." Two days later Monnet was on his way back to France, bearing also a note from Bullitt to La Chambre: "I have the greatest hope that the work you have initiated will not only end with the accomplishment of your program but will also greatly reinforce France and La Paix." Bullitt remained behind for a three-month visit: he vacationed in Cuba in November; he conferred daily with Roosevelt in December; and in January he attended additional White House meetings and testified before congressional committees.

In the week that it took Monnet to cross the Atlantic—he reached Paris on November 4—there was upheaval in the French cabinet over government finances: Paul Marchandeau, the finance minister, who favored the recovery of flight capital by the method Morgenthau had recommended, resigned and was replaced by Paul Reynaud. Daladier, who welcomed the Morgenthau approach to covering the cost of American airplanes, regretted out loud that he had not heard about it earlier, as it would have enabled him to talk Marchandeau out of quitting. With Reynaud as finance minister, Cochran advised Morgenthau on November 17, there would be no effort to recover capital by decree, for Reynaud's sympathies were with the moneyed class, many of whose members had been responsible for the exodus of gold. Daladier pushed ahead anyway, calling a meeting of the Permanent Committee of National Defense to announce there was "the possibility of receiving about a thousand American planes of the latest model in use in the American Army" for 2.5 billion francs ($65 million). Reynaud insisted that there was no new source of funding, noting that the National Defense Ministry already accounted for eighty percent of the budget, and he refused to approve the aircraft purchase until Daladier agreed to raise the 2.5 billion francs by reducing other items in the defense allocation. Daladier did agree, and he met with Reynaud, La Chambre, and Monnet on December 9 to announce the order of one thousand planes for delivery by the following July; then he asked Monnet to return to the United States to study aircraft models and to place an order, provided they were of a caliber to match German models and would be delivered on time. (When he learned he owned stock in companies that stood to realize a profit from the sale of aircraft to France, Bullitt wrote his brother, Orville: "I feel that since I am a government employee, . . . I should not hold stock in any company making munitions or implements of war"; and he asked Orville to sell the stock.)

Monnet and three technicians from the French Air Ministry arrived in Washington on December 16, and they soon discovered that operational U.S. warplanes did not meet their expectations: they lacked the power and maneuverability that would add up to superiority over the *Luftwaffe*. There were, however, two experimental aircraft that might pass the test: the Douglas DB-7 Boston Bomber, which would fly at 300 mph over a one-thousand-mile range, and the P-40 Mohawk, a pursuit plane built by Curtiss-Wright that had been tested at 313 mph, and while not quite as maneuverable as the German Messerschmidt 109, it was more durable. The Frenchmen wished to learn more about the DB-7 and the P-40, but they met stiff resistance, especially from General Arnold, the air commander, who used the Neutrality Act as an excuse; in fact, Hap Arnold guarded his prototypes for fear that the French wanted to buy only a few of them so they could steal the design plans. On the other hand Monnet had the support of Morgenthau, whose concern about the ability of France to pay for the planes had been allayed by assurances that the Daladier government had allocated the necessary $65 million. "They want a thousand planes," said Morgenthau. "They got the cash. They want them before the first of July, and we'll help them all we can. Of course, . . . it all gets down to a question, will the President tell them they can really have the most recent planes."

Arnold acquiesced on the P-40, but he insisted that the DB-7 remain classified for security reasons, informing Morgenthau that he was prepared to defy the president; and he directed his subordinate officers not to divulge military secrets to members of the French air mission. Then Morgenthau reversed himself: "I want to talk with you frankly," he said to Monnet on December 31. "Our mutually good friend Ambassador Bullitt had put me in an almost impossible position. . . . I mean the whole United States Army is opposed to what I am doing, . . . and I just can't continue . . . forcing the United States Army to show planes which they say they want for themselves. . . ." Bullitt, furious at both Arnold and Morgenthau, went to the president, and a meeting at the White House on January 16, 1939, was attended by Morgenthau, Arnold, Woodring, and the other secretaries and chiefs of staff of the military services. "Ambassador Bullitt sat at the President's side," wrote John McVickar Haight, Jr., author of *American Aid to France: 1938–1940.*

Roosevelt reiterated his wish that every effort be made to assist France. Bullitt spoke of time running out and repeated the President's wish. He specifically called for release of the Douglas bomber. Secretary Woodring replied that the plane included many secret elements. . . . The President retorted that he was determined to have the Douglas plane released. It was a tense meeting, and Roosevelt had his dander up.

A formal order was drafted and sent to the secretaries of war, navy, and treasury, and it was clearly implied "they had a choice between compliance and resignation."

The DB-7 was a prized prototype, the first multiengine attack bomber to be developed by the U.S.—the first one hundred production models were not due for delivery until January 1940—so the Air Corps was understandably reluctant to sell it to France. The management of Douglas Aircraft was not so inclined, as it was gratified by the interest of the French in its aircraft (the DB-7 was jointly owned by Douglas and the U.S. government, which had paid for part of its development). Led by Donald Douglas, the president of the company, there was an enthusiastic welcome for two members of the French air mission, Colonel Paul Jacquin and Captain Paul Chemidlin, when they arrived at the Douglas plant in Los Angeles on the morning of January 23. Jacquin was an aerial tactician, who had commanded an experimental squadron in France; Chemidlin was a test pilot assigned to the squadron—brash and cocky and, as one Douglas engineer remembered, "a show-me type fellow."

From the moment they met that morning Chemidlin and John Cable, the Douglas test pilot on the DB-7 project, did not hit it off: it was a case of clashing egos, witnesses recalled. The airplane, Cable bragged, was another hot product of American ingenuity, capable of being flown with one engine crippled; to which Chemidlin responded dubiously, even disparagingly—no plane is designed to fly on one wing, as the tension is liable to knock out the other engine—though he gladly accepted Cable's offer to take him for a ride. Cable had cut his port engine on a previous flight without mishap but had been ordered not to try it again; however, this challenge by a skeptical Frenchman galled him. He made the plane do all he said it could: he flew at full speed at two hundred feet, then climbed to four hundred and did banks and turns; he then cut the port engine, and while flying an erratic pattern made a vertical left-hand bank and a snap roll, at which point the plane went into an earthward spin. Cable tried to jump, but his parachute failed to open and he was killed; Chemidlin rode the DB-7 down, unable to get out, and was severely injured—broken back and other fractures, cuts and contusions—but he survived. Colonel Jacquin, who was one of the first to reach Chemidlin, began speaking excitedly in French, unaware he was being overheard by a newspaper reporter; so while the French pilot was identified as a mechanic named Smithin and rushed to a hospital in Santa Monica, where a "no visitors" sign was placed on the door of his room, the truth was out. A doctor finally confirmed it: the patient was Paul Chemidlin of Paris.

Senator Champ Clark of Missouri, an isolationist, had been assured at a hearing of the Military Affairs Committee by General Malin Craig, the Army chief of staff, that no new American aircraft were being released for foreign export; so when General Arnold testified on January 25, 1939, he was asked by Senator Clark what a Frenchman was doing on a Douglas bomber, "the very latest word in American plane construction," when it crashed on January 23. Arnold replied it had been "at the direction of the Treasury Department." Morgenthau complained to Woodring that he had been "smeared all over the front pages," but he called in newsmen and contended that the proposed contract with France would "activate . . . idle assembly plants and place good hard dollars . . . into the workers' pockets." Roosevelt, noticeably alarmed by the turn of events, called Clark and other members of the Senate committee to the White House and insisted that the selling of airplanes to France was an economic plus for both business and labor; and when it was suggested that it was also an act of helping one nation fight another, the president replied more out of candor than political wisdom: "The frontiers of the United States are on the Rhine." Isolationists were in an uproar: "Good God," Senator Hiram Johnson of California protested to the press, "do you not think the American people have the right to know if they are going down the road to war?" Roosevelt was forced to take the advice of his cautious secretary of state and abandon the plan to expand French air power.

Bullitt, meanwhile, had left Washington, having sent a fifty-seventh birthday greeting to Roosevelt on January 20, ten days early: "I could try to tell you what it means to me to have you in the world; but I think you know. . . . There is nobody like you, and I love you." He had sailed from New York and was at sea at the time of the DB-7 crash, and when reporters tried to contact him in Paris, he was not there: he had gone to Plymouth, England, supposedly to get over a head cold—a transparent fabrication, since England in winter is no place to recover from a sniffle—but actually to let the commotion die down. "The American public knew little of the amazing Bullitt and his one-man stop-Hitler campaign," read a story in *Newsweek*, "until an unscheduled California plane crash revealed that he had engineered, over the protests of War Department professionals, a deal to give France preference over the United States Army on new American-built airplane models."

Marching to War in Europe

WHEN he finally reached Paris, Bullitt was at pains to explain reports that Roosevelt had said the frontier of the United States extended to the French-German border, although the president did believe—this, said the ambassador, is what he had meant—that the French Army was the first line of U.S. defense. Bullitt was, nevertheless, pleased that Roosevelt's remark, even if slightly distorted, had been circulated in Europe: "It is difficult to exaggerate the salutary effect . . . the leakage of your remarks to the Congressmen has had in Europe," he cabled the president on February 3, "no matter how much trouble it may have made for you in the United States." Bullitt also reported that the French government was about to place definite orders—neither he nor the French were aware, apparently, that Roosevelt had decided to halt the aircraft-for-France program—for one hundred Douglas DB-7 bombers plus one hundred fifteen bombers made by Martin and two hundred North American training planes. Bullitt was hell-bent on building a French air arm, though it would have to be from scratch—no less an authority on aviation than Charles Lindbergh had declared that the French aircraft were so bad that they ought to be burned, which even allowing for Lindbergh's pro-German position was an opinion worth hearing—and Bullitt pressed the point on Washington: on February 13 he sent a message to the State Department asserting that a way must be found to circumvent the Johnson Act and allow the French to buy planes on credit. On February 23 he suggested to Roosevelt using an intermediary, Bao Dai, the emperor of the French protectorate of Annam (a part of French Indochina, it was known after 1945 as Vietnam), who as a neutral could obtain credits from the Export-Import Bank or private bankers for the purchase of airplanes. (Bullitt believed he could guarantee the cooperation of the emperor, who was a personal friend—Bao Dai had a home in Switzerland and vacationed often in Paris—but his suggestion was not seriously considered.)

Then, on February 22, Bullitt was delighted to report to Roosevelt that the finance minister, Reynaud, had telephoned and said "he had become convinced that France must make immediately a settlement of her debt to the United States." They would even throw in Clipperton Island in the Pacific, some French interests in the New Hebrides, and "other . . . possessions we might fancy in either the Caribbean or the Pacific," he wrote. "In any event, will you please get your imagination to work furiously on this subject. I wish to God that I could be with you in the White House for one evening. Our inventions would be terrific! As it is, I can only say that if you want any French territory plus ten billion francs in gold, in return for releasing France from . . . the Johnson Act, it looks as if you might be able to get it."

In May Jean Monnet went to Washington to discuss the debt repayment with Roosevelt, who declared: "I do not want to take money out of France at this time." Monnet also met with Morgenthau, but it was a strained discussion, for the treasury secretary had aroused the anger of the French government—and Bullitt's as well—by telling how he had negotiated the tripartite economic agreement of 1936 to Joseph Alsop and Robert Kintner, who wrote an article for *The Saturday Evening Post*. "The American Government has been made contemptible, and the careers of a large number of honorable men . . . have been placed in jeopardy," Bullitt had complained to Roosevelt on April 3; and the following day, in a letter looking ahead to Monnet's visit in May, he wrote: "Don't have Henry the Morgue in on your first conversation. The *Saturday Evening Post* article . . . has made everyone believe that even the most confidential communications with Henry will be published by him."

On March 17, 1939, Bullitt cabled Washington:

. . . Hitler's invasion of Czechoslovakia stunned . . . all Frenchmen. Thought as to future has, however, only begun to crystalize. . . . The invasion . . . ends definitely all possibility of diplomatic negotiations. Seven specific promises by Hitler . . . were broken by this action, and it is no longer possible to have confidence in any promises he may make. . . . Nothing remains but to develop as much armed force as possible, as rapidly as possible. . . . Reports indicate that extreme fear of Hitler is now prevalent throughout Eastern Europe. . . . There is consternation in Poland, but it is believed the Poles will . . . fight if Hitler makes any direct attack. . . . No assistance is expected from the Soviet Union unless Soviet territory is attacked. The French are making every effort to persuade the British to introduce conscription and to prepare for immediate war.

On March 23 Bullitt sent Roosevelt an analysis of the latest developments, a grim assessment, which was factually accurate, allowing for his tendency to make extraordinary evaluations of the national mood of France. "Hitler's invasion . . . produced a curious result," he wrote.

It convinced every Frenchman . . . that Hitler could be stopped by nothing but force. As a result, there is a . . . serenity from one end of France to the other. There is no vacillation or mourning. The spirit of the people is incomparably better than in 1914. . . . The quiet courage . . . in France today is the only manifestation in a long time that has made me proud to be a member of the human race. The German game is obvious and is based on the elementary principle of military strategy that it is wise to strike where your opponents are weakest. . . . Czechoslovakia has gone. Memel has gone [the Lithuanian port on the Baltic Sea, formerly a part of Prussia, had been annexed by Germany], and an effort will be made to establish a virtual protectorate over Lithuania. The Poles then will have three German fronts to defend. . . . If the Poles should cave in without fighting, the next turn would doubtless be that of France. . . . The above is, I believe, the German reasoning. The moral for us is that unless some nation in Europe stands up to Germany quickly, France and England may face defeat, and such defeat would mean the French and British fleets in the hands of the Germans and the Italians. We should then have the Japs in the Pacific and an overwhelming fleet against us in the Atlantic.

As insistently as he had for two years opposed the United States getting involved in another war in Europe, Bullitt now saw it as a distinct possibility. "If European war should begin," he counseled the president,

I believe the American people unanimously would say, "Send supplies to the allies but never, never, never an American soldier." I believe that even though the countries of Europe should fall under German domination, one by one, and even though it should seem that France and England were going to be defeated, the American people would not desire to declare war on Germany unless Germany had committed direct acts of aggression against the United States. . . . I believe, however, that such acts of aggression would be committed and that after not more than a year of European war, the American people would desire to declare war. . . .

Bullitt was proud of the way Roosevelt had handled the Czech crisis and said so in a somewhat condescending tone. "My feeling that we had to say a word for human decency increased in intensity every hour. . . . It was splendidly done and . . . will have some effect at least in Europe. I like also your action in continuing to recognize the Minister of Czechoslovakia. . . . I remember telling you some years ago . . . that, during all the years when Poland had ceased to exist as a sovereign state, the Turkish Sultans invariably invited the Polish Ambassador, who did not exist, to every Court function, and . . . in the presence of the Ambassadors of Germany, Austria, and Russia, the Court Chamberlain announced to His Imperial Majesty the Sultan: 'The Polish Ambassador begs to be excused as he is slightly indisposed.' "

"Both Daladier and Paul Reynaud are convinced that Germany will precipitate general war in Europe before the 15th of May," Bullitt wrote Roosevelt on April 4, adding that he thought it "possible but by no means certain." The point was, however, that Bullitt had become a committed belligerent: "I hope to God that the Neutrality Act will be altered before Congress adjourns," he said in a letter to Judge Moore on May 19, and he considered it "sickening" when Congress failed to act. "The fact is," he wrote Moore in August, "if war starts and France and England do not get supplies from the United States, they will be defeated. As a result, Hitler has been encouraged greatly to act this summer." The same Bullitt who less than a year before had been assailed by President Beneš of Czechoslovakia as an appeaser was being denounced for his hostility by German and Italian spokesmen: "the most ruthless adversary of Hitler," he was called by the Italian ambassador to France, Raffaele Guariglia, on July 4, 1939. Bullitt and Joseph Kennedy in London had both been criticized by the German propaganda office, so Bullitt happily sent Kennedy a medal signifying membership in the Order of the Warmonger, which enraged Kennedy, who was absolutely opposed to the U.S. going to war with Germany.

Bullitt was doing his best to deserve his reputation with the Axis powers: "My guess is that by this time next year you will wish that you had an American Army of two million men ready for action," he had written Roosevelt on March 18; and on March 23 he elaborated on the point:

> The only great army on the side of decency is the French Army; the British have even less of an army than we have, and it is even worse in all respects than our own. . . . [Bullitt was wrong about the British Army, a small but elite force of high caliber.] The vital point, therefore, if war starts, will become the . . . strength of the French Army. Americans will begin to realize that fact . . . when it is too late to create an American army to intervene in time. We ought to create that army now.

Bullitt was, as usual, impatient with the British, who he maintained were "digging their own grave" by depending on volunteers, and he suggested to Roosevelt that he inform the British via Kennedy that "it is of the highest importance that conscription . . . be introduced." He was advised by Hull in a mild rebuke that the president considered this a question of British internal policy and would not "express any opinion with regard thereto." (Bullitt also discussed such sensitive matters with Roosevelt by telephone, and when he became convinced that eavesdroppers were on the line, he dealt with them in a unique way. "Of course the British foreign office is listening," he once said. "You and I know that they are . . . pusillanimous, double crossing, tricky people. . . .")

Roosevelt wrote to Hitler on April 14, 1939, asking for a guarantee of no further aggression: "We recognize complex world problems, which affect all humanity, but we know that study and discussion of them must be held in an atmosphere of peace." Hitler replied in a speech to the Reichstag on April 28, and Bullitt cabled the reaction of Alexis Léger, the secretary-general of the foreign office, who made three points: Hitler had answered Roosevelt's plea not to attack another country by tearing up his nonaggression pact with Poland; he had sounded pointedly more bellicose by denouncing his naval agreement with Britain; and he had shown no intention of permitting justice to interfere with his enslavement of the people of Czechoslovakia. The new issue was Danzig, or Gdansk in Polish, a Baltic port and a Prussian province until it was declared a free city by the Versailles Treaty, united with Poland and administered by the League of Nations.

On April 28, 1939, Bullitt sent a message to the State Department:

Daladier dined with me alone tonight and talked at length about the present situation. He said he believed that Hitler's speech had been designed to create in Poland the same sort of fear of German attack that it had been possible to create in Czechoslovakia. . . . He felt that Hitler had also hoped to obtain a withdrawal of British support for Poland in the matter of . . . Danzig. He was not sure that Chamberlain would not . . . pursue the same course that he pursued with regard to Czechoslovakia. . . . Yesterday the British ambassador had come to see him and had said that in his opinion Hitler's speech left the way open for fruitful negotiations. . . . In . . . Daladier's opinion this was dangerous nonsense. . . . Danzig would merely be the first step for a German domination of Poland. . . . I need scarcely to add that I entirely agree.

As the crisis grew more grave—Hitler's demand for Danzig would lead directly to world war—Bullitt stepped beyond the limits of his position and acted as an intermediary between the Polish and French governments: on April 7 he met at a French resort, Boulogne-sur-Mer, with the Polish ambassador to France, Juliusz Lukasiewicz, and the Polish foreign minister, Jozef Beck, who was returning from talks in London. "For the Poles," Lukasiewicz wrote, "a meeting of our Minister of Foreign Affairs . . . and the American Ambassador in Paris, who was known to be President Roosevelt's right-hand man in . . . foreign affairs, was, from the point of view of British and American public opinion, . . . a most desirable event." Lukasiewicz later advised Bullitt there would be further aggression by Hitler, with Danzig the next objective, and he asked if his government might count on the support of France; Bullitt, after meeting with Daladier, assured the ambassador that Poland could expect French military assistance. Bullitt went even further: "He informed me," Lukasiewicz wrote in a memoir, "that, adopting my views and exercising the authority he was accorded, he had instructed the American Ambassador in London, Joseph Kennedy, to call . . . on Prime Minister Chamberlain, . . . emphasizing categorically the responsibility of the British Government."

On June 28 Bullitt reported to Washington "the Germans were pouring soldiers into Danzig"; Lukasiewicz had told him "that German troops disguised as tourists were being concentrated in such numbers that . . . his Government feared an attempt by Germany to seize Danzig in the very near future." Bullitt heard from Lukasiewicz again on August 3: ". . . he had just received a letter from Beck, who expressed the opinion that Hitler would go on ordering the Nazi leaders in Danzig"—the Nazis had gained control of the legislature in Danzig in 1935—"to create incident after incident until it should be necessary for the Polish Government to take action."

"Between ourselves," Bullitt wrote Judge Moore on April 25, "I have had a rotten time lately because those two vertebrae that the Russian streptococci chewed have been pinching . . . the big nerve that leads to my left arm. . . . I have had acute pain for the past three weeks, and it is difficult to keep working at top speed." Bullitt may have been ailing physically, but he was more likely suffering from the combined effect of hypochondria—Bullitt was in excellent health throughout most of his life, according to his doctor Orville Horwitz—and fatigue from overwork. It was a grueling period, the spring of 1939, with emotional stress added to an enormous workload, and as might be expected Bullitt was not sleeping well: having gone to bed at midnight, he would often arise at 3 A.M., summon Offie to his study, and they would smoke, play chess, and listen to the radio until Bullitt began his daily dictating. His cables to Washington were comprehensive and crammed with details, but on occasion they contained errors, which were not always caused by the pressure of overwork. Bullitt was so often wrong on military matters—he persisted in the belief that the Maginot Line was invincible and that French tanks were superior to German tanks—that there were those in Washington who referred to him as "Misfire Bullitt." The reason arguably was that he only listened to generals of the old school, who later were found responsible for the failure of the French Army to stand against the German advance: Maurice Gamelin, who was relieved as commander-in-chief in May 1940; Maxime Weygand, Gamelin's replacement; and Edouard Réquin, the defeatist troop commander, who had become the inspector general of the Army.

There was more to it, however: a flaw of judgment that affected his analysis—it was an ultimate flaw, if there was one in the man described by *Time* in March 1939 as "President Roosevelt's most trusted adviser on foreign affairs"—and it was the outgrowth of a character trait. Bullitt was impressionable and mercurial, a man of strong yet unsettled sentiments, or as Gordon Wright put it: "He seems to have zigzagged between gloom and hope, even though hope always predominated." Roosevelt had noticed it: "The trouble with Bullitt," he confided to Henry Morgenthau, "is in the morning he will send me a telegram, 'Everything is lovely,' and then he will go out to have lunch with some French official, and I get a telegram that everything is going to hell."

The irony was that Bullitt's strongest sentiment, his hatred of the Soviet Union dating back to his days in Moscow, undercut his grand design in 1939, which was to stop Hitler in his drive to the west and force him to attack Russia to the east. This strategy depended not only on the French-Polish alliance he was personally striving to achieve, but also on a British-French pact with the Soviet Union. "Bullitt's intense anti-Sovietism now took second place to his conviction that the Nazis were the immediate threat," Wright wrote. "He distrusted the Kremlin as much as ever, but he told Daladier that 'in the present situation . . .

no stone should be left unturned, even though one might expect to find vermin under it.' '' But there would be no Allied accord with the U.S.S.R., largely because Bullitt had littered the way to it with remnants of his disgust with the Soviets, causing reluctance to proceed, especially among the British. On April 16 the Soviet Union proposed a mutual security treaty with Britain and France, and negotiations were scheduled in Moscow, although the British approach to them— Bullitt called it "dilatory and almost insulting" in a conversation with the chief diplomatic adviser to the British government, Robert Vansittart—was reflected in instructions to the British delegation, which "recommended proceeding with the greatest prudence, . . . the negotiations . . . to be conducted as slowly as possible . . . to gain time." (One result of the failure of negotiations was the appointment of Molotov as Soviet commissar for foreign affairs in place of Litvinov.)

———————

There were occasional lighthearted exchanges between the ambassador and the president, as the imminence of war—"the grand smash," Bullitt called it in a letter in March 1939—could not suppress Bullitt's splendid wit or Roosevelt's jocular appreciation of the absurd. Daladier had asked his advice on the French birth rate, Bullitt wrote on May 9—France's population had declined, while that of Germany had risen in leaps—and he had suggested having Joe Kennedy, the father of nine, transferred to Paris. "The only low news from Paris this week," he went on to say, "concerns Flandin, . . . Germanophile, . . . ex-Prime Minister. He has faded quickly from the political picture due to the event . . . about two weeks ago. . . . Flandin called on a young lady . . . and was in bed with her when her *amant de coeur* broke into the apartment; beat up Flandin and drove him into the street . . . minus his watch, wallet, and trousers!" In the same letter Bullitt anticipated a visit to the United States of King George VI and Queen Elizabeth of England, saying Kennedy had served Virginia ham and pickled peaches at a recent dinner party in London; the queen had eaten quantities "and expressed a royal desire to become more closely acquainted with the dish when in America." Bullitt had "no other tips to give you," he wrote—earlier he had supplied a list of personal needs of their royal majesties, including, much to Roosevelt's amusement (but to the annoyance of Eleanor Roosevelt, who thought the advice presumptuous), hot water bottles and an eiderdown quilt—"except the obvious one that it is well not to mention the Duke and Duchess of Windsor. . . . Brotherly love is . . . not at fever heat."

There was often a point to Bullitt's light asides: "Amid the bayings and barks of Hitler and Mussolini," he wrote Roosevelt in April 1939, feeling in an anglophobic mood, "it is difficult to turn one's mind to other animals; but I want you to know that I have not forgotten the bar sinister which stands . . . against Man o' War, Gallant Fox and all the other American thoroughbreds." In the event of war, he predicted, "the British would want to sell a large number of horses in the United States"; and what better time to compel them to abandon the "bar sinister," the exclusion of American thoroughbred horses from the British studbook. "I hope you will pass this suggestion along to those who do not care to have our distinguished equines classified as bastards."

"I saw your mother this morning," Bullitt wrote Roosevelt on August 16, 1939, "and she is to dine with me tonight. I have never known her to be in such superb form." He reported, however, that "storm warnings are out in Europe," and on August 24 he cabled: "I told your mother . . . I thought she should return to America today. . . . She agreed and will leave Havre . . . this afternoon." The clearest warning had come from Berlin, where Alexander C. Kirk, the chargé d'affaires—Hugh Wilson, the ambassador, had been recalled in protest of the Nazi persecution of Jews—had heard that an invasion of Poland would begin on August 26, which turned out to be mobilization day for an attack six days later. Kirk dispatched a third secretary of the embassy, Jacob D. Beam, to Paris to advise Bullitt, as he considered the message too important to be sent by telephone or telegraph. "I arrived in Paris and was taken to the chateau at Chantilly," Beam recalled, "where Bullitt was presiding over a dinner party for Jim Farley, the postmaster general. I took him aside and said that Kirk had information, which was pretty good, that the Germans would take off on August 26, at which point he grabbed the telephone, saying he had to alert Daladier right away. I said, 'Hold on a minute, for Christ's sake. This is so secret that it can't be put in writing.' He paid no attention and made the call to Daladier. I was mad as hell and took the first plane to Berlin the next morning."

On August 25, 1939, Bullitt cabled Washington:

Daladier lunched alone with me today and discussed every aspect of the current situation. . . . If Germany should attack Poland, there was no question whatsoever about the result. Both France and England would march at once to the assistance of Poland.

On August 26 Bullitt reported a conversation with Bonnet, the foreign minister, who was ready to concede that the balance of power had shifted to Germany's advantage—on August 23 a Nazi-Soviet pact had been signed—and who told of a meeting between Hitler and Robert Coulondre, the French ambassador to Germany, having moved to Berlin from Moscow. Hitler had seemed agreeable at first, saying he had no claims against France, but from there on it was a diatribe: the French had given carte blanche to the Poles, and the Poles were acting in a manner that no self-respecting state could endure. "Hitler's voice then rose," Bullitt wrote, quoting Coulondre's report to Bonnet, "and he screamed out a series of imaginary Polish atrocities against the German minority in Poland.

After this he said that he would regret war with France but that he was ready for it. . . . If France chose to make a general European war out of the action . . . he would be obliged to take if the Poles . . . continue their present behavior, there would be war." Bonnet had told Bullitt that he considered Hitler's statement to Coulondre "a warning before action." On August 25 Bullitt had cabled solemnly: "Never has any nation confronted a war of the most terrible sort with greater calm or courage."

It would seem that Bullitt's allegiance in the moment of crisis was to France—or more particularly to Daladier—for he said as much in a message to Roosevelt on August 29, at the same time remarking in an unabashed way that the French premier held him in very high esteem. "I have seen Daladier constantly and intimately . . .," he wrote.

I do not telegraph half what he says to me for the simple reason that there is nothing he doesn't say, and some of his remarks would raise hell if they should be known. He is a fine fellow, . . . and he has an altogether too-exalted idea of my own value. In consequence, he asks my judgment about nearly everything of great importance not only in the field of foreign affairs but also in the field of domestic policy. . . . Last Friday, when he lunched with me alone, . . . he told me with tears in his eyes that he had said to General Gamelin . . . that the recovery of France was not due to him, but to me, and added that he didn't know whether there was a God or not, but if there was, and I ever faced Him, I need only say: "I stand on what I did for decency in the world when I was Ambassador in Paris."!!!!

At 2:50 on the morning of September 1, 1939, Roosevelt was awakened by a phone call from Bullitt, who had just talked with Tony Biddle in Warsaw: "Boss," said Bullitt, "the German Army has just marched into Poland." "Then it has happened," said Roosevelt. "Do you think you will talk to Tony again?" "I don't think it will be possible," said Bullitt. Roosevelt alerted the secretary of state immediately. "The moment I recognized the President's voice, I guessed the rest, . . ." Hull recalled.

I said . . . I intended going to my office at once. . . . I drove to the State Department and walked through the deserted corridors to my office at about 3:30. . . . I telephoned . . . Bullitt . . . and Kennedy, . . . asking for their news and appraisal. . . . As reports came in . . . of German bombing of Warsaw and other Polish cities, I . . . sought confirmation. Exactly one week before, Ambassador Bullitt had sent the President . . . a personal message suggesting that immediately after the first shot the President should issue to all nations concerned an appeal to refrain from bombing civilian populations. . . . The President and I agreed that the appeal should be made, and Welles drafted it and had it ready. Bullitt now telephoned again and urged that the appeal be sent at once. We accordingly dispatched it. . . .

September 3, 1939, Bullitt to Washington:

The British Government has just announced that a state of war will exist between Great Britain and Germany at 11 o'clock this morning. . . . The French Ambassador in Berlin will present an ultimatum to the German Foreign Office before noon today, and France as well . . . will be at war with Germany before the close of the day.

Bullitt put the embassy on a wartime footing, which first called for inspecting the reinforced steel and marble building—the $1.5 million structure, just seven years old, was considered one of the sturdiest shelters in Paris—for proofing against bombs and gas. Hubert P. Earle, the son of Bullitt's friend George Earle, had spent the summer working in the embassy, and he recalled that each staff member was assigned to one of three units—a blackout squad, a first aid squad, or a police squad. At night observers were posted on the roof to sound the alarm in case of an air raid; during the day the main embassy hall was a center of frenzy, as American tourists flocked there, trying to book passage home. As he was walking to dinner on the evening of September 3, Earle encountered Bullitt, who invited him for a ride; and at the Hôtel des Invalides they got out of the car and stood on the sidewalk. "The Ambassador lifted his eyes and pointed toward the magnificent gold dome of the Invalides," Earle wrote.

"It will be a frightful thing," he said, "if they bomb our beautiful Paris. I can't bear to think of that dome of the Invalides in ruins, and it seems definitely possible that when war really starts, Paris and the other great capitals of Europe may be blasted off the map." The idea of the city being bombed was not a new one to the Ambassador, because in 1914 he was staying at the home of his aunt . . . and saw the first bombing attack in the history of Paris from the balcony of her home. "A small plane was flying very low over the house-tops," he said. "The people, instead of being terrified, . . . were so curious that they stood in the streets looking up at the plane. . . . It dropped just one bomb, which fell in the street and blew a leg off a little girl."

"Thus far, in France, there is a curious unreality about the war," Bullitt cabled the president on September 8, again imagining loftily what he could not actually observe. "The whole mobilization was carried out in absolute quiet. There were no shouts of 'On to Berlin' . . . to match the shouts of . . . 1914. There was no hysterical weeping of mothers and sisters and children. The self-control and quiet courage has been so far beyond the usual standard of the human race that it has had a dream quality." Bullitt then returned to reality and made a sound prediction: "I expect the Germans to complete soon their destruction of Poland; then to offer peace to France and England. The French and British will reject this proposal and go on fighting. Then the Germans will turn loose on France and England their full air force. . . ." Bullitt had talked that afternoon with Daladier, who said, "If we are to win this war, we shall have to win it on supplies of every kind from the United States. We can hold out for a time without such supplies; but England and ourselves cannot possibly build up sufficient production of munitions and planes to make a successful offensive possible." On September 13 Bullitt reported a meeting between Daladier and Chamberlain in which the British prime minister "had made the impression of a man who had passed from middle age into decrepitude"; but Daladier's disgust with Chamberlain—and it was shared by Bullitt—had to do not with his physical state but with his refusal "to consider the use of British bombardment planes against Germany, . . . stating that he did not wish to provoke German bombardments of Great Britain. . . ."

Also on September 13 Bullitt mailed the president an unusual message. "I enclose herewith a document," he wrote. "On one side you will see the label of a bottle of wine such as does not exist any longer in the world, because the label came from the last bottle in existence, which Daladier and I drank at lunch at my house today. On the back of the label you will find two unimportant signatures, which convey at any rate a lot of admiration and . . . a lot of affection." The inscription read: "Homage to President Roosevelt, 13 September 1939, Ed. Daladier, William C. Bullitt." Roosevelt responded on September 28: "Tell the delightful gentleman who signed that label with you, that, if any similar bottle survives, to keep it until he, you and I can partake of it together as soon as the survival of the democracies is again assured." Roosevelt was optimistic, as always, but Daladier was depressed: "He said that he felt that his political life and probably his personal life . . . could not last more than three months . . .," Bullitt advised Roosevelt on September 16. "The bombardments of France would be so terrible that the French people would . . . drive him from political life and indeed would probably kill him." Bullitt shared with Daladier a sense of defeat— he believed they were witnesses to the end of a great European era—and he was ready to leave Paris. "My work here has nearly ended . . .," he wrote Roosevelt. "I'm feeling rather useless. . . . Tony Biddle won't have a country anymore, and you can make him Ambassador in Paris. You can put me in the Cabinet."

A Rebel Aroused

SLIGHTLY OVER TWENTY YEARS had passed since Bullitt's blowup with President Wilson—about long enough for him to atone for his public tantrum over the terms of the Versailles Treaty—and there were signs of a similar rupture of his association with Roosevelt. Throughout the autumn of 1939 he argued furiously for munitions and airplanes for France—"the French and British together will desire to purchase . . . in the immediate future at least ten thousand planes, . . . none of which exist," he wrote Roosevelt on November 1—and on occasion he was rude and intemperate: "Hurrah for fascism!" he fumed on November 15, his ire aroused by the handling of the offer by France of a Pacific territory as partial repayment of its debt to the United States. Throughout November and December Bullitt persisted in an effort to come to Washington to act in Daladier's behalf in the quest for warplanes, even *after* he had been politely told by the president, ". . . it is not the duty of an Ambassador." Bullitt's behavior was often bold and haughty. He had what seemed an uncanny ability to speak candidly and curtly and to complain indignantly and still stay on the good side of the president, though this evidently was accounted for by the same trait cited by James P. Warburg in an explanation of why Bullitt never achieved his potential stature. "Bullitt was probably the best brain in the State Department," said Warburg, a New York banker who resigned as a delegate to the London economic conference in 1933 in the dispute with Roosevelt over currency policy. "[He] knows Europe, and could be a big factor in this Administration if it weren't for some undefinable quality that stands in his way. He has great influence with the President, but for some reason is never quite taken seriously. . . ."

"We were convinced that the Poles would not stand up against the Germans," said Jacob Beam, speaking for himself and Alexander Kirk, "and Bullitt disagreed completely. We had been reporting that the Poles didn't stand a chance. We gave them two months, and Bullitt was goddamn mad." Bullitt was also angry at his old antagonists, the Soviets: "The Polish Ambassador in Paris [Lukasiewicz] has just informed me," he cabled Washington on September 17, "that last night Molotov summoned the Polish ambassador in Moscow and handed him a note stating that since the Polish Government was no longer able to protect its population bordering on the Soviet Union, Soviet troops would enter Poland for the protection of those populations." Lawrence Steinhardt, the U.S. ambassador in Moscow, advised that the French and British embassies were urging their governments "not to declare war against or break off diplomatic relations with the Soviet Union . . . on the ground that such action would only benefit Germany without helping Poland"; and on September 18 the French and British governments lodged protests in Moscow against "the flagrant aggression" by the Soviet Union. On September 19 Kirk reported from Berlin that German and Russian troops had made contact at Brest: the defeat of Poland had been accomplished in less than three weeks. On September 20 Bullitt reported that the French had been denied the right to cross Belgium to attack Germany and draw German troops from their assault on Poland: "Since the French certainly will not violate Belgian neutrality, the only opening for attack . . . remains the Siegfried Line," he wrote. "To break that line will require vastly more heavy guns, munitions, and airplanes than the French and British now have." Bullitt also reported on September 20 that Daladier and other French leaders believed there was no chance they could win the war if the embargo on arms from the United States remained in effect, and on September 21 Roosevelt addressed a special session of Congress to seek repeal of the Neutrality Act. (The act was not repealed, but on November 4, 1939, it was amended to permit cash-and-carry purchases of war materials by France and Great Britain.)

Bullitt had a talk on September 30 with Léger, who predicted that a German offensive would be "loosed in from five to eight days," and Léger concluded by saying: "The game is lost. France stands alone against three dictatorships. Great Britain is not ready. The United States has not even changed the Neutrality Act. The democracies again are too late." Pessimism was so prevalent, Léger told Bullitt, that Daladier was having difficulty resisting mounting support in the Chamber of Deputies of a withdrawal from the war. "Léger has been consistently on the side of fighting," wrote Bullitt, no doubt recalling the days when he and the chief of the foreign office were at odds over how to deal with Hitler. "The views he expressed today were therefore impressive. . . ." Bullitt reported to Roosevelt on October 4 that Monnet had accompanied Daladier to England for a meeting with Chamberlain on setting up an Anglo-French economic coordinating committee—its primary purpose was to be the purchase of arms in the United States—and he said he had had "a large enough finger in all of this to be able to steer it, in case you have any definite ideas as to what you want or do not want." Hitler addressed the Reichstag on October 6, and Bullitt cabled: "There is not the slightest chance that the French Government will desire to use Hitler's speech . . . as the basis for an armistice." The French had been relieved, however, by signs that a German offensive was not imminent: ". . . the speech has created the impression," Bullitt advised, "that either because of the lateness of the season or because of the attitude of Italy or because of fears as to the future actions of his new partner in crime, Stalin, Hitler may be hesitant about starting an offensive on the western front."

Such hope soon faded, however, as it became apparent that the weather was the crucial factor: "Everyone in Paris is expecting a major German attack to break the moment the present rains stop," Bullitt wrote Roosevelt on October 18. He remained in buoyed spirits all the same: "Our preparations are superb. I have converted a wine cellar in the basement of the embassy residence . . . into an *abri*. It is not in the least bombproof; but I have hung in it the Turkish and Bokharan embroideries that I used to have in my house on the Bosporus, and it is the last word in Oriental style and comfort. . . . Our motto is: 'We don't mind being killed, but we won't be annoyed.' "

On November 1, having been briefed by General Réquin, Bullitt sent Roosevelt a firsthand account of the military situation: "Réquin reported that the rains had been so heavy that all the trenches at the front were completely flooded and unusable. . . . In his opinion, it would be totally impossible for the Germans to launch a major offensive for at least a week." It was the consensus of several French generals, moreover, that even light rains in the week to come "would compel the Germans to postpone any major offensive until next March." Further, it was the belief of officers of the French general staff "that the only way the war can be won in the field will be by a combination of air attack supplemented by tanks." He then repeated the delusion he shared with the French generals: the French heavy tanks "are the best in Europe, . . . and at the front have shown that their armor is not pierced but only dented by the German anti-tank guns." It was the view of the general staff, therefore, "that the missing element is an over-whelming superiority in the air," which could be achieved only by "colossal purchases of planes in the United States."

In the same letter he offered FDR political advice: "Whether you like it or not, you must remain President of the United States throughout this war. I think you know from experience that one of the few principles that I live up to is Montesquieu's statement: 'A flatterer is a dangerous servant for any master.' I am not flattering when I say that there is no other man in the United States who can conduct the affairs of the country with one-half as much intelligence as yourself, . . . and there is no other man who can begin to handle the colossal problems which will arise at the end of the war."

Bullitt then turned to thoughts about his own future: "As you know, I have no objection whatsoever to staying in France. . . . But I honestly believe that I may be able to be of much more use in America. . . . If you agree, the job in which I think I would be useful would be that of Secretary of War. If you do not intend to change the present set-up in the War Department, which incidentally is giving all the Army officers the jitters, you might put me in as midship-mite, otherwise known as Secretary of the Navy. Incidentally, I believe that Tony and Margaret Biddle could handle the . . . job in France perfectly. . . . I have introduced them to everyone from Daladier down, and they have made the most excellent impression." He closed with a note about still another Roosevelt relative: "I had a fine talk with your Aunt Dora this morning. She looks wonderfully well. She says she intends to sail on November 7. . . . "

It was in February 1939 that Bullitt cabled that he had proposed to Reynaud, the French finance minister, introducing an X factor in the negotiations for U.S.

military aid, X standing for "possessions which we might desire for strategic reasons" as partial payment of the French debt; and Reynaud had replied "he felt it would be possible. . . ." However, there was no prompt response from Washington, and on November 15 Roosevelt sent Bullitt a message indicating he was cool to the idea: "I believe that because of the changes in the general situation . . .," he said vaguely, "it would be wiser to abandon any idea of a lease or contract." Bullitt cabled, also on November 15—possibly not in response to the president but in reaction to the delay in Washington—and his anger was unrestrained. He was, he said, "ashamed to go to anyone in the Foreign Office, . . . because your damned Navy Department, after getting me to hornswoggle an island out of the French Government, doesn't have the decency to reply. . . ." Bullitt did blame Roosevelt for vacillating, and he said so bluntly: ". . . when I am under the illusion that I am doing what you want done, which illusion is based on a . . . telegram telling me . . . that you want it done, and I get the French Government to embark on a definite policy, and you kill that policy by . . . reversing yourself without letting me know, . . . I recur to the opposite side of that quotation from Montesquieu in my last letter to you. . . . Hurrah for fascism! What the hell!" Roosevelt's reaction to the extraordinary letter was not recorded.

Bullitt had a three-hour meeting with Daladier on November 23, 1939, in which the French premier insisted that unless the Allies gained supremacy in the air, the war would drag on to the point that there was "a peace of exhaustion and compromise, which would insure the exultant domination of Europe by Germany." The planes must come from America, Daladier declared, or else, as Bullitt put it, "he would unequivocally cease to be Prime Minister. . . . He did not care how much the planes might cost. . . . He would not object to selling Versailles or any other possession of the French Government in order to get planes. . . ." Daladier added that Bullitt must leave at once for Washington to negotiate the airplane purchase, for "the only opinion in which he would have absolute confidence would be my own. It is unpleasant for me . . . to report this sort of thing, which sounds as though I were engaged in attempting to make myself appear more influential than I am; but I feel obliged to report the facts." Hull was flatly opposed to the idea, but he passed it to Roosevelt, who sent Bullitt on November 23 a friendly but stern admonishment:

We both feel certain that it would be a mistake for you to come over here on any such mission because it would be sure to leak out, and it is not the duty of an Ambassador. . . . In regard to purchasing, I am ready to handle the whole matter over here. . . . Our objective is the practical one of not interfering with our own military and naval programs. . . .

Still not willing to give in, Bullitt wrote to Roosevelt on December 11 about a meeting at which Daladier "repeated what I have communicated to you before; He believes that the war cannot be won unless France and England can obtain in the United States ten thousand airplanes . . . during the year 1940. . . . Personally, I agree with Daladier. . . . I believe that this question surpasses all others. . . ." He then quoted Daladier: "At this moment it is of no importance for you to be Ambassador to Paris. Our relations are such that any Secretary of Embassy can carry out the daily business. . . . The one vital problem today is the production of planes in the United States. I implore you to leave for the United States as soon as possible. . . ." Bullitt pressed the point again in a cable to the State Department on December 21, saying that Daladier

was absolutely convinced . . . that there would be no manufacture of planes . . . on any great scale for the account of France and England unless I should return to the United States immediately. . . . I remarked that he was . . . saying that while I would be *persona grata* to him in Washington, I was no longer *persona grata* in Paris. He said . . . that was too crude a way to put it; but . . . he was obliged to say that my presence in Washington now was an absolute essential and my presence in Paris merely a pleasant luxury. Under the circumstances I shall have to be ordered to return to Washington, as I cannot turn up in Paris again. . . .

Hull's reply the following day showed that his patience had been tried—the secretary no doubt suspected that Bullitt was somewhat accountable for the machinations of the French premier—but it was measured and reasonable: "Daladier is asking us to assume greater responsibility than is possible. Practically speaking it might well react against the very purpose he has in mind. Please make this clear to him and explain why we cannot order you home at this time. . . ."

On November 28 Bullitt telephoned Hull with the news that the Soviet Union was about to attack Finland, which it did the following day, and he asked Hull to urge Britain and France to condemn the U.S.S.R. at the League of Nations in Geneva. "I replied to Bullitt . . .," Hull wrote in his *Memoirs*,

that the President and I shared to the full his indignation. . . . But, in fairness, . . . I said, we could not assume the responsibility of urging Britain and France to pursue a certain course of action in their capacity as members of the League. We were not members of the League, and we could not urge Britain and France to take an action we could not take ourselves.

Bullitt decided thereupon to act on his own, and he chortled about it in a letter to the president on December 19. He had been invited by a mutual friend to have lunch with Joseph Avenol, the secretary general of the league, who was no favorite of Bullitt but who suggested meeting at a restaurant known for its excellent oysters. "At least the food would be good," Bullitt wrote,

even though the conversation might be bad. . . . Avenol was just as dead as a dog, as usual. I began to make fun of him about the League and especially the pleasure of working with his Soviet associates. He seemed to have plenty of hatred for his Russian colleagues, so I asked him why he didn't get rid of them. . . . He replied that the League was so dead that it would certainly be impossible to get any action. . . . I told him that if he would carry through, . . . I would undertake to get into motion within two hours the energies necessary to throw the Soviet Union out of the League. . . . Avenol was gloomily skeptical but at least seemed interested in the idea. After lunch I saw Rochat at the Quai d'Orsay [Charles Rochat was the chief of the European section of the French foreign office], and he was even more negative than Avenol. He said that he was certain that any action by the League was out of the question; no nation would have the courage to take up the matter; that Finland would not appeal, . . . etc., etc., whereupon I gave him a lecture . . . on human morality and left to receive the Finnish Minister at my house. He is a nice, timid fellow, and when I asked him why Finland did not appeal to the League, he replied that he felt certain that the League would not dare to take up the aggression. . . . I told him . . . there could be no disadvantage to Finland in making the attempt. . . . The Finnish Minister asked me if he could telegraph his Government what I had said, and I told him that, provided he made it entirely clear that I was speaking as an individual and not in any way as a representative of the Government of the United States, he could telegraph anything he liked to his Government. I then said . . . that he ought to discuss the matter with Avenol at once. He was frightened to talk to Avenol without instructions from his Government. I then told him that I would pick up my telephone immediately, call Avenol, and say that I personally was insisting that they . . . discuss the matter. . . . After thinking hard for about three minutes the poor Finnish Minister said that he would be glad to see Avenol if I made it clear that I was forcing him to see Avenol and if I would not mind his telling his Government that he had seen Avenol only because I had compelled him to. I told him he could make me as an individual responsible for anything. . . . I picked up my telephone and told Avenol that the Finnish Minister was with me; that I was sending the Finnish Minister to his office in my car; and that he would arrive in two minutes. Avenol asked me . . . if I had had any positive reaction from the French Government. I replied that, on the contrary, I had had a totally negative reaction from Rochat, but I was entirely convinced that this . . . would not be Daladier's reaction. Avenol said that he thought I was wrong but hoped I was right because the more he thought about the idea the better he liked it. . . . I had too many other engagements that day to bother about the Finnish business, . . . but the next morning I had an appointment with Champetier de Ribes [a foreign office functionary], and I told Champetier exactly what I had said to Avenol, the Finnish Minister, and Rochat. . . . He repeated to Daladier what I had said, and to everyone's astonishment—except my own—Daladier said that I was entirely right. . . . Daladier went so far as to give immediate orders that the French Government should get in touch with the British Government and say . . . that this was going to be the French line of policy. . . . The British objected, but Daladier went right ahead and called a Cabinet meeting the same afternoon and had the policy approved. . . . Avenol went back to Geneva knowing that he had the full support of the French Government. The Finnish Government replied to the Finnish Minister in Paris that it thought the idea of an appeal to the League a good one. . . . The Finns made their appeal, and the Soviet Union got the boot. . . . [The Soviet Union was expelled from the League of Nations on December 14, 1939.] The moral is: Eat oysters!

Creating a "Hopeless Delusion"

"PLEASE pat God fifty-eight times on the bald spot for me," Bullitt wrote Missy LeHand on Roosevelt's fifty-eighth birthday, January 30, 1940, "and get him to issue that summons which has not yet arrived." There had been a communications mix-up, for the president had sent the so-called summons on January 27, and Bullitt arrived in Washington on February 9, having flown by Pan American clipper from Lisbon. At an intimate dinner at the White House—it was attended by Bullitt, Roosevelt, and Missy LeHand, with whom Bullitt had been having an affair—Bullitt became one of the first to realize that the president was in precarious health. "At the dinner table," according to Carmel Offie, "Mr. Roosevelt collapsed and Dr. McIntire [Ross T. McIntire, the White House physician] was called. . . . Miss LeHand and Bullitt left matters to Dr. McIntire, who described it as a 'very slight heart attack.' "

Bullitt's visit to Washington was further recorded by Harold L. Ickes, the secretary of the interior, an administration insider and a friend and admirer of Bullitt: "Early Saturday morning Bill Bullitt called up," Ickes wrote in his diary.

He had reached Washington the night before and had had dinner with the President. . . . Greatly to my surprise, I found that Bullitt does not want to go back to Paris. He would like to have a job here, but it would have to be a big one. . . . So I said that I would be willing to tell the President that he ought to send Woodring to Paris and make Bill Secretary of War. This would suit Bill right down to the ground.

Ickes did make the recommendation to Roosevelt, who voiced doubts about taking Bullitt away from France, "because not only the officials there but the people depend so strongly on his advice and sympathy."

Bullitt apparently, in private conversations with FDR, had been given reason to believe he was in line for a cabinet post, either to replace Harry Woodring, who was being eased out, or Charles Edison, the son of the inventor, who was quitting as secretary of the navy to run for governor of New Jersey. ". . . I am very thankful to you for a lot of things besides having Anne and myself at the White House," wrote Bullitt on March 20 from Hobe Sound, Florida, where he and his daughter were vacationing, and he mentioned especially "the private thing you said to me. It meant much to me, and it has changed in the happiest way Anne's entire view of the future. I did not realize . . . how lonely she felt, alone in America. And I am deeply grateful that she will not be." (It is altogether likely that Roosevelt had intended to give Bullitt the war or navy job, but when the time came—it was July 1940, and the president was campaigning for an unprecedented third term against a strong tide of isolationism—he decided to appoint two Republicans: Henry L. Stimson, who had been secretary of state in the administration of Herbert Hoover, as secretary of war; and Frank Knox, the 1936 Republican vice presidential candidate, as secretary of the navy.)

Ickes also noted in his diary that at a cabinet meeting Roosevelt had announced that he was sending Sumner Welles, the undersecretary of state, to Europe for consultation with officials in Italy, Germany, Great Britain, and France. "Bill Bullitt had questioned me about this move," he wrote. "Apparently he did not relish the idea . . .," which was an understatement; when Bullitt had dinner with Ickes and his wife and the Welles mission was discussed, he became outraged, announcing he had protested to the president, telling him bluntly that he had declined in the estimation of Premier Daladier for failing to understand fully the situation in Europe. (Ickes mentioned in his diary two other items of interest: Bullitt had told of an angry encounter with Joe Kennedy one afternoon at the State Department, at which Kennedy—whom Bullitt had called to his face "abysmally ignorant on foreign affairs"—had questioned Roosevelt's support of England and France; and Bullitt had given a dinner party at his Washington hotel for Archduke Otto of Hapsburg, the pretender to the Austrian throne—among the other guests in addition to Ickes were Felix Frankfurter, the Supreme Court justice, and Archibald MacLeish, the librarian of Congress—who warned of Hitler's intention to attack the United States.)

"I had hoped the repercussions caused here by Welles' trip would have died down completely before my return," Bullitt cabled Roosevelt from Paris on April 18,

but Reynaud, Daladier, Chautemps, Blum and all the rest of the French politicians . . . have insisted on talking about the trip. They have all said the same thing, . . . that Welles "eulogized" Mussolini . . . and . . . produced the impression that Germany could not be beaten. . . . Daladier said that the impression Welles produced was that you thought Germany was invincible and that France and England ought to try to get a peace of compromise . . . by using the good offices of a great man—Mussolini. Daladier was a bit shocked and sore; Chautemps went so far as to say that . . . the visit had been exceedingly damaging both to your influence in France and to my influence. . . . The present fighting will soon wash out the memory of that visit. But for Heaven's sake, don't again let a Mussolini lemon be sold to you or anyone else. I have been highly restrained in this report since certain of the remarks . . . made to me have been violent in the extreme. Now let's forget the matter for good.

It was not forgotten, certainly not by Bullitt, who "never ceased his attacks on Welles for . . . his efforts to find a formula for a negotiated peace," wrote Joseph P. Lash, the historian and Roosevelt biographer. "It is doubtful, however, that Welles would have ventured any opinion in Europe that he did not believe reflected Roosevelt's own views and hopes. In attacking Welles as bitterly as he did, Bullitt was laying the basis for Roosevelt's subsequent reluctance to give him a new post of consequence." Robert Murphy, the embassy counselor in Paris in 1940, later considered with regret the effect of the incident on the careers of two men, who "were among the State Department's most brilliant . . . representatives at that time . . .," Murphy wrote. "But their misunderstanding aroused so much ill feeling that both men were . . . sidelined at a critical moment in American history."

There was another issue awaiting Bullitt on his return to Paris in April 1940, one he preferred to skirt, for it was a potential embarrassment: ". . . I haven't been asked a question by anyone about the German White Book," he wrote Roosevelt. "It fell completely flat here." The White Book—or "white paper," from an old English term for an official treatise—was a compilation of Polish documents that had been recovered after the invasion by the Germans and published by the foreign office in Berlin in March 1940; it purported to prove—and effectively did, for that matter—that American ambassadors in Europe, notably Bullitt, had encouraged the British and French to support Poland against Germany. One of the documents, a report to Warsaw written on January 16, 1939, by the Polish ambassador to Washington, Jerzy Potocki, contained "a very detailed definition of the attitude taken by the United States towards the . . . European crisis." Potocki had written that Bullitt, who was due to return to Paris in five days, had come to his office and talked for a half hour. "He is sailing with a whole 'trunk' full of instructions, conversations, directions from President Roosevelt . . .," which Potocki outlined, citing Bullitt as attribution: the U.S. unambiguously condemns totalitarian countries; U.S. war preparation will cost "the colossal sum of $1,250 million"; France and Britain must put an end to "any sort of compromise with totalitarian countries"; and they have "the moral assurance that the United States will leave the policy of isolation and be prepared to intervene on the side of Britain and France in case of war."

The charges were immediately denied in Washington, and Bullitt sent Roosevelt and Hull copies of a letter written by Daladier on April 4 attesting that, while he was prime minister, Bullitt had always said France should make her decisions, "knowing that . . . the United States would not enter the war." "Daladier's idea," Bullitt wrote the president, "was that the Germans might continue to attack you and me and that their attacks might be taken up during the campaign by the Republicans. He wished, therefore, to put a letter in your hands that you could publish at any moment you might see fit."

Notwithstanding Daladier's disclaimer—it failed in fact to address the main issue of the White Book—the allegations were essentially fair, as Joe Kennedy in London was willing to acknowledge in 1940 to his friend Charles Lindbergh, who recorded the conversation in his journal: "He [Kennedy] said the reports of the Polish Ambassador, which were captured and published by the Germans, . . . were almost entirely correct as far as the parts which concerned him. . . . He laughed, and said he didn't know about what Bill Bullitt said (but I gathered he felt that was pretty accurate, too)." James V. Forrestal, who became the first U.S. secretary of defense in 1947, wrote in his memoirs that Kennedy believed that Bullitt actually had manipulated Britain and France into war with Germany over the Polish issue. "I asked him about his conversations with Roosevelt and Neville Chamberlain from 1938 on," Forrestal wrote, recalling a talk with Kennedy on December 27, 1945.

> He said Chamberlain's position in 1938 was that England had nothing with which to fight and that she could not risk going to war with Hitler. Kennedy's view: That Hitler would have fought Russia without any later conflict with England if it had not been for Bullitt's urging on Roosevelt in the summer of 1939 that the Germans must be faced down about Poland; neither the French nor the British would have made Poland a cause of war if it had not been for the constant needling from Washington. Bullitt, he said, kept telling Roosevelt that the Germans wouldn't fight. . . .

The furor over the German White Book did not die down: its publication in the United States in the summer of 1940 resulted in investigations by the FBI and a grand jury in New York, and the manager of a German news service was indicted for violating the Foreign Agents Registration Act.

During Bullitt's absence from France the government fell, and Paul Reynaud became premier and president of the Council of Ministers; Daladier joined the cabinet as minister of war, not because there was mutual esteem between him and Reynaud but for pragmatic political reasons. "It is too bad that there should be anything but close friendship between Reynaud and Daladier," Bullitt wrote Judge Moore on April 18, "since the difference in their policies is slight, and they are both able men; but the lady love of each hates the lady love of the other, and from your experience as an old roué you know that venom distilled in a horizontal position is always fatal." On April 28 Bullitt brought Roosevelt up to date on war developments and their disheartening effect on the French leaders: "Both Reynaud and Daladier expect defeat in Norway to produce most serious repercussions. . . . Reynaud foresees his own fall, and Daladier thinks that he as well . . . will be completely discredited and that a defeatist government . . . will come in, with a program of peace at almost any price." But Bullitt for the moment was in a more positive frame of mind: "I think that is much too gloomy a view. The fighting spirit of the French people is untouched, and one defeat will not damage it greatly."

In the letter to Moore on April 18, however, Bullitt had added a postscript in which he admitted: "I am on the end of a long limb and need information and advice." It was one of the rare occasions of his life in which Bullitt admitted to self doubt, and presumably it had to do with the future of France; quite possibly he realized he had been wrong about the fighting spirit of the French, which would be damaged—in fact it would be depleted—by a single defeat. The Germans had overrun the Low Countries in early May, and on the evening of May 15, less than twenty-four hours since the front had broken at Sedan and German tanks had begun pouring through, Bullitt was in Daladier's office. There was a telephone call from General Gamelin, and Bullitt listened as Daladier shouted: "Then you must counterattack at once!" There was silence, and Daladier's face fell: "Then the French Army is finished!" Bullitt cabled Roosevelt immediately: "It seems obvious that unless God grants a miracle, as at the time of the battle of the Marne"—he meant the first battle of the Marne, in September 1914—"the French Army will be crushed utterly."

Bullitt had informed Hull on the morning of May 15 of the gravity of the situation: "The Germans had crossed the Meuse at many points north of Sedan." (While he hoped for another miracle of the Marne, Bullitt also knew the significance of Sedan, a town near the Belgian border where in 1870 Louis Bonaparte, Napoleon III, met decisive defeat in the Franco-Prussian War.) Daladier telephoned Reynaud and "stated that the French troops positively could not hold out . . . against the masses of tanks and airplanes . . . being launched against them, and . . . the battle certainly would be lost quickly unless the troops could be protected from German attacks from the air." Reynaud phoned Winston Churchill, who had replaced Chamberlain on May 10 as prime minister of Great Britain, and he put it bluntly:

. . . since the Germans had broken through into open country, where there were no fortifications whatever on the most direct route to Paris, and since there was nothing to oppose the floods of German planes and tanks except ordinary infantrymen and artillery, the war might be lost in the course of a few days . . . unless the British should send their airplanes . . . at once. Churchill, Reynaud said, had screamed at him that there was no chance of the war being lost, and he . . . had replied that Churchill knew . . . that so long as he . . . should remain Prime Minister, France would fight to the bitter end.

Bullitt sought to assure Washington that France would indeed fight on, as he continued to plead for military aid; and he tried to sustain the French war effort by holding out the hope that U.S. support was on the way. He had little to offer: one hundred used warplanes could be picked up at Halifax, Nova Scotia, Hull cabled Bullitt on May 15, but as Hull noted in his memoirs, ". . . it was too late. . . ." Then Bullitt sent a request to Roosevelt for the sale of twelve old destroyers to France, to which Hull replied on May 16: "In your talks with the appropriate French officials you may point out that for us to sell or lease some of our old destroyers would . . . involve submitting the question to Congress, which for a variety of reasons is not considered opportune." Bullitt was not being sincere with French officials, as Clare Boothe Luce observed—a writer and the wife of Henry R. Luce of *Time*, Mrs. Luce was in Paris during the German offensive—when she was asked by Reynaud at dinner at his apartment about airplane shipments. "I don't think we have any planes to send you," she answered, whereupon the premier turned to Bullitt: "Mr. Ambassador, have you been deceiving us?" Bullitt denied that he had, as he kicked Mrs. Luce in the shin, and Reynaud politely let the matter drop. "In harbouring any anticipation whatever that the United States would instantaneously send him 'clouds of planes,' . . . Reynaud was under a hopeless delusion . . .," wrote Alistair Horne, author of *To Lose a Battle: France 1940*.

For this, the American Ambassador in Paris, William Bullitt, must be held greatly to blame. . . . Bullitt appears to have sinned by misleading both his own country and France as to the true situation of the other; Washington was persuaded by Bullitt that France's fighting capacity was much greater than it was, while through him the French Government was led to expect far greater aid than could possibly have been forthcoming from the United States. . . .

On May 18 Bullitt transmitted to Roosevelt and Hull a message from Reynaud, a formal note of appreciation, which had a bitter edge to it:

The French Government was deeply and profoundly grateful to you for everything that you had done to assist in obtaining available war materials in the United States. It was obvious, however, that with the best will in the world sufficiently great quantities of material could not be obtained in the critical period of the next month to give the French Army the material equality which was essential.

Bullitt added a message of his own (it was quite evident that he had a hand in drafting the Reynaud note): "I entirely agree with Reynaud as to the gravity of the situation." On May 19 Gamelin, who had refused to send his troops against the

Germans in Flanders—let the Belgians and Dutch bear the brunt, he contended—was replaced by Weygand. Nevertheless, on May 28, the day Belgium surrendered, Bullitt was in high spirits again. He had talked with Daladier: "He said that the reaction of the entire French people to the treachery of the King of Belgians had been superb. Morale in France had never been higher than today, and the determination to carry on the war, whatever the cost, had never been stronger. . . ." On May 30, still optimistic, Bullitt made another appeal for aircraft reinforcements, as he cited Allied action at Dunkirk, the scene of a memorable naval evacuation: "The British and French troops . . . today displayed a heroism worthy of the best tradition of both nations. The superiority in quality of the French and British aviators has made it possible for them to establish, whenever numbers are equal or nearly equal, a definite superiority in the air. . . . The war is not lost, and every plane that can be sent today will be worth a hundred next year."

Present at the Surrender

THE WAR *was* lost, as Bullitt knew and as he wrote Roosevelt on the same day of his report to the State Department on Dunkirk, May 30, 1940: "This may be the last letter that I shall have a chance to send you before communications are cut." He still maintained there was a resilience in France: "The morale of the French Army and the civilian population is a vast credit to the human race. . . ." But the French were vastly outnumbered, he wrote, and no longer supported by the British or the Belgians: ". . . in spite of all the courage and character that will go into stopping them, the Germans may reach Paris very soon." There was also a danger of internal disorder, though it was largely imagined by Bullitt, who was letting his Soviet phobia cloud his perspective:

Everyone here believes . . . that the moment the French Government leaves Paris the Communists of the industrial suburbs will seize the city, and will be permitted to murder, loot and burn for several days. . . . Since I am not *persona grata* either to the Communists or to the Nazis, I do not expect to have much influence with either regime, . . . but I shall do my best to save as many lives as possible and to keep the flag flying.

Bullitt advised the president that he had decided he would remain in Paris when it was occupied by German troops, which would raise questions about his judgment, but he was determined: "No American Ambassador in Paris has ever run away from anything, and that I think is the best tradition that we have in the American diplomatic service. . . . In case I should get blown up before I see you again, I want you to know that it has been marvelous to work for you. . . ." Roosevelt had known of Bullitt's intention, having listened to his criticism of Claude Bowers, the ambassador to Spain in 1939, who "had disgraced himself and his country by running away in fear from the seat of a government which he pretended to admire"; yet Bullitt had not raised the point when Tony Biddle deserted Warsaw in September, and Roosevelt understood as well that Bullitt saw Biddle as his imminent successor, wherever the government of France was to be located. "But if the calm of death descends on Paris," he wrote, "I should like to be in very active life trying to prepare the U.S.A. for Hitler's attack on the Americas which I consider absolutely certain. . . . I think the wisest course would be for you simply to announce my appointment, and inform the German Government that you desired my return to the United States to be facilitated. . . ."

Bullitt pressed his case urgently a week later, sending the president what amounted to a demand that he be named secretary of the Navy: "I have no compunctions about saying that when Edison goes out on the twenty-fourth of June, I want to come in on the twenty-fifth. . . . Tony is just as eager to get to work in Paris, . . . and I can promise you with my customary modesty that from my experience here, I now know more about how to get ready for war than anyone except yourself."

He had been acting as if he already did run the Navy, having urged deployment of the Atlantic fleet in the Mediterranean to contain Italy, and then harshly condemning a decision not to take his advice. Hull had cabled simply that such a move "would result in very serious risks and hazards," to which Bullitt replied on May 31: "I believe that if we had sent the Atlantic fleet . . . either to Greece or Tangier when . . . I made the recommendation more than two weeks ago, Mussolini would not have dared to treat pressure of our government to keep him out of the war in the manner that he has. . . . I trust that no member of the American Government is still cherishing, in the words of Reynaud, 'fatuous and naive illusions as to the virtues of Mussolini'. . . . Anything you can do now will leave Mussolini with less strength with which to cooperate with Hitler. . . . At the moment words are not enough. Indeed, unaccompanied by acts they are rather sickening." The president, his patience obviously strained, sent a handwritten note addressed to "Bullitt" and signed "Roosevelt": "I am sorry you keep referring to the Atlantic fleet. . . . I cannot of course give you a list of the disposition of our ships but if you knew it you would not continue fantasies."

On June 3, while Bullitt was at a luncheon at the air ministry, he had a narrow escape: "We were having sherry and biscuits . . . when the air raid siren sounded," he reported,

but since it seemed highly improbable that the Germans had bombarded the center of the City of Paris, instead of seeking the air raid shelter, we went on the balcony to see the planes. A minute later a bomb dropped . . . about a hundred yards from us. Another bomb dropped exactly on the roof of the reception room . . . to which we had withdrawn— obviously it did not explode. . . . Heavy bombs fell on all aides, . . . and we went down to the air raid shelter amid flying glass and plaster. . . . I am entirely uninjured and lost only my hat and gloves, which are sitting at this moment close to the unexploded bomb.

On June 4 he met with Marshal Pétain, the World War I commander, who at eighty-four had returned to the government as vice president of the Council of Ministers. Bullitt filed a summary of Pétain's remarks to Washington:

The threefold superiority of the Germans in manpower was accompanied by a much greater superiority in airplanes and in tanks. The airplane had proved to be the decisive weapon in this war. . . . Against the German attack, which would be made before the end of this week, . . . the French had nothing to oppose but their courage. . . . It was certain that Italy would enter the war. . . . He felt that unless the British Government should send to France to engage in the battle . . . both its air force and reserve divisions, the French Government would do its utmost to come to terms immediately with Germany. . . .

Bullitt was again optimistic when he cabled Roosevelt at midnight on June 5: "Reynaud was enormously pleased by his conversation with you on the telephone this evening. As he told you, the fighting is going well. The French . . . have held all the German attacks in spite of German superiority in material and especially in planes." (Guy La Chambre, who was relieved as air minister in May 1940, contended in retrospect it was not a shortage of aircraft that brought about the defeat of France; rather it was a decision of the high command, expecting a long war, to hold planes in reserve, in addition to an innovative German strategy, which combined air and armored forces.) Reynaud had shaken up his government, having "decided that he must eliminate Daladier, . . . since Daladier was becoming the scapegoat for the difficulties of the French Army. . . ." Reynaud intended to be his own foreign minister, a position Daladier had assumed in May, and he would turn the war ministry over to Charles de Gaulle. "Two weeks ago this general was a colonel in the tank corps," Bullitt explained to Roosevelt. "He showed great initiative and courage in stemming the German advance on Paris. One day last week when I was talking to Reynaud he called him in to introduce him to me. He is a young man who appears to be vigorous and intelligent." The dismissal of Daladier, Bullitt wrote Roosevelt on June 6, had been dictated by Reynaud's inamorata, Hélène de Portès, a Nazi sympathizer. "The people of France . . . deserve better . . . than to be ruled by a Prime Minister's mistress.

. . . In the end she will be shot. Meanwhile, she will rule the roost." (The Comtesse de Portès died on June 28, 1940, in an automobile accident in which Reynaud was seriously injured.)

Bullitt was still cheerful when he cabled Roosevelt, also on June 6, that the pistols George Washington gave to Lafayette had been presented to him in gratitude; and he wrote Judge Moore on June 7 that he had found to his delight that during an air raid he could repair to his wine cellar and sleep peacefully: "I have for years had the feeling that I have had so much more in life than any human being has a right to have, that the idea of death does not excite me. The other day, when those bombs were dropping on our luncheon at the Ministry for Air, I . . . did not have one extra heartbeat." (It was Bullitt's favorite way of explaining that he was impervious to fear, as he had following an aircraft mishap in the Soviet Union in 1934.) On June 8, however, he sounded worried: "Will you please have put on the next Clipper," he cabled Hull, "twelve Thompson submachine guns with ammunition. . . . There is every reason to expect that if the French Government should be forced to leave Paris, its place would be taken by a Communist mob." ("Bullitt's hysteria about Communism," wrote William L. Shirer, author of *The Collapse of the Third Republic*, "which stemmed no doubt from his years as Ambassador to Russia, led to some fanciful reporting.") On June 9 Bullitt went to Domrémy-la-Pucelle, the birthplace of Joan of Arc, to speak at the dedication of a church altar; the next day Domrémy-la-Pucelle was occupied by the Germans.

On June 10, 1940, the Italian foreign minister, Galeazzo Ciano, summoned André François-Poncet, the French ambassador, and announced Italy's entry into the war. "What really distinguished, noble and admirable persons the Italians are to stab us in the back at this moment," Reynaud said to Bullitt, who relayed the premier's remark to Washington; and that evening, in an address at the University of Virginia, Roosevelt declared: ". . . the hand that held the dagger has struck it into the back of its neighbor." Bullitt had cabled the president at midnight on June 9 that he had just had a long conversation with Reynaud.

He said that it had been decided to remove from . . . Paris at once all ministries and services that were not directly involved in the prosecution of the war. . . . He then said that he . . . himself . . . might be compelled to leave Paris in the immediate future and added that he was intensely desirous that I should accompany him. . . . I said . . . that no American Ambassador . . . had ever left Paris and that I had no intention of leaving Paris and . . . would not so long as I thought I could be of use here. He protested that he would have no real means of communication with you. I then stated to him . . . that if I should be cut off from . . . him by the capture of Paris, . . . Ambassador Biddle would be named as my deputy. He replied that this gratified him extremely.

On June 9 Roosevelt had written a cable to Bullitt saying he had decided he should go with the government after all: "I consider it highly desirable that you be in direct contact with the French Government in the event of certain contingencies arising." It was not sent, however; instead a message drafted for the president by Hull went out on June 11:

It is strongly recommended that if all foreign chiefs of mission follow the French Government to its temporary capital, you should do likewise. Because it is impossible here to know last-minute developments or the wishes of the French Government, I must rely on your discretion and assume you will make your decision in the best interests of the United States and of humanity. . . . If in Paris or elsewhere you are cut off from access to the French government, Biddle will temporarily act as representative of United States.

Bullitt reaffirmed his intention to remain in Paris by cable on June 12: "My deepest personal reason . . . is that whatever I have as character, good or bad, is based on the fact that since the age of four I have never run away from anything however painful and dangerous. . . . If I should leave Paris now, I would no longer be myself. . . . It will mean everything always to the French and to the Foreign Service to remember that we do not leave though others do. *J'y suis. J'y reste.*"

On June 11 Bullitt had sent Roosevelt a note: "Please keep this for me—or for yourself if I don't turn up," he wrote, and he enclosed a letter Reynaud had given him at their final meeting on June 10, which while addressed to the president was inscribed, "To my dear friend Wm. C. Bullitt, great Ambassador of a great country." It read: "We shall fight in front of Paris; we shall fight behind Paris; we shall close ourselves in one of our provinces to fight and if we should be driven out of it we shall establish ourselves in North Africa to continue the fight and if necessary in our American possessions." General de Gaulle witnessed Bullitt's farewell call on Reynaud:

I supposed that the United States Ambassador was bringing some encouragement for the future from Washington. But no! He had come to say goodbye. The ambassador was remaining in Paris . . . to protect the capital. But, praiseworthy as was the motive which inspired Mr. Bullitt, the fact remained that during the supreme days of crisis there would be no American ambassador to the French government. The presence of Mr. A. J. Drexel Biddle . . . would not, whatever the qualities of this excellent diplomat, remove the impression . . . that the United States no longer had much use for France.

"I remember an evening with you in the White House, . . ." Bullitt wrote Roosevelt on June 12, "when I said . . . that I felt sure there would be war while I was Ambassador in Paris and that the Germans probably would reach Paris, and that since there would be danger that the Department of State would wish to order me to leave Paris and that I would . . . prefer not to receive such an order since I should have to disobey it. You said you would see to it that I should not receive such order, and I am grateful to you for remembering. . . ."

"It was on Wednesday that the German Army fought over the beautiful grounds surrounding Bill Bullitt's chateau at Chantilly," Harold Ickes wrote in his diary on June 15.

It was almost two years ago to the day that . . . I listened to Bill Bullitt there expounding his views. . . . He thought that the war would be fought to a stalemate. . . . He was wrong. . . . Cabinet yesterday was in the afternoon. The news from France was the worst yet. . . . In order to save Paris from destruction, the French declared it an open city and withdrew all troops. . . . Bill Bullitt stayed on in Paris. . . . I think that this was foolish and a bit spectacular on Bill's part. . . . Just what he could hope to accomplish in Paris, . . . I cannot understand. I wish he had not done this.

When he heard that Bullitt was resolute, Hull went to Roosevelt and argued against it:

I said I . . . thought our Ambassador should go with the French Government. It seemed to me that his influence with the German occupation authorities in Paris would be very small, because his strong anti-Nazi sentiments were well-known. . . . On the other hand, his influence with the French Government might be decisive. The President himself then telephoned Bullitt and said that he and I thought the Ambassador ought to leave Paris with the Government. He made the argument that Bullitt might be murdered by either the Communists or the Nazis. . . . Bullitt said he could not run away from danger and argued the President out of his position.

On June 12, 1940, Bullitt officially became the provisional mayor of Paris, and he went with other diplomats who had remained to the cathedral of Notre Dame, where he sat in the first pew and wept. The city was in chaos: there was a threat of panic as the Germans approached, enhanced by heavy black smoke that billowed on the horizon, though it was the result not of German artillery but of the deliberate setting afire of oil dumps; and Paris was effectively isolated, since communications facilities had been destroyed by the departing military forces. Bullitt could not send a message by telephone or radio, but he learned to his surprise that his embassy could be reached when he got a call from Leland Harrison, the American consul in Berne. He asked Harrison to relay a message to the foreign office in Berlin, which read:

Paris has been declared an open city. . . . All possible measures are being taken to assure the security of life and property. . . . Ambassador Bullitt is remaining in Paris . . . as the representative of the diplomatic corps. Mr. Bullitt hopes to be of any assistance possible in seeing to it that the transfer of the government of the city takes place without loss of human life.

A meeting was set for the morning of June 13 at Porte de Saint-Denis, the northwest gate of Paris, but it was marred by the murder of the chief German representative, an Army colonel, shot by a disgruntled French citizen. The officer had been a friend of Hitler's, and he raged: is this what Bullitt meant by the security of life and property? Bullitt, by utilizing his ample talents as a diplomat—his fluency in German was opportune—was able to arrange a second meeting, which was held without incident; and at dawn on June 14 a procession of German tanks rumbled down the Champs Élysée, followed by the marching troops of the Eighteenth Army, who made it a point to proceed through the Arch of Triumph, as only Napoleon and Woodrow Wilson had before them. When the invaders reached the U.S. embassy, the doorman, George Mitchell, permitted them to install a telephone line; and when Robert Murphy sternly suggested he was carrying American hospitality too far, Mitchell, who had lived in Germany, answered: "They're from Hamburg. They're nice fellas."

Absent at the Capitulation

THE FRENCH GOVERNMENT went to Tours, southwest of Paris, accompanied by Biddle, but it was from Joe Kennedy in London—Kennedy had gone with Churchill to Tours, where the British and French prime ministers met—that Washington got the first report, dated June 12: "You have no doubt received full particulars from Mr. Bullitt," he said mistakenly. "The practical point is what will happen if the French front breaks. . . . Reynaud . . . is for fighting, and he has a young General de Gaulle who believes much can be done. . . . This, therefore, is the moment for you to strengthen Reynaud the utmost you can. . . ." Kennedy cabled again on June 14, having learned details of the Reynaud-Churchill meeting: "Reynaud told Churchill that Weygand was insisting on an armistice; the French Army could not fight any longer. . . . Therefore Reynaud, at insistence of his ministers, must ask England to release France from her agreement not to sign separate peace. . . ." Roosevelt sent a note to Reynaud: ". . . this Government is doing everything in its power to make available . . . material, . . . and our efforts . . . are being redoubled"; but Reynaud needed a greater commitment: ". . . France would make peace unless the United States came in with all sorts of help short of sending an expeditionary force." No such undertaking was contemplated; in fact Roosevelt's message to Reynaud was "not to be published in any circumstances," Hull advised Kennedy. "It was in no sense intended to commit . . . this government to . . . military activities in support of the Allies." On June 15 Biddle cabled Washington from Tours:

> . . . the French government is now faced with two alternatives, . . . to sue for peace, . . . or to move to North Africa and continue the fight. . . . I have heard that Monsieur Reynaud . . . has said that the decision of France to continue the war from overseas depends on your being able to assure the French Government that the United States . . . will come into the war. . . .

On Sunday, June 16, the Council of Ministers met at Bordeaux, and Reynaud was pressed strenuously to seek peace; he refused, having heard from de Gaulle, who was in London, that Churchill had offered a union with free France, an idea that had been suggested to Churchill by Monnet. Reynaud was then asked by President Lebrun to form a new government with a proviso that he ask for an armistice; when he declined, a new government was formed anyway, with Pétain as premier and Weygand as minister of defense. When Biddle met with Reynaud that evening, a decision of the council was imminent: "I said that I assumed . . . a French Government would continue to fight from other shores," Biddle cabled, "even if metropolitan France was occupied by the German Army. He shrugged . . . and looked away." Biddle met again with Reynaud at midnight: "He was calm and entirely himself again—a man relieved of an enormous weight for the future of France. 'I have remained faithful to my word,' he said, 'and loyal to my policy of closest collaboration with Great Britain and the United States. . . .' Pétain will of course immediately seek an armistice by direct approach." The armistice was signed on June 22.

Had Bullitt's absence been a factor? "No one can say what would have been the precise effect of Bullitt's influence," Hull wrote in his *Memoirs*,

> had he been able to exercise it personally on the Government at Tours and Bordeaux. Churchill himself, even by a personal visit to Tours . . . and the offer of a union between Britain and France, was unable to keep France in the war. . . . But then the French Government was angered at the Churchill Government, whereas our own influence with Reynaud and his cabinet was of the highest. I feel that, with Bullitt on Reynaud's side, we should have had a reasonable chance to induce the French Cabinet to continue the fight with the fleet and colonies. Nevertheless, . . . Bullitt was both capable and sincere. And, having the courage of his convictions, he . . . did not hesitate to proclaim and pursue them.

With Paris in German hands, Bullitt had no official status, but he remained for over two weeks, helping American and British citizens depart France. He himself left on June 30 in a five-car caravan with his naval attaché, Roscoe Hillenkoetter, in charge—also in the entourage were Murphy, Offie, and Dudley and Frances Gilroy, personal friends of Bullitt's—and headed south in pursuit of the French government, which had moved again, this time to Clermont-Ferrand. Bullitt spent all day July 1 interviewing officials of the new government and sent a report that evening—considered by George Kennan "one of his most informative and historically important dispatches"—from La Bourboule, where he was lodged in a resort hotel.

The impression which emerges . . . is the extraordinary one that the French leaders desire to cut loose from all that France has represented during the past two generations, that their physical and moral defeat has been so absolute that they have accepted completely for France the fate of becoming a province of Nazi Germany. Moreover, in order that they may have as many companions in misery as possible they hope that England will be rapidly and completely defeated by Germany. . . . Their hope is that France may become Germany's favorite province. . . . As you know, the French Government arrived in Clermont-Ferrand yesterday. Displeased by living arrangements, it left today for Vichy. In view of the disorder none of the statements which were made to me today should be taken as indicating any fixed line of policy or opinion. The truth is that the French are so completely crushed and so without hope for the future that they are likely to say or do almost anything. . . . The simple people of the country are as fine as they have ever been. The upper classes have failed completely.

Bullitt had written, as Kennan commented in 1972, a "uniquely authentic portrayal of the mentality and calculations of the Vichy leaders," drawn from conversations with Pétain, Lebrun, Weygand, and Jean Darlan, the marine minister.

Admiral Darlan was intensely bitter against Great Britain. He said . . . that the British Fleet had proved to be as great a disappointment as the French Army. . . . Darlan went on to say that he felt absolutely certain that Great Britain would be completely conquered by Germany within five weeks. . . . I remarked that he seemed to regard this prospect with considerable pleasure, and when he did not deny this remark but smiled, I said that it seemed to me that . . . the French would like to have England conquered in order that Germany might have . . . many provinces to control. . . . He smiled again and nodded.

With Pétain, Bullitt was deferential, describing him as "calm, serious and altogether dignified." He reported that after an hour "the Marshal asked me to take luncheon with him, and as a result I talked with him for three hours. The Marshal first asked me about conditions in Paris, which I described in great detail. . . . He then said that he desired to thank me most profoundly for having remained in Paris. . . . He said that he personally and all other Frenchmen owed me a deep debt of gratitude. . . ." Pétain "expected Germany to crush England rapidly," although he did not share Darlan's relish for such an eventuality:

"Pétain recognizes that only a defeat of Hitler by some other power can restore independence to France," Bullitt cabled on July 5 from La Bourboule, having had a second meeting with the premier. "He is, therefore, sincerely desirous of a British victory." Pétain also wished to achieve an "equitable mutual understanding" with the United States, as he stated in a message to Roosevelt, which Bullitt transmitted: ". . . it is with confidence that I lay the case before you, Mr. President, whose active friendship for France will not, I am sure, fail my country in the cruel misfortune from which I have undertaken to extricate it."

On July 13, 1940, Bullitt cabled Washington from Madrid:

At five o'clock in the evening on July 10, Jeanneney [Jules Jeanneney, president of the French Senate] announced the vote which terminated the existence of the French Republic. I left the next morning. . . . The death of the French Republic was drab, undignified and painful. The deputies and senators met in the theater of the Casino at Vichy at 12 o'clock. . . . It took an hour and a half to count the ballots. . . . Jeanneney read the fatal figures and declared the session of the National Assembly closed. As he pronounced the word, "closed," a voice . . . cried, *"Vive la République, quand même!"*

Bullitt also cabled from Madrid: "Both Blum and Reynaud had the courage to come to Vichy for the National Assembly in spite of the real danger involved. I called on them both. Blum was full of courage and despair. Reynaud, his head bandaged and one eye still bloody from the automobile accident in which his fiancée, the Countess de Portès, was killed, was a broken man. He said . . . he might soon be in prison because of the arrest of his two private secretaries, who were stopped . . . at the Spanish frontier carrying a large suitcase filled with twenty million francs in paper, a considerable quantity of gold, jewels, and Reynaud's most private personal files. . . . He swore to me that he had given no orders . . . to take any of these things." (Blum and Reynaud as well as Daladier were interned and tried in 1942 for having taken France to war unprepared, but were not convicted; however, they remained in German custody until the end of the war in 1945.)

There had been a disquieting incident when Bullitt and his party reached Spain: the officer in charge of the Spanish border questioned the identity of the Gilroys—Dudley Gilroy was a retired British army officer and the manager of a racing stable at Chantilly; Frances Gilroy, a Philadelphian, was a friend of Bullitt's from childhood—who were traveling as Bullitt's butler and maid. "She is not a maid," declared the officer, apparently noticing Mrs. Gilroy's elegant appearance. "Of course not," huffed Offie. "Don't you understand that the ambassador has a mistress?"

VII

Envoy to
Limbo

Bringing Home the War

B U L L I T T left Lisbon July 15 on the Pan American clipper for New York, and because the plane was grounded by engine trouble at Horta in the Azores for four days—transatlantic air travel was still unreliable and a bit risky—he had time to take stock. As he had recently written to Judge Moore, Bullitt had had "so much more in life than any human being has a right to have," and indeed there had been some exhilarating experiences, though for each he had paid a price: leading the secret mission to Moscow in 1919 to meet with Lenin, which precipitated the break with Wilson; negotiating the Roosevelt-Russian diplomatic accord, followed by a posting to Moscow for three wretched years; representing his government in Paris during a crucial period, which ended with the fall of his beloved France. For Bullitt there was a sense of enormous personal defeat as of mid-1940, but he was a man of enduring confidence, and it can be assumed that at age forty-nine he looked to the past with satisfaction and to the future with positive expectation. Future historians would judge his record in public life, although contemporary critics had already formed an opinion—he was brilliant but difficult (James P. Warburg, a New York banker and long time acquaintance, found him "utterly unscrupulous—the kind of fellow who rather prided himself on being unscrupulous"); as for his future as an official of government, there was not to be one—Bullitt had reached the climax of his career. That he would virtually disappear from public view within months of his return to the United States was attributable in large measure to his impetuosity in personal working associations: ". . . he was intolerant," a relative of Bullitt's observed privately; he would develop passionate attachments to people, but "when they would not come up to his impossible expectations, he would discard them." Bullitt considered his professional colleagues intellectual inferiors, and his contempt for them was often unconcealed: he had openly castigated his counterparts in three major European capitols—Joseph Kennedy in London, Joseph Davies in Moscow, and William Dodd in Berlin; he would later be at odds with John Cudahy over U.S. entry into the war, and his friendship with Tony Biddle would be strained by rivalry; finally he would demand the dismissal of Sumner Welles, the undersecretary of state, and he would no longer be welcome at the White House.

There were other dignitaries aboard the "Dixie Clipper" bound from Horta to New York, although none so notable as Bullitt, whose arrival was front-page news in *The New York Times*. One was John G. Winant, chairman of the International Labor Organization in Geneva and a former governor of New Hampshire (the ILO was an adjunct of the League of Nations, so Winant was not on good terms with Bullitt); another was former Empress Zita, the widow of the last monarch of Austria and the mother of Bullitt's friend Archduke Otto of Hapsburg (Bullitt enjoyed the company of royalty and presumably got along well with Empress Zita). On arrival at La Guardia Field on Saturday, July 20, Bullitt held a twenty-minute news conference—an exception to "his customary practice of being uncommunicative to reporters," it said in the *Times*—and he stepped out of line by enunciating U.S. policy toward the Vichy French government. "Marshal Pétain is universally respected in France, as he is throughout the world," Bullitt declared. "He is doing his best to bring order out of desperate disorder. . . ." Bullitt then stopped himself, saying: "As for the future, I do not want to say anything. First, I must speak to the President and the Secretary of State." But when a reporter referred to France as a "fascist state," actually run by the pro-German vice premier, Pierre Laval, Bullitt gave the *Times* its headline for Sunday morning: "FRANCE OF PETAIN IS NO FASCIST STATE." "I don't know if it is right to call it a fascist state," he was quoted as saying. "Marshal Pétain has a tremendous reputation, and he is thoroughly honest and straightforward. . . . Pétain is absolutely the boss. He is trying to do his best in an extraordinarily difficult situation." Police motorcycles, sirens blaring, then escorted the ambassador to Pennsylvania Station in Manhattan—he had been met at the airport by his daughter, Anne, and his brother, Orville, and his wife—and he spent the night with them in Philadelphia.

Bullitt briefed President Roosevelt over Sunday supper at the White House, and news accounts of what they discussed were misleading: a possible return to France by Bullitt (which was out of the question); and recognition of the Pétain government (which Bullitt had made a touchy subject by his untimely remarks at the airport). They did talk at length about the threat of a German invasion of the Americas, which was first on Bullitt's agenda: Hitler would attack South America by Christmas, having defeated Great Britain, he predicted, as a steppingstone to the continental United States. (American military commanders had for years considered the possibility of a German invasion via Mexico, but Roosevelt was not convinced that Britain would yield so easily.) Bullitt presented the president with a serious dilemma: even had he agreed that a German attack was imminent, he was running for reelection at a time when isolationism prevailed in the nation (96 percent said no to a Gallup poll question in January 1940 as to whether the U.S. should declare war on Germany, and a majority doubted that Hitler, if he were to conquer Britain, would invade the United States).

Roosevelt invited Bullitt to Hyde Park, and they went together July 22 on a presidential train, which again exposed Bullitt to the press. He insisted that the relationship of the U.S. government with the French government of Pétain was "exactly the same" as it had been with the government of Paul Reynaud. "We have never broken off relations," he said, noting that Robert Murphy was the chargé d'affaires of the embassy in Vichy; but Roosevelt in a press conference on July 23 was noncommittal, and when asked if Bullitt would be returning to France, he said the ambassador had earned a vacation. "I cannot understand Bill's attitude toward the Pétain government," Harold Ickes wrote in his diary on August 3, 1940.

He seems to think of it as a free and independent government of a sovereign state, but the President, as he told the Cabinet, . . . does not so regard it. . . . Neither do I so regard it. Without consulting the Department of State, Bill at a press interview said that he thought the Pétain government ought to be recognized by this country, and would be. I do not think that it should be, although that has already been done in effect, and certainly Bill was out of order in making an announcement of foreign policy which properly should have come either from the State Department or from the President. But then Bill has always been an *insurrecto* so far as the State Department is concerned.

"How well do you know Billy Bullitt?" Roosevelt demanded of Francis B. Biddle, the solicitor general, as they cruised on the Potomac River on the yacht *Mayflower* in late summer 1940. ". . . [W]ithout waiting for an answer," wrote Biddle in a memoir—Biddle, of course, was one of Bullitt's oldest friends— "[he] went on to say that Billy was all wet about Pétain. He had given out a statement when he got back from France that Pétain was a great national hero, which he was not. He was a shrewd old peasant who had decided to sell France to the Germans, and had been able to twist Bullitt around his finger." Roosevelt had another score to settle with Bullitt, involving Marguerite "Missy" LeHand, who had been his personal secretary for twenty years, to whom he was devoted, and with whom Bullitt had been having a romance since his days in the Soviet Union. ("Well, Russia is recognized, Bullitt goes as ambassador," Eleanor Roosevelt wrote to her friend Lorena Hickock in 1933. "I wonder if that is why F.D.R. has been so content to let Missy play with him! She'll have another embassy to visit next summer anyway.") They had even considered marriage: "The one real romance of her life was William C. Bullitt, . . ." Roosevelt's eldest son, James, told biographer Nathan Miller, "but he broke off their engagement." Roosevelt, according to Miller, never forgave Bullitt.

While they were at Hyde Park, Roosevelt asked Bullitt to deliver an address on foreign policy at a meeting of the American Philosophical Society in Philadelphia on August 18. Bullitt was an appropriate choice, for it was the society that welcomed home Benjamin Franklin, the first ambassador to France, in 1785, but Roosevelt had an ulterior motive: knowing Bullitt would speak out on the threat to U.S. security and that he would be widely heard, he reasoned that the response to the speech would be a fair test of the national mood. Bullitt went quietly to New Hampshire, to Camp Pasquaney, where he had spent summers as a youth: "Bill . . . entered into the life of the camp, . . ." recalled Charles Stanwood, the camp director, "taking boys on canoe expeditions . . . and telling stories of his global adventures. Although we did our best to follow his request that his presence be kept a secret, persistent reporters somehow discovered he was at Pasquaney. . . ." (". . . Ambassador William C. Bullitt was camping in the woods today near Newfound Lake," the Associated Press reported from Bristol, New Hampshire, on August 8.) "Bill didn't help hide his whereabouts," Stanwood explained—Stanwood wrote about Bullitt's visit in a history of the camp—

for he telephoned President Roosevelt every morning. . . . Right after breakfast he would crank up our country line to summon the operator in Bristol. . . . To the operator he would simply say, "Get me the White House in Washington. This is Bullitt speaking. . . . Hello, White House? Bullitt speaking. Get me the President. . . . Good morning, Frank. You ought to be up here. The weather's wonderful. Come on up for a swim." Then there would be a long silence, while the President apparently talked at length about many things. . . . I gathered that . . . the President was urging Bill to hurry with the writing of something. . . . Bill often said, "Yes, it's coming along. I'm working on it." All of us at the camp knew he was writing something, for almost every day he spent much of the afternoon at the old Sigma Alpha House, usually returning to the main camp with what were obviously the pages of a manuscript.

Bullitt submitted a draft of his address on August 13: a rousing call upon Americans to respond to reality, it was approved by the president and by Undersecretary of State Welles, and two million copies were printed for distribution. Late on a Sunday afternoon Bullitt appeared before four thousand people gathered in Independence Square, surrounded on the flag-draped platform by family, friends, and colleagues: his daughter, Anne, and brother, Orville; Tony Biddle, just back from France; John Cudahy, whose last post had been Brussels; and Francis Biddle, the solicitor general. "America is in danger," Bullitt said simply.

It is my conviction . . . that the United States is in as great peril today as was France a year ago. And I believe that, unless we act now, decisively, to meet the threat, we shall be too late. . . . The French wanted no more war. And when the German propagandists told the French that they would buy peace with Germany by making one concession after another, the French believed them.

Bullitt, who had been misled by assurances of the French generals that the Maginot Line was impregnable, compared French dependence on that "tremendous obstacle" to a similar attitude in the United States.

Today we hear Americans . . . arguing that the dictators will never so wish to invade the Americas as to cross the Atlantic, which is regarded as such a tremendous obstacle. They ask us to ignore the fact that the Atlantic is an obstacle only so long as the European exits to the Atlantic are controlled by a nation which is genuinely friendly to us. . . . The truth is that the destruction of the British Navy would be the turning of our Atlantic Maginot Line. Without the British Navy, the Atlantic would give us no more protection than the Maginot Line gave France after the German troops had marched through Belgium. . . . What stands today between the Americas and the unleashed dictatorships? The British fleet and the courage of the British people. How long will the British fleet be able to hold the exits from Europe to the Atlantic? I cannot answer that question, nor can any man. . . .

It is as clear as anything on this earth that the United States will not go to war, but it is equally clear that war is coming toward the Americas. . . . On the tenth day of last May the people of France were as confident as are the people of the United States today that their country could not be conquered. Three days later, on the thirteenth of May, the Germans had smashed through the center of the French Army, and France was doomed. . . . Why are we sleeping, Americans? When are we going to wake up? When are we going to tell our Government that we want to defend our homes and our children and our liberties, whatever the cost in money or blood? . . . When are we going to tell them that we want to know what are our duties, not what are our privileges? When are we going to say to them that we don't want to hear any longer about what we can get from our country, but we do want to hear what we can give to our country?

("And so, my fellow Americans, ask not what your country will do for you; ask what you can do for your country," said John F. Kennedy in his inaugural address in 1961. President Kennedy's biographer, Arthur M. Schlesinger, Jr., attributed the statement to a quotation from Rousseau, which Kennedy had written in a notebook in 1945: "As soon as any man says of the affairs of the state, 'What does it matter to me?' the state may be given up as lost.")

Isolationists in the Senate denounced the address and Bullitt himself—ironically he was most loudly criticized for Communist sympathies—in floor debate on August 19. ". . . [T]here has been no man in the government service . . .," said Burton K. Wheeler, Democrat of Montana, "who has been friendlier to the Russian government"; and the "aid-to-Britain" forces, Wheeler declared, were forgetting that "the bones of our boys are still fertilizing the fields of France." "Is not this the same Bullitt," demanded Champ Clark, a Missouri Democrat, "who was utterly repudiated as a diplomatic agent by President Woodrow Wilson because of association with . . . and admiration for Lenin, Trotsky, and the bloody-handed murderers of the Communist Revolution in Russia?" In the House of Representatives John C. Schafer of Wisconsin, a Republican, called Bullitt "a multi-millionaire, New Deal, international, unchristian, warmongering ambassador," who ought to be put in prison. Supporters of Bullitt, what few there were in Congress, were quite silent—Senator Joseph F. Guffey, a Pennsylvania Democrat and a friend of Bullitt's, urged his colleagues and all American citizens to read the speech—but *The New York Times* applauded Bullitt's stand and the way he had stated it: while the words had been said before, it said in an editorial, they had seldom been said so well.

It had been agreed, Bullitt later wrote, that Roosevelt would address the nation within days of the Philadelphia speech, reiterating the threat of war. "But he did not. . . . It was a presidential election year. His White House advisers persuaded him that if he told the truth, he would lose the election." Roosevelt won the election in a landslide—449 electoral votes to 82 for Wendell L. Willkie, the Republican.

Eased Out of a Job

HAROLD ICKES noted in his diary on October 7 that Carmel Offie had called Ickes's wife, Jane, to say that Bullitt was restless and unhappy.

He has no status in Washington and is becoming sensitive about his anomalous position to the degree that he is not going around or seeing people. . . . Offie hoped that I would talk to the President in Bill's behalf. I did so, but the response was not encouraging. The President said that Bill had wanted to know what was to be done with him, and . . . the President proposed to make no moves until after the election. The President scoffingly said to me: "Bill wants to be Secretary of State, and I can't do that." In explanation, he said that Bill talked too much, and I got the impression that he also thinks that Bill is too quick on the trigger.

Ickes made another entry on November 17:

Jane and I had lunch with Bill Bullitt. . . . He, too, had sent his resignation to the President, and it had been promptly rejected. [With the president's reelection, resignations of ranking officials were pro forma.] Bill at once gave it out to the newspapers and got a lot of publicity. I did not tell . . . Bill that the President had declined to accept mine. Bill does not know what he is going to do. He wants to get into the Cabinet. He told us that the President had offered to send him to London as Ambassador but that he had declined the offer. His reason is that his daughter, Anne, has reached the age where she needs some social life, and he has no way of providing this except personally. The thought had occurred to him that Frank Knox would be a good man for London. . . . What Bill has in mind is that if Knox is sent to London, the President will then make him Secretary of the

Navy. According to Bill the President offered this post to him before he appointed Knox. Frank Knox would make a good Ambassador to London. . . . I would be willing to encourage both the President and Frank Knox to bring about this result, but frankly I do not think that Bullitt would make a good Secretary of the Navy. I doubt whether he could sit long enough at a desk to do any kind of an executive job. . . .

Bullitt's announcement on November 13, 1940, that he was quitting came during a period of uncertainty and change in the U.S. diplomatic ranks in Europe, and not just in the conquered nations such as France, Poland, and Belgium: William Phillips was ill and was being replaced as ambassador to Italy by Alexander Kirk; and Joseph Kennedy, who had been at odds with Roosevelt over backing Britain in the war—Ickes referred to Kennedy as a "wet blanket," a "defeatist"—resigned and said he intended to devote his time to keeping the United States neutral. Roosevelt might well have offered Bullitt Kennedy's post in London—Bullitt would not have lied about it to Ickes—but he might also have anticipated that Bullitt would decline. The reality was that the president had wangled his way out of a predicament: he had disposed of two opinionated and outspoken ambassadors—that Kennedy and Bullitt argued from opposite sides of the neutrality issue made little difference—either of whom could have undermined his subtle strategy of preparing for war while running for reelection when antiwar sentiments prevailed. With Kennedy Roosevelt was able to be straightforward: he summoned him to the White House to talk politics, and Kennedy told reporters on the way out that he would support the president for a third term. (It was years later that Kennedy revealed what he got in return: a promise by Roosevelt to support Joseph P. Kennedy, Jr., as governor of Massachusetts after the war.)

With Bullitt Roosevelt chose to be devious: "Resignation not accepted," he wrote on November 9. "We will talk about that and the future later. Hope to see you very soon." Roosevelt had in fact already decided to appoint as ambassador to the Vichy government of France William D. Leahy, a former chief of naval operations, as Bullitt had learned in a roundabout way: he had heard from Murphy in Vichy that Welles had requested an *agrément* for Admiral Leahy from the French government. Bullitt was very displeased, as he told the president by telephone on the evening of November 9: "I thought you said this afternoon that I was to remain as Ambassador to France and go off on a holiday until December 15. It's known all over town now and puts me in a fine spot." "Bill, believe it or not," Roosevelt replied, "I forgot all about it. It's entirely my fault. I wouldn't blame Welles entirely. . . . Welles went ahead this afternoon. . . . It's all right, though, Bill, because you remain as Ambassador until the appointment is made." Bullitt countered: "Yes, but what on earth am I going to do after you put me in that awful position? Leahy is now Ambassador—after I told the press this after-noon that I was remaining Ambassador to France. . . . What am I going to say to the press? This is shocking." "Sure, I understand, Bill. Damn the press. Just say you're still Ambassador, and I'll say the same thing to the press tomorrow." Bullitt was sad and exasperated: "Well, my dear fellow, I don't hold anything against you for it. I never have held anything against you in my life. . . . I had better tell the press simply that I am returning to private life. . . . Well, this certainly is a funny one, if anything ever was funny. It certainly leaves me in a spot."

Bullitt went to Philadelphia, and on November 18 he received a telegram at the Rittenhouse Club from Pa Watson—General Edwin M. Watson was Roose-velt's appointments secretary—who said a fifteen-minute meeting with the presi-dent had been scheduled for the following morning, though Watson later told Bullitt by phone it had been changed to November 20 at 12:45 P.M. "Bill Bullitt drove out to see me yesterday . . .," Ickes wrote on November 23. "He had had a talk with the President. . . . The President kept telling Bill that he did not want him to get out of the Administration, but apparently there was nothing definite that he could offer. He assured Bill that he was going to do a lot of rearranging, but Bill is a little skeptical, . . . as am I." Bullitt made a swift and graceful exit, having rented a home in the Philadelphia suburb of Penllyn, and he sent Roose-velt a note on December 28 asking that his resignation be accepted, so his personal belongings might be shipped from Paris. "It was a joy to see you in such fine form," he wrote of their parting session together. Roosevelt sent a reply dated January 7, 1941: "Your letter of resignation as Ambassador to France is before me. It is with great reluctance that I accept it. . . ."

Sounding Off on the Sidelines

THE JOB in London had been open since Kennedy's resignation on December 1, and according to press speculation Bullitt was the most likely successor—if Roosevelt had discussed London with Bullitt and Bullitt had declined, it was not made public—with Tony Biddle also being considered. (There was a report as well in *The Philadelphia Inquirer* that both Bullitt and Biddle were seeking to succeed Josephus Daniels, who was retiring as ambassador to Mexico; and while

Bullitt might not have accepted the post, it was true that he and Biddle had become friendly competitors.) On January 20, 1941, however, the day of Roosevelt's inauguration, it was announced that John G. Winant, a liberal Republican and an advocate of the New Deal, would be the ambassador to Great Britain, and Biddle would go to London to represent the United States with the exiled governments of nations that had fallen to Hitler: Poland, Belgium, Norway, the Netherlands, Czechoslovakia, and Yugoslavia. (Bullitt proved that he and Biddle were still good friends by permitting Offie to be assigned to him as a third secretary.)

Bullitt was out of a job but not out of the limelight: he was a central figure in the debate in Congress over the lend-lease bill, in which the charge was revived that U.S. diplomats had encouraged the Allies to resist the German advance. The specific allegation in hearings of the House Foreign Affairs Committee—it was made most vocally by Charles Lindbergh, who had emerged as a leading antiwar spokesman—had to do with secret commitments of American aid. Bullitt went before the committee on January 25 and issued a denial as far as France was concerned, claiming the allegations had originated with German propagandists; and he produced the letter Daladier had written to Roosevelt on April 4, 1940, saying Bullitt had advised him that the United States would not enter the war. Bullitt, of course, was begging the question: he had repeatedly made commitments of U.S. aid to the French; and he probably perjured himself when he denied the assertion of Jerzy Potocki, the former Polish ambassador to Washington (Potocki's report was contained in the German White Book), that he said he had been instructed by Roosevelt to urge Polish resistance. Bullitt also infuriated the isolationists with his sharp tongue. The opponents of lend-lease, he observed after the hearing, suffered from "political dementia praecox," to which Senator Wheeler responded: "Bullitt ought to know," obviously referring to his undergoing analysis with Freud in the 1920s. Bullitt was at the White House—to confer and to celebrate—the day the lend-lease bill was passed, March 11, 1941. (Lend-lease was, Bullitt wrote in 1948, entirely Roosevelt's idea, "that stroke of political genius which served so greatly in winning the war"; and he recalled a discussion in August 1940 of ways to finance aid to Great Britain. "Bill," said the president, "if my neighbor's house catches fire, . . . and I am watering the grass in my back yard, and I don't pass the garden hose over the fence to my neighbor, I am a fool. How do you think the country and the Congress would react if I should put aid to the British in the form of lending them my garden hose?")

Once Bullitt was cut loose from the government, he spoke out loudly and often, starting at the University of North Carolina at Chapel Hill on the evening of January 7, 1941, the effective date of his resignation. It was a thoughtful address, not a strident call to arms, tailored to the disposition of an audience made up of members of the International Relations Club; at the same time it was directed to the everyday American, for it was broadcast nationwide over NBC radio. "For the first time in our history," Bullitt said,

the war machines of Europe can reach the Western Hemisphere in a few hours. The physical isolation in which we have lived and developed our own way of life is at an end. Whether we like it or not—and most of us don't like it because we were happy with our isolation—the earth has been so contracted by the airplane that in a very real sense all the nations of the world have become our neighbors.

He then spoke of moral change in the world, which he called "even more bewildering than the geographical change." There had once been "a community of moral doctrine," which put restraints upon nations: "All were ashamed to kill, . . . to be cruel, to lie, to break their pledged word." But the moral doctrine no longer existed: the Bolsheviks in Russia had instituted "a government based on secret police and firing squads under which only an obedient slave can enjoy relative security"; the Fascists in Italy "installed the lie, the pledged word given and broken"; and the Nazis "under the leadership of a genius of evil . . . turned their backs on all the moral teachings of Christ, Mohammed, Confucius, and Buddha, and announced that the highest virtue was to be hard, and that there was one master race—the German—which was superior to all other races. . . ." To the list of totalitarian states Bullitt added Japan: ". . . to prove their moral superiority," he asserted, the Japanese "began to disembowel the Chinese with their bayonets"; and he noted that on September 27, 1940, Germany, Italy, and Japan "leagued themselves together by an agreement signed in Berlin," which posed, he declared, "the threat of ultimate war against us." Bullitt stressed the inevitability of war: "No bridge of understanding can be built between our nation and the totalitarian states, because a minimum of good faith is . . . necessary. . . . The dictators have proved . . . that we cannot believe a word they say or trust a pledge they make." He cited finally the examples of European nations that "did everything they could to avoid displeasing the Nazis; but they were attacked as ruthlessly as if they had acted with outright hostility to Germany. . . . Yet those who cannot bear to look at the harsh reality still comfort themselves by dreaming that we can get close to the dictators and establish happy cooperation. . . ." Such delusion reminded him of an old limerick:

> There was a young lady of Niger
> Who went for a ride on a tiger;
> They came back from the ride,
> With the lady inside
> And a smile on the face of the tiger.

On February 18 at a dinner of the Phi Beta Kappa association in New York City Bullitt urged that the U.S. warplane production rate be doubled: "If the Germans, by controlling the air, should be victorious, . . . the Nazi dream of a German super-race ruling over a world of unarmed slaves might well become a reality." He denounced anyone who would have America stand aloof from Great Britain, warning there were "powerful totalitarian elements in South America only waiting for the disappearance of the British Navy to invite the cooperation of Germany." At the Overseas Press Club on February 27 he charged that the United States "had done worse than any man had reason to expect" in providing war materials for its own defense. "If we were fully aware of the danger that threatens us," he said, "we should at this hour be producing every element of defense that we need . . . with as great speed as though we were at war."

An article by Bullitt appeared in *Life* on April 21, and in it he described Hitler as "the embodiment of danger to us": ". . . the Nazis alone of all potential aggressors . . .," he wrote, "aim to establish their tyranny over the entire earth. . . . So long as Hitler remains a conqueror, force and force alone will rule the world." Why had he not already struck?

We in the U.S. have not been attacked by Hitler and his allies—for one reason and one only: they have not been able to get at us. . . . If Great Britain should be conquered, we would be in danger of immediate attack. . . . If the British Navy should be eliminated, we would be left with a one-ocean navy for the defense of the coastlines of two oceans. . . . We could not . . . use our Navy effectively to . . . prevent a Latin American state lying south of the Equator from setting up a totalitarian government and cooperating with Hitler. . . . Our Navy would face the Japanese Navy in the Pacific and a Hitler-controlled navy in the Atlantic based on Dakar [the capital of French West Africa], . . . which is much closer to the bulge of Brazil than is our Caribbean base at Guantanamo. . . . What can we do to keep Great Britain from being throttled? The popular answer . . . is "convoy to Great Britain." . . . But a convoy does not mean a few destroyers accompanying a fleet of merchant ships and, by their mere presence, scaring off submarines and airplanes. To convoy means to send and to use destroyers, cruisers, aircraft carriers, planes. It means German planes and submarines firing, and our ships and planes firing back. It means that we should be fighting—although not at war unless Hitler should declare war on us. German and Italian armed forces fought in Spain . . . against the forces of the Spanish Government, but neither Germany nor Italy was ever technically at war with Spain. . . . We have, therefore, totalitarian precedent if we should convoy, and we might be fighting but not technically at war. . . . But we have to recognize that the step from fighting to being at war is short. . . . There is no easy way by which we can escape from war with Hitler. We cannot get off this planet.

"Bill Bullitt called up, and I asked him to lunch with me," Ickes wrote on April 26, 1941.

He continued to be pessimistic about the war—more pessimistic than anyone with whom I have come in contact. And the dreadful part is that I don't know that he may be right. . . . He seemed to doubt whether England would be able to withstand Germany, and he said that within four years our Government would be something entirely different from what it is today. . . . Bill doesn't like the Hopkins setup [Harry L. Hopkins, special assistant to the president, was Roosevelt's closest adviser], and he doesn't understand any more than the rest of us do the President's apparent inertia. He keeps insisting that the President is too tired to do anywhere near what he undertakes to do. And when he gets tired he dumps important matters into the lap of another man, who is not only tired but physically below par—Hopkins. [Harry Hopkins suffered from a digestive disorder and died of it in 1946.]

Bullitt was less impatient with the president in early June, according to another diary notation by Ickes, because he had gone to lunch at the White House and had been "one of the family"; and Roosevelt had at least listened to his advice. "Bill told him just how he felt about the international situation . . .," Ickes wrote.

He believes that if we do not actually get into this war in an effective way, England is all too likely to fall, and then we will be left alone to fight with the chances heavily against us. According to Bill, the President knows this too. But . . . the President will continue to play his luck. . . . He is waiting for an incident, fully conscious . . . that none may come before it is too late. Bill agrees with me that the Germans will not give us an incident until they are good and ready. . . . Bill made a suggestion to the President that I think was as novel as it was excellent. It was that the President go to Congress . . . with a carefully prepared address, . . . saying in effect that, unless Congress by adverse joint resolution directed him otherwise, he would go to war with Germany at the end of twenty-four hours. . . . The President said that he could carry a majority in the Senate with a plan like this, but he was doubtful about the House. As usual, he showed no disposition to venture.

———————

Bullitt meant it when he told Roosevelt he wished to remain in the United States to shepherd his daughter's introduction to society. Anne was seventeen, a graduate in June of the Foxcroft School, and while she would have preferred going to college—she was accepted at Vassar for the fall of 1941—her father was insistent, though for an unusual reason. "You'll do parties for a year," he ruled. "If you don't, you'll spend the rest of your life wondering if you should have. If you do, you'll realize how empty and meaningless they are." There was a debutante ball for Anne on June 12 at the exclusive Sulgrave Club in Washington, followed by several parties in Philadelphia, including an all-night dance at Meadow Farm, the commodious home Bullitt had rented in Penllyn with Anne's coming-out year in mind. "Anne would please you," he wrote George Biddle, who was still living in Croton-on-Hudson, New York, and was a recognized artist. "She passed her examinations for Vassar but decided that she wanted instead to go to the School of Industrial Art in Philadelphia and is now working from nine to four each day there. . . . The business of being a debutante gets attended to on Saturdays and Sundays. She really has some talent but has sense enough to know she is never going to be a great artist, and I think, wisely, intends to do some sort of commercial work. She is just as direct, simple and unspoiled as ever and entirely worthy of her godfather." (Anne's version of how it was decided she would not go to college was at variance with her father's: "He did not like intellectual women," she said simply. He disapproved just as firmly when she announced she wanted to become an actress, and it was *his* decision that she would study to be a commercial artist.)

The owner of Meadow Farm, Bullitt's landlord and next-door neighbor, was R. Sturgis Ingersoll, his old friend and the brother of Orville Bullitt's wife, Susan. Ingersoll heard on the radio early one morning of Hitler's attack on the Soviet Union—Operation Barbarossa, named for the twelfth-century German monarch, Frederick I, was announced by Joseph Goebbels, the Reich propaganda minister, on June 22—and he rushed across a field still in pajamas to break the news to Bullitt, who was drinking coffee with his houseguest, John Wiley. "Here indeed were the experts," Ingersoll wrote in a memoir. (Wiley had come home from Riga when Latvia was incorporated into the U.S.S.R. in 1940.) "Whatever their conclusion might be, it would constitute news from the horse's mouth. . . . Bill opened by saying that Stalin had liquidated all his top generals. The question narrowed down to how many weeks would it take for Hitler to rule Russia from Moscow. Bill opined three weeks; Wiley, more cautious, said: 'No, Bill, make it six.' They settled on five." Bullitt evidently was recalling the poor performance of the Red Army in its invasion of Finland in late 1939, not realizing that Stalin had since undertaken an extensive rebuilding program.

"I called Bill Bullitt . . . at his home near Philadelphia," Ickes wrote on June 28.

I wanted to know what his reaction was to the declaration of war against Russia by Hitler. He did not believe that Russia could withstand Hitler for any great length of time. But . . . he felt that this was a golden opportunity for us to participate in an active way that could strengthen Great Britain's position before Hitler returns to the assault of Great Britain. . . . Bill does not believe that the Red Army is particularly efficient or well trained, and he suspects that some of the Russian generals are in the pay of Hitler. . . . Bill thinks that the Russians will fight bravely for their own land but said that they are "peasant soldiers," who are not prepared to engage in a mechanized war with the Germans.

Bullitt wrote to Roosevelt on July 1, urging him to announce promptly that "the German attack on the Soviet Union makes it essential for us to produce with greater speed than ever, since Germany may soon have all the resources of the

Soviet Union at her disposal, . . ." and that "Communists in the United States are just as dangerous enemies as ever, and should not be allowed to crawl into our productive mechanism. . . ."

"The wrongness of Bullitt's predictions about Russia's power of resistance impeached his political advice," wrote Joseph Lash, and his reputation for reliability was further diminished by the accurate assessment of his successor as ambassador to Moscow, Joseph Davies. "It was symptomatic of the relative standings of Bullitt and Davies at the White House at the time of the Harriman mission," Lash observed, "that Roosevelt had Davies as a guest at his press conference, . . . a sure sign of presidential confidence." (W. Averell Harriman, a wealthy businessman and a friend of both Roosevelt and Harry Hopkins—Harriman and Bullitt had been contemporaries at Yale—had led a U.S.-British delegation to the Soviet Union to discuss lend-lease aid, and Harriman reported that "Hitler will never destroy Russia.") Bullitt may have been mistaken—it was all the more irritating for him to realize that Davies had based his judgment on the advice of the military attaché in Moscow, Colonel Faymonville, whom Bullitt had called a "Bolshevik lover"—but he was in accord with the majority of perceptive observers. ". . . Davies stood virtually alone in his faith in the Red Army," wrote Richard H. Ullman, author of an analysis of Davies's dealings with the Soviets.

Most . . . diplomats in Moscow at the time of the German attack believed that the Russian leadership had been fatally weakened by the purges. Why was Davies right . . .? Davies thought the Soviet Union was stronger than his . . . colleagues believed it to be partly because he did not understand its weaknesses as fully as they did. [It is also true that Davies was ambassador to Moscow for only about a year, having left there in 1938.] With more realistic theories to guide them, they were better able to discern the disabilities of the Soviet system. . . . But the shroud of secrecy was too heavy, with the result that they overestimated Russia's weaknesses, while Davies merely overlooked them. Thus Davies was right for the wrong reasons. . . .

Roosevelt sent Hopkins to Moscow in July, and on the strength of his estimate of the Russian resolve to resist the German advance it was decided that lend-lease assistance would be sent to the U.S.S.R. No strings were attached to it, however, and with this Bullitt took great exception. ". . . [W]hen the President was urged . . . by myself and others," he later wrote,

to give Lend-Lease aid to Stalin only after the Soviet dictator had given formal, written pledges to respect the eastern boundary of Europe as it existed in August 1939, . . . it seemed reasonable to believe that the President would act favorably on the suggestion. But the President rejected the suggestion on the ground that, although there was no doubt that Stalin would make such promises, there was equally little doubt that Stalin would break the promises as soon as it might suit him. . . .

The Atlantic Charter, a declaration of world peace, "which will afford to all nations the means of dwelling in safety within their own boundaries . . .," was signed by Roosevelt and Churchill on August 14; but as Bullitt later lamented, no guarantee had been obtained from Stalin to abide by its terms. "The President and the Prime Minister feared," Bullitt wrote in 1946, "they might have some difficulty in persuading Stalin to adhere to the Charter because it was difficult to square the Soviet Union's aggressions against Finland, Estonia, Latvia, Lithuania, Rumania and Poland. . . ."

On the day that Roosevelt and Churchill, at a historic meeting at sea, signed the Atlantic Charter, Bullitt addressed an American Legion convention in Altoona, Pennsylvania, and flatly affirmed that the United States would be at war "sooner or later"; and he clearly indicated the risk would be less if involvement was immediate. "The grim truth is that . . . we face war," he declared. "Either the dictators and their system of tyranny . . . will go down or we and our democratic way of life will go down." On October 23 Bullitt was for the first time publicly critical of the Roosevelt administration, and he chose as his forum a meeting of the Union League of Philadelphia, whose Republican members applauded loudly when he said the U.S. should declare war on Germany at once. "We are going to war whether you like it or not," he said. "The alternatives are clear. Either we say, 'Let Hitler conquer the world,' or we say, 'We go to war.' I say alternatives, but I don't mean that. We are going to war." The Republican presidential candidate in 1940, Wendell Willkie, had been "out ahead of the Administration in the line of truth," he maintained, and Roosevelt had failed to go "hard enough and far enough" to meet the Nazi threat.

I am a completely unregenerate Democrat, who will always vote the Democratic ticket. I take it that is why I have been invited here: that you feel the seriousness of the question of the day, so that whether a man is a Republican or a Democrat is swallowed up. The situation confronting America is, in the words of Franklin, "If we don't hang together, we will hang separately." It is a situation that must be faced by Republicans and Democrats alike.

In *The New York Times* on October 24, 1941, on the same page that carried an account of Bullitt's address to the Union League in Philadelphia, there was a report from Washington on the appearance of John Cudahy before the Senate Foreign Relations Committee to oppose an amendment to the Neutrality Act to permit the arming of American merchant vessels. Cudahy's pro-German sentiments were well known: he had been dismissed from the Foreign Service upon his return from Brussels in the summer of 1940 for having expressed the view that the average German soldier had conducted himself decently during the occupation of Belgium. He proposed in his testimony to the Senate committee that the U.S. take no side in the war but offer itself as a mediator, for he was convinced that Hitler—he had met with the Nazi leader on June 5, 1941, the last American to have been granted an audience—had no ambition to strike across the Atlantic. Cudahy was, of course, in complete disagreement with his old friend Bullitt, and on October 30, at an America First rally at Madison Square Garden in New York—a rally at which Lindbergh declared, ". . . there is no danger to this country from without; . . . our only danger lies from within. . . ."—Cudahy was a featured speaker; and he again called for a peace conference mediated by the United States. (Cudahy, from a family in the meat packing business in Cudahy, Wisconsin, had been a pacifist since he served as an officer with the American expeditionary forces at Archangel during the Russian civil war in 1919: he considered war to be "the sheer madness of human destruction. . . ." After the U.S. entered the war with Germany, he became the chief of civil defense in Wisconsin, and on September 6, 1943, he died in a fall from a horse, which Bullitt believed to be suicide.)

"Bill Bullitt came in, . . . and it was a Bill Bullitt in distress," Ickes wrote in his diary on September 20.

He had been to see the President and had finally learned definitely that there was no place for him in the preparedness organization. Bill was terribly hurt. He was being game about it, and he told about his interview with the President with a laugh, but it wasn't a merry laugh. It seems the President has been stringing Bill ever since he resigned as Ambassador to France. Bill held himself available because the President insisted that it was his full intention to call him into service in some important post. One first-class job after another would appear, . . . and the President would talk tentatively to Bill about it, indicating that now Bill was to be put to work, and then someone else would get the appointment. Twice, Bill told me, he had had attractive offers from private business. . . . On each occasion, when he went to consult the President, he was told that he must not take the job because the President was counting upon using him and couldn't get along without him. . . . Bill finally saw the President . . . to force the issue. He had begun to suspect that he was being given the run-around. The President told him that he had wanted to use him but that no position had offered itself that was commensurate with Bill's standing and abilities.

Bullitt had suggested to Roosevelt, according to Ickes, that Harry Hopkins "was responsible for his exclusion," and when the president denied it, "Bill told him that four people had related to him incidents, . . . which proved to him that it was Harry's doing. The President said: 'You may say to these people that the President of the United States says that this is a damned lie.' "

"For eighteen months I have been going double time and the administration has been going half time," Bullitt wrote George Biddle on November 1. "I don't know whether that is out of step or out in front. Probably a bit of both."

Sent to Observe the War

TO HIS SURPRISE Bullitt was summoned to the White House on November 18 and asked by Roosevelt to go as his personal representative to Africa and the Middle East—from French Equatorial Africa to Iran—and report on hostilities there, in particular the efforts of the British to reverse the successes of Field Marshal Erwin Rommel, the commander of the German desert forces. "The idea of an American operation against North Africa was one dear to President Roosevelt . . .," wrote William L. Langer, author of *Our Vichy Gamble*, in assessing the significance of Bullitt's trip. "The entire region was of obvious and vital interest to the United States and offered the possibility of establishing a base for operations on the continent of Europe."

Bullitt was delighted by the idea of being an ambassador-at-large, and he promptly felt justified in offering some top-level policy advice to the president, who was about to receive a visit from the British prime minister. "Don't let Churchill get you into any more specific engagements than those in the Atlantic Charter," he wrote on December 5, the day he departed. "Try to keep him from engaging . . . vis-à-vis Russia. The Treaties—if made—will be as difficult for you to handle as the secret Treaties were for Wilson." He was scheduled to return via the Far East—"I hope . . . you will see the Generalissimo [Chiang Kai-shek] . . .," Roosevelt had written on December 2—but that idea would be overtaken by events. Bullitt was in Trinidad on December 7, 1941, and he first heard of the Japanese attack on Pearl Harbor as he entered the residence of the British governor, Sir Hubert Young. "I have been forbidden . . .," Young exclaimed, "to have played together my national anthem and your national anthem, and now I can as we are allies." A military band played "The Star-Spangled Banner" and "God Save the King," and the governor, as Bullitt described it, "grew purple and exploded."

Bullitt was regarded, it had been reported in *The New York Times*, "as a keen judge and analyst of political and military trends"—there were those, having read his accounts of the last days of the French republic, who would disagree— and he approached his assignment with customary gusto. "The British are handling the situation here better than was indicated by the reports . . .," he cabled from Cairo—all of his messages were marked "strictly confidential for the President"—on December 21. "I believe [they] are doing as good a job as can be expected with the inadequate means at their disposal against a determined enemy led by a soldier of genius. Rommel has again escaped an excellent trap set for him. . . ." (Rommel continued his advance until he was defeated at Alamein in October 1942.) Bullitt then made the first of several recommendations—they were sound, as developments would show, albeit premature—that manpower and munitions supplies be augmented in the area:

> In view of the vital importance of North Africa for an ultimate attack on Italy and Germany and in view of the importance of having a British Army on the eastern border of Tunisia, rather than a German army, . . . I believe that (1) it would be folly to withdraw forces of any kind . . . now; (2) that the forces now here should be strengthened in any way that will not reduce forces which are vitally needed at other points.

It was a whirlwind tour—Bullitt would make his headquarters in an airplane, Roosevelt had said to reporters before he left—to Beirut, Bethlehem, Jerusalem, Palestine, Bagdad, and Teheran; and on December 27 he cabled: "I returned to Cairo yesterday from Syria, Lebanon, and Palestine. In those countries all is quiet on the surface but seething underneath. There is no sign whatsoever of reconciliation between the Arabs and Jews in Palestine." He had conferred at length with Oliver Lyttelton, the British minister of state for the Middle East, and General Georges Catroux, the Free French commander, and their subordinates. "The British are confident that they will be able to reach the border of Tunisia in about six weeks," he reported.

> In consequence, Lyttelton and all the British generals, General Catroux and all the French officers talk to me constantly about the problem of getting Tunisia and all the rest of French North Africa to side with us at the moment of the arrival of the British forces on the Tunisian frontier. . . . The Frenchmen with whom I have talked agree that there will be no chance of getting the French of North Africa to come over to our side unless we can send an American Expeditionary Force to Casablanca. We should probably have to send one hundred thousand men—to be safe against German attack through Spanish Morocco—and we should have to take the Azores, Madeira and the Canaries and maintain a large naval force and air force for the protection of transport.

Bullitt and Lyttelton sent a joint message to Washington on December 31, having consulted with Catroux, on the "possible invasion of Tunisia": "Catroux put the minimum force necessary . . . at six divisions. . . . We would emphasize that this is a preliminary telegram . . . sent . . . to reach you while the Prime Minister is . . . in Washington. . . . [Roosevelt and Churchill were conferring.] It appears however . . . that if resources are available in the near future the planning must start at once."

Bullitt was back in Washington on January 31, 1942. He talked with the press after lunch with the president but had little to relate, even when asked if he and Roosevelt had discussed a recent German counteroffensive in Libya. He did say he had spent four days at the front, "in exactly the territory which the Germans have now taken back"; and while he was camped outside Bengasi, Libya, he was bombed "a little bit."

Down and Out in Anger

IT WAS the worst of times for Bullitt, as he returned to private life and inactivity, all the more so for his brief experience of war and the opportunity to advise the president as to its conduct. He believed his recommendations were being ignored—he had no way of knowing that a major Allied landing at Casablanca in November 1942 would mark the first commitment of American ground forces in the war with Germany—and he was sounding as anxious as he had from Paris in May 1940. "I find that almost everyone concerned with military matters in Washington is convinced . . . that we must reinforce the air arm in the Near East," he said in a memorandum to Roosevelt on March 13, "but I cannot find the will to divert aircraft from other points. It seems to me urgent that this question should be reexamined. . . . It may already be too late." He was probably unaware, too, that the chief of staff at the War Department, General George C. Marshall, agreed with him: "The urgency of Ambassador Bullitt's concern as to the Middle East is justified," Marshall said in a report to the president.

> From a military viewpoint, the region invites attack, and its loss would permit junction by sea between the Japanese and the Germans with . . . disastrous consequences. . . . Of course, the meat of the situation for us is the urgent necessity of meeting our responsibilities in the Southwest Pacific, the reinforcement of Alaskan defenses, and, above all, the gathering of air power in England.

Bullitt met with Roosevelt on April 8, and his bitterness—more because he had not been given another important assignment than for the absence of action on his proposals for North Africa (he had been named chairman of the board of the General Aniline and Film Corporation, a German company annexed by the government, a meaningless position)—was reflected in a memo addressed to no one but written for the record that evening.

He [Roosevelt] said that I had made him feel as if he had seen the entire area with his own eyes, and he wanted me to go out there and be his eyes and ears again. . . . I said that I was fully in accord with Secretary Stimson. [The secretary of war had argued that owing to a decision not to send the necessary support to the Middle East, Bullitt ought not to return there.] I certainly would not go out to the Near East and lie either to the military or civilian leaders, . . . and if I told them the truth, they would be plunged into despair. The President then said that I could go out and refuse absolutely to discuss any military or naval questions. . . . I laughed quite sincerely at this and said that any such idea was simply idiotic; that no one in the entire Near East ever discussed anything except the military situation. . . . The only thing people were interested in was whether or not they could preserve their lives and the countries they were living in from Hitler's domination. . . . The President then said he was trying to send me out to buy him a pair of pants, and I had to go out for a fur coat. . . . I then said to the President that I positively would not go on a mission in which I did not believe, based on a policy that I thought was disastrously mistaken. . . . I then said . . . that I had no desire to continue to have a high paid job with a large title and have no work to do; that I had completed . . . all the tasks that had developed out of my recent mission and that I wished to know what, if anything, he wanted me to do. The President said that he had been thinking of me lately entirely in connection with the Near East and that he would have to turn his mind on where he wanted me to work if I would not go to the Near East. . . . We then discussed a number of posts that I might occupy. . . . The President said that he would send for me in the near future.

Bullitt still held Roosevelt in high esteem: "Dear Franklin," he had written on March 4, "When I saw you at the service in St. John's Church this morning"—St. John's was an Episcopal church a short distance from the White House—"I wanted deeply to shake your hand and say, 'God bless you.' Since I could not, I do it now." If the president was being less than candid in his assurances—and clearly he was—it was simply because Bullitt was difficult to place in the bureaucracy: his hauteur had made him unpopular not only with government officials but with others to whom Roosevelt listened. When it was mentioned by Vice President Henry A. Wallace in the spring of 1942 that Bullitt wanted to be put in charge of a consolidated information service that was being created, the president's response was succinct: he had checked with newspapermen, and they did not like him. Wallace, on the other hand, had studied Bullitt carefully during their brief acquaintance and admired him, though with reservations. "Bullitt is a vivid kind of person," he wrote, "whose heart seems definitely in the right place, but I would judge from looking at him that he probably has been drinking a little too much in recent years and that he never in his life has done enough work with his hands or lived enough with the rank and file of the people to understand the world as it is. . . ."

Wallace's wisdom, if it had been offered, might have dampened Bullitt's political aspirations, which had been dormant since he had declined to run for governor of Pennsylvania in 1938, but were revived when his name came up again in 1942. "We are headed . . . for certain defeat unless complete unity is worked out before the primaries," wrote Attorney General Francis Biddle to Roosevelt on February 23, 1942. "All of the candidates must retire except the one agreed on. I believe that the only man with a chance for success is Billy Bullitt." Bullitt was opposed, however, by Senator Guffey, who was convinced he would not pull the labor vote—Catholic support was also in doubt, Biddle admitted, because "Bill has been twice divorced and has written a dirty book"—and the president remained uncommitted. "You and Tony should know that I think I have saved you from the Governorship of Pennsylvania," FDR wrote Margaret Biddle, the wife of the ambassador to the exile governments in London, on March 13. "The fact is that . . . nobody has agreed on anybody. . . ." Bullitt did not actively seek the nomination—he did, however, contest Guffey's point and wrote Roosevelt on February 21 that the state labor leaders "want me and say that I am the only person who stands a chance of winning"—but he attempted to use the support he had received as a bargaining chip. "I am in a quandary," he wrote Roosevelt on March 26.

> You will recall that when we talked two weeks ago, you agreed that for me to run in the primary . . . was absolutely out of the question, and you said that you would get hold of Stimson and have me put on the Combined Chiefs of Staff Committee. . . . As I said to you, I would a thousand times rather do that job than be Governor of Pennsylvania. . . . Inasmuch as the decision . . . will have to be made today, . . . I would like to know what you really want.

Bullitt was not the nominee for governor, nor did Secretary of War Stimson appoint him to the committee; and when on April 20 he went directly to Stimson to volunteer for active military duty, he was turned down, presumably because he was too old. Finally, in a tone more resigned than angry, Bullitt wrote the president: "To do nothing to help defeat the enemies of our country is intolerable, and I am therefore seeking another field of service."

There was a rumor meanwhile that Bullitt was in financial straits—all the stories of his vast wealth were spurious, and he had been spending far in excess of his earnings—and was without a place to live in Washington. Henry Wallace heard it from Evalyn Walsh McLean (the same Mrs. McLean who had visited Moscow in 1934 and had driven Bullitt to distraction by announcing she would wear the Hope diamond in public). "Mrs. McLean said Bill Bullitt was busted," Wallace wrote in his diary on April 2, "and that Cissy Patterson . . . had said she was going to put Bill up in the upper story of her home." Mrs. Patterson, the publisher of *The Washington Times-Herald*, despised Roosevelt for the very foreign policy that Bullitt had espoused, but while she argued with Bullitt, she cherished their friendship. "I didn't suppose this world held anyone as fascinating—just for *me*—as that man," she had written of their romantic encounter on the Riviera in the 1920s. But she was also a friend of Martin Dies of Texas, the chairman of the House Committee on Un-American Activities, to whom Bullitt's politics were shaded in pink; and Dies warned Cissy Patterson, according to Wallace, that if Bullitt moved in, "Washington sentiment would laugh them both out of town." Instead, Bullitt turned to Offie, who had completed his assignment with Biddle in London: "Bill is living in Offie's house in Georgetown," Wallace noted on May 20—Offie was frugal, and he had begun to invest his savings in Washington real estate. "Bill said that Offie had sponged off him for many years, and now he was sponging off Offie."

Bullitt suffered an added personal mishap in September 1942 when jewelry belonging to his daughter was stolen from the home of a friend in suburban Philadelphia. The theft was reported to the FBI, and while several suspects were identified in a two-year investigation—there was a principal suspect, but the evidence against her was insufficient—the case was not solved.

"Settling in the Navy"

"THIS MOMENT has come something where you can be of real service," Roosevelt wrote Bullitt on June 17, 1942.

> Cordell Hull tells me that it seems advisable . . . to bring Johnson [Nelson T. Johnson, minister to Australia] home. . . . As you know, he was very successful in China, . . . but I would rather have a little more active fighting type of person in Australia today. I realize this is not an Embassy, but it is far more important in wartime than almost any Embassy in peacetime. I spoke to Cordell about your going, . . . and I hope, and he hopes, that you will agree to it.

Bullitt tersely refused the offer in a reply written June 18, saying he had taken a job as special assistant to the secretary of the navy. "For this reason—and others—I cannot accept the post which you kindly suggested in your . . . letter. . . ." The "and others" was meant to let Roosevelt know that he considered a posting to Canberra tantamount to diplomatic exile, and he was affronted by the implication that he had not been "of real service" in previous assignments. "I am most happy," he wrote, "to have found a spot—however minor—in which I can render real war service." He went to work at the Navy Department on June 22, and on June 23 he called Henry Morgenthau to invite him to dinner, evidently no longer angry about the magazine article on the economic crisis in France. "I want to let you know that I've taken a new job . . .," he said. "I'm settling in the Navy. . . . I'm on some work here which really pleases me intensely because it's direct war work, no more nonsense. I finally managed to get released yesterday from my noble title of Personal Representative of the President with the rank of Ambassador for All Countries, which is utterly meaningless. . . ." Was Bullitt ingenuous? Did he really believe that Frank Knox would have made him his special assistant without an okay from the White House? ". . . I know you will do a grand job for the Navy," Roosevelt wrote on June 22, obviously pleased that the question of whither Bill Bullitt had been resolved.

Bullitt's duties in the Navy were never clearly specified to the public. "The duties of Mr. Bullitt's office are for such special assignments as the Secretary of the Navy may make," read the official announcement; and an assumption by some members of the press—the columnist Drew Pearson, for one, who was no friend of Bullitt—that he was a public relations adviser was quite wrong. The caption of a photograph in *The New York Times* on August 12, showing Bullitt in London with the commander of U.S. forces in Europe, Lieutenant General Dwight D. Eisenhower, identified him as "Presidential Roosevelt's special envoy," and that may have been accurate. He had gone in mid-July to a war conference in London—it was a high-level meeting with the delegation from Washington consisting of Harry Hopkins, General Marshall, Admiral Ernest J. King, the chief of naval operations, and Bullitt—and he carried a letter from Roosevelt to Churchill, which read: "My old friend, Bill Bullitt, will arrive in London the latter part of this week. As you know each other I need only say that I am sure he will receive every cooperation and facility." Bullitt met for lunch at 10 Downing Street with Churchill on July 17; he had dinner with Charles de Gaulle, the Free French leader, on July 20; and he conferred on at least two occasions— on July 31 and August 13—with General Eisenhower, who confided how upset he was over the state of war planning.

"The whole picture was now so mixed up," Bullitt wrote, "that he thought it was just a God damned mess." There had been a dispute over where to concentrate military action: General Marshall favored an assault on the coast of France; the British, still mindful of the carnage in World War I—millions of lives lost at Verdun and the Somme in 1916 alone—preferred to confront the Germans in North Africa; and Admiral King believed a concerted effort against Japan would be the wisest course. Roosevelt settled the issue by sending a directive to

Hopkins that the North African option would be adopted, and it was this decision that prompted Eisenhower to ask Bullitt to carry a message to Marshall, who had returned to Washington. "The General said that he would appreciate it greatly if immediately on arriving in Washington I would see General Marshall and would say to him: That he, Eisenhower, didn't like the revised plans any more than General Marshall liked them. . . . So far as he was concerned, he had received the order to try to carry out the operation, and he would carry it out. . . ."

Bullitt had not been silent during the war plans debate: he had sided with King and argued for an attack on Japan, which infuriated Marshall, who ordered him banned from the meetings. The U.S. ambassador to Great Britain, John Winant, was also angry at Bullitt for what he considered his meddling: "When Bullitt came around, Winant would sound off," recalled Jacob Beam, who became Winant's private secretary after leaving Berlin. "They did not like each other." A more serious charge was that Bullitt was prone, having had a few cocktails, to reveal secret information, and word of his indiscretions filtered back to Washington. "Winant said that when Bill Bullitt was in England," Vice President Wallace noted, "he spoke too freely, that he spilled military secrets, which made him *persona non grata* with the British military people. . . ." Eisenhower learned from another source that Bullitt was a possible security risk, and he issued a top-secret message to his staff just prior to the North African landing in November. A French official, he warned, had learned of planned American operations in French Morocco. "This French official stated further that he had heard the same thing from Mr. Bullitt while the latter was in London. These things are most disturbing. . . . I request that the most drastic measures be instituted to insure secrecy."

To add to the problem, the meddlesome Offie was in London, having been temporarily assigned to the Navy Department as Bullitt's assistant. Offie had somehow become aware of the decisions of the military strategists—it is reasonable to suspect that he learned of the plan to land in North Africa from Bullitt— and he walked out of the American embassy one afternoon and said within earshot of several people, "Well, it's set for November." Offie was immediately seized by U.S. Army counterintelligence agents, and it took no little persuading—by Bullitt and by embassy officials such as Beam—to obtain his release.

Bullitt went to Dublin on August 19 to confer with Eamon de Valera, the Irish prime minister, then returned home; on arrival in New York he declined to discuss his trip and left promptly for Washington, where he made a report to Secretary Knox. Its content was not revealed, but from another briefing by Bullitt, which was preserved—it was to Secretary of War Stimson on September 1, and Stimson kept notes—it can be deduced that one of his principal assignments was to report on submarine warfare. The outlook, based on conversations with air and naval commanders in Britain, was discouraging: the Germans had three hundred submarines, one hundred of which were at sea and one hundred-fifty in training in the Baltic Sea; and while they had lost one hundred subs so far, they were replacing them at a rate of twenty to twenty-eight a month.

Prescription for a Postwar Policy

IN RESPONSE to a request from Roosevelt on November 19, 1942, that he submit his "views on the machinery of preparation for civil administration in occupied territories," Bullitt wrote a series of reports, the third of which—it was dated January 29, 1943—contained his proposals for a postwar strategy generally. "He predicted with startling accuracy," wrote George Kennan, "the situation to which the war would lead if existing policies continued to be pursued. . . ." In a cover letter to the president, Bullitt wrote: "It is as serious a document as I have ever sent you. I hope you will read it." The document said in part:

In what countries in Europe may we reasonably hope to set up de facto administrations, followed by de jure governments, that will work for a world of liberty, democracy and peace? The answer to this question lies largely in Stalin's hands. He may set up Soviet governments in many of the countries in which we now expect to set up democratic governments. . . . Many people . . . have said lately that Stalin has changed his political philosophy. He is said to share your views expressed in the Atlantic Charter, and to favor the Four Freedoms. It is stated that he has abandoned all idea of world communism and is ready to dissolve the Comintern. He is said to want no annexations but to be interested only in security. He is reported to be determined to have the Soviet Union evolve in the direction of liberty and democracy, freedom of speech and freedom of religion. We ought to pray to God that this is so. . . .

The most careful search for factual evidence to support the thesis that Stalin is a changed man reveals none. . . . We find no evidence; but we find in all democratic countries an intense wish to believe that Stalin has changed—a wish we share. "Therefore, we have to suspect that this view is a product of the fatal vice in foreign affairs—the vice of wishful thinking. . . . Wishful thinking has produced the following logic: Because the Red Army has fought magnificently, the Soviet Union is a democratic state; . . . because Stalingrad has been defended with superb heroism, there is no O.G.P.U. (secret police). The reality is that the Soviet Union, up to the present time, has been a totalitarian dictatorship in which there has been no freedom of speech, no freedom of the press, and a travesty of freedom of religion; in which there has been universal fear of the O.G.P.U. and Freedom from Want has been subordinated always to the policy of guns instead of butter. . . .

Stalin places first the welfare of the Soviet State and treads softly, therefore, in extending communism to other countries; but there is no evidence that he has abandoned either the policy of extending communism or the policy of controlling all foreign communist parties. . . .

Even if Stalin has not changed, as we pray he has, . . . we may be able to set up throughout Europe the sort of democratic administrations we want. We have to demonstrate to Stalin—and mean it—that while we genuinely want to cooperate with the Soviet Union, we will not permit our war to prevent Nazi domination of Europe to be turned into a war to establish Soviet domination of Europe. . . . When Germany collapses, we must (1) be in a position to prevent . . . the flow of Red amoeba into Europe; (2) set up in occupied or liberated countries in Europe democratic administrations which, working together, will be strong enough to provide the requisite defense against invasion by the Soviet Union. No single state in Eastern Europe can be made strong enough to resist . . . without the support of other states. A combination of feeble states will be inadequate. . . . We are obliged, therefore, in setting up administrations, . . . not only to set up democratic administrations but also to lay the groundwork for a combination of . . . governments in Europe strong enough to preserve democracy. . . .

The British unfortunately—as well as some Americans—are in the grip of an idea which, if adopted as a policy, would result in such enfeeblement . . . of Europe that Soviet domination would be easy. Many British officials are saying now that they intend to disarm totally every nation on the Continent of Europe, . . . and maintain peace in Europe by having Europe guaranteed by the United States, Great Britain and the Soviet Union—all fully armed. This is not the old British policy of the Balance of Power . . . but a new one of the Balance of Impotence. . . .

The final answer to the Balance of Impotence Policy is that it is too disreputable to be avowed in time of war, and no policy too disreputable to be . . . exposed to public discussion can acquire the support of world public opinion or form the basis for world peace. If the Soviet Union as well as Europe could be disarmed, an argument might be made (an unwise argument at best) for establishing an Anglo-Saxon armed dictatorship over all the earth. But the Soviet Union cannot be disarmed. Since this is so, Europe cannot be made a military vacuum for the Soviet Union to flow into. . . . The balance of power, which it is the interest of Great Britain and ourselves to seek, is the balance between an integrated Europe (with Germany and Italy disarmed) and the Soviet Union. An integrated democratic Europe, pacific but armed, is a vital element for the creation of world peace. How can such a Europe be achieved? The first prerequisite is complete agreement between Churchill and yourself that it is desirable to create such a Europe. . . .

We shall never again have as much influence on Great Britain and the Soviet Union as we have today. Today they are dependent on us for their lives. . . . Our influence over Great Britain and the Soviet Union will decrease in direct proportion to our approach to

victory over Germany. On the day Germany surrenders, our influence . . . will reach zero.
. . . By using the old technique of the . . . carrot and the club, you might be able to make
Stalin move in the direction in which we want him to move. You would have a substantial
carrot: War aid of all sorts; post-war aid for rebuilding; . . . genuine security . . . through
agreements to maintain peace. . . . Your club would have lead in it, not cotton: You could
intimate that you might have to turn our major war effort against Japan instead of Germany; intimate a . . . diminution or cessation of war aid to the Soviet Union; . . . intimate
that you would find it too difficult from the point of view of domestic politics to agree to
post-war aid; . . . intimate, also, full opposition to predatory Soviet policy in Europe and
Asia. . . .

Men at some times are masters of their fate. You have your power now—and while
you have it you must use it. You will lose it the day Germany collapses. Wilson could have
written his own ticket before the Armistice of 1918. You may be able to write yours—now.

In a frank conversation with Henry Wallace in late January 1943, Bullitt
explained his misgivings about the British: Anthony Eden, once again the foreign
secretary, had offered Russia the Baltic states—Estonia, Latvia, Lithuania—to
make amends for not being able to send forces to fight the Germans. Hull, said
Bullitt, was strongly opposed to the concession, with Roosevelt in agreement,
but Wallace told him another version of the president's attitude: "I told Bill the
President had the idea that the Baltic States should be in Russia's economic
sphere and that five years after the war a plebiscite should be held. Bill said this
was an utterly cockeyed idea."

Bullitt also let the vice president know his recommendations for a drastic
reshuffling of top government officials (in his January 29 memorandum to Roosevelt he had commented that "Hull's authority . . . has been nibbled at . . . by
various subordinates" and that the secretary ought to be given orders "to dismiss
any and every member of his Department . . . that he chooses"): "Bill would
like to see Sumner Welles, Adolf Berle, and Dean Acheson [an assistant secre-
tary] fired, and Cordell Hull given carte blanche." Bullitt had for some time
believed that the coordination of peace plans should be handled by someone in
the White House, but he had now reached the conclusion—he had changed his
mind because the someone in the White House was Harry Hopkins, who was a
"babe in the woods" in foreign affairs—"that the only place to have this work
done was in the State Department. . . ." But that was impossible, he told Wallace, because there were four State Departments: "One under Hull, one under
Welles, one under Berle, and one under Acheson."

Bullitt's freely expressed views on war planning were causing controversy. In a memo to Roosevelt on May 12, just prior to a visit to Washington by Churchill, he questioned the basic Allied strategy, which was, as he summarized it, "to hold Japan in check . . . and, . . . while doing this with the minimum forces required, to concentrate all remaining forces for the destruction of the armed power of Germany." It was a strategy based, he maintained, on an assumption that "after the defeat of Germany, the Soviet Union and Great Britain will turn all their strength . . . against Japan. . . ." There was a probability, however, that "we shall get no help from the Soviet Union and only conservative assistance from Great Britain. . . . Furthermore, it is certain that, if we have a hard war to fight against Japan, . . . we shall have no decisive voice in the settlement of Europe." The memo was circulated to top officials of the War and Navy departments and to certain members of Congress, and it was applauded by advocates of a so-called America-first policy: Senator Albert B. Chandler of Kentucky, for one, quoted from it extensively in a speech demanding that the U.S. undertake immediately an all-out war on Japan. It was also challenged by Churchill, who addressed a joint session of Congress on May 19, 1943: ". . . let no one suggest that we British have not at least as great an interest as the United States in the unstinting and relentless waging of war against Japan. And I am here to tell you that we will wage that war side by side with you, . . . while there is breath in our bodies and while blood flows through our veins."

On June 16 Drew Pearson claimed in a column that Secretary Stimson, "shocked by Bullitt's lack of faith and his criticism of our Allies," had written on a copy of the memo, "The author . . . does not serve the purposes of his country." Bullitt protested in a letter to Stimson the day the column appeared in *The Washington Post*, demanding to know "whether or not you ever wrote on any paper prepared by me the words attributed to you by Pearson"; and Stimson replied he had read the memo and had "disagreed fundamentally with its conclusions," but the note he had written "differed entirely from Pearson's purported copy, which is a complete fabrication." Stimson concluded by saying: "I did not challenge your patriotism." Before responding to Bullitt, however, Stimson had telephoned Felix Frankfurter and said that while he had disapproved of the Bullitt memo, the Pearson column "doesn't represent my general views"; but he had forgotten the details of the incident and wondered if he had talked about it with Frankfurter or had shown him the memo. Frankfurter replied: "I never saw this memorandum. I didn't know about it."

Frankfurter, too, had been annoyed with Bullitt and for a related reason: "I'm not a fellow who cuts relationships because he has disagreements, . . ." he said by phone to Stimson, "and . . . I was going to have a long talk with him because he has been talking very foolishly. . . . I have a letter from an absolutely reliable friend, who wrote me that Bullitt is giving this emphasis on the European theater as against the Pacific theater, attributing that emphasis to the undue Jewish influence in the Administration. . . ."

———

Roosevelt was impressed but perplexed by Bullitt's postwar planning analysis, and he sought other opinions: for example, he had Welles consult with Eden, who disagreed completely and insisted that the surest way to "pave the way for international cooperation" was to continue to cultivate friendly relations with the Soviet Union. Bullitt went straight to Roosevelt to press his case, and the president responded: "Bill, I don't dispute your facts. . . . I don't dispute the logic of your reasoning. I just have a hunch that Stalin is not that kind of man. Harry [Hopkins] says he's not and that he doesn't want anything but security for his country, and I think that if I give him everything I possibly can and ask nothing from him in return, *noblesse oblige*, he won't try to annex anything and will work with me for a world of democracy and peace." Bullitt told Roosevelt bluntly that "when he talked of *noblesse oblige*, he was not speaking of the Duke of Norfolk but of a Caucasian bandit, whose only thought when he got something for nothing was that the other fellow was an ass. . . ." Roosevelt replied brusquely, controlling his anger: "It's my responsibility, not yours, and I'm going to play my hunch."

Banished by St. Peter

———

B ULLITT'S AVERSION to Sumner Welles grew in proportion to his frustrated ambition—"Bullitt wanted Welles's job," asserted Grace Tully, Roosevelt's private secretary and closest staff confidante after Missy LeHand had a crippling stroke in June 1941—but it was based also on his loyalty to R. Walton Moore, who despised Welles for his part in pushing him from a position of power in the Department of State. On April 20, 1937, Moore wrote Bullitt that the Senate had passed a bill creating for him the office of department counselor, making way for the president to name Welles undersecretary. "Apparently, Mr. Welles has won his fight, . . ." Moore reported, "and . . . I shall win the consolation race. . . . I heard someone say that if Welles is to be Under Secretary, the logical thing would be to replace him as Assistant Secretary by his spokesman, Drew Pearson. They are two persons whom I hold in utter contempt. . . ."

Bullitt and Welles were contemporaries, a year apart in age: Welles had gone to Groton, the prep school Bullitt had disparaged ("Every Groton fellow I know is a snob"); he was at Harvard, class of 1914, when Bullitt was at Yale; as with Bullitt his diplomatic career flourished when Roosevelt was elected president; and inevitably he and Bullitt became competitors. Had Bullitt fully understood Roosevelt's biases, he might not have chosen Welles as an adversary, for while the president delighted in watching his underlings vie, he was doggedly loyal to his own kind; and Welles, more than anyone in his administration, was of his own kind. Not only had he gone to Groton and Harvard, as had Roosevelt, but his mother and Roosevelt's mother-in-law had been best of friends, and Welles was a page in the wedding of Franklin and Eleanor in 1905. When Roosevelt was governor of New York, beginning in 1929, their professional association was firmed, and Welles, aware that Roosevelt aspired to national leadership, activated his interest in Latin America: it was Welles who inspired the "good neighbor" policy, which President Roosevelt unveiled in 1933.

Welles, like Bullitt, was a superb diplomat and an accomplished linguist—it was said that he could hold his tongue in French, Italian, German, and Spanish—and he served in Latin American embassies: he was sent to Havana in 1933, for example, to guide the forming of a government following a revolt against the dictator, Gerardo Machado. But unlike Bullitt he preferred to remain in Washington, where he had the president's ear; and by 1941, the year of Bullitt's comedown, he was regarded as first in line to succeed Hull as secretary of state. (Not with the support of the incumbent secretary, however: "Hull came to distrust Welles and finally to hate him," wrote Francis Biddle, the attorney general.) Welles did have a weakness, which Bullitt knew about, as did many people in Washington: he was a latent homosexual; and on a special train to Alabama for the funeral of Speaker of the House William B. Bankhead, in September 1940, he got drunk and propositioned a sleeping car porter. Word of the incident had been withheld from the news agencies, but Roosevelt was so fearful of a scandal that he ordered a special Secret Service detail for Welles, to guard against a recurrence. Meanwhile Bullitt, through friends in executive positions with the Southern Railway, obtained documentation of Welles's indiscretion, including an affidavit from the porter.

Judge Moore died on February 8, 1941, and on April 23 Bullitt had a meeting with Roosevelt, which Bullitt recorded afterward:

I . . . said to the President that Judge Moore had sent for me on his deathbed and charged me with a duty which I could not evade, however unpleasant. . . . The Judge had asked me . . . to see to it that the President was informed with regard to the contents of certain papers. I went on to say that one of these papers gave in brief form the information that the Judge desired to communicate to the President. . . . I then handed the President the document. . . . The President read the first page . . . and looked over the other pages and finally said, "I know all about this already. . . . There is truth in the allegations." . . . I then said that Judge Moore had felt that the maintenance of Welles in public office was a menace to the country since he was subject to blackmail by foreign powers; . . . and that the Judge was also convinced that . . . a terrible public scandal might arise at any time, which would undermine the confidence of the country in . . . the President. The President said that he did not believe that any newspaper would publish any information about this matter. . . . I replied that Judge Moore had thought that the scandal would not arise as a result of newspaper publication but that there would be a demand for criminal prosecution of Welles. . . . I added that the Secretary of State had said to me . . . that he considered Welles worse than a murderer. . . . I added that the morale in the Department of State . . . was being ruined. . . . I repeated that blackmail of high government officials guilty of crimes of this nature had been used often . . . to oblige such men to act as traitors. . . . The President said that he was fully aware of the danger, but there was for him a different question. . . . Welles was useful in the State Department. . . . I replied that I questioned the utility of Mr. Welles. . . . I added that I . . . wanted to work on licking Hitler . . . but that under no circumstances would I take any position in the Department of State . . . until he . . . dismissed Welles. At this point the President . . . summoned General Watson. I rose and remarked that I would expect to hear from him . . . and took my leave. The President, when General Watson entered the room, said: "Pa, I don't feel well. Please cancel all my appointments for the rest of the day."

Roosevelt had reason to suspect that Bullitt was misrepresenting the facts when he said he was doing a "deathbed duty" for Judge Moore, for there was evidence in an FBI report—dated January 30, 1941, to Roosevelt from J. Edgar Hoover, the FBI director—that Bullitt had been trying to bring the Welles matter to the president's attention for some time. The FBI had been ordered by Roosevelt to investigate the incident, which occurred on September 18, 1940, on the trip to Jasper, Alabama, and Hoover reported personally to Roosevelt on January 29, 1941. "I told the President . . . the sum and substance of the facts concerning the incident . . .," Hoover wrote in his report.

I then told the President that there were some other developments . . . which I thought he should know. I told him that about two weeks ago, Senator Wheeler [Burton K. Wheeler of Montana] had told a newspaper man that Ambassador Bullitt had told a friend of Wheeler's about the incident. . . . Senator Wheeler expressed indignation that such a

vicious story was being circulated. . . . According to Wheeler, Bullitt did not want to
report the incident to the President because . . . anyone who took bad news to the
President "would get his own legs cut off." Bullitt, according to Wheeler, was endeavoring to get Judge Moore of the State Department to tell the President about the
incident. . . .

In May 1943, during the debate over relations with Russia, Bullitt sought an
appointment with Roosevelt, and he was told by General Watson there was a
matter the president wanted him to discuss with Stephen Early, the White House
press secretary. Bullitt also made a record of his meeting with Early, which
occurred May 5:

> . . . the President had received reports that I had talked with the Secretary of State and
> other people about the "unfortunate weaknesses" of Sumner Welles. I replied that I had
> discussed this subject . . . with the President himself; that I had taken a number of
> documents into the President's office; . . . that the President had read one of them and had
> then said that he knew that Welles was guilty of the criminal behavior alleged. . . . Mr.
> Early said that the allegation which had now come to the President's ears was that I had
> turned over . . . a large number of documents with regard to the Welles case to a hostile
> newspaper publisher. . . . Mr. Early said, to be specific, that the allegation was that I had
> turned over the documents to Cissy Patterson, publisher of the *Washington Times-Herald*.
> I replied that that was a complete lie. I added that I had known Mrs. Patterson for over
> thirty years and that we had remained on a friendly footing, . . . always disputing on
> political matters but remaining friends. . . . I said that I had gone to the President in the
> first instance to warn him that . . . Welles would be his Achilles Heel and that he must
> dismiss him both for his own good and for the good of the country. I said that I had
> observed that the President had resented my remarks . . . and that our intimate friendship
> had ended. . . .

Hull for his own reasons had been trying to get rid of Welles, and in his
explanation of how the dismissal finally transpired he made no mention of the
incident on the train or Bullitt's role, although he was certainly aware of both. "In
the late spring of 1942," Hull wrote in his memoirs, "Welles delivered two
addresses on foreign affairs that tended to commit this Government to new lines
of . . . policy. . . . I called Welles to my office on June 29 . . . and pointed out to
him that no Under Secretary . . . ever had the function of giving out new foreign
policy. . . ." The conversation cleared the air for the time being, Hull noted, but
the two men continued to differ, and as the war proceeded, the issues became

crucial: the designation of a Western Hemisphere neutrality zone, for example. "In early summer, 1943," Hull recalled, "the President himself realized that the situation . . . could not continue. . . ." As he was about to depart for a conference with Churchill in Quebec in August, Roosevelt called Welles to his office, and it is evident from Welles's letter of resignation that his inability to get along with Hull was not the real reason for Roosevelt's decision. "Since talking with you the other day," Welles wrote on August 16, "it has seemed very clear to me that the present hue and cry . . . will continue unless this step is taken immediately. . . . Whatever you think the best course in this situation I will of course loyally follow. But I want you to know that so long as I live I shall never forget the friendship and kindness you showed me in our last talk."

Roosevelt announced on September 25 he had accepted Welles's resignation, omitting the customary statement of regret, but he revealed his sentiments privately. Adolf Berle, who as the senior assistant secretary took over for Welles, went to see the president on the day Bullitt had been summoned. "He said Bullitt had just been there," Berle remembered. "That on Bullitt's entry he had appointed himself St. Peter. Two men came up: Sumner Welles, and after chiding him for getting drunk, he let him in. The second was Bullitt. After paying due tribute to what Bullitt had done, St. Peter accused him of having destroyed a fellow human being and dispatched him to Hell." Roosevelt confided his resentment to Henry Wallace over lunch at Warm Springs, Georgia, in August 1944. "He said Bill Bullitt was perfectly terrible," Wallace recalled. "I asked him why. He said because of that awful story he spread all over town about Sumner Welles. He said Bill ought to go to hell for that."

When he was questioned by the FBI in 1953 in an unrelated investigation, an espionage case, Bullitt for some reason claimed he had broken with Roosevelt in 1941 in a dispute over policy toward the Soviet Union. The fabrication remained unexplained—the dispute over Stalin's intentions occurred in the spring of 1943, and it did not precipitate a falling-out—unless it can simply be attributed to Bullitt's inclination to shape history.

There were those who considered it curious that Bullitt would use homosexuality as the basis for his criticism of Welles, because they believed that his trusted secretary, Carmel Offie, was gay.

Offie served in Italy during the war and in Germany during the occupation, and in 1947 he joined the Central Intelligence Agency (Roscoe Hillenkoetter, the naval attaché in Paris, had become CIA director). In 1948 Offie became the deputy to Frank Wisner, head of the Office of Policy Coordination, but he was soon to be purged for his sexual inclinations: when Senator Joseph R. McCarthy in February 1950 attacked the State Department as being an employer of Communists, he also alluded to a security risk in the CIA, and he was talking about Offie, though not by name. McCarthy had learned from police records that Offie had been arrested in Washington for immoral loitering, and Offie's dismissal was ordered by Allen W. Dulles, the CIA director in 1953, over Wisner's objections.

Humiliated in Philadelphia

B EFORE their falling-out, Bullitt was urged by Roosevelt to run for mayor of Philadelphia, traditionally a Republican city in a state that had not elected a Democrat in the seventy-year period from the Civil War to the Depression year 1935, when Pennsylvania voters sent Joseph Guffey to the Senate and made Bullitt's friend George Earle governor. Bullitt announced his candidacy on July 17, 1943: "Eggpated William Christian Bullitt . . . tossed his top hat in the political ring," it was noted in *Time*; on July 23 he resigned from the Navy Department; and on September 14 he was nominated in a Democratic primary. He ran on an ambitious platform—rebuilding the city, new housing for the poor, cleaning up the rivers, eliminating the local income tax—but his campaign was misdirected: for example, he took a *Life* photographer on a downtown tour, pointing out substandard housing, littered streets, and water pollution. "Philadelphians are not proud of their sewers dumping into the Schuylkill River, their considerable acreage of slums, their broken water mains and other civic liabilities," wrote a reporter for *The New York Times*. "But they consider them problems for Philadelphia, not dirty linen to be exposed in a magazine of great circulation."

Even more costly to Bullitt's cause was a Republican smear tactic, which was slanderous yet effective, for there was at least a tinge of truth to each of the allegations of a thirty-page pamphlet, "Who *Is* William C. Bullitt?" Bullitt, first, had praised the Kaiser on his trip to Germany during World War I; he had broken confidence with a dying President Wilson in 1919; he had divorced Ernesta

Drinker, the daughter of a noted educator, to marry Louise Bryant, the widow of his intimate friend, the Communist John Reed; he had written a scurrilous book, in which he voiced an elitist political philosophy ("Every civilization ever made has been imposed by a few aristocrats," he had written); and in 1933 his "immediate arrest on charges of violating the Logan Act" was demanded in the United States Senate. When he was ambassador to the Soviet Union, his parties "eclipsed in bizarre splendor even those given by the rich Red officials"; he "had flitted much about the European capitals on mysterious missions" and had reversed himself on relations with Russia, leading the U.S. ambassador to Germany to question his mentality; and in Paris he gave a party at which six-hundred guests "downed 490 bottles of choice champagne." He was accused of "tactless phrases" by Churchill in 1939; he had tried to obtain airplanes for the French to the detriment of U.S. preparedness; he was an admirer of Pétain, "the Fascist collaborator," and of Nazis (a photograph of Bullitt walking side by side with Goering at the funeral of Pilsudski, the Polish chief of state, in 1935 was published as proof); and in 1940, ignoring the order of Secretary of State Hull, "he remained in Paris and helped the Nazi troops occupy the city," later applauding the conduct of the German Army. Finally, in his "vague position of 'special assistant' in the Navy Department, . . . he managed to draw upon himself the irate criticism of high placed policy-making officials," and the Pearson column on Stimson's reaction to his memorandum of May 12, 1943, was cited under the heading: " 'Does Not Serve . . . His Country'—HLS." It was also charged that he was not a resident of Philadelphia, though in registering to vote, "Bullitt gave 1811 Walnut St., which is the rich and exclusive Rittenhouse Club, as his residence"; and he never paid state property taxes: "Mr. Bullitt does not know the most elemental facts about Philadelphia, because he never lived in Philadelphia since boyhood."

J. David Stern, the publisher of *The Philadelphia Record* and Bullitt's campaign manager, was disgusted by the dishonesty of the polemic and frantic because the pamphlet appeared on October 28, just five days before the election. Stern called Roosevelt that day to ask for help, and Roosevelt agreed to send a letter of rebuttal. Dated October 29, it read: "I think that pamphlet about Bill Bullitt is a mass of falsehoods. . . . He attended the funeral of Marshal Pilsudski as representative of the United States. When you or I attend a funeral we walk . . . in the procession with anybody we are told to walk with." (Bullitt walked with Goering because protocol called for the procession to be in alphabetic order, and in French, the diplomatic language, *Amérique* follows *Allemagne*.) "In the case of the fall of Paris," said the president further, communications with the United States were practically broken off. He did the obvious and right thing to do—use every effort to save Paris and its civilian population from destruction and death. He followed the action of the American Ambassador in 1914, . . . Myron Herrick, . . . when Paris was threatened by the Germans. . . . This attack on Bullitt is another piece of dirty political falsification.

Roosevelt's letter was of little help—Stern did not receive it until late Sunday, October 31, and was able to print it in only one third of Monday's edition of *The Record*—and Bullitt lost by 64,000 votes, a landslide, to Bernard Samuel, who had been acting mayor since the death of the Republican incumbent. In Stern's opinion it was Bullitt's manner that accounted for his defeat: he was an excellent speaker, said Stern, "but his aristocratic appearance and . . . accent fitted into the Republican picture of a social snob." Bullitt came to believe that Roosevelt had intentionally set him up for the humiliation, and he had few kind words for his old boss thereafter (he did, however, send the president a bottle of brandy and a card at Christmas in 1943). It was not a coincidence, moreover—although there were ideological reasons—that within a few years Bullitt became a Republican.

Off for a "Small Adventure"

BULLITT met on February 1, 1944, with Hull, who had suggested to Roosevelt the day before, according to Bullitt, "that I should be used in a position of real importance," to which the president replied that he was displeased with "the way I had acted in the Welles affair." Hull told Roosevelt "that if I had done anything to help get Welles out of the picture, he, the President, should be grateful to me; that he and himself . . . had been sitting on a keg of dynamite for two years." Roosevelt asked what job there might be for Bullitt, and Hull proposed "that as Ambassador-at-Large I should be put in charge of all our relations from Dakar and Casablanca through the Mediterranean to Teheran. He said that the President had said . . . he would think it over." Bullitt and Hull next met on March 11, and again Bullitt recorded their talk:

I . . . asked Cordell what the substance of his conversation had been with the President. . . . He said that he had taken to the President a memorandum, . . . saying that I was to be appointed Ambassador-at-Large. . . . Hull said that . . . he had been . . . certain that the President would concur since the President had already told him twice that this was okay. He said that he did not know what had happened, but it was evident that the President had changed his mind. . . . He said that he . . . had argued with him . . . and that the President had finally written on the memorandum, "Why not Minister to Saudi Arabia?" . . . Hull went on to say that he had the impression definitely that the President knew perfectly well that I would not accept such a post, and . . . his . . . proposing that it should be offered to me was merely a stall. . . . We went on to discuss the general international . . . situation. Hull said that he was at his wit's end. . . . He said that he was trying to make a good record of friendliness toward the Russians; . . . and that he was trying . . . to keep some hand on our larger international policies. He added that he still did not know what had happened at Teheran [the Teheran meeting of Roosevelt, Churchill, and Stalin had occurred in late November 1943]. . . . He added that the President seemed to be cut off from his advisers. . . .

Clare Boothe Luce said it crisply in a reminiscing conversation: "So Sumner Welles was dropped. But they also dropped Bill. He couldn't get another job. The news went around that he was the kind of guy who brought up that kind of story." There were those in addition to Hull who thought that Bullitt's eclipse was regrettable. George Earle came to Washington in May 1944 to submit a plan, offered to him by a group of anti-Hitler Germans, which he believed would end the war and also stem a Soviet advance into central Europe; and while he waited at the White House to see Roosevelt, he discussed the plan with James Forrestal, who had just been named secretary of the Navy (Frank Knox died on April 28). "My God, George," Forrestal remarked, "you and I and Bill Bullitt are the only ones around the President who know the Russian leaders for what they are."

Earle, having served his term as governor of Pennsylvania, 1935–1939, became the minister to Bulgaria and remained in Sofia until the German takeover in 1941. He then joined the Navy, and it was while he was in Istanbul, Turkey, as the naval attaché, an intelligence post, that he was approached by anti-Hitler German conspirators, including Franz von Papen, a former chancellor, who was the ambassador to Turkey. Roosevelt was not interested in the von Papen plot: "Stop worrying . . .," he said to Earle in May 1944. "We are getting ready for this Normandy landing. . . . Germany will surrender in a few months." Earle replied that the menace in Europe was not German but Russian, and like Bullitt he would not be mollified. Roosevelt did not appreciate criticism of his policy of cooperation with the Soviet Union, and to get Earle out of the way he had him assigned to American Samoa as assistant governor.

Bullitt decided to apply again for an Army commission and wrote to Stimson on May 1, 1944, noting that he had been rejected for combat duty two years before because of his age.

I wonder now if I might not be acceptable for active military duty of another sort in France. I speak French almost as easily as English and have had experience in maintaining most friendly relations with French civilians and military men in difficult hours. Could I serve in liaison with the French forces? . . . The fight to drive the Germans out of France is my fight in a peculiar degree. I profoundly want to get into it actively.

He ended the letter almost plaintively: "Cannot the Army use me?" When he had not heard from Stimson by May 12, he wrote again, wondering if his request had "gone astray," and on May 18 the secretary finally sent him a terse note: "I am very sorry to say that I see no possibility that the Army will be able to use your services. . . ." As determined as he ever had been, Bullitt offered to serve with the Free French Army, and he got an altogether different sort of response from General de Gaulle, writing from Algiers on May 25: "Come now! Good and dear American friend. Our ranks are open to you. You will return with us into wounded Paris. Together, we will see your star-spangled banners mingled with our tricolors." Bullitt was thrilled: "I am off . . . for a small adventure," he wrote George Biddle from his home in Washington. He mentioned it was no longer necessary for him to guide his daughter's social life: "Your godchild is in fine form. . . . She is going to teach French and algebra at Foxcroft during the absence of her husband in the South Pacific." (Anne had recently married Caspar W. B. Townsend, Jr., of Philadelphia.)

En route to North Africa Bullitt wrote two articles for *Life*, which appeared in August and September, and they were curiously dissimilar in point of view and tone. In the first, "The Future of France," he was decidedly optimistic:

The chances are that France will become a democratic republic with a stronger executive than before the present war but with a bill of rights that will ensure personal liberty. Recovery will require control of economic life by the national government for some years, and there will be a strong tendency to maintain control by the state of banking, insurance, communications and the basic production of coal, iron, steel and electrical power. An effort will be made by the government to raise the birth rate and to encourage immigration. Public health and social services will be emphasized. . . . The parties of the Left will have to govern by coalition, and since the Radicals stand primarily for liberty, the Communists for equality and the Socialists for fraternity, the sum total of their approach to life may not differ greatly from the old slogan: *Liberté, Egalité, Fraternité*. France as a whole will not be the soft France produced by the victory of 1918 but the hard France produced by the defeat of 1871. The iron of the German occupation has entered into the soul of France. The French have learned that to be free in the world today it is necessary to be strong.

In the second report, however—it was written from Rome, and Bullitt was severely criticized for visiting the capital of a defeated Axis enemy (Italy surrendered in September 1943), while the war with Germany continued—he stated publicly the warnings he had sent Roosevelt of a Soviet-dominated Europe, as he cast the piece as a picture of the future.

What is that picture as seen from Rome? It is an old picture which had been familiar to Romans since the time of the Caesars—a picture of western Europe . . . threatened by hordes of invaders from the East. . . . Today . . . Rome sees again approaching from the East a wave of conquerors. And dominating the hearts and minds and, indeed, the talk of all men throughout Italy is the question: "Will the result of this war be the subjugation of Europe by Moscow instead of Berlin?"

Events in Poland had set the pattern, Bullitt declared: "The Italians, being of the same race as Machiavelli, cannot conceal a regretful admiration for the skill with which Poland is being subjected to the aims of Soviet imperialism." Eight months before the end of World War II Bullitt had fired the first shot of the Cold War—he also proposed a confederation of nations to withstand the Soviet onslaught, which in five years would become reality in the form of the North Atlantic Treaty Organization, or NATO—and the reaction was harsh, not only in Moscow but also in the United States. Max Lerner, a left-wing political writer, denounced Bullitt as a man "of unsavory fame," and he attacked the article in *Life*:

. . . it is the first time, outside of the pages of the lunatic fascist press, . . . that the slimy whispered agitation for a split between America and its Russian partner in the war has found articulate expression. It is the first time that anyone with a veneer of respectability . . . has uttered a direct call for a war between England and America on one side and Russia on the other.

On August 15, 1944, the de Gaulle forces landed on the south coast of France, and by August 28 they had captured the port cities of Toulon and Marseilles; they drove slowly northward along the Rhone River, fighting over the rugged terrain of the Vosges Mountains, until they were slowed to a standstill by winter weather. Bullitt was awarded the rank of commandant, equivalent to an American major— as an honorary citizen of France he was able to accept the commission and retain his U.S. citizenship—and assigned to the staff of General Jean de Lattre de Tassigny, the invasion commander. (Known to his men as *le roi Jean*, King John, de Lattre was an illustrious French officer: a cavalry lieutenant in World War I, who fought the Germans with a saber his grandfather had used in the Napoleonic wars, and the commander of a division in 1940, who heroically resisted the German advance. He was imprisoned by the Vichy government in 1943 but escaped, was rescued by the British and flown to England; he then joined de Gaulle in Algeria.) Paris had been liberated on August 25, and Bullitt hitched a ride there on an American bomber: he insisted he was fully familiar with the countryside and would navigate, but he guided the flight beyond Paris and within range of enemy fire and was ordered by the pilot to take a passenger seat.

On October 14 Bullitt wrote his brother, Orville:

I am in Paris on a mission . . . and return to the front tomorrow. Nothing since 1919 [he was referring to the meeting in Moscow with Lenin] has given me so much satisfaction as the job I am doing now, and I haven't felt so well in twenty years. . . . We crossed from Italy in an infantry landing craft—two nights in the hold with eighty others, . . . and I joined General de Lattre de Tassigny at his . . . headquarters. . . . Since then I have spent about twenty hours a day with him—as he doesn't care for sleep and I go . . . wherever he goes. As you know he is Commander-in-Chief of the First French Army—the only French Army. He is a great fellow. . . . He goes into the front line constantly with your humble brother along—so . . . I have a chance to be in the scrap both at the planning end and the execution. . . . I have been able to be of some real service at various times. . . . I do jobs . . . from the highest level to the lowest, including the interpreting when General Marshall or some other big fish comes along. The hours are long and the discipline absolute and the physical life hard. We have no heat or hot water. . . . But his chef is superb, and I picked up a lot of the best wines in Burgundy. . . . Paris is a bit sad as there are no lights and no restaurants except in a few hotels—but the French are as delightful as ever. . . . My house at Chantilly is intact and my servants still there. The apartment in Paris is dirty but o.k. Nearly all my close friends have survived, and I have been kissed more times than I shall ever be again. . . .

Bullitt returned to the U.S. embassy, unlocking the gates that had been shut for over four years, and as he mounted a balcony and made a victory gesture, he was loudly cheered by a gathering of Parisians. Bullitt realized they probably had mistaken him for General Eisenhower—there was a resemblance, with his similar build and bald head, even though he was wearing a French uniform—but he accepted the ovation. Bullitt wrote his brother, again from Paris, on December 13: "We have been cold and dirty for three weeks and had no water to drink—and I have been cleaning my teeth in Cordon Charlemagne 1941 at 250 francs a bottle!" And on December 18, along with a Christmas greeting, he reported on the prospect of peace: "The Boches are still fighting like tigers and will have to be beaten in field after field, and that will not be a short job, but I think that six or eight months . . . ought to cover it. . . ."

Roosevelt, Churchill, and Stalin met at Yalta in Russian Crimea in early February 1945, but Bullitt would not realize until later the significance of the meeting: had Roosevelt heeded his warning of January 29, 1943, he might have been able at Yalta—at a time when the U.S.S.R. still depended on the U.S. for support—to force Stalin to desist in Central Europe. Carmel Offie was a witness to the aftermath of Yalta—Offie had become an aide to Robert Murphy, who, having served as minister to French North Africa, had been appointed the U.S. civilian representative with the Allied command in Italy—and he recorded his personal impressions in a letter to Orville Bullitt. "I saw Mr. Roosevelt for the last time . . .," Offie wrote

on board the *Quincy* in Algiers Harbor. . . . He looked ghastly, sort of dead and dug up. The same reaction was had by . . . Kirk, our Ambassador in Rome. . . . Harry Hopkins was carried off the *Quincy* on a stretcher and, accompanied by Chip Bohlen, was flown to Marrakesh to get strength enough to be flown to the United States. Pa Watson, who died en route to the United States, was under an oxygen tent. . . . As Kirk said, . . . this is really a ship of death. . . .

Roosevelt died of a cerebral hemorrhage at Warm Springs, Georgia, on April 12, 1945.

On January 9, 1945, Bullitt was injured during the battle for Alsace province—he was struck by a vehicle, and his left leg, hip, back, and ribs were "somewhat damaged," as he understated it in a letter to Orville Bullitt on February 20—but he had said nothing about it and had tried to ignore the pain. "The result was that after about nine days I was totally unable to stand up." After three weeks in a field hospital he returned to duty: "I went up again to the Rhine, but after doing Alsace with de Gaulle and de Lattre my leg went bad again, and I was sent to Paris for treatment at the American Hospital. My leg is much better. . . . The pain in my back and hip is almost gone. . . ." He was not telling the truth, as the back injury—he had actually splintered a vertebra—would cause a lifelong disability, but he was determined not to quit the war. "I am extremely anxious to get back to the front," he wrote his brother, "and shall not stay in Paris one day more than necessary. . . . De Gaulle asked me if I didn't want to fly home to get fixed up, but I told him I wanted to visit Berlin first." Bullitt rejoined the First Army in March and accompanied it into Baden-Baden, on the German side of the Rhine; and at a dinner, in jest, de Lattre made him the military governor of the resort city (gullible American correspondents took the appointment seriously). The Germans surrendered on May 7, 1945—at a ratification ceremony in Berlin on May 8 de Lattre was present in the name of France—and Bullitt was awarded the Croix de Guerre and the Legion of Honor. When they parted in July, Bullitt presented de Lattre with a sword, which was inscribed: "To my friend Jean, whom I shall never forget."

There was a victory parade up the Champs Élysées on July 14, Bastille Day, and right behind the lead command car, de Lattre's, three cars abreast carried the officers of the First Army staff; in the one on the right sat Commandant Bullitt, his arms folded, his thoughts only to be presumed. The officer sitting next to him, Commandant André Chamson, sent his impression to Orville Bullitt: "I think that for the former Ambassador of the United States . . . this passage across Paris in all the intoxication of a victory . . . was a thrilling adventure."

"The Great Globe Itself"

BULLITT'S BREAK with his own government was complete by the time he returned to the United States in 1945: he would make a fleeting effort to become an adviser—possibly a sort of roving ambassador—to the new president, Harry Truman. Truman said no, having asked his aide Clark Clifford for an assessment, and Clifford learned that Bullitt had a reputation for coveting other men's jobs. So Bullitt decided to put his thoughts on paper—they were bitter thoughts, yet there was validity to them—and he turned them into a book, which he appropriately titled *The Great Globe Itself*, from the lines of Shakespeare in *The Tempest*:

> And, like the baseless fabric of this vision,
> The cloud-capp'd towers, the gorgeous palaces,
> The solemn temples, the great globe itself,
> Yea, all which it inherit, shall dissolve; . . .

The book was a scathing appraisal of Roosevelt's last days and of the late president's fateful foreign policy:

Power was in the hands of the people of the United States such as no people had ever held before. . . . We wanted peace and we could have used our power to move toward peace. . . . But we stood like a carnivorous dinosaur, . . . who had a body the size of a locomotive, teeth a foot long—and a brain the size of a banana. He perished from the earth. We too shall perish from this earth if we cannot understand our present predicament and act in accordance with our vital interests. . . .

Bullitt blamed the predicament on Roosevelt personally, in particular for his actions at Yalta:

The weary President was on the verge of thrombosis. . . . He was not at his best and, in a moment of weakness, gave the Kurile Islands and control of the Chinese ports of Port

Arthur and Darien to the Soviet Union and agreed to let Stalin slip into the proposed United Nations Organization as "independent states" the Soviet Ukraine and White Russia, which are less independent than the states of California and Massachusetts. And he made the agreement to recognize . . . a government of Poland satisfactory to the Soviet Government. . . . He also secured Stalin's signature to another joint declaration of noble principles which, like the Atlantic Charter, contained no specific, detailed commitments.

Of Roosevelt's recent death Bullitt wrote that God had been kind to him:

He died before the actions of the Soviet Government in Poland, Hungary, Austria, Rumania, Bulgaria, Yugoslavia, the portion of Germany occupied by the Red Army, Iran, Manchuria and Korea . . . forced him to admit that he had lost his gamble. . . . Stalin had remained unconverted. The events of 1945 proved beyond . . . doubt that the Atlantic Charter and the Yalta Declaration had been to Stalin merely . . . ready-made suits of sheep's clothing which he could wear until he no longer needed a camouflage. Stalin had remained faithful to Lenin's teaching: "It is necessary to use any ruse, cunning, unlawful method, evasion, concealment of truth." The war was over, but there was no sign of peace. The President's "great design" had failed.

In the book Bullitt exhibited once again a remarkable ability to "see the future," and in this case he saw doom: he was among the first—he and J. Robert Oppenheimer, who visualized the awful potential of the instrument of destruction he had helped develop—to see that mankind was in jeopardy. "After the next World War . . . there may be no after," Bullitt wrote in a foreword to the book, and he illustrated the point with a parable:

. . . The human race is destroyed by atomic bombs. Two aviators remain alive, chasing each other around the earth in jet planes. Over a forest in Africa, propulsive energy exhausted, first one, then the other, crashes at the foot of a high tree in the branches of which sit an aged chimpanzee and his mate. The old ape shrugs his shoulders, turns wearily to his wife and says, "There you are, Ma; now we have to start all over again."

The Great Globe Itself, published by Scribner's in 1946, was not a critical success: it was "inadequate and not sufficient to inspire confidence," in the opinion of Orville Prescott of *The New York Times*; a "naively hysterical little book," asserted Louis Gannett in *The New York Herald Tribune*. Bullitt himself was lambasted in *The Nation* for stirring up feeling that would lead to a revival of fascism in Europe; the book was called "reckless" in *Commonweal*; and the noted historian, Henry Steele Commager, took strenuous exception: ". . . so gross are the distortions, so fallacious the arguments, so immoral the proposals of this book, that it can only serve to promote misunderstanding." There was a favorable commentary, however, in *The Saturday Review*, by John Barkham: "Bullitt, who knows the score, says: Stop Stalin before it's too late. . . . With that view this reviewer . . . has no quarrel."

Of all the Washington hierarchy, oddly enough, one man who stood by Bullitt and was willing to listen to him at length was Henry Wallace—wild-eyed Wallace, who had been dropped from the Democratic ticket in 1944 for being too radical and too pro-Soviet. (The convention in Chicago settled on Senator Truman of Missouri as Roosevelt's running mate, and after the election Wallace agreed to become secretary of commerce.) On February 12, 1946, Wallace wrote in his diary:

> . . . I had a very interesting luncheon with Bill Bullitt, who is very anti-Russian and who obviously had me in to try to make me anti-Russian also. Bill . . . proceeded to get down to the business of attacking Russia. . . . He said he was a good Democrat, and he felt my domestic policies were marvelous. He thought my foreign policy was pretty bad. . . . I told him my foreign policy was based fundamentally on the idea of avoiding World War III and doing our part towards raising the standard of living in the backward areas of the world. He was very critical of Stalin's recent speech. [A hard-line declaration of policy on February 9, in which the Soviet leader had stressed the production of national defense materials.] I told him that . . . this was accounted for in some measure by the fact that . . . our military was getting ready for war with Russia. . . . We were challenging him, and his speech was taking up the challenge. . . . [Bullitt] said the Russians were like an amoeba, . . . surrounding that which they could digest. . . . He then proclaimed that the proper policy of the United States was to put indigestible particles in their path. He said because . . . the United States had the atomic bomb we could come down firm with Russia. . . . I said I thought that was where the trouble had begun; that after we got the atomic bomb and acted the way we did, the Russians felt it necessary to enter upon an armaments race. . . . I asked Bullitt what he would propose doing. He suggested setting up a western European federation of all the countries which have democratic forms of government. I said I thought that sounded like a good idea. . . . I told him . . . the best way to handle the Russians was to demonstrate to the countries surrounding Russia that our system would furnish the common people . . . more good things of life than the Russian system. . . . Bill said, "Yes, I agree with you, . . . but we must go beyond and be prepared to . . . stop Russia with a strong hand. . . ." I said, . . . "It seems to me that that way leads to World War III. . . ."

"My back has been absolutely hellish for the past week," Bullitt wrote his doctor and cousin, Orville Horwitz, on April 5, 1946. "I got it pulled out by an osteopath yesterday and it is somewhat better, but I suspect we shall have to consider some sort of operation." Horwitz confirmed his hunch, notifying Bullitt that the X rays showed "a definite dislocation," and a surgical spine fusion was performed in September by Dr. Harrison L. McLaughlin at Columbia Presbyterian Hospital in New York. While in the hospital, Bullitt was asked by an intern during a routine examination how long he had suffered from leukemia, an awkward way for him to learn that he had the dread disease. Bullitt telephoned

Horwitz in a fury, demanding to know why he had not been told, and Horwitz answered he must have overlooked it in his diagnosis. "Nonsense," said Bullitt. "You've never made a misdiagnosis in your life." Horwitz had not missed it, as he then revealed to Bullitt: he had chronic lymphatic leukemia, which in its early stages shows no symptoms and requires no treatment; and it quite likely had been caused by X rays of Bullitt's stomach during his illness in 1912. Horwitz explained he had not told Bullitt because he believed there was no reason to alarm him.

Nineteen forty-seven was a crucial year for U.S.-Soviet relations. On March 12 President Truman proposed $400 million in military and economic aid to Greece and Turkey, but his intent went well beyond fortifying anti-Communist resolve in those two countries. His message to Congress would be remembered as an enunciation of the Truman Doctrine: "I believe it must be the policy of the United States to support free peoples who are resisting subjugation by armed minorities and by outside pressures." Then, in an address at Harvard on June 5, George C. Marshall, the wartime chief of staff whom Truman named secretary of state in 1947, announced the European Recovery Program, later known as the Marshall Plan.

George F. Kennan, who had ascended to senior diplomatic rank since serving with Bullitt in Moscow—second secretary in Prague, second secretary in Berlin, counselor in Lisbon, and minister-counselor in Moscow—was assigned by Marshall in April 1947 to direct a State Department policy planning staff. Kennan thus had a key role in formulating the Marshall Plan, and he articulated a policy of containment of the Soviet Union, which was interpreted by some—the columnist Walter Lippmann, for one—as a combative stance in all areas of the world threatened by Soviet aggression; therefore it was an extension of the Truman Doctrine. Kennan regretted the misunderstanding: ". . . I do not think in terms of doctrines," he wrote in retrospect. "I think in terms of principles." His purpose, he declared, had been to avoid a war by allowing Soviet ambitions to moderate. "The Soviet leaders, formidable as they were, were not supermen. Like all rulers of all great countries, they had their internal contradictions and dilemmas to deal with. Stand up to them, I urged, manfully but not aggressively, and give the hand of time a chance to work." Kennan and Bullitt were on opposing sides in the debate, for Bullitt applauded the Truman Doctrine as one constructive step by an administration that was not acting aggressively enough. Appearing before the House Committee on Un-American Activities on March 24, 1947, he testified that if Russia had the atomic bomb, "it would already have been dropped on the United States." (Kennan and Bullitt would in the end be able to share memories of a mutual experience: Kennan was appointed ambassador to Russia in 1952, but he soon was at odds with the Kremlin leaders and was declared *persona non grata* for antigovernment remarks after only five months in Moscow.)

Finally realizing that he was at an impasse in Washington, at least so long as the Roosevelt-Truman administration was in office, Bullitt returned to the occupation at which he had started in 1914, journalism. He had favorably impressed Henry R. Luce, the editor-in-chief of *Time*, *Life*, and *Fortune*—one important reason was that Bullitt and Luce saw eye to eye on the Red menace—and it was virtually assured that he would be hired by Time Inc. as a foreign affairs consultant. The editors of the magazines protested vehemently, however, for Bullitt was a public figure whose political attitudes were well known; and Luce backed down, passing the task of telling Bullitt to his assistant, Allen Grover. When he was told, Grover recalled, "Bullitt looked bewildered at first and then said: 'Well, you finally got me, and some day I'm going to get you.' " Nevertheless, the *Life* editors were quite willing to assign Bullitt to write articles on developments overseas, which kept him on the move for the rest of the year. In late April 1947 he went to Paris for a reassessment, returning to New York on May 13; the trip had been "entirely personal," he said to reporters, and he was en route to Washington to attend the wedding of his daughter on May 31. (Having divorced Caspar Townsend the year before, Anne Bullitt was being married to Nicholas Duke Biddle, the son of Anthony J. D. Biddle, Bullitt's old friend and fellow European envoy.)

Bullitt's report, "France in Crisis" (*Life*, June 2, 1947), indicated a marked shift since he had predicted three years before, also in *Life*, that the parties of the left would govern by coalition. ". . . [A]ll the power that Stalin's international machine can muster," he now wrote, "is being used . . . to crush democracy in France and to install a puppet government obedient to the Soviet dictator." He was even losing confidence in de Gaulle, who had been elected president in 1945: "Into exhausted France rode General de Gaulle to be greeted as a savior—the redemption of the past, the hope of the future. . . . Never has a man stood on a higher pinnacle of adoration than de Gaulle the day he entered Paris. . . . He knew that the Communists felt sure they could destroy him, but he believed he was stronger than they. So he was—at first." The Communists had already won the first round: they had opposed and harassed de Gaulle "until his patience gave out and, in January 1946, he resigned." The Communists emerged as the strongest party in France in elections in November 1946, with 169 deputies out of 618, but a coalition government under Paul Ramadier, a protégé of Léon Blum, continued to rule by coalition. "Today," Bullitt wrote,

Ramadier, a moderate Socialist, heads a government composed of Socialists, M.R.P.'s [members of the Popular Republican Movement] and Radicals. . . . If he succeeds in bringing prices down and holding the franc at its present level, France may hope to move painfully through two or three hard years to a solid recovery. If, on the other hand, the Communists choose to prevent orderly recovery by loosing a series of "slowdown strikes" or "bottleneck strikes" or even a general strike, recovery will be long delayed. . . .

A postponed recovery would be tragic, Bullitt wrote, and he briefly mentioned another reason for concern: in the French protectorate of Annam, in Indochina, 115,000 troops, almost half the French Army, were engaged in a guerrilla war with the forces of the Communist revolutionary Ho Chi Minh.

First American in Vietnam

BULLITT went to Asia in July 1947, stopping first in Tokyo to visit Tommy White, his Army pilot in Moscow, who was an Air Force major general and chief of staff for the Far East; he then spent two months touring China, the scene of civil war between the Nationalists, whose authority had been absolute since 1930, and the Communists. Bullitt regarded the Red challenge as an eastern counterpart of Stalin's aggression in central Europe: the Soviet Union, he declared in *Life*, was "striving to reduce China to the status of a satellite, . . . using the Chinese Communists as instruments of . . . power politics." He blamed Roosevelt, who he contended had broken a pledge to Chiang Kai-shek, the Nationalist ruler, to return to China territories that had been annexed by Japan: ". . . at Yalta . . . President Roosevelt signed with Marshal Stalin and Prime Minister Churchill, secretly, behind the back of China, an agreement by which vital rights of China in . . . Manchuria were sacrificed to Soviet imperialism." He also cited the role of George Marshall, who as ambassador to China in January 1946 negotiated a truce in the civil war, which was broken by the Communists in April—they had used the hiatus to reorganize their forces, Bullitt asserted—when they overran Changchun, the capital of Manchuria. "The final verdict on General Marshall's actions in China," Bullitt wrote, "must be that never was a distinguished soldier sent on a more hopeless and unwise political mission."

The article in *Life*, published on October 13, prompted an angry response by Andrei Vyshinsky, the Soviet deputy foreign minister and United Nations representative, who already had named Bullitt as one of a number of American warmongers (also included on Vyshinsky's list were James Forrestal, recently named secretary of defense, and George Earle). Bullitt had joined the "China lobby," an ad hoc group of business and military leaders and members of Congress, who believed that U.S. policy was, as Bullitt phrased it, "marked by a weary and petulant inclination to 'let China stew in her own juice.' " His article in *Life*, wrote H. Bradford Westerfield, a noted foreign policy analyst, was "the opening gun in the . . . assault on the administration's conduct of relations with China." Bullitt would not be quieted by public exposure, quite the opposite: on November 29, along with eleven other former ambassadors—including Josephus Daniels, James W. Gerard, and William Phillips—he signed a telegram to Secretary Marshall and the Senate Foreign Relations Committee calling for military and economic aid to China; on December 10 he wrote to *The New York Herald Tribune* to protest a column by Walter Lippmann, an erstwhile friend, in which Lippmann had called action to prevent a Communist conquest of China "diplomatic boondoggling"; and on December 17 he was one of several prominent China lobbyists—others were General Albert C. Wedemeyer, former commander of U.S. forces in China, and Representative Walter Judd of Minnesota—to testify before the Senate Appropriations Committee.

Bullitt had finally decided to abandon the Democratic Party, and he wrote in March 1948 to Louis Wehle, the New York lawyer who had introduced him to Roosevelt in 1933: "Marshall . . . is still blocking any genuine cooperation between the American and Chinese government. I am afraid we shall have to take him apart." Wehle was supporting Thomas E. Dewey, the Republican governor of New York, who was running for president against Truman, and he wrote back in October that Bullitt could expect to be undersecretary of state in a Dewey administration; whereupon Bullitt became a Republican and remained one after Dewey lost the election.

Bullitt had gone from China to Annam, or Vietnam as it would be known, as an official guest of the French government, owing not so much to his being a former ambassador as to his having served with the French First Army, whose troops were engaging the Communist guerrillas. (General de Lattre de Tassigny was not in Vietnam in 1947, but he would come later as overall military and political leader.) "Not one in a hundred Annamites is a Communist," Bullitt wrote in an article that appeared in *Life* on December 29,

but all decent Annamites want independence; and just as General de Gaulle was followed by millions of Frenchmen who disagreed with his political views, because he was the symbol of resistance to Hitler, so today Ho Chi Minh, the Communist leader of the Annamite fight for independence, is followed by millions of Annamites. . . . In consequence the Annamites fight and die . . . in a war in which victory . . . can lead only to a replacement of the yoke of France by the terrible yoke of Stalin.

Bullitt then expressed a thought that would be accepted as a credo by Americans who would follow him to Vietnam when the war became their responsibility, and it would haunt them: ". . . the worst disaster which could befall the French, the Annamites and the civilized world would be . . . to surrender to Ho Chi Minh and his Communist comrades." Bullitt believed he had a solution to offer: cooperation between the French and the Vietnamese nationalists.

Since there is no conflict between the real interests of France and the Vietnamese nationalists, . . . what prevents their reconciliation? The answer is to be found in Paris. Ignorance of the situation in Vietnam is almost as great in Paris as in Washington. . . . Is it too much to hope that France can find within herself . . . something of the spirit that led her once to spread liberty throughout Europe?

His idea was to rally Vietnamese nationalists in support of a non-Communist leader, and he inserted U.S. financial backing into the scheme, provided France would promise Vietnamese independence. He presumed there would be an American "hand in the matter," for "larger issues are at stake" than the interests of France. "As the immediate neighbor of South China, Vietnam is vital to the defense of the Far East against the aggressions of Soviet imperialism."

Bullitt's choice as the leader-designate was also favored by nationalists with whom he had met in Saigon and Hanoi: he was Bao Dai, the hereditary emperor, who had abdicated when Ho Chi Minh was proclaimed president of the Vietnam republic in 1945. Bao Dai (his name in English means guardian of greatness) was in exile in Hong Kong, enjoying a carefree life; but he had already responded to the pleas of a delegation of his countrymen: "To avoid bloodshed, I renounced the throne of my ancestors. . . . Now . . . you have revealed to me the whole picture of your miseries. . . . I shall exert the full weight of my authority to mediate in the conflict. . . ." Bullitt visited Bao Dai, stopping in Hong Kong en route from Vietnam, and he learned the emperor had his reservations: "I will neither be a puppet of the French nor a lemon for the Americans to squeeze."

Dai did agree to talk with French authorities, and Bullitt flew to Paris to arrange a meeting, which was held in December 1947 aboard a French naval ship in the Bay of Along, north of the Vietnamese port of Haiphong. When Bao Dai demanded a firm pledge of independence, the French high commissioner for Indochina, Emile Bollaert, hedged, and Bao Dai, disgusted, went to his home in Switzerland for a "vacation." Further efforts by the French failed to appease Bao Dai, so Bullitt took it upon himself in a typically bold way to resolve the differences. ". . . Bao Dai was meeting with William Bullitt in Switzerland," wrote Philippe Devillers, an authoritative French historian. "Bao Dai told Bullitt that the French conditions were not acceptable and that he wouldn't enter into negotiations until these conditions were changed. Bullitt had incited Bao Dai to negotiate a reasonable understanding with the French, letting it be understood that at that time the United States would . . . give him support. . . ."

Stanley Karnow, author of a comprehensive history of the war in Vietnam, wrote that in late 1948 a new French high commissioner for Indochina, Léon Pignon, favored firmness, but Pignon

> foresaw that the Communists, advancing across China, would soon arrive at the Viet-namese frontier to bulwark the Vietminh [the Vietnam Independence League of Ho Chi Minh]. He also reckoned that the United States would help France more readily if a liberal French policy were adopted. Thus he carried a set of fresh proposals to Bao Dai, who was lolling at his château on the Côte d'Azur. Bao Dai went to Switzerland to consult with his main American promoter, William Bullitt, who counseled him that he could count on U.S. support if he extracted real concessions from the French. Though Bullitt had no authority to speak for the United States, both Bao Dai and Pignon believed him to be representing the official American view, and this influenced them.

The "Bao Dai solution," for which Bullitt could take credit, was achieved with the signing of the Élysée Agreement on March 8, 1949, but it was no solution at all. "What they call a Bao Dai solution turns out to be just a French solution," said the emperor himself, resenting the retention by France of control of his country's finances and defense. As much to blame as anything, though, was the behavior of Bao Dai, who governed from his lodge in the Vietnamese mountain resort of Dalat, or from the Côte d'Azur, and who transferred large sums of money to Swiss and French banks. Alexander Werth, the Paris corre-spondent of *The Times* (London), depicted a different Bao Dai, cunning and complex, as he had been viewed by Frenchmen living in Vietnam:

> They will tell you . . . that he hates the French, and while he is a weak, though not stupid, man who finds it hard to . . . take any kind of initiative himself, he has a sneaking admiration for Ho Chi Minh and the Resistance, and would like nothing better than to see them drive the French out of Indochina. He would then like to retire. . . . The job of Emperor, it is said, was forced upon him by the French urged on by the Americans, notably Mr. Bullitt.

Bullitt was perhaps justified in his assurances of U.S. support, for it was forthcoming: Washington promptly recognized the Bao Dai government, and much of the money the emperor set aside for his own future was in American aid dollars. (It was also with the support of U.S. agents in Saigon that Bao Dai was deposed in 1955.) By 1954, when the French departed in defeat, the United States share of the cost of the war in Vietnam was already greater than 78 percent.

VIII

Exile

One Way to "Stop the Rot"

IN JUNE 1947 Bullitt was awarded an honorary degree by Georgetown University in Washington, and he delivered a commencement address reminiscent of his speech in Philadelphia in August 1940, urging an awakening to the Nazi menace; this time, though, his assessment of the world was bleaker, his call for action more alarming—there was also the difference that he was now speaking for himself, not the President—as the world had entered the nuclear age. "You step today onto a field of battle . . . ," he told the graduating class.

There is war and famine in China and Indo-China. . . . There is murder in the Holyland. There is fear of invasion in Turkey, and hunger and fear in Greece. Undernourished Italy is trembling on the verge of civil war. Germany is as famished as Hitler made all the countries he invaded. Hungary is being crushed. Austria is starving. Exhausted France is living in dread of her Communists. Great Britain is grimly bearing privation. . . . Into this sick body of mankind the Soviet Government, . . . through . . . its world-wide Communist conspiracy, . . . is instilling the belief that there can be no peace on earth until all the peoples of the world have been conquered for Communism. . . . Therefore, . . . you step today onto a field of battle. On the issue of that battle depends the survival of Christian civilization. . . .

The key to survival, Bullitt maintained, was keeping the Soviet Union "constantly confronted by superior force," which might have astonished anyone who recalled his warning a decade earlier that development of the bombing plane would destroy European civilization: "Today it is only the superiority of our air force and our possession of the atomic bomb that prevent Stalin from ordering the Red Army to occupy all Europe. And let us remember always that the most legitimate and praiseworthy use of force on this earth is to hold the field to permit the growth of moral ideas." (The U.S. lost much of its advantage in August 1949, when the U.S.S.R. detonated an atomic device, but regained it in November 1952 by successfully testing a hydrogen weapon.)

Bullitt's fears for China were realized, although it was not a Soviet victory, as he had predicted in *Life* in October 1947: in September 1949 Chinese revolutionaries established the People's Republic, with Mao Tse-tung as its chief of state, and by April 1950 Chiang Kai-shek ruled only Taiwan, where he had established his regime, and the islands of Matsu and Quemoy. Bullitt was indignant: he still blamed George Marshall for what he considered capitulation; and he was not appeased in the least by the appointment as secretary of state of Dean Acheson—Acheson, Harvard Law and a protégé of Felix Frankfurter, had become undersecretary in 1945—who decided against granting $1.5 billion in aid to the Chinese Nationalists. When the one top-ranking official whom he still respected, James Forrestal, committed suicide in 1949 and was replaced as secretary of defense by Marshall, Bullitt's severance with the administration was complete. He did not turn his back on his country, as he had in the 1920s—he still had a house in Washington and a farm in Massachusetts—but he went often to Paris, where he had kept his apartment, and he bought a seaside cottage in Taiwan, next door to the vacation home of Chiang Kai-shek.

While away much of the time, Bullitt continued to be interested in the internal security issue as he viewed it—the Communist threat—and he figured prominently in the case of Alger Hiss, a State Department official who was convicted of perjury in January 1950. Questioned by the FBI in October 1949 at his home in Ashfield, Massachusetts, Bullitt said he had been told by a French official that Hiss was a Communist, and he later identified his source as Edouard Daladier, when he was the premier of France. Bullitt said further he had relayed the information to Stanley K. Hornbeck, Hiss's superior, and in the trial Hornbeck testified that Bullitt had described Hiss as a "fellow-traveler." When John W. Davis, the Democratic candidate for president in 1924, appeared on behalf of Hiss, a headline in *The New York Times* read: "EX-PRESIDENTIAL NOMINEE HEADS 6 CHARACTER WITNESSES FOR MAN BULLITT CALLED A RED."

In April 1952 Bullitt participated in a radio discussion of the Communist threat, sponsored by the Georgetown University Forum, with Richard M. Nixon, a Republican senator from California, who charged at the outset that in six years "we have lost 600 million people to the Communists. . . ." "I think we began falling down a long time ago," Bullitt commented, "when our government adopted the policy of trusting the Soviet Union. . . ." It was not until 1947, when Stalin threatened to take Turkey,

> that Truman enunciated . . . the Truman doctrine, . . . that is to say, the policy of containing Soviet efforts to expand. However, we didn't follow out the necessary consequences of that doctrine. . . . We have concentrated, the administration has concentrated, its attention so completely to Europe that it has allowed Asia to go, and there is now a most threatening situation there. . . . You have a war on in Indochina, . . . and it is a very bloody war.

Bullitt was asked by a Georgetown professor about U.S. military capabilities in Asia. "Well, I don't believe we should attempt to use American troops in Indochina," he replied. "The fact is that . . . the physical conditions are . . . ill adapted to a white physique. It is a country of stifling heat, malaria mosquitoes, and swamps and small streams and rice paddies, and white soldiers down there are definitely less effective than yellow soldiers. . . . We should arm the Vietnamese as rapidly as possible. . . ." "You mean . . .," asked Nixon, "we . . . should not . . . use our ground forces?" "Certainly not," said Bullitt.

Nixon ran for vice president in 1952 with Eisenhower on the Republican ticket, which Bullitt supported, saying, again at a meeting at Georgetown—Bullitt had agreed to serve on a council of lay advisers to the president of the Catholic university—that with General Eisenhower as president the country would be better able to survive the peril of Communist conquest. Eisenhower was elected, and Bullitt tried to exert influence on the foreign policy of the new administration; but his anti-Communism was as excessive for most Republicans as it had been for the Democrats: invitations to presidential assistant Sherman Adams were brusquely rejected by the former governor of New Hampshire, who scrawled a note on one of them, to a dinner on March 7, 1953: "Tell him Mrs. Adams is ill." Bullitt would be heard, however—the Communist threat was a dominant issue in the spring of 1953, with the war in Korea still being fought and with Senator Joseph R. McCarthy of Wisconsin engaged in his relentless Red-baiting crusade—as he was in May at a convention of businessmen in Chicago. "When the Soviet Government offers peace and friendship to a non-Communist state," Bullitt declared,

> it always intends to end the friendship by driving a dagger into the back of its new friend. . . . Today the Soviet Government fears our international bombers, our atomic bombs, and our hydrogen bombs. . . . The Soviet leaders know that today they would lose a war against us. . . . This chance may be our last. When the Soviet Government possesses the weapons it needs to destroy us by a surprise attack, it will not hesitate to attack. If our Government should fail to employ the present period of our relative impunity to seize the initiative, . . . we may incur the destruction of our country. . . . No war, hot or cold, was ever won by forces which feared to take the offensive.

War with the Soviet-supported North Koreans and the Red Chinese had about ended by June 1953, and Bullitt was in Seoul—he had long been a friend of Syngman Rhee, the president of the Republic of Korea—and an armistice was soon to be signed. He suspected that the U.S. had again backed down—the peace was based on an agreement to partition Korea at the thirty-eighth parallel—as he wrote in the September issue of *The Reader's Digest*:

> We all want to end the American casualties; but if we do that in such a way as to deal death to Korea, no man in Asia will respect us or dare to be our friend. Before many years have passed, the Communist conspirators in the Kremlin will add another 700 million Asians to the war power of the 800 million slaves they now rule. Then, too late, we shall know that Syngman Rhee was right when he wanted to win the Korean War.

In August 1954 Bullitt argued in *Look* for an attack by the Nationalists on the Chinese mainland, supported by the United States (the editors of the magazine were careful to note they did not agree), for the only alternative to such an attack was an H-bomb war with the Soviet Union. "We are in mortal peril," he wrote.

The Soviet Government is constructing hydrogen bombs and intercontinental bombers as fast as it can, in order to inflict on us a nationwide H-bomb Pearl Harbor. [Actually the U.S.S.R. did not test a hydrogen bomb until late 1955.] It will not stop. It can only be stopped. Our skies will be filled with death unless we either destroy the productive center of the Soviet Union before they produce enough bombs and bombers to annihilate us, or swing the world balance of power strongly against the Soviet Union, so that when it possesses those weapons of annihilation, it will not dare to use them. Liberation of the mainland of China, which is the key to all Asia, would produce such a swing in the balance of power.

Bullitt attended a stag dinner at the White House on May 31, 1955, and in a letter of appreciation to Eisenhower he could not resist the opportunity—it would turn out to be his last—to advise a president, sternly and condescendingly. "Today in Europe as well as Asia," he wrote on June 8,

we are courted for our money but regarded as brainless and soft. Our world position has disintegrated with extraordinary speed ever since the then-despised Chinese Red Army defeated the U.S. Army at the Yalu River, drove it back to the 38th parallel, there broke our national will to win. . . . We have now destroyed the superb morale of the Koreans, and we are engaged in destroying the morale of the Nationalist Chinese. In spite of our strong words, the tragedy of Indo-China is moving to a gruesome climax. Japan is drifting away from us. Only a little more appeasement is needed to hand the remainder of Asia to the Communists. We need only permit the Red Chinese Air Force to bomb Matsu and Quemoy with impunity. . . . On the other hand, if we tell the Russians . . . that as soon as any one of the islands is bombed we will knock out the Red airfields in the area, we shall stop the rot.

The Wages of Age

IN TAIWAN in the summer of 1954 Bullitt aggravated the injury to his back in a fall while mountain climbing: both legs were paralyzed, and he was in acute pain.

He was put in traction and could only travel in a prone position; fortunately for him a Chinese general assigned to the embassy in Washington had just died, and a coffin was being sent for return shipment of the body, so it was used to transport Bullitt home. He had made his last trip to Taiwan—he donated his house there to an order of Catholic nuns—but not for reasons related to his health: his friendship with Chiang Kai-shek had been breached over a seemingly trivial dispute. A servant had entertained in Bullitt's house during his absence and without his permission, which was a crime under Chinese law; Bullitt objected to prosecution, but Chiang insisted, and Bullitt never spoke to him again. It was one of many associations that Bullitt abandoned in later life, although the causes of incompatibility were usually more complex than the misbehavior of a houseboy. He had a propensity for forsaking friends, especially those he had come to know professionally, explained his cousin Orville Horwitz. "He just would not abide anything less than a first-rate mentality," said Horwitz,

except in the case of his gardener or his cook. . . . He burned most of his bridges, although some of us—his brother, Orville, Tommy White, and I—refused to get mad at him, realizing he was just testing us. Orville just refused to argue with him. I loved Bill, and I went to him at one point—he must have been nearly seventy by then—and I said, "You can do any damn thing to me, but you're never going to lose my friendship." Bill found it necessary to disagree with people he really loved, and it took me a long time to figure out why. It was this: if he liked you, he thought you were God, and anything you did was perfect; so as soon as you did something that wasn't perfect, he took it as a personal affront.

It seemed that the mightier the man the more Bullitt enjoyed rebuking him. Admiral Arthur W. Radford, the chairman of the Joint Chiefs of Staff, was anxious in the mid-1950s to enlist him for a series of television broadcasts to boost public awareness of the need for military preparedness; and he went to see him in Ashfield, Massachusetts, for that purpose. Radford asked Orville Horwitz to come along and to tell Bullitt the project would be good for his health, and Horwitz agreed. "Radford really admired Bill," Horwitz recalled,

and he told him how desperately he was needed, but Bill gave one excuse after another for not doing it, so I got kind of blunt and said he ought to get off his duff and do something constructive. Bill got mad as hell at both Radford and me, and he ordered us to leave the house, as he stomped off to his room. It was 2:30 in the morning, and Radford asked me, "What do we do now?" I answered that we should just go to bed, for by morning Bullitt would forget all about it, which is exactly what happened. Radford was deeply offended, though, and he never forgave Bill.

The rift with Charles de Gaulle was the result of a serious disagreement over relations with China: de Gaulle, who had been elected president of France in 1958 under a new constitution that endowed him with vast authority, decided in

1964 to recognize the People's Republic of China, which meant a diplomatic break with the Nationalist government. Bullitt protested vigorously—by this time, still an honorary citizen of France, he was living in Paris most of the time—and he became enraged when the French government turned the Chinese embassy over to the Communists and sent troops to evict the Nationalists, confiscating their files, including secret intelligence reports. He demanded and got an appointment with de Gaulle, whom he called a *salaud*, a slob if translated politely; and relations between the two men were no longer cordial.

———

Bullitt's health was a subject of mounting concern as he reached his mid-sixties, with his broken back the disability of most urgent concern: upon returning from Taiwan in 1954, he spent four months in a hospital for hydrotherapy, and he then went to Hot Springs, Virginia, for convalescence. "I have now tried out that belt for a couple of weeks," he wrote in September to Harrison McLaughlin, the surgeon who had fused his spine in 1946, "and find that it at least eliminates the sensation of having the bottom of my spine become a bowl of pebbles." In March 1955 McLaughlin turned the case over to another New York specialist, Preston Wade (spine surgery was still an innovative procedure, and patients were often referred by one doctor to another). "Many thanks for taking on William Bullitt," McLaughlin wrote Wade. "I hope he does not give you too much trouble." McLaughlin added a note about Bullitt's leukemia, advising that a hemotologist had found it "quite benign." But in the fall of 1959 the prognosis changed, prompting Dr. Horwitz to write to a fellow internist, who had also examined Bullitt: ". . . his spleen became enlarged, and he developed several lymph nodes in his neck and groin." Leukemia therapy was effective, reducing Bullitt's white blood cell count from 100,000 to 10,000, though he was plagued with skin cancers, which were removed on a routine schedule. When leukemia reappeared in 1960, the drug dosage was increased, and a cancer specialist at the University of Pennsylvania Hospital, John W. Frost, wrote on March 5 to Horwitz: "I am hopeful that we will again have . . . a good remission. . . ."

A Final Vendetta

━━━━━━━

IN 1964 Bullitt decided the time had come to publish the psychological study of Woodrow Wilson, written by him and Sigmund Freud, and he went to Houghton

Mifflin of Boston with a contract signed by him and Freud in 1932. It gave him an exclusive right to select an American publisher and awarded him two-thirds of the proceeds. Why at this late date did he wish to publish the book? A reason for the delay was that he did not want it to appear during the lifetime of Wilson's widow, Edith Galt Wilson, who died in 1961, but there was more to it: he had withheld the book in 1932 out of concern for its effect on his government career, which was no longer of interest to him in 1964. "I think he published it out of sheer boredom," said Orville Horwitz, perhaps an adequate explanation; nevertheless, Bullitt's own rationale, stated in a signed foreword, is enlightening:

> In the spring of 1932, . . . when our manuscript was ready to be typed, Freud made textual changes and wrote a number of passages to which I objected. After several attempts we decided to forget the book for three weeks, and to attempt then to agree. When we met, we continued to disagree. I wished to return to the United States to participate in Franklin D. Roosevelt's campaign for President, and I believed that I would never again find time to work on the manuscript. . . . I suggested that, since neither of us was entirely impervious to reason, it was likely that some day we would agree; meanwhile the book should not be published. . . .

Freud was forced to leave Vienna after the *Anschluss* in 1938, and Bullitt met him at the railroad station in Paris; he "suggested that we might discuss our book once more after he was settled in London. I carried the manuscript to Freud and was delighted when he agreed to eliminate the additions he had written. . . . Once more I visited him in London and showed him the final text, which we had both accepted. . . . I did not see Freud again. He died in 1939."

There was another reason Bullitt wanted the book published, and it had to do with propriety: in 1956, the year of the one hundredth anniversary of the births of both Wilson and Freud, Ernest Jones, who had been an assistant to Freud and was his biographer, tried to obtain the manuscript, and Bullitt reacted impulsively. "I'll tear the damn thing up before I give it away," he told Orville Horwitz, who contended that he had no right to destroy the book, for it belonged to posterity. "Something written by Sigmund Freud should not be the property of one person," Horwitz argued. "It would be as if one person owned the 'Mona Lisa.'" Bullitt disagreed with his cousin: "No, it belongs to me."

Prospective publication of *Thomas Woodrow Wilson—A Psychological Study* precipitated a long and acrimonious argument between Bullitt and Freud's heirs—notably his daughter Anna and son Ernst—over the content of the manuscript; and eventually the question was raised as to the actual authorship of the book, at which point the battle was joined by many of Freud's loyal followers. The publisher, Houghton Mifflin, became arbiter of the dispute—first, because

Bullitt refused to deal directly with the Freuds; second, because the company's reputation was at stake over the extent of Freud's participation in the work.

A Houghton Mifflin editor, Alick Bartholomew, was assigned to work with the Freuds, and Bartholomew heard from Ernst Freud in a letter dated August 25, 1965, from London. "My sister Anna Freud and myself feel that the manuscript in its present state is in dire need of careful editing," he wrote. "Although the Foreword and Introduction as well as the historical treatment are excellent, the psychoanalytical interpretation is full of unnecessary repetitions. . . ." He said his sister would be in the United States in October—she was to receive an award at the White House—and would be willing to meet with a Houghton Mifflin representative. Bartholomew met with Anna Freud and learned a lot—about the Freud-Bullitt collaboration and about Bullitt (Anna Freud, a near contemporary of Bullitt, had gotten to know him in Vienna). "She respects him a great deal," wrote Bartholomew in a memorandum on October 14, 1965, "and said that forty years ago, though tremendously personable and charming, he was also frightfully arrogant."

Bartholomew's report on the meeting with Anna Freud was significant, as it was the one detailed record of the Freud family position, which ultimately would be disregarded in the rush to publish the book: it addressed both the presentation of content and the question of authorship. "Sigmund Freud apparently regarded the Wilson book essentially as Bullitt's," Bartholomew wrote, "and his role as a cooperator rather than co-author. . . . There were no notes about the book amongst Freud's papers, and Bullitt had the only manuscript, . . . with every chapter signed by both. Freud realized that if the book were published too soon, it would hurt Bullitt's career, and therefore left the timing of publication entirely in Bullitt's hands." Bartholomew noted that Bullitt had sent a copy of the manuscript to the Freuds in April 1965—it was the copy he had submitted to Houghton Mifflin the previous year—"saying he had not yet approached a publisher, but felt the time had come to arrange publication." (Bartholomew did not comment on the evidence that Bullitt had lied to the Freuds.) Bartholomew had obviously been impressed by Anna Freud's assertions, though aware that she had a vested interest beyond being Freud's daughter: "The Wilson book is very important to Freudian thought," he wrote, "as it contains the only psychoanalysis that Freud ever attempted of an important living figure." But Bullitt, according to Anna Freud, had turned it into

a kind of parody by thoughtlessly repeating phrases like "passively toward this father" and "identification with Jesus Christ." The repetition of psychoanalytical formulae became an incantation. Miss Anna Freud feels most strongly that the publication of the manuscript as it is would be harmful to her father's contribution to scientific thought. He was a stickler for precision of thought and economy of words.

Bartholomew had one final observation, which indicated that Anna Freud, while logical in her position and deserving of greater consideration, would yield. "Perhaps Bullitt has made sufficient changes to satisfy Anna," he wrote. "I somehow doubt it. If not, then she will insist we delay publication until after Bullitt's death [whether or not Anna Freud knew Bullitt had only a year or two to live, she was powerless to effect such a delay]. Meanwhile, the Freuds will sign the contract, believing that Mr. Bullitt's formidable daughter would probably obstruct revision less than she would contract negotiation."

The contract was signed on December 3, 1965, and on March 17, 1966, Bartholomew, still reflecting the position of the Freud family, wrote another memo:

> Our publishing contract with William Bullitt and the Freud Estate gives each party an equal voice in approval of the final manuscript. The present behavior of Ambassador Bullitt makes it difficult for the Freuds to have "equal time." . . . I believe we should make a great mistake in assuming that the Freuds will ultimately accept any Bullitt version of the original manuscript. . . . I believe the only position we can for the moment justify to the Freuds is that Mr. Bullitt is unwilling to see any changes made in the original manuscript. . . . But we must tell them that and see what they say—we cannot just assume that they cannot do anything about it. . . .

Bartholomew at this point made a very important statement, for it addressed the lasting issue, the authorship:

> Bullitt wrote this book with psychoanalytical material provided by Sigmund Freud. Freud has the status of co-author, but it is still Bullitt's book. It is possible to make a case that Bullitt "used" Freud when he wrote this book. It is certainly a fact that Freud withheld his approval of it for seven years until the year before his death, when he was in the position of "beneficiary" to Bullitt (who was largely instrumental in getting him out of Vienna). What this could conceivably mean to the publisher is that *Thomas Woodrow Wilson* might be ill received by the psychological profession. . . .

The psychological profession, especially as it included disciples of Freud, would indeed resent the way Freud had been used. In Bullitt's defense there would be the recollection of Orville Horwitz, who edited the manuscript in 1932 and took note that each page had been initialed by both Freud and Bullitt. "I know they wrote the book together," said Horwitz,

> though it is conceivable that Bill put it into better English. It's obvious too that Bill assembled the facts and that he and Freud analyzed them together. A lot of Freudians don't want to believe that Freud could be so critical of an American president. They forget that he was a patriotic Austrian and was probably more angry at Wilson than Bill was, because as a result of the Versailles Treaty Austria ended up with a small plot of land around Vienna.

The Freuds notified Houghton Mifflin on July 18, 1966, that they were disassociating themselves from the book. "I feel that under the circumstances," wrote Ernst Freud, "we have to agree to the Bullitt version of the *Wilson*, to be published as it stands. This is a pity as it would have been much more acceptable with the slight alterations."

Proceeding to publication in the fall of 1966, Houghton Mifflin still was concerned with the extent of Freud's role, and a company executive, Benjamin C. Tilghman, was assigned to investigate. Tilghman's efforts would end inconclusively—he would discover that the manuscript was retyped in 1939, "an amalgam of . . . two sets of notes and corrections . . .," but there was "no manuscript which contains . . . the original text plus two sets of corrections"— but his meetings with Bullitt were enlightening. Tilghman drove to Ashfield, Massachusetts, on September 11, and he was shown by Bullitt the signed manuscript, which "was in a letter case and inside the top of the case there was a typewritten note which said, in effect, that the enclosed manuscript was not to be published in its present form." Tilghman passed along Bullitt's explanation in a memorandum dated October 18:

> Bullitt said he met Freud in London in 1939 and Freud agreed to delete a long addition he had made. . . . He also agreed to remove some of the . . . smaller additions, but others now seemed to Bullitt improvements and . . . were retained. In addition, Bullitt . . . had some corrections . . . and these were approved by Freud. Bullitt then took the revised signed manuscript back with him to Paris and had his secretary retype it. This retyped version was given to Freud . . . who approved it. Bullitt said that Freud was quite ill by now. My interpretation of Bullitt's story is that he is not absolutely sure whether . . . Freud read every single line, . . . but Bullitt said there was no doubt that Freud was urged to read it, that he had plenty of time to do so, and that he did not in any way withhold his consent to publication.

Tilghman sensed, however, that Bullitt was not being completely straightforward: "I asked Bullitt if there had been any changes made in the 1939 manuscript after the retyping. He said that there was no need to worry about that and that I now knew everything I needed to know." Tilghman was left in a quandary: "I could not establish in any graphic way the fact and nature of Freud's participation."

Tilghman wrote to Bullitt on October 24, 1966, to say that questions were being raised by scholars who had seen the manuscript. "The most direct questions asked have come from a professor who is a scholar of Freud's writing and life. The professor has asked us about the terms used in the book. He says that many are unknown to him and differ from the terminology he knew of in Freud's writings. . . ." Tilghman was worried and said so:

Even though publication is still far off, there is already a considerable amount of interest in the book. It now seems to us certain that there will be strongly conflicting views. Such a situation is by no means always detrimental. It is, though, important to prevent further doubts about the book's authenticity. I am afraid that if speculation on that point continues, the result will be reviews which will obscure your clear look at Wilson and the importance of the book.

Bullitt telephoned Tilghman on October 26, and it seemed not to bother him that the opposition forces were gathering: they now numbered Erik H. Erikson, the famed Freudian psychologist at Harvard, and Barbara W. Tuchman, the renowned historian. "He replied," Tilghman wrote, "that he did not think that gasps from people like this were worth anything." At the end of a memo dated November 9, 1966, Tilghman said to David Harris, the managing editor of Houghton Mifflin: "I cannot see that we are any closer to authenticating the manuscript than we were at the very beginning."

The book was published in December 1966, accompanied by a selection in *Look* on December 13, which consisted of Bullitt's foreword; a digest of Wilson's life, compiled by Bullitt from 1,500 pages of notes; and a section of the book dealing with the Paris peace conference in 1919. The *Look* publication appeared to settle the question of who had written what: the narrative was essentially Bullitt's work while Freud had interjected psychoanalytical commentary and had reviewed the chapters, signing them and making margin notations. In the foreward Bullitt also shed more light on the collaboration, going back to a meeting with Freud that he placed in Berlin in 1930.

He asked me what I was doing, and I told him I was working on a book about the Treaty of Versailles. . . . He astonished me by saying he would like to collaborate with me in writing the Wilson chapter. I laughed and remarked that the idea was delightful but bizarre. . . . To bury Freud on Wilson in a chapter of my book would be to produce an impossible monstrosity: the part would be greater than the whole. . . . Freud persisted. . . . He could not do the research necessary for an analysis of Wilson's character; but I could do it easily, since I had worked with Wilson and knew all his close friends and associates. . . . We started to work on our book at once. . . .

The biographical digest indicated the direction of Bullitt's bias:

In physique, Tommy resembled his mother, Jessie Woodrow Wilson. He was thin, sallow and weak, and his eyes were exceptionally deficient. Moreover, in his childhood, he began to suffer from the indigestion that harassed him all his life. His passionate love of his father was the core of his emotional life. . . . The minister was the great man of the Presbyterian upper middle class to which the Wilsons belonged. Five times a day, the father prayed to God, while the family listened. . . . After the family moved to Augusta, Georgia, young Tommy sat in the fourth pew and gazed up into the face of his "incomparable father" with rapt intensity. . . . So completely did he take into his heart the teachings of his father, that for the remainder of his life, he never allowed himself to entertain religious doubt for an instant. . . . Early, the father became convinced that his son would be a great man, and he did not conceal this belief from Tommy or from anyone else. In spite of his meager income, he kept his son in absolute economic dependence on him for twenty-nine years. And Tommy was content to be so kept.

The excerpt from the book contained some Freudian flourishes, such as: "In the psychic life of man, a force is active that we call libido—the energy of the Eros"; but the essence of the chapter was Bullitt's account of Wilson's actions in 1919. "At some time between the Armistice negotiations and his arrival in Paris," Bullitt wrote,

he decided to fight for the peace he wanted not with . . . masculine weapons but with the weapons of femininity, not with force but with persuasion. All the Allied nations were living on supplies and credits from America. But to use those powerful economic . . . weapons involved a fight of precisely the sort he had never made and could not make. . . . He had never dared to have a fist fight in his life. All his fighting had been done with his mouth. . . . Throughout the early morning of April 4, Wilson writhed in his bed, vomiting, coughing, . . . fighting for breath. . . . But the torment in his body was perhaps less terrible to him than the torment in his mind. He faced alternatives both of which were horrible to him. He could break his promises and become the tool of the Allies, not the Prince of Peace, or he could hold to his promises, withdraw the financial support of the United States from Europe. . . . He shrank from the possible consequences of wielding his masculine weapons.

Bullitt then quoted from his letter of resignation to President Wilson on May 17, 1919: ". . . our Government has consented now to deliver the suffering peoples of the world to new oppressions, subjections, and dismemberments—a new century of war."

The book aroused a loud reaction among historians, psychologists, and officials whose government experience also dated back to the Wilson years, such as Allen W. Dulles, who served with the American peace delegation in 1919 and later became the director of the Central Intelligence Agency. Dulles, who had entered Princeton when Wilson was the university's president, found a "deep note of bitterness" in the book's conclusions, which to him amounted to a flawed portrayal. "Certainly, it does not describe the Wilson I knew," wrote Dulles in the same issue of *Look* that carried the book excerpt. "The authors have described Wilson . . . as an ugly, unhealthy, 'intense' Presbyterian, with a neurotic constitution and with little interest in the amenities of life. . . . Yet during his Princeton days, the students considered him the most popular teacher there. . . ." Prior to the Paris peace conference, Dulles recalled, he had worked with Bullitt assembling material for Wilson's Fourteen Points. "I also saw Bullitt often . . . at the Conference. Bullitt is a man who espoused causes and individuals and then turned from them abruptly. . . ." Dulles was quick to explain that he was not a disinterested observer: "As I am charging others with prejudice, I must admit my own. The admiration I first gained for Wilson as an inspiring teacher during my Princeton days undoubtedly colors my own thoughts. . . ." (Dulles did not mention another reason for resenting Bullitt's actions in 1919: Robert Lansing, whose resignation as secretary of state was precipitated by Bullitt's testimony before the Senate Foreign Relations Committee, was his uncle.)

"The book can either be considered a mischievous and preposterous joke, a sort of caricature of the worst that has come from psychoanalytic ideologues," wrote Harvard psychiatrist Robert Coles in *The New Republic*, "or else an awful and unrelenting slander upon a remarkably gifted American president. I fear it is meant to be the latter. . . ." Coles understandably was inclined to defend Freud and offered the opinion that "it is overwhelmingly Bullitt's work: the style, the use of words, the content, the tone. . . ." He was even willing to suspect that Freud had been duped: "Perhaps he . . . trusted some of his friends too much—because it can be argued that William Bullitt's twisted vendetta against Woodrow Wilson may actually be an underhanded assault on psychoanalysis and Sigmund Freud." Barbara Tuchman called the book "good psychology but bad history; bad because it is invalid, dangerous because it misleads us," she wrote in *The Atlantic*. ". . . [I]t makes the contradictions in Wilson's behavior fall into place with an almost audible click. But as an overall estimate of the whole man it is lamentable, and as an interpretation of events it falls to pieces." A "disastrously bad book," Erik Erikson wrote in the first of a two-part series in *The New York Review of Books*, and Erikson joined others in the psychoanalytic profession wishing to minimize Freud's responsibility. ". . . [T]he text now printed must be ascribed to Bullitt," Erikson wrote, "because he either transcribed or wrote, translated or caused to be translated, every word of it. He 'showed Freud the final text' in London in 1938, eight years after the beginning of the collaboration. Freud was in the last year of his life. He was a desperately sick man . . . and an émigré, by then deeply grateful to Bullitt. . . ." The second part of the series was written by Richard Hofstadter, the historian, who listed three reasons he was irritated by the book: "its indefiniteness about the details of authorship, a certain persistent insensitivity in thought and style, and a punitive tone, which gives it the aspect of a vendetta carried on in the name of science."

Other reviews were uniformly negative. "What is ultimately unfortunate about this book," wrote Robert Sussman Stewart, author of a history of psychoanalysis, in *The New York Times Book Review*, "is that the general public will conclude that this study is a model of psychoanalytic procedure and that psychoanalysis itself has no place in the interpretation of history or in the reconstruction of biographical material." "It would be hard to find a literary collaboration more ill conceived than this one," wrote the reviewer in *Time*. And in a column in *Newsweek*, Raymond Moley, who had had a hand in obtaining for Bullitt a State Department position in 1933, wrote: "Apparently much of this book is of Bullitt's composition. His clumsy use of Freudian jargon gives him a cruel weapon to pay off a forty-eight-year-old grudge." "This is a strange document," wrote George Steiner in *The New Yorker*. "It is of obvious yet uncertain psychological and historical interest. But it also suggests that psychoanalysis *à distance* is not a very sound exercise." A. J. P. Taylor, the British historian, put it quite bluntly in *The New Statesman*: "The book is a disgrace as a scientific exercise. The two authors had no means of analysing Wilson except on the basis of second-hand knowledge, and therefore they guessed. . . . Moreover they wrote in disillusion and hate. . . . The book therefore contributes nothing to historical understanding."

So Close to Greatness

BULLITT was never aware of the critical assault on his book: the cancer had advanced to a terminal stage by January 1967—on February 2 he was admitted to the American Hospital in Neuilly, a suburb of Paris—and the reviews were withheld by Horwitz and Offie, who were in Paris along with Anne Bullitt and Orville and Susy Bullitt. Orville wanted to take his brother back to Philadelphia, and arrangements had been made with Pan American for an aircraft with a bed, but there were severe snowstorms all along the U.S. east coast, Orville Horwitz recalled. "I didn't want to see us stranded in Iceland," he said, "so I went to Bill and asked if he really cared about going back, and he said, 'Hell no.' It was then that I said good-bye, and I'll never forget his last words to me. 'I just want to tell you,' he said, 'that it has been a great privilege to know you, and I don't know how I could have gotten through life without you.' "

On the day Bullitt died, February 15, 1967, Secretary of Defense Robert S. McNamara announced in Washington that the bombing of military targets in North Vietnam had been resumed after a six-day pause. McNamara emphasized that the bombing in itself would not win the war, and he said that an enemy buildup in South Vietnam seemed to have leveled off.

Bullitt's body was flown to Philadelphia, and he was buried following an Episcopal ceremony on February 20 at the Church of the Holy Trinity on Rittenhouse Square. Bullitt's funeral was attended by his family and a few dignitaries—James A. Farley, the former Democratic Party chairman; Arthur W. Radford, the ex-chief of the Joint Chiefs of Staff; and Richard M. Nixon, a future president—but otherwise his death, as had much of his life, went largely unnoticed. All the pity, for he was a prophet—he was intelligent, even brilliant, and he had a remarkable ability to see the future: he was correct in his objection to the Versailles Treaty, sensing it would enable a man like Hitler to start another general war in Europe; he understood Stalin for the villain he was and foresaw the Cold War; and he worried with reason about human extinction in a nuclear era. Bullitt's perception of the implications of Soviet expansion resulted in his most estimable piece of work, which was a letter to President Roosevelt on January 29, 1943. "He predicted with startling accuracy," wrote George F. Kennan, "the situation to which the war would lead if existing policies continued to be pursued. . . . This letter . . . had no counterpart . . . as a warning . . . of the effective division of Europe which would ensue if the war continued to be pursued on the basis of the concepts then prevailing. . . . It deserves a place among the major historical documents of the time." Bullitt's main point was emphatically stated: "We have to demonstrate to Stalin—and mean it—that while we genuinely want to cooperate with the Soviet Union, we will not permit our war to prevent Nazi domination of Europe to be turned into a war to establish Soviet domination of Europe. . . ."

Roosevelt did not listen, as President Wilson had not heeded Bullitt's advice in 1919—Bullitt made poor judgments, too, as in 1940 after the fall of France, when he publicly supported the government of Marshal Pétain—and FDR by 1944 no longer had need of his counsel. Bullitt turned to other forums: he spoke publicly, and in 1946 he wrote a book bitterly critical of Roosevelt, now dead, for having "wasted the . . . opportunities" for world peace. But he was again prophetic: "After the next war . . . there may be no after." He had by this time moved to the extreme anti-Communist right: in 1947 he said at a congressional hearing that if the Soviet Union had the atomic bomb, "it would already have been dropped on the United States"; and in 1949 he made American involvement in the war in Indochina inevitable by assuring the emperor of Vietnam, Bao Dai, he could depend on U.S. support, if he would lead a nationalist government. "Our world position has disintegrated . . .," he wrote President Eisenhower in 1955, "ever since the then-despised Chinese Red Army defeated the U.S. Army at the Yalu River, drove it back to the 38th Parallel, there broke our national will to win. . . ." Having advised three wartime presidents over forty years of international tension, Bullitt had had his last say, damning the truce in Korea.

George T. Boswell, who wrote a doctoral dissertation at Texas Christian University on Bullitt in 1972, viewed his career as Greek tragedy:

> . . . those qualities . . . which enabled him to rise to a position of great influence . . . also insured his ultimate downfall. He carried within him the seeds of his own destruction. . . . The ultimate tragedy . . . was that Bullitt's talents went largely unused during those years when the United States transformed itself from an isolated observer of international affairs into the leading world power. . . . The real loser was not Bullitt, it was the nation.

Had Bullitt been more moderate in the expression of his ambition—if there was a single incident that ruined his career, it was the disaccord with Sumner Welles—he might have become a superlative secretary of state, who could have stopped Stalin in Central Europe and avoided the Cold War; instead he saw conspiracies where there were none and squandered his greatness. Bullitt was a member of a generation of Americans whose fathers had built an industrial and mercantile colossus, affording them the privilege of wealth and station. As George Kennan wrote, he was one of the "remarkable group of Americans, born just before the turn of the century, . . . a striking generation, full of talent and exuberance. . . ." There was as well, however, a mutual tendency toward ultimate destruction. "The civilization of the 1930s and 1940s was not strong enough to support their weight. They knew achievement more often than they knew fulfillment, and their ends . . . tended to be frustrating, disappointing, and sometimes tragic." Bullitt came close to greatness, for he had the promise of greatness; that he failed to realize that promise was a tragedy.

BIBLIOGRAPHY

Baltzell, Edward Digby. *Philadelphia Gentlemen*. Philadelphia: University of Pennsylvania Press, 1979.

Berle, Adolf A. *Navigating the Rapids*. New York: Harcourt Brace, 1973.

Biddle, Francis B. *In Brief Authority*. Garden City: Doubleday, 1962.

Biddle, George. *An American Artist's Story*. Boston: Little, Brown, 1939.

Bohlen, Charles E. *Witness to History*. New York: Norton, 1973.

Bowen, Catherine Drinker. *Family Portrait*. Boston: Little, Brown, 1970.

Brook-Shepherd, Gordon. *November 1918*. Boston: Little, Brown, 1981.

Bryant, Louise. *Mirrors of Moscow*. New York: T. Seltzer, 1923.

Bullitt, Ernesta. *An Uncensored Diary from the Central Empires*. Garden City: Doubleday, 1917.

Bullitt, Orville. *For the President, Personal and Secret*. Boston: Houghton Mifflin, 1972.

Bullitt, William C. *The Bullitt Mission to Russia*. New York: Huebsch, 1919.

———. *The Great Globe Itself*. New York: Charles Scribner's Sons, 1946.

———. *It's Not Done*. New York: Harcourt Brace, 1926.

———, and Freud, Sigmund. *Thomas Woodrow Wilson—A Psychological Study*. Boston: Houghton Mifflin, 1967.

Burns, James MacGregor. *Roosevelt: The Soldier of Freedom*. New York: Harcourt Brace, 1970.

Burt, Nathaniel. *The Perennial Philadelphians*. Boston: Little, Brown, 1963.

Canby, Henry Seidel. *Alma Mater: The Gothic Age of the American College*. New York: Rinehart, 1936.

Cole, Wayne S. *Charles A. Lindbergh and the Battle Against American Intervention in World War II*. New York: Harcourt Brace, 1974.

Craig, Gordon A., and Gilbert, Felix. *The Diplomats*. Princeton: Princeton University Press, 1953.

de Gaulle, Charles. *War Memoirs*. New York: Viking, 1955.

Devillers, Philippe. *Histoire du Viet-Nam de 1940 à 1952*. Paris: Éditions du Seuil, 1952.

Dodd, William E., Jr., and Dodd, Martha. *Ambassador Dodd's Diary*. New York: Harcourt Brace, 1941.

Earle, Hubert P. *Blackout*. Philadelphia: Lippincott, 1939.

Farley, James A. *Jim Farley's Story*. New York: McGraw-Hill, 1948.

Farnsworth, Beatrice. *William C. Bullitt and the Soviet Union*. Bloomington: Indiana University Press, 1967.

Feis, Herbert. *1933: Characters in Crisis*. Boston: Little, Brown, 1966.

Fischer, Louis. *Men and Politics*. New York: Duell, Sloan and Pearce, 1941.

———. *Russia's Road from Peace to War*. New York: Harper, 1969.

Forrestal, James V. *The Forrestal Diaries*. New York: Viking, 1951.

Friedlander, Saul. *Prelude to Downfall*. New York: Knopf, 1967.

Gamelin, Maurice G. *Servir*. Paris: Plon, 1946–47.

Gardner, Virginia. *Friend and Lover*, 3 vols. New York: Horizon, 1983.

Gerard, James W. *My Four Years in Germany*. New York: George H. Doran, 1917.

Goerlitz, Walter. *The German General Staff*. New York: Frederick A. Praeger, 1953.

Goldman, Eric. *Rendezvous with Destiny*. New York: Knopf, 1952.

Haight, John McV. *American Aid to France*. New York: Athenaeum, 1970.

Halliday, Ernest M. *The Ignorant Armies*. New York: Harper, 1960.

Hemingway, Ernest. *Selected Letters*. New York: Charles Scribner's Sons, 1981.

Horne, Alistair. *To Lose a Battle: France, 1940*. Boston: Little, Brown, 1969.

Hull, Cordell. *The Memoirs of Cordell Hull*, 2 vols. New York: Macmillan, 1948.

Ickes, Harold L. *The Secret Diaries of Harold L. Ickes*, 3 vols. New York: Simon and Schuster, 1954.

Ingersoll, R. Sturgis. *Reflections at Eighty*. Philadelphia: Lippincott, 1977.

Johnson, Owen. *Stover at Yale*. New York: Grosset and Dunlap, 1912.

Jones, Ernest. *The Life and Work of Sigmund Freud*. New York: Basic Books, 1957.

Jones, Thomas. *A Diary with Letters*. Oxford: Oxford University Press, 1954.

Kaplan, Justin. *Lincoln Steffens*. New York: Simon and Schuster, 1974.

Karnow, Stanley. *Vietnam*. New York: Viking, 1983.

Kennan, George F. *Memoirs*, 2 vols. Boston: Little, Brown, 1967.

Kilbom, Karl. *Memoires*. Stockholm: Tilden, 1954.

Kraft, Barbara S. *The Peace Ship*. New York: Macmillan, 1978.

Langer, William L. *Our Vichy Gamble*. New York: Knopf, 1947.

Lansing, Robert. *War Memoirs*. Indianapolis: Bobbs-Merrill, 1935.

Lash, Joseph P. *Love, Eleanor*. Garden City: Doubleday, 1982.

———. *Roosevelt and Churchill*. New York: Norton, 1976.

Lerner, Max. *Public Journal*. New York: Viking, 1945.

Lindbergh, Charles A. *The Wartime Journals*. New York: Harcourt Brace, 1970.

Lukasiewicz, Juliusz. *Diplomat in Paris*. New York: Columbia University Press, 1970.

Lyons, Eugene. *Assignment in Utopia*. New York: Harcourt Brace, 1937.

Martin, Ralph G. *Cissy: The Extraordinary Life of Eleanor Medill Patterson*. New York: Simon and Schuster, 1979.

Medvedev, Roy. *Let History Judge*. New York: Random House, 1973.

Miller, Nathan. *FDR: An Intimate History*. Garden City: Doubleday, 1983.

Moley, Raymond. *After Seven Years*. New York and London: Harper & Brothers, 1939.

Monnet, Jean. *Memoirs*. Garden City: Doubleday, 1978.

Murphy, Robert. *Diplomat Among Warriors*. New York: Doubleday, 1964.

Paillat, Claude. *The Illusions of the War*. Paris: Robert Laffont, 1979.

Phillips, William. *Memoirs*. Boston: Beacon, 1952.

Ponomarov, B. N., *et al*. *History of the Communist Party of the Soviet Union*. Moscow: Foreign Languages Publishing House, 1960.

Powers, Thomas. *The Man Who Kept the Secrets*. New York: Knopf, 1979.

Reynaud, Paul. *Mémoires—1936–1940*. Paris: Flammarion, 1963.

Roazen, Paul. *Freud and His Followers*. New York: Knopf, 1975.

Roosevelt, Franklin D. *FDR, His Personal Letters—1928–1945*, 3 vols. New York: Duell, Sloan and Pearce, 1950.

Schlesinger, Arthur M., Jr. *A Thousand Days*. Boston: Houghton Mifflin, 1965.

Shirer, William L. *The Collapse of the Third Republic*. New York: Simon and Schuster, 1969.

Slosson, Edward E. *Great American Universities*. New York: Macmillan, 1910.

Steffens, Lincoln. *Autobiography of Lincoln Steffens*. New York: Harcourt Brace, 1931.

Stern, J. David. *Memoirs of a Maverick Publisher*. New York: Simon and Schuster, 1952.

Tansill, Charles C. *Back Door to War*. Chicago: Henry Regnery, 1952.

Taylor, Telford. *Munich: The Price of Peace*. Garden City: Doubleday, 1979.

Thayer, Charles W. *Bears in the Caviar*. Philadelphia: Lippincott, 1951.

Wallace, Henry A. *The Price of Vision*. Boston: Houghton Mifflin, 1973.

Watson, Mark S. *The United States Army in World War II*. Washington D.C.: Department of the Army, 1950.

Wedemeyer, Albert C. *Wedemeyer Reports!* New York: Holt, 1958.

Wehle, Louis B. *Hidden Threads of History*. New York: Macmillan, 1953.

Westerfield, H. Bradford. *Foreign Policy and Party Politics*. New Haven: Yale University Press, 1955.

Whitehead, Don. *The FBI Story*. New York: Random House, 1956.

Widener, Peter A. B. *Without Drums*. New York: G. P. Putnam's Sons, 1940.

Wolf, Edwin, and Whiteman, Maxwell. *The History of the Jews of Philadelphia*. Philadelphia: The Jewish Publication Society of America, 1956.

NOTES

FOREWORD

p. xiii. A treaty "which makes certain future wars, . . .": Beatrice Farnsworth, *William C. Bullitt and the Soviet Union*, 68.

pp. xiii–xiv. ". . . impossible monstrosity . . . the part would be greater than the whole. . . .": William C. Bullitt and Sigmund Freud, *Thomas Woodrow Wilson—A Psychological Study*, vi.

p. xiv. "He knew every European statesman. . . .": *The New York Times*, February 16, 1967.

They made "an ideal team": Louis B. Wehle, *Hidden Threads of History*, 114–115.

French government members "seem to be greatly pleased. . . .": Bullitt to Roosevelt, October 5, 1936, PSF file, B-43, Roosevelt papers, Hyde Park, N.Y.

"Bullitt practically sleeps with the French cabinet.": Harold L. Ickes, *The Secret Diaries of Harold L. Ickes*, Vol. 3, 123–124.

". . . he asks my judgment. . . .": Bullitt to Roosevelt, August 29, 1939, PSF file, B-43, Roosevelt papers, Hyde Park, N.Y.

p. xv. "No American Ambassador in Paris has ever run away from anything. . . .": Bullitt to Roosevelt, May 30, 1940, PSF file, B-43, Roosevelt papers, Hyde Park, N.Y.

"When are we going to say . . .?": *The New York Times*, August 19, 1940.

"For eighteen months I have been doing double time. . . .": Bullitt to George Biddle, November 1, 1941, Biddle papers, Library of Congress.

p. xvi. Hull "considered Welles worse than a murderer": Bullitt memorandum, April 23, 1941, Orville Bullitt, *For the President*, 513.

"Stand where you are. . . .": James McGregor Burns, *Roosevelt: The Soldier of Freedom*, 350.

"We have seen the future. . . .": Lincoln Steffens, *Autobiography*, 799.

"When Germany collapses . . .": Bullitt to Roosevelt, January 29, 1943, PSF file, B-34, Roosevelt papers, Hyde Park, N.Y.

The Bullitt memo "deserves a place among the major historical documents. . . .": George F. Kennan, introduction to *For the President*, xiv.

"The events of 1945 . . .": William C. Bullitt, *The Great Globe Itself*, 26.

CHAPTER I

p. 3. "A career *away* from Philadelphia is out of bounds . . .": Nathaniel Burt, *The Perennial Philadelphians*, 69.

pp. 3–4. "Proper Philadelphia was busy assimilating . . .": Edward Digby Baltzell, *Philadelphia Gentlemen*, 392.

p. 4. "At the very center of town . . .": Burt, *op. cit.*, 193.

p. 5. ". . . a little touch of Jewishness . . .": Burt, *op. cit.*, 65.

. . . Penrose was elected to the state legislature . . . "because of his ability to cultivate . . .": Baltzell, *op. cit.*, 140.

"Since colonial times . . .": Baltzell, *op. cit.*, 38.

p. 6. Samuel Gross . . .: Burt, *op. cit.*, 112–13.

"Philadelphia's gradual decline . . .": Baltzell, *op. cit.*, 90.

Coal: "It has been a dirty business . . .": Burt, *op. cit.*, 199.

"A few far-sighted Philadelphians . . .": Baltzell, *op. cit.*, 105.

p. 7. "Mother lived on the right side of the Market Street tracks.": P. A. B. Widener, *Without Drums*, 10.

p. 10. "The entrance to the place . . .": diary of John C. Bullitt.

p. 11. . . . the Bullitt charter "had been drawn by an expert . . .": *The Autobiography of Lincoln Steffens*, 408.

p. 13. "If Haym Salomon had not escaped . . .": Edwin Wolf and Maxwell Whiteman, *The History of the Jews of Philadelphia*, 101.

p. 14. "Thomas Cooper informed me . . .": ibid., 312.

p. 17. "Greene Towne, which will never be burnt . . .": William Penn in *The Story of Rittenhouse Square*, 9.

p. 19. "My earliest recollection of Bill . . .": R. Sturgis Ingersoll, *Recollections at Eighty*, 77. "I was so excited . . .": Hubert P. Earle, *Blackout*, 113.

CHAPTER II

p. 29. ". . . the professional spirit prevails . . .": Edward E. Slosson, *Great American Universities*, 45–46.

"I'm frankly aristocratic . . .": Owen Johnson, *Stover at Yale*, 27.

p. 30. "There was no fiercer competition . . .": Henry Seidel Canby, *Alma Mater: The Gothic Age of the American College*, 73–74.

p. 33. "I cannot remember a single distinguished figure . . .": letter from John McClenahan to Orville Bullitt, June 2, 1964.

p. 37. . . . the explicit allusions "aroused considerable controversy . . .": Orville Bullitt, *For the President*, 16.

p. 38. "The doctor said that the only thing that might make her eat again . . .": John McClenahan to Orville Bullitt, June 2, 1964.

"There was much rushing to and fro . . .": James W. Gerard, *My Four Years in Germany*, 106–107.

p. 39. "We retreated to Warsaw . . .": John McClenahan to Orville Bullitt, June 2, 1964.

p. 40. Bullitt's grandmother's jewels and what happened to them: from an interview with Anne Bullitt, October 10, 1983.

p. 43. Schwimmer became Hungarian ambassador to Switzerland: report based on FBI internal security investigation, May 27, 1942.

p. 51. "My sister's early ambition . . .": Catherine Drinker Bowen, *Family Portrait*, 130.

p. 54. . . . a "solemn warning . . .": *The New York Times*, January 16, 1916.

pp. 58–59. Bullitt interview with Count Stephen Tisza, premier of Hungary: Edward M. House collection, Yale University Library.

pp. 59–61. Bullitt interview with Gottlieb von Jagow, German foreign secretary: Edward M. House collection, Yale University Library.

p. 63. "He is . . . the sharpest of the American correspondents. . . .": Walter Lippmann, Lippmann papers, Yale University Library.

". . . worse or better Germany . . .": *The New Republic*, October 28, 1916.

p. 65. "Ernesta is very ill . . .": Bullitt to Lippmann, Lippmann papers, Yale.

p. 66. "The German offensive can be stopped . . .": Bullitt to House, January 22, 1917, House collection, Yale.

pp. 67–68. ". . . the Russian 'terror' will far surpass . . .": Robert Lansing, *War Memoirs*, 342.

p. 68. ". . . the Left heard its own words . . .": Bullitt to President Roosevelt, June 1, 1939, PSF file, B–43, FDR Library, Hyde Park, N.Y.

"I wish I could see Russia . . .": Bullitt to House, May 20, 1918. House collection, Yale.

p. 69. ". . . Today we are fighting Great Russia . . .": Bullitt to House, September 20, 1918, House collection, Yale.

p. 70. "The time is rapidly approaching . . .": Bullitt to House, September 12, 1918. House collection, Yale.

"I have just read the President's address . . .": Bullitt to House, September 27, 1918, House collection, Yale.

CHAPTER III

pp. 73–74. "What am I going to get killed for?": Beatrice Farnsworth, *William C. Bullitt and the Soviet Union*, 12–13.

p. 74. "Out of a billion five hundred sixty-five million people . . .": Gordon Brook-Shepherd, *November 1918*, 29.

Ludendorff: Walter Goerlitz, *The German General Staff*, 197.

p. 76. "Everyone is entirely in the dark . . .": Bullitt diary, Yale University Library.

p. 77. "An enormous crowd, dominated by passions . . .": Claude Paillat, *The Illusions of the War*, 39.

p. 80. ". . . to cure him of his Bolshevism . . .": Robert Lansing, *Desk Diary*, February 16, 1919, Lansing papers, Library of Congress.

p. 81. "You are hereby directed to proceed to Russia . . .": Bullitt, *The Bullitt Mission to Russia*, 4.

". . . Bullitt . . . came bouncing up to ask me how I'd like to go to Russia . . .": Lincoln Steffens, *Autobiography*, 791–92.

p. 83. "What differentiates spying from collecting information?": Karl Kilbom, *Memoirs*.

p. 84. "Are you empowered to negotiate?": Steffens, *op. cit.*, 793.

p. 85. Shatov encounter: Steffens, *op. cit.*, 793.

p. 86. "The Red terror is over. . . .": Bullitt, *The Bullitt Mission to Russia*, 58–59.

"There is already a Lenin legend. . . .": Bullitt, *op. cit.*, 63.

p. 87. "They had heard in their village. . . .": Bullitt, *op. cit.*, 63–64.

He ". . . seized the opportunity. . . .": Bullitt, *op. cit.*, 53.

p. 88. "Lenin's proposal meant . . .": *Life*, March 27, 1944.

"You must do your utmost for it . . .": Bullitt to House, March 18, 1919, House collection, Yale.

p. 89. "We can produce such famine. . . .": Bullitt to House, March 17, 1919, House papers, Yale.

Lenin: "When we proposed a treaty to Bullitt . . .": John Silverlight, *The Observer* of London (Orville Bullitt, *For the President*, 9).

p. 90. "It was a disappointing return . . .": Steffens, *op. cit.*, 799.

p. 91. "We had a long discussion . . .": Bullitt before the Senate Committee on Foreign Relations, *The Bullitt Mission to Russia*, 65.

p. 92. "this last beautiful fight on Russia": Bullitt to Walter Lippmann, April 1, 1919, Lippmann papers, Yale.

p. 94. "Some of us had resigned. . . .": Adolf A. Berle, letter to Upton Sinclair, December 27, 1939, Berle papers, Hyde Park, N.Y.

pp. 94–95. "Bullitt was not to be mollified . . .": Steffens, *op. cit.*, 801–802.

p. 95. "I was one of the millions who trusted . . .": Bullitt, *The Bullitt Mission to Russia*, 96–97.

p. 98. "I do not think that Secretary Lansing is at all enthusiastic about the League of Nations . . .": Bullitt, *The Bullitt Mission to Russia*, 102.

p. 99. "I felt sure that I was right about . . . the Treaty of Versailles, . . .": Bullitt, undated memorandum, Orville Bullitt, *For the President*, 13–14.

CHAPTER IV

pp. 103–104. "I see Bill Bullitt, in retrospect . . .": George F. Kennan, introduction to Orville Bullitt, *For the President*, xv–xvi.

p. 104. ". . . handsome, urbane, full of charm and enthusiasm . . .": George F. Kennan, *The New Yorker*, February 25, 1985.

p. 105. ". . . Bill wanted places all over . . .": Orville Horwitz interview, August 28, 1984.

". . . posthumous idealization of John Reed . . .": Virginia Gardner, *Friend and Lover*, 236.

p. 106. "Dear Miss Bryant," letter exhibited by Anne Bullitt in an interview, October 10, 1983.

pp. 107–08. "It is a very difficult thing. . . .": Louise Bryant, an unpublished memoir, Bryant papers, Syracuse University Library, Syracuse, N.Y.

p. 108. "We called on the American Ambassador. . . .": Louise Bryant, "Christmas in Petrograd 1917," Bryant papers, Syracuse, N.Y.

"Russia is wonderful now . . .": Louise Bryant to John and Marguerite Storrs, November 19, 1917.

p. 109. "I am exiled here . . .": Louise Bryant to John and Marguerite Storrs, March 15, 1920, John Storrs collection, Archives of American Art, Washington, D.C.

"Five days before he died . . .": Louise Bryant to Max Eastman, November 14, 1920 (published in the *Liberator*, February 1921).

p. 110. "You may picture me as the lord of the old estate . . .": Bullitt to his brother, Orville, quoted by Gardner, *Friend and Lover*, 241–42.

p. 111. "He settled down to enjoy the wines . . .": Justin Kaplan, *Lincoln Steffens*, 264.

p. 112. "I live a useless life . . .": Gardner, *op. cit.*, 246.

p. 113. "Our little Turk . . .": Bryant to John Storrs, July 1924.

"When Bill began his psychoanalysis . . .": Gardner, *op. cit.*, 248.

p. 114. "He had a very long analysis . . .": Gardner, *op. cit.*, 253.

psychoanalysis of James and Alix Strachey: Paul Roazen, *Freud and his Followers*, 346.

". . . how shocking our country is . . .": Bryant to Storrs, May 26, 1925.

p. 115. "The book aroused considerable controversy . . .": Orville Bullitt, *For the President*, 16.

"She found him awfully hard to take . . .": Gardner, *op. cit.*, 310.

pp. 115–16. Bullitt's affair with Cissy Patterson: Ralph G. Martin, *Cissy*, 217.

p. 117. "Louise seemed perfectly at ease . . .": Gardner, *op. cit.*, 263.

"Louise talked nonstop . . .": ibid.

". . . a big Jew from Yale . . .": Ernest Hemingway, *Selected Letters*, 268.

"I have a feeling we were all rather desperate . . .": Gardner, *op. cit.*, 265.

"I have been quite ill again . . .": Gardner, *op. cit.*, 267.

p. 118. Bullitt-Bryant divorce: Gardner, *op. cit.*, 270–71.

"I have not written . . . because I have been so ill . . .": Gardner, *op. cit.*, 278.

"Once I was playing . . . the *'Unfinished'* Symphony . . .": interview with Anne Bullitt, October 10, 1983.

p. 119. How he weathered the stock market crisis: interview with John Bullitt, September 6, 1983.

"Bill was never rich . . .": Orville Bullitt, *For the President*, xliii.

p. 120. ". . . if you deal with bright people . . .": interview with Orville Horwitz, August 28, 1984.

Bullitt's first encounter with Freud: Gardner, *op. cit.*, 248.

pp. 120–21. "It is a full study of Wilson's life . . .": Ernest Jones, *The Life and Work of Sigmund Freud*, 150–51.

p. 121. "It is interesting to know that your plans . . .": House to Bullitt, July 31, 1930, House collection, Yale.

p. 122. "Tomorrow F and I go to work . . .": Bullitt to House, October 26, 1930, House collection, Yale.

"The book is at last finished . . .": Bullitt to House, April 29, 1932, House collection, Yale.

pp. 123–24. Marian Newhall Horwitz: from interviews with Orville Horwitz.

p. 124. "I should . . . be glad to have you show Roosevelt my letter . . .": Bullitt to House, January 9, 1932, House collection, Yale.

pp. 124–25. "I get many letters from abroad . . .": House to Bullitt, December 28, 1931, House collection, Yale.

p. 125. "Masaryk has invited me to visit him . . .": Bullitt to House, May 27, 1932, House collection, Yale.

p. 126. He would claim outright years later that he had gone to Russia at Roosevelt's request: Bullitt to Milton De Kalb Brogley, University of Wisconsin, December 5, 1947.

"The future American ambassador . . . came to Moscow . . .": Eugene Lyons, *Assignment in Utopia*, 499–500.

p. 127. "Bill Bullitt writes from the Berkshires . . .": George Biddle, *An American Artist's Story*, 253.

"I proposed . . . that he and I formulate the principles . . .": Louis B. Wehle, *Hidden Threads of History*, 113–14.

p. 128. "The Governor said the right things . . .": Bullitt to House, September 17, 1932, House collection, Yale.

"There was a certain community of social background . . .": Wehle, *op. cit.*, 114–15.

p. 129. "There is your man for Paris.": Wehle, *op. cit.*, 119–20.

Bullitt's inquiry to Hanfstaengl about Hitler: John McClenahan to Orville Bullitt, June 2, 1964.

Bullitt's secret mission to Europe: *The New York Times*, January and February, 1933.

p. 130. "Damn near sent you to jail for twenty years, hey, boy?": Jack Alexander, *The Saturday Evening Post*, March 18, 1939.

". . . how genuine was his jovial friendship with Roosevelt . . .": Herbert Feis, *1933: Characters in Crisis*, 104.

p. 131. "He was pleasant, keen-minded, idealistic, and widely informed . . .": Raymond Moley, *After Seven Years*, 136.

"We've been working about twenty hours a day . . .": Bullitt to House, May 13, 1933, House collection, Yale.

p. 132. Bullitt advising Roosevelt that Litvinov had asked about renewed relations: Bullitt to Roosevelt, July 8, 1933, PSF file, B–68, Roosevelt papers, FDR Library, Hyde Park, N.Y.

p. 133. "In some respects we stood to gain more than Russia . . .": Cordell Hull, *Memoirs*, vol. I, 296.

"A Virginian, with the amiable spirit . . .": Feis, *op. cit.*, 308–309.

pp. 133–34. Recognition negotiations: papers of Henry Morgenthau, Jr., FDR Library, Hyde Park, N.Y.; also Bullitt to Hull, October 11, 1933, PSF file, B–68, Roosevelt papers, Hyde Park, N.Y.

pp. 134–35. Correspondence between President Roosevelt and President Kalinin of the Soviet Union: PSF file, B–67, Roosevelt papers, Hyde Park, N.Y.

p. 136. Settlement of debt questions: Robert F. Kelley memorandum, July 1933.

"Restless and mercurial in his thinking . . .": Eric Goldman, *Rendezvous with Destiny*, 324.

p. 137. "I think we were a bit too gentle with him, . . .": Bullitt to Roosevelt, November 15, 1933, PSF file, B–68, Roosevelt papers, Hyde Park, N.Y.

p. 138. "In fact, Bullitt was not ideal for the Russian post . . .": Beatrice Farnsworth, *William C. Bullitt and the Soviet Union*, 109.

House to Bullitt, November 18, 1933; Bullitt to House, November 22, 1933: House collection, Yale.

CHAPTER V

p. 141. "I think you know what a joy it is . . .": Bullitt to Roosevelt, December 6, 1933, PSF file, B–68, Roosevelt papers, Hyde Park, N.Y.

"Bullitt is a striking man . . .": Kennan, *The New Yorker*, February 25, 1985.

p. 142. "As the old American friend of new Russia . . .": Janet Flanner, "An American in Paris," *The New Yorker*, December 18, 1938.

pp. 143–44. Bullitt's reception in Moscow: Bullitt to the Department of State, December 24, 1933 and January 1 and 4, 1934, PSF file, B–68, Roosevelt papers, Hyde Park, N.Y.

p. 145. "Litvinov's entire preoccupation . . .": Bullitt to Hull, January 1, 1934, PSF file, B–68, Roosevelt papers, Hyde Park, N.Y.

". . . the Russians . . . played upon his weakness . . .": Farnsworth, *op. cit.*, 109–10.

p. 146. "Bullitt . . . had come with high hopes and enormous enthusiasm . . .": Kennan, *Memoirs: 1950–1963*, 119–20.

p. 147. "[Roosevelt] attached little importance to these particular issues . . .": Kennan, *Memoirs: 1925–1950*, 56–57.

p. 148. "Soviet partnership with America against Japan was Stalin's hope . . .": Louis Fischer, *Russia's Road from Peace to War*, 219.

"a man of great appeal . . .": Charles E. Bohlen, *Witness to History*, 15.

p. 150. "It was a Russian Victorian pomposity . . .": Orville Bullitt, *For the President*, 80.

pp. 150–51. ". . . the first months witnessed a confusion . . . a struggle full of hilarity and good spirits . . .": Kennan, *Memoirs: 1925–1950*, 63–64.

p. 152. A trip to famine-ravaged villages: Charles W. Thayer, *Bears in the Caviar*, 67–68.

p. 153. "He had been in the Ukraine . . .": interview with Elbridge Durbrow, December 6, 1983.

"I miss Washington . . .": Bullitt to R. Walton Moore, March 29, 1934, Group 55, Box 3, Moore papers, FDR Library, Hyde Park, N.Y.

p. 154. "I am deeply sorry . . .": Bullitt to Roosevelt, May 18, 1934, PSF file, Roosevelt papers, Hyde Park, N.Y.

"It is now quite apparent that Litvinov . . .": Moore to Bullitt, April 10, 1934, Moore papers, Hyde Park, N.Y.

p. 155. ". . . oral promises . . . are not to be taken seriously": Bullitt to Hull, March 28, 1934, PSF file, B–67, Roosevelt papers, Hyde Park, N.Y.

p. 156. ". . . the categorical refusal of the Soviet Government . . .": Bullitt to Department of State, June 4, 1935.

p. 157. Lolya Lepishinkaya, a "tame Russian": Durbrow interview, December 6, 1983.

pp. 157–58. Incident at picnic in the park: Anne Bullitt interview, October 10, 1983.

p. 158. "We are staggering along here . . .": Bullitt to Moore, June 14, 1934, Moore papers, Hyde Park, N.Y.

pp. 159–60. "My first long flight in the airplane . . .": Bullitt to Moore, June 14, 1934, Moore papers, Hyde Park, N.Y.

p. 160. "I am a little late in telling you . . .": Roosevelt to Bullitt, August 14, 1934, PSF file, B–67, Roosevelt papers, Hyde Park, N.Y.

"I have no copy here . . .": Bullitt to Moore, June 19, 1934, Moore papers, Hyde Park, N.Y.

pp. 160–61. "The President felt that this was not necessary . . .": Bullitt to Department of State, July 17, 1934, PSF file, B–67, Roosevelt papers, Hyde Park, N.Y.

p. 161. "There was a complete breakdown . . .": Moore to Francis B. Sayre, assistant secretary of state, July 19, 1934, *Foreign Relations of the United States: The Soviet Union, 1933–39*. Washington: U.S. Government Printing Office, 1952, 119.

"I added that if his position. . . . insoluble.": Bullitt to Department of State, March 21, 1934, PSF file, B–34, Roosevelt papers, Hyde Park, N.Y.

". . . the big water jump . . .": Bullitt to Moore, May 4, 1934, Moore papers, Hyde Park, N.Y.

p. 162. "The nub of the matter is this . . .": Bullitt to Department of State, May 21, 1934, PSF file, B–67, Roosevelt papers, Hyde Park, N.Y.

Litvinov counteroffer: Bullitt to Department of State, April 2, 1934, PSF file, B–68, Roosevelt papers, Hyde Park, N.Y.

". . . wholly unacceptable . . .": Hull to Bullitt, April 5, 1934.

pp. 162–63. "I had a completely unsatisfactory discussion with Litvinov . . .": Bullitt to Department of State, April 8, 1934, PSF file, B–68, Roosevelt papers, Hyde Park, N.Y.

p. 163. "If the U.S.S.R. asserted counter-claims . . .": Moore to Bullitt, May 15, 1934, Moore papers, Hyde Park, N.Y.

"Was the basic disagreement touched upon . . .": Bullitt to Department of State, May 2, 1934, PSF file, B–68, Roosevelt papers, Hyde Park, N.Y.

"The answer . . . is in the negative . . .": Hull to Bullitt, May 3, 1934, PSF file, B–67, Roosevelt papers, Hyde Park, N.Y.

p. 164. "I have just spent a most unsatisfactory hour with Litvinov . . .": Bullitt to Department of State, June 16, 1934, PSF file, B–68, Roosevelt papers, Hyde Park, N.Y.

p. 165. "I venture to suggest . . .": Bullitt to Department of State, September 13, 1934, PSF file, B–68, Roosevelt papers, Hyde Park, N.Y.

Skvirsky proposal: Bullitt to Department of State, September 15, 1934, PSF file, B–68, Roosevelt papers, Hyde Park, N.Y.

"Considering that Litvinov . . . made no objection . . .": Hull to Bullitt, September 17, 1934, PSF file, B–68, Roosevelt papers, Hyde Park, N.Y.

p. 166. "Litvinov . . . accompanied me to the first polo match . . .": Bullitt to Department of State, July 27, 1934, PSF file, B–68, Roosevelt papers, Hyde Park, N.Y.

Bullitt regarded as not serious: Louis Fischer, *Men and Politics*, 303.

p. 167. "Stalin was not sincere . . .": Roy Medvedev, *Let History Judge*, 309.

"In the course of a very long . . . conversation . . .": Bullitt to Department of State, July 27, 1934, PSF file, B–68, Roosevelt papers, Hyde Park, N.Y.

"Stalin would not support Litvinov's refusal . . .": Bullitt to Department of State, September 9, 1934, PSF file, B–68, Roosevelt papers, Hyde Park, N.Y.

pp. 167–68. "There can be no objection to your talking with Stalin . . .": Hull to Bullitt, September 15, 1934, PSF file, B–68, Roosevelt papers, Hyde Park, N.Y.

p. 168. "Oh, it will be worked out some way.": *Complete Presidential Press Conferences of Franklin Delano Roosevelt*, Vol. 4, 88–92, September 26, 1934.

"I then got up to leave . . .": Bullitt to Department of State, October 10, 1934, PSF file, B–68, Roosevelt papers, Hyde Park, N.Y.

pp. 169–70. "My first impression of Bullitt . . .": diary of J. Graham Parsons, embassy officer in Tokyo in 1934.

p. 170. Bullitt's report on meetings with Chiang Kai-shek: Bullitt to Department of State, December 14, 1934, PSF file, B–43, Roosevelt papers, Hyde Park, N.Y.; also Orville Bullitt, *For the President*, 100.

pp. 170–71. Bullitt-Morgenthau telephone conversation, December 21, 1934: Morgenthau papers, Hyde Park, N.Y.

p. 171. "Troyanovsky . . . rejected my proposal . . .": Hull to John C. Wiley, January 31, 1935, PSF file, B–68, Roosevelt papers, Hyde Park, N.Y.

p. 172. "Litvinov said that he had long since accepted . . .": Wiley to Department of State, February 5, 1935, Wiley papers, FDR Library, Hyde Park, N.Y.

"I have carefully avoided going to the Quai d'Orsay . . .": Bullitt to Moore, April 7, 1935, Moore papers, Hyde Park, N.Y.

p. 174. "Litvinov then said . . .": Bullitt to Department of State, May 16, 1935, PSF file, B–67, Roosevelt papers, Hyde Park, N.Y.

"However, he does only an irreducible minimum of work . . .": Bullitt to Moore, April 25, 1935, Moore papers, Hyde Park, N.Y.

p. 175. ". . . an astonishingly successful party . . .": Bullitt to Roosevelt, May 1, 1935, PSF file, B–68, Roosevelt papers, Hyde Park, N.Y.

Scene at Spaso House: Charles W. Thayer, *Bears in the Caviar*, 156–64.

pp. 175–76. George Andreytchine: Bullitt to Roosevelt, April 13, 1934, May 1, 1935, PSF file, B–68, Roosevelt papers, Hyde Park, N.Y.; Roosevelt to Bullitt, May 21, 1934, PSF file, B–68, Roosevelt papers, Hyde Park, N.Y.

pp. 176–77. "So many wild stories . . . about my illness . . .": Bullitt to Moore, June 2, 1935, Moore papers, Hyde Park, N.Y.

p. 177. Kennan and the letter of Neill S. Brown: Carroll Kilpatrick, "An American in Russia: 1850," *The Virginia Quarterly Review*, Spring 1952.

"I went on to say . . .": Bullitt to Department of State, October 8, 1934, PSF file, B–67, Roosevelt papers, Hyde Park, N.Y.

p. 178. Bullitt contacted by Louis Fischer: Bullitt to Department of State, July 2, 1935, PSF file, B–67, Roosevelt papers, Hyde Park, N.Y.

"At this moment . . .": Bullitt to Moore, July 15, 1935, Moore papers, Hyde Park, N.Y.

Thayer incident in Odessa: Durbrow interview, December 6, 1983.

p. 179. Radek and the issue of the Comintern: Bullitt to Moore, July 15, 1935, Moore papers, Hyde Park, N.Y.

p. 180. ". . . would like to have your recommendations . . .": Hull to Bullitt, August 19, 1935, PSF file, B–68, Roosevelt papers, Hyde Park, N.Y.

Such a break "would satisfy the indignation . . .": Bullitt to Hull, August 21, 1935, PSF file, B–68, Roosevelt papers, Hyde Park, N.Y.

"The President and I feel that it is necessary to make a formal written protest . . .": Hull to Bullitt, August 23, 1935, PSF file, B–67, Roosevelt papers, Hyde Park, N.Y.

pp. 180–81. "I handed our note of protest . . .": Bullitt to Department of State, August 25, 1935, PSF file, B–67, Roosevelt papers, Hyde Park, N.Y.

p. 181. "Touching the suggested protest to the Soviet . . .": Moore to Bullitt, August 27, 1935, Moore papers, Hyde Park, N.Y.

Soviet-American relations "inevitably will be extremely distant and frigid . . .": Bullitt to Moore, August 30, 1935, Moore papers, Hyde Park, N.Y.

p. 182. "Ragusa remains surrounded . . .": Bullitt to Moore, October 2, 1935, Moore papers, Hyde Park, N.Y.

"Kelly and I lunched with Litvinov alone today . . .": Bullitt to Department of State, November 9, 1935, PSF file, B–67, Roosevelt papers, Hyde Park, N.Y.

p. 183. "He met the American correspondents every day . . .": Louis Fischer, *Men and Politics*, 308.

"His remarks about Russia were directly contrary . . .": William E. Dodd, *Ambassador Dodd's Diary*, 277–78.

"I was delighted to know. . . . shambles.": Bullitt to Moore, November 9, 1935, Moore papers, Hyde Park, N.Y.

pp. 183–84. "War in Europe is regarded as inevitable . . .": Bullitt to Department of State, July 19, 1935, PSF file, B–68, Roosevelt papers, Hyde Park, N.Y.

p. 184. "I saw Litvinov yesterday . . .": Bullitt to Moore, February 22, 1936, Moore papers, Hyde Park, N.Y.

Stalin "evaded the issue . . .": Bullitt to Department of State, March 1, 1936, PSF file, B–43, Roosevelt papers, Hyde Park, N.Y.

pp. 184–85. "Stalin considers it sound strategy . . .": Bullitt to Department of State, April 20, 1936, PSF file, B–43, Roosevelt papers, Hyde Park, N.Y.

p. 185. ". . . an astonishingly loathsome Jew . . .": Bullitt to Moore, February 22, 1936, Moore papers, Hyde Park, N.Y.

"Russia is a good country for pine trees . . .": Bullitt to Moore, March 30, 1936, Moore papers, Hyde Park, N.Y.

"Of course, I am ready to go anywhere . . .": Bullitt to Moore, April 8, 1936, Moore papers, Hyde Park, N.Y.

"I know how anxious you are to have some definite work . . .": Roosevelt to Bullitt, April 21, 1936, PSF file, B–43, Roosevelt papers, Hyde Park, N.Y.

pp. 185–86. "I shall plan to leave here on May 15 . . .": Bullitt to Moore, May 9, 1936, Moore papers, Hyde Park, N.Y.

p. 186. "Mr. Bullitt told me. . . ." J. Edgar Hoover memorandum, Don Whitehead, *The FBI Story*, 160–61.

CHAPTER VI

p. 189. "I always expected to be Ambassador to France.": Columbia University Oral History, William Adams Delano transcript, 64.

Resignation of Jesse I. Straus: Robert K. Straus, letter to Brownell, December 30, 1983.

"I was, of course, distressed . . .": Bullitt to Moore, October 5, 1936, Moore papers, Hyde Park, N.Y.

"I didn't have anything to say . . .": Bullitt to Roosevelt, October 5, 1936, PSF file, B–43, Roosevelt papers, Hyde Park, N.Y.

"Bullitt will be popular in Paris . . .": *L'Europe Nouvelle*, October 17, 1936.

p. 190. "Damnit! That's just like Franklin.": Columbia University Oral History, James A. Farley transcript.

pp. 190–91. The country was in a sorry state: William L. Shirer, *The Collapse of the Third Republic*, 296–98.

p. 191. "I got away to a good start with Blum.": Bullitt to Roosevelt, October 24, 1936, PSF file, B–43, Roosevelt papers, Hyde Park, N.Y.

Thwarting aid to the Spanish Republicans: Thomas Jones, *A Diary with Letters*, 210–11.

"Bullitt practically sleeps with the French cabinet.": Harold L. Ickes, *The Secret Diaries of Harold L. Ickes*, vol. 3, 123–24.

"If he erred . . .": Robert Murphy, *Diplomat Among Warriors*, 32.

p. 192. "Bullitt was closer than anyone . . .": James A. Farley, *Jim Farley's Story*, 194.

"Blum came personally . . .": Bullitt to Roosevelt, November 8, 1936, PSF file, B–43, Roosevelt papers, Hyde Park, N.Y.

"Bullitt dispatched couriers throughout Europe. . . .": James A. Farley, *Jim Farley's Story*, 194.

"I wish you would . . . get Ray Atherton . . .": Bullitt to Roosevelt, October 24, 1936, PSF file, B–43, Roosevelt papers, Hyde Park, N.Y.

p. 193. "Blum wants to reach an understanding with Germany . . .": Bullitt to Roosevelt, October 24, 1936, PSF file, B–43, Roosevelt papers, Hyde Park, N.Y.

"There is no feeling of crisis . . .": Bullitt to Roosevelt, November 8, 1936, PSF file, B–43, Roosevelt papers, Hyde Park, N.Y.

p. 194. "When Dodd leaves Berlin . . .": Bullitt to Roosevelt, November 8, 1936, PSF file, B–43, Roosevelt papers, Hyde Park, N.Y.

". . . the policy of Great Britain is to keep the continent of Europe divided . . .": Bullitt to Hull, April 30, 1937, *Foreign Relations of the United States, 1937*, vol. 1, 84–86.

p. 195. "In all this intellectual chaos and impending doom . . .": Bullitt to Roosevelt, November 24, 1936, PSF file, B–43, Roosevelt papers, Hyde Park, N.Y.

"I rather agree. . . .": Adolf A. Berle, *Navigating the Rapids*, 320.

"Liking the dramatic side of foreign affairs . . .": Cordell Hull, *Memoirs*, vol. 1, 790.

"the sort of house that was built . . .": Bullitt to Moore, November 8, 1936, Moore papers, Hyde Park, N.Y.

p. 196. "We shall . . . have to stop . . . entertaining visiting firemen.": Bullitt to Moore, November 8, 1936, Moore papers, Hyde Park, N.Y.

". . . obligatory speeches that I have to make.": Bullitt to Roosevelt, November 8, 1936, PSF file, B–43, Roosevelt papers, Hyde Park, N.Y.

"Everyone in France, including Blum . . .": Bullitt to Roosevelt, November 24, 1936, PSF file, B–43, Roosevelt papers, Hyde Park, N.Y.

pp. 196–97. ". . . the President is not a god . . .": Bullitt to Moore, November 29, 1936, Moore papers, Hyde Park, N.Y.

p. 197. "Czechoslovakia, clearly, . . .": Bullitt to Roosevelt, November 24, 1936, PSF file, B–43, Roosevelt papers, Hyde Park, N.Y.

Blum's hope for "reconciliation with Germany": Bullitt to Roosevelt, December 7, 1936, PSF file, B–43, Roosevelt papers, Hyde Park, N.Y.

An effort to disparage Ambassador Dodd: *ibid*.

The "new element" of aerial bombardment: Bullitt to Roosevelt, December 20, 1936, PSF file, B–43, Roosevelt papers, Hyde Park, N.Y.

p. 198. "Your mother is in tremendous form . . .": Bullitt to Roosevelt, September 7, 1937, PSF file, B–43, Roosevelt papers, Hyde Park, N.Y.

"There is increasing evidence . . .": Bullitt to Moore, January 8, 1937, Moore papers, Hyde Park, N.Y.

"I have been disgusted for many years . . .": Bullitt to Roosevelt, December 8, 1936, PSF file, B–43, Roosevelt papers, Hyde Park, N.Y.

p. 199. British aim to keep France and Germany from reaching an understanding: Bullitt to Roosevelt, May 28, 1937, PSF file, B–43, Roosevelt papers, Hyde Park, N.Y.

p. 200. "It is my honest opinion . . .": Bullitt to Moore, November 29, 1936, Moore papers, Hyde Park N.Y.

Polish threat to the Bolsheviks: Maurice Gamelin, *Servir*, vol. 2, 230.

p. 201. "Blum said that Litvinov had assured him . . .": Bullitt to Hull, May 20, 1937, *Foreign Relations of the United States, 1937*, vol. 1, 94.

Condition of the French economy: Shirer, *op. cit.*, 321.

p. 202. The French found Bullitt "witty, ingratiating and genuinely friendly. . . .": Jack Alexander, *The Saturday Evening Post*, March 11, 1939.

pp. 202–03. "I have found the pleasantest country place in France . . .": Bullitt to Roosevelt, May 28, 1937, PSF file, B–43, Roosevelt papers, Hyde Park, N.Y.

p. 203. "The latest inside information . . .": Roosevelt to Bullitt, August 5, 1937, PSF file, B–43, Roosevelt papers, Hyde Park, N.Y.

"If it were not for Chantilly . . .": Hubert P. Earle, *Blackout*, 111.

Ernest Hemingway, a guest at Chantilly: Anne Bullitt, October 10, 1983.

". . . he turned somersaults on the lawn!" Bullitt to Roosevelt, July 23, 1937, PSF file, B–43, Roosevelt papers, Hyde Park, N.Y.

"a jellyfish with lots of common sense": Bullitt to Roosevelt, October 24, 1936, PSF file, B–43, Roosevelt papers, Hyde Park, N.Y.

"I had a conversation with Chautemps this afternoon . . .": Bullitt to Department of State, July 2, 1937, *Foreign Relations of the United States, 1937*, vol. 1, 347–48.

p. 204. "Delbos and Blum are more or less in despair . . .": Bullitt to Roosevelt, May 10, 1937, PSF file, B–43, Roosevelt papers, Hyde Park, N.Y.

p. 204. "Paris has become a madhouse . . .": Bullitt to Roosevelt, May 28, 1937, PSF file, B–43, Hyde Park, N.Y. (Shakespeare quotation, "It's poor picking between rotten apples," varies slightly from original in *The Taming of the Shrew*, Act I, Scene 1: "There's small choice in rotten apples.")

Burdens "almost intolerable": Bullitt to Moore, June 2, 1937, Moore papers, Hyde Park, N.Y.

Praise for Hillenkoetter: Bullitt to Moore, July 5, 1937, Moore papers, Hyde Park, N.Y.

". . . I will accept no invitations . . .": Bullitt to Moore, *ibid*.

p. 205. Impressions of the Windsors: Bullitt to Roosevelt, November 4, 1937, PSF file, B–43, Roosevelt papers, Hyde Park, N.Y. Report of a romance between Bullitt and the Duchess of Windsor is from an interview in 1984 with Eleanor Davies Ditzen, the daughter of Joseph E. Davies.

"I am delighted with my appointment . . .": Arthur Bliss Lane to Bullitt, July 14, 1937, Yale University Library.

p. 206. "It is high time we were represented by a gentleman . . .": Bullitt to Moore, November 24, 1937, Moore papers, Hyde Park, N.Y.

Bullitt hearing rumor that Joseph Davies was seeking his job: Bullitt to Moore, November 24, 1937, Hyde Park, N.Y.

"Davies to Brussels was a stroke of genius . . .": Bullitt to Roosevelt, January 10, 1938, PSF file, B–43, Roosevelt papers, Hyde Park, N.Y.

pp. 206–07. Criticizing Dodd for his anti-German attitude: Bullitt to Roosevelt, November 23, 1937, PSF file, B–43, Roosevelt papers, Hyde Park, N.Y.

p. 207. "I cannot tell you how delighted . . .": Bullitt to Roosevelt, December 7, 1937, PSF file, B–43, Roosevelt papers, Hyde Park, N.Y.

"I am convinced you won't have Moore long . . .": Bullitt to Roosevelt, November 3, 1937, PSF file, B–43, Roosevelt papers, Hyde Park, N.Y.

"He seems to have been shelved completely . . .": Bullitt to Roosevelt, January 10, 1938, PSF file, B–43, Roosevelt papers, Hyde Park, N.Y.

"The three days at Nîmes were really grand . . .": Bullitt to Roosevelt, November 3, 1937, PSF file, B–43, Roosevelt papers, Hyde Park, N.Y.

"It is a good sonnet . . .": Roosevelt to Bullitt, November 11, 1937, PSF file, B–43, Roosevelt papers, Hyde Park, N.Y.

pp. 207–08. "I talked with Norman Davies . . .": Bullitt to Roosevelt, November 2, 1937, PSF file, B–43, Roosevelt papers, Hyde Park, N.Y.

p. 208. "Colonel Beck stated to me . . .": Bullitt to Department of State, *Foreign Relations of the United States, 1937*, vol. I, 162–63.

pp. 208–09. "You will remember . . .": Bullitt to Roosevelt, November 23, 1937, PSF file, B–43, Roosevelt papers, Hyde Park, N.Y.

p. 209. "Goering said . . . there was not direct conflict . . .": Bullitt to Department of State, *Foreign Relations of the United States*, *1937*, vol. I, 170–74.

pp. 209–10. "The atmosphere in Berlin today . . .": Bullitt to Roosevelt, November 23, 1937, PSF file, B–43, Roosevelt papers, Hyde Park, N.Y.

pp. 210–11. ". . . that the United States, Great Britain and France . . .": Bullitt to Roosevelt, December 7, 1937, PSF file, B–43, Roosevelt papers, Hyde Park, N.Y.

p. 211. ". . . completely run down and should have a vacation . . .": Carmel Offie to Missy LeHand. December 3, 1937, PSF file, B–43, Roosevelt papers, Hyde Park, N.Y.

"Orders duly received . . .": Bullitt to Roosevelt, January 10, 1938, PSF file, B–43, Roosevelt papers, Hyde Park, N.Y.

pp. 211–12. Events in Europe: Shirer, *op. cit.*, 331n.

p. 212. The foreign office was . . . "prepared to go to any limit": Edwin Wilson, chargé d'affaires in Paris, to Department of State, March 14, 1938, *Foreign Relations of the United States, 1938*, vol. I, general. Washington: U.S. Government Printing Office, 1955, 35–36, 483.

". . . if a reasonable attitude was assumed . . .": von Ribbentrop to Hitler, March 10, 1938, *Documents on German Foreign Policy, 1918–1945*, Series D (1937–1945), vol. I, 268–69.

"When I asked [San Quentin] . . .": Bullitt to Roosevelt, January 10, 1938, PSF file, B–43, Roosevelt papers, Hyde Park, N.Y.

p. 213. "I could scarcely hear what you said . . .": Bullitt to Roosevelt, February 25, 1938, PSF file, B–43, Roosevelt papers, Hyde Park, N.Y.

Bullitt candidacy vetoed: Alexander, *The Saturday Evening Post*, March 11, 1939.

Rescue of Freud from Vienna: Ernest Jones, *The Life and Work of Sigmund Freud*, 220, 226–27.

"We may have a complete blow-up . . .": Bullitt to the Department of State, April 24, 1938, PSF file, B–43, Roosevelt papers, Hyde Park, N.Y.

p. 214. "Call to the White House . . .": Bullitt to Roosevelt, May 20, 1938, PSF file, B–43, Roosevelt papers, Hyde Park, N.Y.

"Bullitt further advised . . .": Bullitt to Roosevelt, May 21, 1938, PSF file, B–43, Roosevelt papers, Hyde Park, N.Y.

"The French General Staff estimates . . .": Bullitt to Roosevelt, May 12, 1938, PSF file, B–43, Roosevelt papers, Hyde Park, N.Y.

p. 215. "Here at Chantilly . . .": Bullitt to Roosevelt, June 13, 1938, PSF file, B–43, Roosevelt papers, Hyde Park, N.Y.

"May God . . . prove that you are wrong.": Roosevelt to Bullitt, June 25, 1938, PSF file, B–43, Roosevelt papers, Hyde Park, N.Y.

pp. 215–16. German armored warfare strategy: Alistair Horne, *To Lose a Battle*, 34–36, 47–51, 71–72, 133, 182–84.

p. 216. "The impression I gathered . . .": Bullitt to Department of State, *Foreign Relations of the United States, 1938*, vol. 1, 509.

p. 216. "He knows that if he grants autonomy now to the Sudeten Germans . . .": Bullitt to Roosevelt, June 13, 1938, PSF file, B–43, Roosevelt papers, Hyde Park, N.Y.

pp. 217–18. Bonnet "being pressed extremely hard by the Spanish government . . .": Bullitt to Department of State, PSF file, B–43, Roosevelt papers, Hyde Park, N.Y.

p. 218. A "very private letter, which requires no answer . . .": Bullitt to Roosevelt, June 21, 1938, PSF file, B–43, Roosevelt papers, Hyde Park, N.Y.

pp. 218–19. "I have never been much angrier in my life . . .": Bullitt to Roosevelt, June 14, 1938, PSF file, B–43, Roosevelt papers, Hyde Park, N.Y.

p. 219. "but Sumner tells me . . .": Roosevelt to Bullitt, June 15, 1938, PSF file, B–43, Roosevelt papers, Hyde Park, N.Y.

"The President has now let me know . . .": Bullitt to Hull, June 30, 1938, PSF file, B–43, Roosevelt papers, Hyde Park, N.Y.

"I don't know whose diseased brain . . .": Bullitt to Roosevelt, June 30, 1938, PSF file, B–43, Roosevelt papers, Hyde Park, N.Y.

"the greatest Bolshevik lover at large . . .": Bullitt to Roosevelt, November 23, 1937, PSF file, B–43, Roosevelt papers, Hyde Park, N.Y.

p. 220. "Both Daladier and Bonnet fought the Treaty of Versailles . . .": Bullitt to Department of State, September 15, 1938, *Foreign Relations of the United States, 1938*, vol. 1, 601.

"Daladier said to me yesterday . . .": Bullitt to Department of State, June 23, 1938, *Foreign Relations of the United States, 1938*, vol. 1, 526.

"He is inclined to believe that the dispute is unsolvable . . .": Bullitt to Department of State, July 18, 1938, *Foreign Relations of the United States, 1938*, vol. 1, 533.

pp. 220–21. "I am living at Chantilly altogether . . .": Bullitt to Moore, July 19, 1938, Moore papers, Hyde Park, N.Y.

p. 221. "The French government is now convinced . . .": Bullitt to Roosevelt, August 17, 1938, PSF file, B–43, Roosevelt papers, Hyde Park, N.Y.

". . . the Germans have one million eight hundred thousand men mobilized . . .": Bullitt to Roosevelt, August 31, 1938, PSF file, B–43, Roosevelt papers, Hyde Park, N.Y.

The French "would order immediate mobilization . . .": Bullitt to Department of State, September 8, 1938, *Foreign Relations of the United States, 1938*, vol. 1, 581.

Lindbergh estimate of German air power: Wayne S. Cole, *Charles A. Lindbergh and the Battle Against American Intervention in World War II*, 52.

Reaction in France to the meeting at Berchtesgaden: *Foreign Relations of the United States, 1938*, vol. 1, 600.

"If you have enough airplanes . . .": Bullitt to Roosevelt, September 20, 1938, PSF file, B–43, Roosevelt papers, Hyde Park, N.Y.

pp. 221–22. "Bill Bullitt just telephoned . . .": Bullitt message relayed to Roosevelt, September 23, 1938, PSF file, B–43, Roosevelt papers, Hyde Park, N.Y.

p. 222. Urging an appeal to the chiefs of state: Bullitt to Department of State, September 24, 1938, *Foreign Relations of the United States, 1938*, vol. 1, 642.

"My own thought was . . .": Cordell Hull, *Memoirs*, vol. 1, 590–91.

Roosevelt message to Hitler, September 26, 1938: *Foreign Relations of the United States, 1938*, vol. 1, 658.

"I am so delighted this evening . . .": Bullitt to Roosevelt, September 28, 1938, PSF file, B–43, Roosevelt papers, Hyde Park, N.Y.

"In itself the Munich Agreement . . .": Telford Taylor, *Munich: The Price of Peace*, xiii.

p. 223. "If I had three or four thousand aircraft . . .": Jean Monnet, *Memoirs*, 590–91.

"Munich threw Bullitt and Daladier . . . together . . .": Gordon Wright, "Ambassador Bullitt and the Fall of France," *World Politics*, October 1957, 66.

pp. 223–24. "If war should begin . . .": Bullitt to Roosevelt, September 28, 1938, PSF file,

B–43, Roosevelt papers, Hyde Park, N.Y.

pp. 224–25. The effect of Bullitt's argument: Mark S. Watson, *The United States Army in World War II*, 131–32.

p. 225. Morgenthau's opposition to Bullitt's plan: John McV. Haight, *American Aid to France*, 30.

pp. 225–26. Bullitt and Monnet to Washington to meet with Morgenthau: Morgenthau diary, October 26, 1938, Morgenthau papers, Hyde Park, N.Y.

p. 226. "I have the greatest hope . . .": Bullitt to Guy La Chambre, French air minister, Haight, *op. cit.*, 35.

Cochran report to Morgenthau, November 17, 1938: Haight , *op. cit.*, 37.

p. 227. "They want a thousand planes . . .": Morgenthau staff conference, December 20, 1938, Haight, *op. cit.*, 37.

"Ambassador Bullitt sat at the President's side . . .": Haight, *op. cit.*, 84–85, 91–92.

p. 228. The crash of the Douglas DB–7: Haight, *op. cit.*, 84–92.

pp. 228–29. Senate hearings: Haight, *op. cit.*, 93–96.

p. 229. "The American public knew little of the amazing Bullitt . . .": *Newsweek*, April 24, 1939.

p. 230. "It is difficult to exaggerate the salutary effect . . .": Bullitt to Roosevelt, February 3, 1939, PSF file, B–43, Roosevelt papers, Hyde Park, N.Y.

Asserting that a way must be found to circumvent the Johnson Act: Bullitt to Department of State, February 13, 1939, PSF file, B–43, Roosevelt papers, Hyde Park, N.Y.

Using Bao Dai as an intermediary: Bullitt to Roosevelt, February 23, 1939, PSF file, B–43, Roosevelt papers, Hyde Park, N.Y.

Reynaud plan to pay French war debt: Bullitt to Roosevelt, February 22, 1939, PSF file, B–43, Roosevelt papers, Hyde Park, N.Y.

p. 231. Joseph Alsop and Robert Kintner: "The Great World Money Play," *The Saturday Evening Post*, April 8, 1939.

"The American government has been made contemptible . . .": Bullitt to Roosevelt, April 3, 1939, PSF file, B–43, Roosevelt papers, Hyde Park, N.Y.

"Don't have Henry the Morgue in on your first conversation . . .": Bullitt to Roosevelt, April 4, 1939, PSF file, B–43, Roosevelt papers, Hyde Park, N.Y.

p. 231. ". . . Hitler's invasion of Czechoslovakia stunned . . . all Frenchmen . . .": Bullitt to Department of State, March 17, 1939, PSF file, B–43, Roosevelt papers, Hyde Park, N.Y.

pp. 231–32. "Hitler's invasion . . . produced a curious result . . .": Bullitt to Roosevelt, March 23, 1939, PSF file, B–43, Roosevelt papers, Hyde Park, N.Y.

p. 232. "My feeling that we had to say a word for human decency . . .": Bullitt to Roosevelt, March 18, 1939, PSF file, B–43, Roosevelt papers, Hyde Park, N.Y.

"Both Daladier and Paul Reynaud are convinced . . .": Bullitt to Roosevelt, April 4, 1939, PSF file, B–43, Roosevelt papers, Hyde Park, N.Y.

"I hope to God that the Neutrality Act will be altered . . .": Bullitt to Moore, May 19, 1939, Moore papers, Hyde Park, N.Y.

"The fact is if war starts . . .": Bullitt to Moore, August 9, 1939, Moore papers, Hyde Park, N.Y.

p. 233. "the most ruthless adversary of Hitler": Saul Friedlander, *Prelude to Downfall*, 74.

"My guess is that by this time . . .": Bullitt to Roosevelt, March 18, 1939, PSF file, B–43, Roosevelt papers, Hyde Park, N.Y.

"The only great army on the side of decency . . .": Bullitt to Roosevelt, March 23, 1939, PSF file, B–43, Roosevelt papers, Hyde Park, N.Y.

"Of course the British foreign office . . .": Ickes, *op. cit.*, vol. 2, 602.

"We recognize complex world problems. . . .": Roosevelt to Hitler, April 14, 1939, *Foreign Relations of the United States, 1939*, vol. 1, 133.

pp. 233–34. The reaction of Léger to Hitler speech: *Foreign Relations of the United States, 1939*, vol. 1, 159–60.

p. 234. "Daladier dined with me alone tonight . . .": Bullitt to Department of State, April 28, 1939, *Foreign Relations of the United States, 1939*, vol. 1, 177.

"For the Poles . . .": Juliusz Lukasiewicz, *Diplomat in Paris*, 182–83, 185.

"the Germans were pouring soldiers into Danzig . . .": Bullitt to Department of State, June 28, 1939, *Foreign Relations of the United States, 1939*, vol. 1, 194–95, 202.

p. 235. "Between ourselves . . .": Bullitt to Moore, April 25, 1939, Moore papers, Hyde Park, N.Y.

"He seems to have zigzagged between gloom and hope . . .": Wright, *op. cit.*, p. 80.

pp. 235–36. "Bullitt's intense anti-Sovietism now took second place . . .": *ibid.*

p. 236. Britain's "dilatory and almost insulting" approach to the Soviet Union: Charles C. Tansill, *Back Door to War*, 528–29.

"The only low news from Paris this week . . .": Bullitt to Roosevelt, May 9, 1939, PSF file, B–43, Roosevelt papers, Hyde Park, N.Y.

pp. 236–37. "Amid the bayings and barks . . .": Bullitt to Roosevelt, April 19, 1939, PSF file, B–43, Roosevelt papers, Hyde Park, N.Y.

p. 237. "I saw your mother this morning . . .": Bullitt to Roosevelt, August 16, 1939, PSF file, B–43, Roosevelt papers, Hyde Park, N.Y.

"I told your mother . . .": Bullitt to Roosevelt, August 24, 1939, PSF file, B–43, Roosevelt papers, Hyde Park, N.Y.

Warning from Berlin: interview with Jacob Beam, June 28, 1984.

"Daladier lunched with me today . . .": Bullitt to Department of State, August 25, 1939, *Foreign Relations of the United States, 1939*, vol. 1, 365.

Conversation with Bonnet: Bullitt to Hull, August 26, 1939, PSF file, B–43, Hyde Park, N.Y.

p. 238. "Never has any nation . . .": Bullitt to Hull, August 25, 1939, PSF file, B–43, Roosevelt papers, Hyde Park, N.Y.

"I have seen Daladier constantly and intimately . . .": Bullitt to Roosevelt, August 29, 1939, PSF file, B–43, Roosevelt papers, Hyde Park, N.Y.

"The moment I recognized the President's voice . . .": Hull, *op. cit.*, vol. 1, 671–72.

p. 239. "The British Government has just announced that a state of war will exist . . .": Bullitt to Department of State, September 3, 1939, *Foreign Relations of the United States, 1939*, vol. 1, 415.

"The Ambassador lifted his eyes . . .": Earle, *Blackout*, 206–07.

"Thus far, in France . . .": Bullitt to Roosevelt, September 8, 1939, PSF file, B–43, Roosevelt papers, Hyde Park, N.Y.

p. 240. Daladier's disgust with Chamberlain: Bullitt to Roosevelt, September 13, 1939, PSF file, B–43, Roosevelt papers, Hyde Park, N.Y.

"I enclose herewith a document . . .": Bullitt to Roosevelt, September 13, 1939, PSF file, B–43, Roosevelt papers, Hyde Park, N.Y.

"Tell the delightful gentleman . . .": Roosevelt to Bullitt, September 28, 1939, PSF file, B–43, Roosevelt papers, Hyde Park, N.Y.

"The bombardments of France would be so terrible . . .": Bullitt to Roosevelt, September 16, 1939, PSF file, B–43, Roosevelt papers, Hyde Park, N.Y.

"My work here has nearly ended . . .": Bullitt to Roosevelt, September 8, 1939, PSF file, B–43, Roosevelt papers, Hyde Park, N.Y.

p. 241. "Bullitt was probably the best brain . . .": James P. Warburg, Columbia University Oral History, Warburg transcript, 232.

"We were convinced that the Poles would not stand up . . .": Beam interview, June 28, 1984.

"The Polish Ambassador in Paris . . .": Bullitt to Department of State, September 17, 1939, PSF file, B–43, Roosevelt papers, Hyde Park, N.Y.

p. 242. "Since the French certainly will not violate Belgian neutrality . . .": Bullitt to Department of State, September 20, 1939: *Foreign Relations of the United States, 1939*, vol. 1, 445.

"The game is lost. France stands alone . . .": Bullitt to Department of State, September 30, 1939, quoting Léger: *Foreign Relations of the United States, 1939*, vol. 1, 460.

"a large enough finger in all of this . . .": Bullitt to Roosevelt, October 4, 1939, PSF file, B–43, Roosevelt papers, Hyde Park, N.Y.

"There is not the slightest chance . . .": Bullitt to Department of State, October 6, 1939, *Foreign Relations of the United States, 1939*, vol. 1, 504.

"Everyone . . . is expecting a major German attack . . .": Bullitt to Roosevelt, October 18, 1939, PSF file, B–43, Roosevelt papers, Hyde Park, N.Y.

p. 243. Military status report; political advice; plea for a cabinet post: Bullitt to Roosevelt, November 1, 1939, PSF file, B–43, Roosevelt papers, Hyde Park, N.Y.

p. 244. "ashamed to go to anyone in the Foreign Office . . .": Bullitt to Roosevelt, November 15, 1939, PSF file, B–43, Roosevelt papers, Hyde Park, N.Y.

The planes must come from America, Daladier declared: State Department document 851.248/296, November 23, 1939.

"We both feel certain that it would be a mistake . . .": Roosevelt to Bullitt, November 23, 1939, PSF file, B–43, Roosevelt papers, Hyde Park, N.Y.

p. 245. Daladier "repeated what I have communicated . . .": Bullitt to Roosevelt, December 11, 1939, PSF file, B–43, Roosevelt papers, Hyde Park, N.Y.

Daladier "was absolutely convinced . . .": Bullitt to Department of State, December 21, 1939, PSF file, B–43, Roosevelt papers, Hyde Park, N.Y.

"Daladier is asking us to assume greater responsibility . . .": Hull to Bullitt, December 22, 1939, PSF file, B–43, Roosevelt papers, Hyde Park, N.Y.

"I replied to Bullitt . . .": Hull, *op. cit.*, vol. 1, 710.

pp. 246–47. "At least the food would be good. . . . The moral is: Eat oysters!": Bullitt to Roosevelt, December 19, 1939, PSF file, B–43, Roosevelt papers, Hyde Park, N.Y.

p. 247. "Please pat God . . . on the bald spot . . .": Bullitt to Missy LeHand, January 30, 1940, PSF file, B–43, Roosevelt papers, Hyde Park, N.Y.

"At the dinner table, Mr. Roosevelt collapsed . . .": Orville Bullitt, *For the President*, 398.

"Early Saturday morning Bill Bullitt called up . . .": Ickes, *op. cit.*, vol. 3, 132–33, 136.

p. 248. ". . . I am very thankful to you . . .": Bullitt to Roosevelt, March 20, 1940, PSF file, B–43, Roosevelt papers, Hyde Park, N.Y.

"Bill Bullitt had questioned me about this move . . .": Ickes, *op. cit.*, vol. 3, 138. Bullitt-Kennedy row: Ickes, *op. cit.*, vol. 3, 147.

Dinner for Archduke Otto of Hapsburg: Ickes, *op. cit.*, vol. 3, 148–49.

pp. 248–49. "I had hoped the repercussions . . .": Bullitt to Roosevelt, April 18, 1940, PSF file, B–43, Roosevelt papers, Hyde Park, N.Y.

p. 249. ". . . never ceased his attacks on Welles . . .": Joseph P. Lash, *Roosevelt and Churchill*, 91–92.

Two men who "were among the State Department's most brilliant . . .": Murphy, *op. cit.*, 35.

". . . I haven't been asked . . . about the German White Book . . .": Bullitt to Roosevelt, April 12, 1940, PSF file, B–43, Roosevelt papers, Hyde Park, N.Y.

"He is sailing with a whole 'trunk' full of instructions . . .": report of Jerzy Potocki in German White Book, 32.

p. 250. "Daladier's idea was that the Germans might continue to attack you . . .": Bullitt to Roosevelt, April 12, 1940, PSF file, B–43, Roosevelt papers, Hyde Park, N.Y.

"He [Kennedy] said the reports of the Polish Ambassador . . .": Charles A. Lindbergh, *The Wartime Journals*, 420.

"I asked him about his conversations with Roosevelt . . .": James V. Forrestal, *The Forrestal Diaries*, 121–22.

Furor over the German White Book did not die down: J. Edgar Hoover to Edwin M. Watson, secretary to the president, August 7, 1940; *The Washington Evening Star*, March 11, 1941.

pp. 250–51. "It is too bad . . .": Bullitt to Moore, April 18, 1940, Moore papers, Hyde Park, N.Y.

p. 251. "Both Reynaud and Daladier expect defeat in Norway to produce . . .": Bullitt to Roosevelt, April 28, 1940, PSF file, B–43, Roosevelt papers, Hyde Park, N.Y.

"I am on the end of a long limb . . .": Bullitt to Moore, April 18, 1940, Moore papers, Hyde Park, N.Y.

"It seems obvious . . .": Bullitt to Roosevelt, May 15, 1940, Shirer, *op. cit.*, 680.

"The Germans had crossed the Meuse . . .": Bullitt to Hull, May 15, 1940, *Foreign Relations of the United States, 1940*, vol 1, 220–21.

p. 252. Bullitt . . . continued to plead for military aid: *Foreign Relations of the United States, 1940*, vol. 1, 221, 223–24, 230.

"In harbouring any anticipation . . .": Alistair Horne, *To Lose a Battle*, 641, 641n.

"The French Government was deeply and profoundly grateful to you . . .": Bullitt to Roosevelt and Hull, May 18, 1940, *Foreign Relations of the United States, 1940*, vol. 1, 236–38.

p. 253. "He said that the reaction . . .": *ibid.*

"The British and French troops . . . today displayed a heroism . . .": Bullitt to Department of State, PSF file, B–43, Roosevelt papers, Hyde Park, N.Y.

"This may be the last letter . . .": Bullitt to Roosevelt, May 30, 1940, PSF file, B–43, Roosevelt papers, Hyde Park, N.Y.

p. 254. "No American Ambassador in Paris has ever run away . . .": *ibid.*

"I have no compunctions . . .": Bullitt to Roosevelt, June 7, 1940, PSF file, B–43, Roosevelt papers, Hyde Park, N.Y.

"I believe that if we had sent the Atlantic fleet . . .": Bullitt to Hull, May 31, 1940, Orville Bullitt, *op. cit.*, 445–46.

"I am sorry you keep referring to the Atlantic fleet . . .": Roosevelt to Bullitt, May 31, 1940, PSF file, B–43, Roosevelt papers, Hyde Park, N.Y.

p. 255. "We were having sherry and biscuits . . .": Bullitt to Department of State, June 3, 1940, PSF file, B–43, Roosevelt papers, Hyde Park, N.Y.

Bullitt's meeting with Pétain: *Foreign Relations of the United States, 1940*, vol. 1, 238–40.

"Reynaud was enormously pleased . . .": Bullitt to Roosevelt, June 5, 1940, Orville Bullitt, *op. cit.*, 451.

"Two weeks ago this general was a colonel in the tank corps . . .": Bullitt to Roosevelt, June 5, 1940, *ibid.*, 452.

pp. 255–56. "The people of France deserve better . . .": Bullitt to Roosevelt, June 6, 1940, PSF file, B–43, Roosevelt papers, Hyde Park, N.Y.

p. 256. Request for submachine guns: Bullitt to Hull, June 8, 1940, PSF file, B–43, Roosevelt papers, Hyde Park, N.Y.

"Bullitt's hysteria about Communism . . .": Shirer, *op. cit.*, 456, 681–82.

"What really distinguished, noble and admirable persons . . .": Bullitt quoting Reynaud, to Hull, June 10, 1940, *Foreign Relations of the United States, 1940*, vol. 1, 244.

"He said that it had been decided . . .": Bullitt to Roosevelt, June 9, 1940, PSF file, B–43, Roosevelt papers, Hyde Park, N.Y.

p. 257. "I consider it highly desirable . . .": Roosevelt to Bullitt, June 9, 1940, PSF file, B–43, Roosevelt papers, Hyde Park, N.Y.

"It is strongly recommended . . .": Hull to Bullitt, June 11, 1940, PSF file, B–43, Roosevelt papers, Hyde Park, N.Y.

"My deepest personal reason . . .": Bullitt to Hull, June 12, 1940, PSF file, B–43, Roosevelt papers, Hyde Park, N.Y.

"Please keep this for me . . .": Bullitt to Roosevelt, June 11, 1940, PSF file, B–43, Roosevelt papers, Hyde Park, N.Y.

"I supposed that the United States ambassador was bringing some encouragement . . .": Charles de Gaulle, *The War Memoirs*, 61.

pp. 257–58. "I remember an evening with you in the White House . . .": Bullitt to Roosevelt, June 12, 1940, PSF file, B–43, Roosevelt papers, Hyde Park, N.Y.

p. 258. "It was on Wednesday that the German Army . . .": Ickes, *op. cit.*, vol. 3, 209.

"I said I . . . thought our Ambassador should go with the French Government . . .": Hull, *op. cit.*, vol. 1, 790–91.

pp. 258–59. Bullitt message to Berlin: "Paris has been declared an open city. . . .": Orville Bullitt, *For the President*, 471.

p. 259. Negotiating the surrender of Paris, June 13–14, 1940: William L. Shirer, *The Collapse of the Third Republic*, 776–79; Robert Murphy, *Diplomat Among Warriors*, 45.

"You have no doubt received full particulars . . .": Kennedy to Hull, June 12, 1940, *Foreign Relations of the United States, 1940*, vol. 1, 247–48.

"Reynaud told Churchill . . .": Kennedy to Hull, June 14, 1940, *ibid.*

". . . this Government is doing everything . . .": Roosevelt to Reynaud, June 13, 1940, *ibid.*, 248.

pp. 259–60. ". . . France would make peace unless . . .": Reynaud to Washington, *ibid.*

Roosevelt's message to Reynaud was "not to be published": Hull to Kennedy, June 13, 1940, *ibid.*

p. 260. ". . . the French government is now faced with two alternatives . . .": Biddle to Hull, June 15, 1940, *ibid.*, 256–57.

"I said that I assumed . . . a French government would continue to fight from other shores . . .": Biddle to Hull, June 16, 1940, *ibid.*, 261.

"He was calm and entirely himself again . . .": Biddle to Hull, June 16, 1940, *ibid.*

"No one can say . . .": Hull, *op. cit.*, 791.

p. 261. "one of his most important . . . dispatches . . .": Kennan, introduction to *For the President*, xi.

"The impression which emerges . . .": Bullitt to Roosevelt and Hull, July 1, 1940, Orville Bullitt *op. cit.*, 481–87.

p. 262. "Pétain recognizes that only a defeat of Hitler . . .": Bullitt to Hull, July 5, 1940, Orville Bullitt, *op. cit.*, 488–89.

"At five o'clock in the evening on July 10 . . .": Bullitt to Hull, July 13, 1930, PSF file, B–43, Roosevelt papers, Hyde Park, N.Y.

"Both Blum and Reynaud had the courage . . .": Bullitt to Hull, July 13, 1940, Orville Bullitt, *op. cit.*, 491–92.

Incident at the Spanish border: Anne Bullitt interview, October 10, 1983.

CHAPTER VII

p. 265. Observations of James P. Warburg: Columbia University Oral History, Warburg transcript, 232.

p. 266. "Marshal Pétain is universally respected in France . . .": *The New York Times*, July 21, 1940.

p. 267. "I cannot understand Bill's attitude . . .": Ickes, *The Secret Diaries*, vol. 3, 277.

"How well do you know Billy Bullitt?" Frances B. Biddle, *In Brief Authority*, 135.

"Well, Russia is recognized, Bullitt goes as ambassador . . .": Joseph P. Lash, *Love, Eleanor*, 172.

"The one real romance of her life . . .": Nathan Miller, *FDR*, 213n.

p. 268. "Bill entered into the life of the camp . . .": Charles Stanwood, in an unpublished history of Camp Pasquaney.

pp. 268–69. "America is in danger . . .": *The New York Times*, August 19, 1940.

p. 269. ". . . ask not what your country will do for you . . .": Arthur M. Schlesinger, Jr., *A Thousand Days*, 4–5.

pp. 269–70. Bullitt denounced in Congress: *The New York Times*, August 20, 1940.

p. 270. "But he did not . . .": *Life*, August 30, 1948.

"He has no status in Washington . . .": Ickes, *op. cit.*, vol. 3, 343–44.

pp. 270–71. "Jane and I had lunch . . .": Ickes, *op. cit.*, vol. 3, 369–70.

p. 271. "Resignation not accepted . . .": Roosevelt to Bullitt, November 9, 1940, PSF file, B–43, Roosevelt papers, Hyde Park, N.Y.

pp. 271–72. "I thought you said . . .": Bullitt memorandum, November 9, 1940, Orville Bullitt, *For the President*, 505–06.

p. 272. "Bill Bullitt drove out to see me yesterday . . .": Ickes, *op. cit.*, vol. 3, 374.

"It was a joy to see you in such fine form . . .": Bullitt to Roosevelt, December 28, 1940, Orville Bullitt, *op. cit.*, 509.

"Your letter of resignation . . . is before me . . .": Roosevelt to Bullitt, Orville Bullitt, *op. cit.*, 510.

p. 273. Lend-lease debate in Congress: *The New York Times*, March 2, 1941.

"that stroke of political genius . . .": *Life*, August 30, 1948.

p. 274. "For the first time in our history. . . .": Address by Bullitt before the International Relations Club of the University of North Carolina, January 7, 1941, Morgenthau Diaries, Hyde Park, N.Y.

p. 275. "If the Germans . . .": *The New York Times*, February 19, 1941.

"If we were fully aware of the danger that threatens us . . .": *The New York Times*, February 28, 1941.

". . . the Nazis alone . . . aim to establish . . .": *Life*, April 21, 1941.

pp. 275–76. "Bill Bullitt called up . . .": Ickes, *op. cit.*, vol. 3, 486–87.

p. 276. "Bill told him just how he felt . . .": Ickes, *op. cit.*, vol. 3, 538–39.

Debutante party for Anne Bullitt: *The New York Times*, June 13, 1941.

pp. 276–77. "Anne would please you . . .": Bullitt to George Biddle, October 13, 1941, Biddle papers, Library of Congress.

p. 277. "He did not like intellectual women." Anne Bullitt interview, October 10, 1983.

"Here indeed were the experts . . .": R. Sturgis Ingersoll, *Reflections at Eighty*, 78.

"I called Bill Bullitt . . .": Ickes, *op. cit.*, vol. 3, 550.

pp. 277–78. ". . . the German attack . . . makes it essential . . .": Bullitt to Roosevelt, July 1, 1941, PSF file, B–43, Roosevelt papers, Hyde Park, N.Y.

p. 278. "The wrongness of Bullitt's predictions . . .": Lash, *Roosevelt and Churchill*, 444.

". . . Davies stood virtually alone . . .": Richard H. Ullman, "The Davies Mission and United States-Soviet Relations, 1937–1941." *World Politics*, January 1957, 238–39.

". . . [W]hen the President was urged . . .": *Life*, August 30, 1948.

p. 279. Signing of the Atlantic Charter: *The New York Times*, August 15, 1941.

"The President and the Prime Minister feared . . .": Bullitt, *The Great Globe Itself*, 16.

"The grim truth is . . .": *The New York Times*, August 15, 1941.

"We are going to war . . .": *The New York Times*, October 24, 1941.

pp. 279–80. John Cudahy: Ernest Halliday. *The Ignorant Armies*, 212–13.

p. 280. America First rally in New York: *The New York Times*, October 31, 1941.

"Bill Bullitt came in . . .": Ickes, *op. cit.*, vol. 3, 615–16.

pp. 280–81. "For eighteen months I have been going double time . . .": Bullitt to George Biddle, November 1, 1941, Biddle papers, Library of Congress.

p. 281. "The idea of an American operation against North Africa . . .": William L. Langer, *Our Vichy Gamble*, 285.

"Don't let Churchill get you into any more specific engagements . . .": Bullitt to Roosevelt, December 5, 1941, Orville Bullitt, *op. cit.*, 531.

"I hope . . . you will see the Generalissimo . . .": Roosevelt to Bullitt, December 2, 1941, *ibid.*

"I have been forbidden . . .": *ibid.*, 532.

"as a keen judge and analyst . . .": *The New York Times*, November 26, 1941.

pp. 281–82. "The British are handling the situation here . . .": Bullitt to Roosevelt, December 21, 1941, PSF file, B–34, Roosevelt papers, Hyde Park, N.Y.

p. 282. "I returned to Cairo . . .": Bullitt to Roosevelt, December 27, 1941, PSF file, B–34, Roosevelt papers, Hyde Park, N.Y.

"Catroux put the minimum force necessary . . .": Bullitt to Roosevelt, December 31, 1941, PSF file, B–34, Roosevelt papers, Hyde Park, N.Y.

p. 283. Bullitt at the front: *The New York Times*, February 1, 1942.

"I find that almost everyone concerned . . .": Bullitt to Roosevelt, March 13, 1941, Orville Bullitt, *op. cit.*, 548–49.

"The urgency of Ambassador Bullitt's concern . . .": Marshall to Roosevelt, March 18, 1942, Orville Bullitt, *op cit*, 550.

p. 284. "He [Roosevelt] said that I made him feel . . .": Bullitt memorandum, April 8, 1942, Orville Bullitt, *op. cit.*, 551–53.

"When I saw you . . . in St. John's Church . . .": Bullitt to Roosevelt, March 4, 1942, *ibid.*, 548.

"Bullitt is a vivid kind of person . . .": Henry A. Wallace, *The Price of Vision*, 61–62.

p. 285. "We are headed . . . for certain defeat . . .": Francis B. Biddle to Roosevelt, February 23, 1942, Orville Bullitt, *op. cit.*, 547–48.

"You and Tony should know. . . .": Roosevelt to Mrs. Anthony J. D. Biddle, March 13, 1942, *FDR, His Personal Letters—1928–1945*, 1296.

State labor leaders "want me and say . . .": Bullitt to Roosevelt, February 21, 1942, *ibid.*, 546–47.

"I am in a quandary . . .": Bullitt to Roosevelt, March 26, 1942, PSF file, B–43, Roosevelt papers, Hyde Park, N.Y.

"To do nothing to help defeat . . .": Bullitt to Roosevelt, April 20, 1942, PSF file, B–43, Roosevelt papers, Hyde Park, N.Y.

"Mrs. McLean said Bill Bullitt was busted . . .": Henry A. Wallace diary, April 2, 1942, Columbia University Oral History, Wallace transcript, 1476.

p. 286. "I didn't suppose the world held anyone . . .": Ralph G. Martin, *Cissy*, 217.

"Bill is living in Offie's house . . .": Wallace diary, May 21, 1942, *op. cit.*, 1592.

Theft of Anne Bullitt's jewels: FBI memorandum, A. Rosen to E. A. Tamm, September 7, 1944.

"This moment has come something . . .": Roosevelt to Bullitt, June 17, 1942, PSF file, B–34, Roosevelt papers, Hyde Park, N.Y.

"For this reason . . . I cannot accept . . .": Bullitt to Roosevelt, June 18, 1942, PSF file, B–34, Roosevelt papers, Hyde Park, N.Y.

p. 287. "I want to let you know . . .": Bullitt to Henry Morgenthau by telephone, June 23, 1942, Morgenthau diaries, Hyde Park, N.Y.

". . . I know you will do a grand job . . .": Roosevelt to Bullitt, June 22, 1942, OF file, B–799, Roosevelt papers, Hyde Park, N.Y.

"The duties of Mr. Bullitt's office . . .": *The New York Times*, June 24, 1942.

"President Roosevelt's special envoy . . .": *The New York Times*, August 12, 1942.

"My old friend, Bill Bullitt . . .": Roosevelt to Churchill, Orville Bullitt, *op. cit.*, 559.

pp. 287–88. "The whole picture was now so mixed up . . .": Bullitt memorandum, August 1942, Orville Bullitt, *op. cit.*, 559–61.

p. 288. "When Bullitt came around, Winant would sound off . . .": interview with Jacob Beam, June 28, 1984.

"Winant said that when Bill Bullitt was in England . . .": Wallace diary, February 1943, *op. cit.*, 1592.

"This French official stated further . . .": General Eisenhower to G–2, August 19, 1942, Eisenhower papers, Abilene, Kansas.

"Well, it's set for November": Beam interview, June 28, 1984.

Bullitt to Ireland and U.S.: *The New York Times*, August 16 and 21, 1942.

pp. 288–89. Bullitt report on German submarine strength: papers of Henry L. Stimson, Yale University Library.

p. 289. "He predicted with startling accuracy . . .": Kennan, introduction to *For the President*, xiv.

pp. 289–91. "It is as serious a document as I have ever sent you . . .": Bullitt to Roosevelt, January 29, 1943, PSF file, B–34, Roosevelt papers, Hyde Park, N.Y.

p. 291. "I told Bill . . .": Wallace, *The Price of Vision*, 171–73.

pp. 291–92. The basic Allied strategy . . . "to hold Japan in check . . .": Bullitt to Roosevelt, May 12, 1943, Orville Bullitt, *op. cit.*, 591–94.

p. 292. ". . . let no one suggest that we British . . .": Churchill to join session of Congress, May 19, 1943.

"The author . . . does not serve the purposes of his country.": Secretary of War Stimson quoted by Drew Pearson, *The Washington Post*, June 16, 1943.

"whether or not you ever wrote . . .": Bullitt to Stimson, June 16, 1943, Stimson papers, Yale.

"I did not challenge your patriotism . . .": Stimson to Bullitt, June 17, 1943, Stimson papers, Yale.

"I'm not a fellow who cuts relationships . . .": Felix Frankfurter by telephone to Stimson, June 16, 1943, Stimson papers, Yale.

p. 293. "Bill, I don't dispute. . . . I'm going to play my hunch.": *Life*, August 30, 1948.

"Bullitt wanted Welles's job. . . .": Grace Tully in a telephone interview with Will Brownell, 1977.

"Apparently, Mr. Welles has won his fight . . .": Moore to Bullitt, April 20, 1937, Moore papers, Hyde Park, N.Y.

p. 294. "Hull came to distrust Welles . . .": Biddle, *In Brief Authority*, 182.

pp. 294–95. "I . . . said to the President that Judge Moore . . .": Bullitt memorandum, April 23, 1941, Orville Bullitt, *op. cit.*, 512–14.

p. 295. "I told the President . . . the sum and substance . . .": J. Edgar Hoover, FBI report, January 30, 1941.

p. 296. ". . . the President had received reports that I had talked . . .": Bullitt memorandum, May 5, 1943, Orville Bullitt, *op. cit.*, 514–15.

"In the late spring of 1942 . . .": Hull, *Memoirs*, vol. 2, 1227–31.

pp. 296–97. "Since talking with you the other day . . .": Welles to Roosevelt, August 16, 1943, PSF file, B–96, Roosevelt papers, Hyde Park, N.Y.

p. 297. "He said Bullitt had just been there. . . .": Adolf A. Berle, *Navigating the Rapids*, 829.

"He said Bill Bullitt was perfectly terrible . . .": Wallace, *The Price of Vision*, 383.

Bullitt's explanation of his break with Roosevelt: FBI report, November 13, 1953.

p. 298. "Eggpated William Christian Bullitt . . . tossed his top hat . . .": *Time*, July 17, 1943.

Pictorial report on Philadelphia blight: *Life*, October 18, 1943.

"Philadelphians are not proud of their sewers . . .": *The New York Times*, October 31, 1943.

pp. 298–99. "Who *Is* William C. Bullitt?": pamphlet published by the Republican Central Campaign Committee of Philadelphia, PSF file, B–34, Roosevelt papers, Hyde Park, N.Y.

pp. 299–300. "I think that pamphlet . . . is a mass of falsehoods . . .": Roosevelt to J. David Stern, October 29, 1943, PSF file, B–34, Roosevelt papers, Hyde Park, N.Y.

p. 300. "but his aristocratic appearance . . .": J. David Stern, *Memoirs of a Maverick Publisher*, 269.

". . . the way I had acted in the Welles affair . . .": Bullitt memorandum, February 1, 1944, Orville Bullitt, *op. cit.*, 602.

pp. 300–01. "I . . . asked Cordell what the substance of his conversation had been with the President . . .": Bullitt memorandum, March 11, 1944, Orville Bullitt, *op. cit.*, 603–04

p. 301. "So Sumner Welles was dropped . . .": interview with Clare Boothe Luce, November 1976.

"My God, George, you and I and Bill Bullitt . . .": James V. Forrestal to George H. Earle, May 1944, Albert C. Wedemeyer, *Wedemeyer Reports!*, 417.

Earle and the von Papen plot: Wedemeyer, *op. cit.*, 416–17.

p. 302. "I wonder now if I might not be acceptable for active military duty . . .": Bullitt to Stimson, May 1, 1944, Stimson papers, Yale.

Wondering if his request had "gone astray": Bullitt to Stimson, May 12, 1944, Stimson papers, Yale.

"I am very sorry to say . . .": Stimson to Bullitt, May 18, 1944, Stimson papers, Yale.

"Come now! Good and dear American friend . . .": Charles de Gaulle to Bullitt, May 25, 1944, Orville Bullitt, *op. cit.*, 604–05.

"I am off . . . for a small adventure . . .": Bullitt to George Biddle, undated.

"The chances are that France will become a democratic republic . . .": *Life*, August 14, 1944.

p. 303. "What is that picture as seen from Rome? . . .": *Life*, September 4, 1944.

". . . it is the first time . . .": Max Lerner, *Public Journal*, 286.

p. 304. "I am in Paris on a mission . . .": Bullitt to Orville Bullitt, October 14, 1944, Orville Bullitt, *op. cit.*, 606–07.

"We have been cold and dirty for three weeks . . .": Bullitt to Orville Bullitt, December 13, 1944, Orville Bullitt, *op. cit.*, 609.

"The Boches are still fighting like tigers . . .": Bullitt to Orville Bullitt, December 18, 1944, Orville Bullitt, *op. cit.*, 610.

p. 305. "I saw Mr. Roosevelt for the last time . . .": Carmel Offie to Orville Bullitt, February 1945, Orville Bullitt, *op. cit.*, 611.

"The result was that after about nine days . . .": Bullitt to Orville Bullitt, February 20, 1945, Orville Bullitt, *op. cit.*, 612–13.

p. 306. "I think that for the former Ambassador . . .": Orville Bullitt, *op. cit.*, 614.

Clifford learning of Bullitt's reputation for coveting other men's jobs: telephone interview with George Elsey, August 1984.

"Power was in the hands of the people . . .": Bullitt, *The Great Globe Itself*, 151–52.

pp. 306–07. "The weary President was on the verge of thrombosis . . .": Bullitt, *op. cit.*, 24.

p. 307. "He died before the actions of the Soviet Government . . .": Bullitt, *op. cit.*, 26.

"After the next World War . . . there may be no after.": Bullitt, *op. cit.*, vii.

Parable of the human race destroyed: Bullitt, *op. cit.*, v.

"inadequate and not sufficient to inspire confidence . . .": *The New York Times*, July 21, 1946.

"naively hysterical . . .": *The New York Herald Tribune*, July 16, 1946.

Bullitt . . . was lambasted . . .: *The Nation*, October 12, 1946.

The book was called "reckless": *Commonweal*, August 9, 1946.

". . . so gross are the distortions . . .": *The Weekly Book Review*, July 14, 1946.

"Bullitt, who knows the score . . .": *The Saturday Review*, July 13, 1946.

p. 308. ". . . I had a very interesting luncheon with Bill Bullitt . . .": Wallace, *The Price of Vision*, 546–48.

"My back has been absolutely hellish . . .": Bullitt to Orville Horwitz, April 5, 1946, Horwitz medical file, Philadelphia.

X rays showed "a definite dislocation": Horwitz to Bullitt, June 27, 1946, Horwitz medical file.

pp. 308–09. Diagnosis of leukemia: interview with Orville Horwitz, July 26, 1983.

p. 309. Truman Doctrine: President Truman, message to Congress, March 12, 1946.

". . . I do not think in terms of doctrines . . .": Kennan, *Memoirs: 1925–1950*, 364.

". . .[the atomic bomb] would already have been dropped. . . .": hearings before the House Committee on Un-American Activities, March 24, 1947; reported in *The New York Times*, March 25, 1947.

p. 310. "Bullitt looked bewildered . . .": interview with Allen Grover, August 5, 1984.

". . . [A]ll the power that Stalin's international machine can muster . . .": *Life*, June 2, 1947.

p. 311. "striving to reduce China to the status of a satellite . . .": *Life*, October 13, 1947.

pp. 311–12. Bullitt denounced by Vyshinsky: *The New York Times*, September 27, 1947.

p. 312. "the opening gun in the . . . assault . . .": H. Bradford Westerfield, *Foreign Policy and Party Politics*, 261.

Telegram calling for aid to China: *The New York Times*, November 30, 1947.

Protesting Lippmann column: *The New York Herald Tribune*, December 10, 1947.

Testifying as China lobbyist: *The New York Times*, December 18, 1947.

"Marshall . . . is still blocking . . .": Bullitt to Louis Wehle, March 13, 1948, Wehle papers, Roosevelt Library, Hyde Park, N.Y.

pp. 312–13. "Not one in a hundred Annamites is a Communist . . .": *Life*, December 29, 1947.

p. 313. "To avoid bloodshed, I renounced the throne . . .": *Time*, October 6, 1947.

pp. 313–14. ". . . Bao Dai was meeting with William Bullitt in Switzerland . . .": Philippe Devillers, *Histoire du Vietnam de 1940 à 1952*, 453n.

p. 314. Pignon "foresaw that the Communist . . .": Stanley Karnow, *Vietnam*, 175.

"What they call a Bao Dai solution . . .": *ibid*.

"They will tell you . . . that he hates the French . . .": Alexander Werth, *The Nation*, May 13, 1950.

CHAPTER VIII

p. 317. "You step today onto a field of battle . . .": Georgetown University commencement address, June 9, 1947.

p. 318. Bullitt's warning that Alger Hiss was a Communist: FBI report, October 7, 1949; *The New York Times*, December 14, 1949.

"I think we began falling down a long time ago . . .": Georgetown University Forum, April 20, 1952.

p. 319. "Tell him Mrs. Adams is ill.": notation on an invitation, March 7, 1953.

"When the Soviet Government offers peace and friendship . . .": *Vital Speeches of the Day*, May 1953, 532.

"We all want to end the American casualties . . .": *The Reader's Digest*, September 1953.

p. 320. "We are in mortal peril . . .": *Look*, August 24, 1954.

"Today in Europe as well as Asia . . .": Bullitt to Eisenhower, Eisenhower papers, Abilene, Kansas.

p. 321. "He just would not abide anything less . . .": interview with Orville Horwitz, August 28, 1984.

"Radford really admired Bill . . .": *ibid*.

p. 322. "I have now tried out that belt . . .": Bullitt to Dr. Harrison McLaughlin, September 4, 1954, Horwitz medical file.

"Many thanks for taking on William Bullitt . . .": Dr. McLaughlin to Dr. Preston Wade, March 22, 1955, Horwitz medical file.

". . . his spleen became enlarged . . .": Dr. Horwitz to Dr. Dwight Dill, October 27, 1959, Horwitz medical file.

"I am hopeful that we will again have . . . a good remission . . .": Dr. John W. Frost to Dr. Horwitz, March 5, 1960.

p. 323. "In the spring of 1932 . . .": from the foreword, *Thomas Woodrow Wilson—A Psychological Study*.

"I'll tear the damn thing up before I give it away . . .": Horwitz interview, August 28, 1984.

p. 324. "My sister Anna Freud and myself feel . . .": Ernst Freud to Houghton Mifflin, August 25, 1965.

"She respects him a great deal. . . .": Alick Bartholomew of Houghton Mifflin, memorandum, October 14, 1965.

p. 326. "I feel that under the circumstances . . .": Ernst Freud to Houghton Mifflin, July 18, 1966.

p. 327. "I cannot see that we are any closer . . .": Benjamin C. Tilghman of Houghton Mifflin, memorandum, November 9, 1966.

pp. 327–28. Excerpts from the Bullitt-Freud book: *Look*, December 13, 1966.

pp. 328–29. "Certainly, it does not describe the Wilson I knew . . .": Allen W. Dulles, *Look*, December 13, 1966.

p. 329. "The book can either be considered . . .": Robert Coles, *The New Republic*, January 28, 1967.

"good psychology but bad history . . .": Barbara W. Tuchman, *The Atlantic*, February 1967.

"disastrously bad book": Erik H. Erikson, *The New York Review of Books*, February 9, 1967.

"its indefiniteness about the details . . .": Richard Hofstadter, *Ibid.*

pp. 329–30. "What is ultimately unfortunate . . .": Robert Sussman Stewart, *The New York Times Book Review*, February 9, 1967.

p. 330. "It would be hard to find a literary collaboration more ill conceived . . .": *Time*, January 27, 1967.

"Apparently much of this book . . .": Raymond Moley, *Newsweek*, February 20, 1967.

"This book is a strange document . . .": George Steiner, *The New Yorker*, January 21, 1967.

"The book is a disgrace . . .": A. J. P. Taylor, *The New Statesman*, May 12, 1967.

"I didn't want to see us stranded in Iceland . . .": Orville Horwitz interview, July 26, 1983.

pp. 330–31. "Mr. Bullitt, an Episcopalian . . .": *The Catholic Standard and Times*, February 24, 1967.

p. 331. "Mr. Bullitt was received into the Catholic Church . . .": *The Catholic Standard and Times*, March 17, 1967.

p. 332. ". . . those qualities . . . which enabled him . . .": George T. Boswell, " 'Buddha Bill': The Roller-Coaster Career of William C. Bullitt": unpublished doctoral dissertation, Texas Christian University, 1972.

He was one of the "remarkable group of Americans . . .": Kennan, introduction to *For the President*, xvi.

INDEX